HAWAII

BY *Edward Joesting*

HAWAII

AN UNCOMMON HISTORY

W · W · NORTON & COMPANY · INC ·  NEW YORK

Library of Congress Cataloging in Publication Data

Joesting, Edward, 1925–
    Hawaii: an uncommon history.

    Bibliography: p.
    1. Hawaii—History.   I. Title.
DU625.J63   919.69   66–11646
ISBN 0-393-00907-6

W. W. Norton & Company, Inc., 500 Fifth Avenue, New York, N.Y. 10110

   6 7 8 9 0

For Harriette

CONTENTS

Photographs appear following page 162

INTRODUCTION

THIS BOOK IS NOT a conventional history, and to distinguish it from others I have used the word "uncommon" in the title. By using this word I hope to call attention to two major points.

The first concerns the technique used in writing the book. General histories traditionally include the major social, political, economic, and military events of nations. To cover such highlights even briefly leaves little room to probe people or to explore the intrigue and moving forces behind events.

This book does not attempt to cover all the highlights of Hawaii's past. I have, rather, selected a series of episodes and have written about these in some depth. A series of episodes forms a chapter and represents Hawaii during a certain era. Episodes sometimes revolve around a certain event—for example, the annexation of Hawaii by Great Britain in the 1840s—or around an individual, such as Jack London in the early 1900s. This selective technique allows a deeper, more human look into Hawaii's past than is possible with a general history.

The second purpose for using the word "uncommon" is to convey the idea that this book includes historical information not previously available to the.general reading public. New information appears to an increasing degree as the book progresses. The amount of new information available about the late nineteenth century is substantial, and the abundance of written and printed materials concerning the twentieth century is added to such a wealth of oral history that a major problem has been that of selection.

EDWARD JOESTING

Honolulu, Hawaii

ACKNOWLEDGMENTS

Hawaii is an agreeable place in which to write a book. Being an isolated island chain, it possesses a certain sense of remoteness which is cherished by many writers. The physical surroundings are pleasant, and people are generous in the assistance they give the serious historical researcher.

Among those who helped me with research were Janet Bell, Agnes Conrad, Sophie Cluff, Jean Dabagh, Yasuto Kaihara, Helen Lind, Lela Goodell, Janet Azama, Margaret Titcomb, Jacob Adler, Jean Stevens, and Kathy Crockett.

Those who helped by reading the entire manuscript, or portions of it, include Ann and Harry Zeitland, Walton Wimberly, Phyliss and Murray Turnbull, Betty and O. A. Bushnell, Gavan Daws, and Marion Kelley.

William J. Lederer gave encouragement during the difficult time when the book was being conceived.

Errors of fact, of omission, of interpretation and faults in style are solely the responsibility of the author.

HAWAII

The Islands of
HAWAII

Hanalei

KAUAI

Waimea · Lihue

NIIHAU

OAHU

Pearl Harbor · Honolulu · Kalaupapa

MOLOKAI

Wailuku

Lahaina

LANAI   *MAUI* · Hana

Kohala

Kawaihae · Hilo

Kailua

HAWAII

Kealakekua
Bay

Ka'u

South Point

Chapter One

THE DREAM REMAINED THE SAME

THE ISLANDS OF HAWAII are the children of the gods. The Mother of the Gods and the God of Light dwelt in the sky, and when their first child was born it dropped into the sea and became the island of Hawaii. Another child was conceived and it became the island of Maui. The island of Kahoolawe followed.

After bearing these three children the Mother of the Gods returned to Tahiti, but the God of Light remained, and by another woman the island of Lanai was born. By a third woman the island of Molokai was born. When the Mother of the Gods heard of this infidelity, she returned from Tahiti, and to spite her former mate she lived with another man. By him she conceived and bore the island of Oahu.

At last the Mother of the Gods and the God of Light were reunited, and she became pregnant with the child which became the island of Kauai. Then followed the islands of Niihau, Kaula, and Nihoa. The Mother of the Gods now became barren, and the creation of the Islands of Hawaii was completed.

Geologists take a somewhat less romantic view of the creation of the Hawaiian Islands. They say the minute fingers of land which now reach above the ocean's surface are the result of a laborious travail which has gone on so long that it is beyond human comprehension. Over eons of time, so long that no one can estimate within tens of thousands of years, the Islands of Hawaii were heaved up from the deep blackness of the sea.

Perhaps it all started when two immense blocks of rock on the ocean's floor wrenched apart, creating pressures which pushed mountainous flows of molten lava and ash upward. With the wrenching came earthquakes felt around the vast perimeter of the Pacific Ocean. The pressures of the eruptions were so great that they overcame the weight of the water which pushed down from above. Many square miles of molten rock were thrust upward in intermittent outflowings. Periods of activity were followed by times of quiet.

Hundreds of thousands of years passed between the time the first eruptions occurred on the ocean floor and the day molten lava finally broke the surface of the ocean. Towering geysers of steam shot into the air; the sea boiled and hissed as white hot liquid rock gushed forth. From 13,000 feet down in the Pacific Ocean, land had finally been thrust upward into the light of the sun.

The first islands to appear in the empty sea were in the far northwestern end of the Hawaiian chain. The little atoll called Kure might have been the first to emerge. In a southeast line other volcanoes pierced the blue-green surface of the sea. Some became dormant soon after they reached the ocean's surface, while others, particularly in the middle section of the chain, rose thousands of feet into the air and for a time stood prominently on the horizon. Many volcanoes worked up to great heights but did not rise above the surface. Today, to the west of the island of Hawaii are four submerged peaks, the highest of which rises to within 2,460 feet of the surface. The area surrounding these peaks quickly falls off to depths of 12,000 feet or more.

At the southeast end of the chain active volcanoes steadily worked upward. Sometimes the outpourings of adjacent volcanic cones joined to form one large island. The island of Oahu is the result of two such separate volcanoes, which today bear the names of the Koolau and the Waianae mountain ranges. The island of Maui was formed by two volcanoes, and at one early time Maui was joined to the neighboring islands of Lanai, Kahoolawe, and Molokai. Molokai, in turn, was formed by two volcanoes. The island of Hawaii is made up of five volcanoes which poured molten rock into the sea until the watery channels between were filled high with lava and one large island emerged.

Geologists guess that in the past hundred years enough lava has flowed forth from the mountain of Mauna Loa, on the island of Hawaii, to raise the height of its peak between three and six feet. At this rate of development, without making any allowances for erosion, it would have taken roughly 250,000 to 500,000 years for Mauna Loa to build to its present height from sea level. And it took additional hundreds of thousands of years for the mountain to have risen from the ocean floor to sea level.

The 1,500-mile-long string of islands emerged in utter loneliness, for Hawaii is the most isolated of all major island groups in the world. The North American continent is some 2,100 miles distant. To the north the Aleutian Islands are only slightly less remote, and the nearest high islands in the south are the Marquesas, 2,000 miles away.

The land itself was uninviting and sterile, a combination of lifeless fields of gray lava, pock-marked with coarse brown and red cinder cones. In the beginning there were no plants, no insects, no animals, just the harsh raw colors of the new land. Slowly life did come, at nature's own deliberate pace. Perhaps the first minute plant seeds were blown on the upper air currents, landing by accident in a pocket where soil had collected between lava rock boulders. Perhaps the first plant or insect floated to Hawaii on a log which had been uprooted in a storm far away and had been swept by ocean currents to Hawaii. Perhaps a bird alighting after a long flight dropped the first seed or brushed away a tiny land shell which had clung to its wings. Eventually insects and plant life arrived in all of these ways.

One new family of plants or insects might have arrived and survived every 10,000 or 20,000 years. Once they had become established, there were few natural enemies to fight off. As the families spread into the cool highlands, into the wet valleys and arid lowlands, many species developed, each conditioned to its particular environment. Nowhere else in the world would so many species evolve from so few basic families of plants and animals.

All the forces of disintegration had been at work on the Island chain from the moment the first outcroppings poured forth from a rent in the ocean floor. The tremendous weight of the water above and the relentless action of currents must have carried away whole mountains of molten rock. In the northwest and central parts of the chain some islands collapsed and settled far below the surface when the weight of the land above was too great for the porous rock foundations below.

Once land appeared above the surface of the sea, other destructive forces came into action. Rains eventually wore away the more porous lava and cut knife-like valleys deep into the land. Heavy rain storms turned the sea around the islands brown with soil which had been carried away. As lava fields deteriorated into soil, winds blew great red clouds of earth away. The shores of the islands were buffeted by the waves of the open ocean, undermining chunks of land which tumbled into the sea, leaving high cliffs where once there had been gentle slopes. The same destructive forces can be seen today. After a heavy rain the waters within the reef on the leeward side of Molokai are clogged with mud washed down from the mountains. The towering red clouds of top soil which are blown out to sea from the central plain of Maui must look the same today as they did a hundred centuries ago.

During a glacial age, when the waters of the north lay deeply frozen, the level of the seas was lowered, and land was exposed which had previously been covered. During this age a twenty-square-mile ice cap covered Mauna Kea, the peak which stands 13,796 feet above the sea on the island of Hawaii. Ice extended about 3,200 feet down from the summit and was between 150 and 350 feet thick. Its terrific weight pressed down on the mountain top until some 25,000 to 30,000 years ago. Then the season of perpetual winter passed, and water which had been frozen again filled the oceans, causing the level of the seas to rise some 1,000 feet above the present height. Gradually the oceans receded to their current level.

While the land was being worn away, quite a different kind of force was at work in certain waters surrounding the Islands. Coral reefs were building in offshore shallows where the water temperature remained between 73 and 78 degrees Fahrenheit. The reefs were made up of billions of cells from tiny lime-producing sea creatures, and they formed barriers as hard as concrete. Not only was the water temperature critical, but the coastal shelf could not fall off too quickly into the sea. In water more than 240 feet deep reef coral will grow slowly if at all.

The volcanoes in the northwestern two thirds of the Hawaiian chain became inactive. The islands which remained above the surface were reduced to low lying atolls or steep pinnacles of rock. But to the southeast the building of the Islands continued through volcanic eruptions. Haleakala, on the island of Maui, last erupted in about 1750. Volcanic activity continues today on the island of Hawaii, where occasional streams of lava flow downward into the sea, adding to the size of the island in the pattern of past centuries.

The contour of the land, as it rose above the sea, was little different from what it is today. Much of the raw colored earth became covered with a thousand shades and tints of green plants and trees. Above the green stood the high gray cliffs, eroded into accordion-like indentations which, with the aid of sun and shadow, appear razor sharp from a distance.

No man knew of this strange, rich, and rugged land. No human eye had seen the jagged heights, nor had any person breathed the heavy moist air which carried the smell of damp earth and foliage far out to sea. The distant ancestors of the people who would first sight Hawaii might then have been half a world away, perhaps somewhere in the midlands of India or in the coastal lands of southeastern Asia. These obscure people were emerging just as relentlessly as the volcanoes had pushed up the Islands their descendants would inhabit.

It is unlikely we shall ever be able to search out definitely the distant origins of the Hawaiians or of the larger Polynesian family to which they belong. Nineteenth century missionary-oriented historians speculated they might have sprung from the ten lost tribes of Israel. Dr. Peter Buck, the famous Polynesian anthropologist, believed that words in the Polynesian vocabulary possibly carried back to Egypt, to Mesopotamia, the kingdom of Baluchistan, and to an ancient part of India called Vrihia. From India some group of people moved slowly eastward, through Burma and Thailand to the tip of the Malay Peninsula—forced ever onward by hostile tribes or by some illusory dream of eventually discovering an idyllic homeland. As they migrated they intermarried with various tribes. Such mixing of peoples changed the physical appearance of their progeny and deeply influenced their crafts and religion. Still another theory suggests the ancestors of the Polynesians moved down the southeast coast of Asia toward the islands of Indonesia.

Wherever they came from, a group of people must have descended on Indonesia, and here they encountered a profoundly different environment. The great land mass of Asia had been left behind. Now they were an island people, and their world was an intricate lace work of islands and watery channels. They took to the sea in dugout canoes, venturing across the narrow waterways which are the highways of Indonesia. They must have remained for many generations, because the Polynesian vocabulary includes words which clearly had their origin in Indonesia.

Indonesia was not destined to be their final home. They turned eastward, reaching Polynesia either by way of Micronesia or by sailing along the northern coast of New Guinea. They did not set off in any great organized way, but rather it appears that groups departed eastward in a sporadic fashion. It is very possible that the islands of Tonga, on the western border of Polynesia, were inhabited by 1000 B.C. In the Western world it was still 800 years before Rome would emerge as a great power.

Long before these sailors reached Polynesia, they had committed themselves to a life dominated by the sea. They became expert fishermen, and they knew how to search the protected reef areas for the wide variety of sea life to be found there. When they sailed off on new voyages of discovery, they carried seedlings of the most useful plants with them. The sounds, moods, and rhythms of nature became part of them, and they came to think of the deep ocean, the currents which swept like rivers through the seas, the winds, the fish, and the ocean birds as living, intelligent companions.

By the time they crossed the imaginary borders into Polynesia, these adventurers had evolved the distinctive features which they would maintain for centuries. In color they were brown-bronze, considerably darkened by the glare of the sun. They were often grizzled and leathery by their mid-twenties. Their hair was black and sometimes wavy. Their faces were broad and their eyes large and dark. Life was strenuous, and the hardy ones who survived were often physically large men and women. Size was a virtue among both men and women, and the latter often stood over six feet in height and weighed more than 200 pounds. In modern times anthropologists have pondered the classification of the Polynesian among the peoples of the world. They call him Europoid, probably because he fits that category only slightly better than he does either the Negroid or Mongoloid mold.

The vast area of the Pacific called the Polynesian Triangle is another modern label. It is an arbitrary division created by scientists because the peoples within this area share similar customs and crafts and speak a related language. The imaginary boundaries of the Triangle run from New Zealand in the south to the Hawaiian Islands in the north. The base of the Triangle runs from New Zealand in the west to tiny Easter Island in the east, which lies far off the coast of South America. The eastern border of the Triangle runs from Easter Island north to the Hawaiian Islands, the apex of the Triangle.

The first Polynesian islands sighted by the earliest voyagers might well have been the Samoan group which lies just inside the central border of the Triangle. The high green islands of Samoa, abundantly provided with water and good soil, were indeed an inviting sight to the immigrants. Here, perhaps, was their final idyllic homeland. In anticipation they bestowed on the largest island of the group the revered name of Savai'i.

So long ago did the first settlers come to Samoa that all stories of discovery of the islands were subsequently lost from memory, so the Samoans originated their own story of how they came to be on their islands. The god Tagaloa had thrown stones down from heaven into the sea. When he had finished with his amusement, he sent his daughter down in the form of a snipe to see if any of the stones were above water. After much searching she found land and reported to her father that a vine was growing on the land. When the vine withered and rotted, worms appeared and these worms evolved into the men and women of Samoa. Remembering the visit of the snipe, the Samoans considered themselves to be of divine origin.

Nearly all the food plants and domesticated animals which became so important throughout Polynesia were first brought to Samoa by way of Fiji and other neighboring islands to the west. Smuggling them out was not always easy. An ancient Samoan legend tells of Samoan visitors to Fiji who feasted on pork and, before departing for their home, requested that they be allowed to carry pigs with them. The Fijians would not allow this, but they did supply the visitors with two dressed hogs as provisions for their return trip. The Samoans were able to conceal within the abdominal cavities several small suckling pigs which escaped the eyes of the Fijians, and so pigs were introduced to Polynesia.

South of Samoa some 200 islands dot the sea. They are called the Tonga group, for the most part a collection of small, low atolls, which were first reached by Polynesians at about the same time that Samoa was being settled. Soon these scattered little islands could not support their bursting populations, and so their people looked with envy toward the larger and richer islands of Samoa. At some early date legends tell of war-like tribes from Tonga invading and conquering their larger neighbors. About 1050 A.D. the Tongans were temporarily driven back to their home islands, but they returned again to overcome the Samoans and to exact tribute from them until about 1275, when the two sons of Savea, the first of the great line of Malietoa rulers, decided they had had enough of Tongan domination.

One day the two young Samoan warriors went, as usual, to pay tribute to the Tongan ruler, but instead of following the familiar ritual they walked boldly to the canoe of the Tongan chief and pulled the mooring stick out of the ground. This was a deadly insult, an insult so great that it was a declaration of war. In the battles which followed the Tongans were gradually forced off one island after another.

After making his final stand, the legends say, the defeated Tongan ruling chief stood in his canoe and called to the victorious Samoans who lined the shore: "Congratulations, thou hero! I am pleased with your fighting. I shall return no more as a warrior. But I will come back as your guest." This amounted to a peace treaty, and it is considered to remain in effect to this day.

With age the Samoan civilization became highly formalized. The craftsmen, who made a profession of building the familiar round thatched houses, formed a strong and honored guild. Their fees were high, and one of their conditions of work was that good food be served them during the period of construction. Those who did the tattooing, that necessary and painful experience every respectable Samoan male went through, formed another guild. Expert fishermen, canoe makers, and other specialists joined in other strong guilds.

Today we assume that many of the gods worshipped in Polynesia were deified chiefs who had been famous navigators or warriors. As the Polynesians expanded through the Pacific, they carried their favored gods with them, and so the fame of certain deities spread far. Four major gods were dominant through most of the Triangle: Tane was the divine ruler of trees, birds, insects, and canoes; Tu was god of war; Rongo was god of agriculture, food, and peace; Tangaroa was god of fishermen and sailors. In addition thousands of other gods were worshipped by certain craftsmen, by families, or by chiefs who ruled whole islands. And having a family god did not preclude a person from worshipping any other number of gods as well, whose help was sought in every important event in life.

Religion was both emotional and practical. The Polynesians held firmly to their gods, but they were far from inflexible. At one time the people of Tahiti chose to migrate to the Cook Islands and were overwhelmed by the fanatic worshippers of 'Oro, who decreed they must give up their god, Tane. There were numerous other occasions when gods were abandoned, since they were really only super-super human beings, who did have weaknesses, and a chief would change gods if he felt he had paid proper homage but had not received adequate help in return. At such times a chief might adopt the god of a successful neighboring chief.

The chiefs who led the numerous expeditions which explored the Polynesian world must have had varied reasons for sailing into unknown oceans. Perhaps an ambitious lesser chief wanted to rule without interference from the high chiefs above him, or the population of an island might have outgrown its food supply. A chief defeated in war was customarily given an opportunity to gather together his followers and sail off in search of a new home. And certainly many a young chief set forth seeking adventure and fame. Whatever the reasons may have been, explorers continued through the heart of the Triangle toward its eastern limits, settling on hundreds of islands along the way. One of these early, intrepid mariners sailed against winds and currents to Hiva, a distant group of islands which an old chant called the "World of Light."

The "World of Light" was much later renamed the Marquesas by the Spaniards. They were precipitous, rugged volcanic islands without friendly offshore coral reefs. There were few plateaus or broad valleys to make farming and travel easy. The settlers lived in deep valleys which opened onto boisterous seas. The sun reached the valley floors for only a short time each day, and arthritis became a common malady of people who lived there.

As the population increased each valley became the home of an independent tribe. The pressure to survive caused the inhabitants of one valley to view the inhabitants of all other valleys as their enemies. Warriors frequently made forays into a neighboring valley to plunder and kill. Life was a constant war as tribes fought to hold their valleys against attackers and to wreak such revenge on their neighbors as they could.

The Marquesas are stern, cruel islands, and the people took on the character of their land. They became one of the sturdiest, cruelest, and most aggressive races in all of Polynesia. The warriors were proud men who carved intricate designs in their massive ironwood war clubs. The bodies of most men and women were tattooed bluish-black from hairline to toe with elaborate designs. The men tied brief loin cloths around their middles, wore ankle bands woven from human hair, and hung ornaments of pearl shell about their necks. Carved whale teeth discs were placed in their slit ear lobes and the weight stretched the lobes to their shoulders.

Warriors shaved the sides of their heads clean with a shark's tooth, and the remaining tufts of hair on top of the head were bound in one or two tight knots which resembled horns. On ceremonial occasions the Marquesans rubbed their tattooed bodies with scented coconut oil. Some carried skulls which had been cleaned and dried and then wrapped tightly in bark cloth. Eyes, nostrils, and mouth were painted on the prize skull which they swung along at their sides with a cord passed through the nose and mouth. They assembled on massive stone platforms which were up to 200 feet square. These platforms were surrounded by the carved images of gods—square, heavy-featured idols with big almond shaped eyes and gaping mouths.

The ancient Marquesan looked demonic, and he lived up to his appearance. In war he was a relentless, cruel warrior who neither gave nor expected quarter. Raiding parties often had the sole purpose of hauling off men, women, and children who were sacrificed to appease the appetites of the gods. A human victim served another purpose, for the Marquesans relished few things as much as a hearty meal of human flesh.

Their fierceness bred a certain independence among the people, something not commonly found in Polynesia. While tribes were usually governed by hereditary chiefs, there was a deep feeling of autonomy among the people. A man of ability could more easily rise to a position of importance in the Marquesas than elsewhere in Polynesia if he had a strong arm and intelligence.

Building the great voyaging canoes which carried the Polynesians about the Pacific required skill, and the success of each step along the way was insured by religious ceremonies. The stone adzes used to cut the trees which would serve as hulls were placed in a temple the night before work began so they would absorb strength for their tasks. At dawn the sleeping adzes were carried to the sea and dipped in the water to awaken them.

The construction of the ocean-going canoe was the domain of honored craftsmen. They hollowed the logs so the hulls would be thick enough to be strong, yet thin enough to be light. To the accompaniment of special chants, side boards were lashed to the canoe with braided sennit so the vessel would stand high and keep out the sea. A platform was constructed amidships connecting the two hulls, and here a grass thatched house was often built to shelter women and children on long voyages. On one of the high upturned bow or stern pieces might be lashed the image of a special god. A mast, a sail of plaited matting, paddles, bailers, and stone anchors completed the equipment. A good canoe would stretch seventy to eighty feet long and could carry sixty people on an ocean voyage.

When the ship was launched, it was made to drink sea water by being rocked back and forth until the ocean broke over bow and stern. With this the vessel had been dedicated to the god of the sea. The canoe was given a name and so was the great paddle which was used to steer it. So intertwined was the construction of a canoe with religious observance that when work was completed, no one could doubt that it was destined to sail on some divine mission.

Legends tell us of a remarkable civilization which developed on the island which in ancient times was called Havai'i and which is now known as Ra'iatea. On this island, which is some 120 miles east of Tahiti, a powerful priesthood evolved which organized a uniform system of religion, history, and language which was adopted by most of central Polynesia. The district of Opoa on Havai'i became the home of the priesthood, and here chiefs and priests came annually from as far away as the Marquesas Islands to carry on discussions. Opoa is a high peninsula with lovely bays on either side. The renowned temple called Taputapuatea was here, dominating the district of Opoa. The temple name meant "Sacrifices from Abroad," and so sacred was this temple that boulders from here were carried hundreds of miles across the sea to serve as corner stones for new temples. Such a boulder, with a human victim buried beneath, gave a new temple great prestige.

Close to the beach where the visiting canoes landed was a smaller temple, which was called "Landing Place for Sacrifices." Nearby stood the "White Rock of Investment," a great shaft of stone nine feet high. Ranking chiefs were lifted atop this stone and invested with the sacred girdle of their class. Four men had been buried alive beneath the pillar of rock to serve as guardians of the temple.

When the day of the annual gathering came, the canoes of the visiting chiefs waited beyond the reef at the mouth of the sacred channel which led to the lower temple. When all the canoes had assembled, they entered the channel in pairs, signaling to one another on deep toned drums and with conch shell trumpets. The visitors brought gifts of various kinds, but the most important offerings were human beings. The victims had been killed and disemboweled at sea before the canoes entered the channel. When the canoes touched the shore, some of the corpses were strung up by ropes to branches of nearby trees. The remaining victims were used as rollers over which the canoes were dragged up on dry land. Long before the canoes entered the channel the women, children, and old people of Opoa had retreated inland, hauling their domestic animals with them. So grim was this time, say ancient legends, that even the wind dared not make a disturbing noise.

Several days of strict religious ceremonies followed the arrival of the visitors. If distracting noises or a slight commotion of any kind interrupted the perfection with which the services were conducted, atonement would have to be made, usually in the form of a human sacrifice. After such a sacrifice had been made, the services would start once more. When they had been completed to perfection, discussions of all kinds would take place. On a great stone platform at the temple of Taputapuatea the religious ceremonies and discussions were held. It was a grisly setting, because the hollow eyes of hundreds of warriors stared down on the assembly: skulls had been wedged and stacked in every available crack in the stone temple.

The annual gatherings went on for many generations, but the unbending rule of the priesthood inevitably led to disagreement. It finally happened when a visiting chief got into an argument with a priest of Opoa. The chief killed the priest and secreted his body, but the priest was missed, and when his body was found the murderer barely escaped to sea in his canoe. The incident had tremendous repercussions throughout central Polynesia. So important was the event that it became a part of the mythology of peoples as far away as New Zealand. After this incident the number of persons attending the annual gatherings decreased, although Havai'i remained the cultural and political center of the Society Islands for some time. Long after the power of the priests of Opoa had vanished, people on distant islands repeated a saying which acknowledged the importance of this island: "We are seed scattered hither from Havai'i."

A thousand years before the power of Havai'i began to wane, a voyaging canoe had set out from the Marquesas Islands, bound northward in search of new lands. There was nothing to distinguish this canoe from the many others which sailed forth on long ocean voyages from numerous islands in Polynesia. The name of the chief is not recorded, nor that of the canoe or the people aboard. We do not know why they left their homes, but they did sail across a sea which for 2,000 miles lay nearly unbroken by islands. Day after day dawned on an empty horizon, and even the confidence of the bravest voyager must have been shaken. Onward they came into an ocean no Polynesian had seen before.

They hoped to find that fabled homeland—that land their ancestors had so often thought they had discovered. In Samoa they had called it Savai'i, in Tonga it was Hawai, the islanders on Rarotonga called it Avaiki, and in the Society Islands the center of power was Havai'i. Hawaiki had been the mystical homeland from which they had come ages ago and the place to which they would depart after death. The pronunciation had changed as their language had changed, but the dream remained the same. Now they searched far off to the north in hopes of finding their Hawaii.

Chapter Two

SOMEWHERE TO THE NORTH
WAS AN UNKNOWN LAND

Each winter flights of mottled brown-gold birds migrate south from their breeding grounds in Alaska and Siberia. The birds are golden plovers, and annually their instincts lead them south over the 2,000 miles of open ocean to Hawaii. Some of these birds go no farther, but many others continue on for another 2,000 miles or more to other islands in Polynesia. No one knows for how many centuries golden plovers have made this annual trip.

The yearly arrival of these land birds would not have gone unnoticed by the Polynesians, who were sensitive to every nuance of nature. They must have concluded that somewhere to the north was an unknown land which was the summer home of these birds. When at last an adventurous chief sailed away to the north, eventually coming upon the Islands of Hawaii, the successive flights of birds could well have been the major indication that land could be found somewhere in that direction.

That historic first voyage was certainly one of agonizing physical hardship. As the days passed the terrible suspicion must have grown in the minds of the voyagers that somehow they had missed the land, or perhaps that there were no islands in this sea at all. Then one day the little company beheld a fantastic sight. There, high above the blue-gray mist of the horizon, they saw the towering mountain of Mauna Loa. Suddenly everyone must have been laughing and confident. On that day the peak of Mauna Loa was perhaps crowned with a mysterious cap of snow, a thing unknown to them. As they sailed closer, the huge mountain and its slopes became clear. They saw endless varieties of green foliage broken by wide harsh streaks of black and gray where recent lava flows had poured downward from vents high up on the mountain side.

Certainly they were wary as they came ashore. Perhaps they would be attacked by those who lived here. But their fears disappeared when they found no trace of other human beings. They stood on a virgin island vaster than any they dreamed existed, and now they possessed it. They dragged the water-logged canoe onto the smooth boulders of the shore and probably found shelter in a nearby cave. These voyagers had completed an historic trip, for they had sailed thousands of miles over uncharted seas in an age when most of the world's sailors refused to venture beyond the sight of land.

This new island home abounded in strange plants and birds, many of which existed nowhere else in the world. The plants offered little in the way of food, but the fruit of the pandanus tree was edible, as was the pith of the tree fern and berries from bushes. There was no reason to worry, because the seedling plants which the voyagers carried with them quickly grew in the warm and moist soil of the new land. The abundant sea life along the rocky shore was an immediate source of food, and the pigs, dogs, and chickens which the voyagers had brought along multiplied quickly.

The collection of plants which were carried to Hawaii included all those which had been important to life in the southern islands: wild ginger, the bottle gourd, taro, ti plant, sugar cane, the candlenut tree, several varieties of banana, coconut, two kinds of mulberry plants, bamboo, mountain apple, turmeric, arrowroot, several varieties of yams, the sweet potato, and breadfruit. Since Hawaii's climate was similar to that of their former homes, the plants flourished. As these plants spread through the Islands, the balance of nature was upset, and many of the more sensitive native plants disappeared.

The size of the island of Hawaii and its varieties of climate must have been a source of amazement. Away to the northwest another island was visible, and the newcomers crossed the narrow channel to Maui and explored that untouched island. Beyond they found another and yet another island, each offering endless room and unbelievably lavish resources to a people who had known only the smaller crowded islands of southern Polynesia.

As time passed they gave descriptive names to the land and to the surrounding seas. The dry island which lies in the shadow of Maui and which receives little rain was called Kahoolawe, meaning roughly "the red dust blowing," because the wind blew clouds of dust into the sea. Mauna Kea means "white mountain," probably because of the patches of occasional snow there. Some prefixes were repeated time and time again. *Hono* means harbor, *mauna* means mountain, *wai* means water, *pu'u* means hill, and *pali* means cliff. The names of the channels were as important as the names given the land. The name of the channel between Maui and Kahoolawe means "the way to Tahiti," because sailors took their bearings here before setting forth on the long voyage to the southern islands.

Radiocarbon tests from the earliest known camp sites indicate that immigrants were in Hawaii by 750 A.D. and that all the major islands were well populated by 1000 A.D. In this spacious land of plenty the Marquesans did not have to pursue their old warlike ways in order to survive, and they became a peaceful people. There was always land for the other chiefs who arrived with followers, and it is likely they lived in relative peace for some time. Such a happy existence could not continue indefinitely, however. It changed when fierce chiefs from Tahiti and other islands in the Society group found their way to Hawaii. Soon they had brought the original settlers under their control.

When the Society Island chiefs conquered the original inhabitants of Hawaii, they possibly created the basis for a series of legends which have survived to this day. These legends are about the Menehune, a group of dwarf-like people who stood two to three feet tall. Their living places were the deep valleys and mountain wildernesses. The Menehune were said to appear only at night, and during the period between dusk and the first crow of a cock, which signaled dawn, they performed prodigious building feats. They completed temples, called heiaus, irrigation ditches, and giant fishponds all within the course of one night by forming a human chain and passing the needed boulders from quarry to building site. If they were disturbed, the job was abandoned. Today certain ancient ruins, particularly on the island of Kauai, are attributed to the Menehune.

If the legends of the Menehune have a basis in fact—and most legends do—perhaps the trials the original settlers experienced after they had been subdued by the Society Islanders is the basis. The Tahitian equivalent of the word Menehune means commoner, and the conquerors certainly viewed the subdued as inferior, or mere commoners. The defeated Islanders could have been driven into the narrow valleys and rugged mountains. Over generations of time it is possible they became smaller in stature as food and living conditions remained poor. The stone work construction which they had done earlier continued to be attributed to them, but storytellers would have found it more dramatic to say it was mysteriously done at night.

One legend states that the Menehune people were pushed northward onto the island of Kauai and their king became alarmed because his people were intermarrying with the newcomers. He ordered them all to sail away with him in search of a new homeland. To the northwest of Kauai are the small barren islands of Necker and Nihoa. On these islands the ruins of terraces, stone implements, and images of gods have been discovered. If it is true that the Menehune did leave the major islands, it is possible they dwelt on the tiny islands of Necker and Nihoa until they found they could not subsist there. Then they might have sailed forth again into the unknown ocean just as their ancestors had done for countless generations.

In Tahiti the new lands in the north became known as Hawai'ia, meaning "Burning Hawaii," because of the fiery volcanoes which were active there. Travel between the Society Islands and Hawaii continued for some centuries. Then for some unknown reason it came to an end. It is believed a priest named Paao was one of the last persons of importance to travel to "Burning Hawaii." He arrived from that stronghold of the priesthood, Havai'i, around 1275 A.D., about the time Marco Polo had found his way to China. Paao was shocked to learn that the blood of the high chiefs in Hawaii had been sullied through intermarriage with commoners. This was an intolerable condition which Paao felt duty bound to correct. He sailed back to his home and returned with a high-born chief who reputedly did much to restore the respect due high chiefs on the island of Hawaii. But Paao was not content with simply restoring the dignity of the chiefs. He carried back with him other customs reminiscent of the obdurate rule of the chiefs of Havai'i. Among these was a new design for heiaus, the brutal custom of human sacrifice, and the use of the red feather girdle to add grandeur to the investiture of kings.

The civilization of ancient Hawaii was unified and given a sense of order through the "kapu" system. The word *kapu* is the Hawaiian variation of the word *tabu* or *taboo*. If something was kapu, it was forbidden or set aside as sacred by religious custom. Kapu systems were common among primitive peoples the world over, but nowhere else was the system as highly developed as in Polynesia. The system touched every phase of life. It was kapu for women to eat pork, bananas, or turtle meat. It was kapu for women to eat in the company of men. Certain kapu ceremonies were sacred and essential, such as those required at the time of birth and on the death of a family member. To break these absolute laws meant swift retribution, usually death.

The degree of kapu, or sacredness, a chief possessed was equal to his rank. A very high chief might possess the "kapu moe," and runners would go before him waving a ti leaf branch shouting the words "Kapu moe!" Everyone within sight of the chief would immediately fall flat on the ground until the chief had passed. When containers holding the water for the chief's bath, or when his clothing, food, or anything else belonging to a kapu moe chief passed by, the people fell to the ground. For the shadow of a commoner to fall across that of a ranking chief was forbidden. It was kapu to wear a loin cloth of a chief or to enter his house by the private side entrance. To violate any of these brought an automatic death sentence. The kapus which pertained to the chiefs reflected the fact that they were descendants of the gods, and their persons were sacred. Chiefs of lower rank were paid less deference, because the degree of kapu they possessed was less.

The gulf which separated the chiefs, or alii, and the commoners had to be accepted. No one dared question the fact that chiefs were descendants of the gods. Theoretically the chief who possessed the most distinguished lineage was king, although in actual practice competing chiefs might settle the issue on the battlefield. A king ruled over each major island and all land belonged to him. He appointed chiefs to govern sections of land, and these chiefs again divided the land under them among lesser chiefs.

A chief's genealogy was all important in determining where he stood in the hierarchy. The rank of a person's mother and father counted equally, and when it was impossible to find a woman of equal rank to marry, a high chief might marry his own sister. The child born of such a union would increase the high rank of his parents. Since genealogies were so vital, men of special ability memorized the long ancestries of important chiefs, starting centuries back with the gods who were their forefathers. These men squatted before their chiefs and chanted the ancestral succession as well as the historical events which had happened along the way.

Chiefs held life and death authority over their subjects, but they also realized that they must rely on commoners for support in wartime and as suppliers of food and goods. The commoners did not belong to the land, as they did in medieval Europe, and if conditions became intolerable they could leave and seek a home on the lands of a more lenient neighboring chief. As a practical matter the commoner found it safer to pay his taxes, carefully observe the kapus, and stay out of the way of the alii unless he had some special reason to seek their favor. The alii in turn avoided situations where commoners might unwittingly break vital kapus. If a chief provided a rude kind of justice in settling disputes, was a brave soldier in war time, and gave his people a certain sense of security, he would receive the commoners' respect and affection. A complicated interdependence evolved between chief and commoner over the centuries, remnants of which still exist today.

On occasions of state the chiefs were a truly stirring sight. Not only were chiefs quickly distinguished by their proud bearing, but they were identifiable from afar by their colorful apparel. They wore capes and cloaks made from thousands of brilliant red and yellow feathers tied to fine nets of braided sennit. The texture was as smooth as velvet. They wore impressive helmets, again covered with feathers tied to a basket-like framework. Often the helmets had sweeping crests similar in looks to the traditional helmets worn by ancient Roman soldiers. Indeed, the crests of the helmets might have symbolized the comb of the fighting cock. Nowhere else in Polynesia had the people developed such a high degree of artistry and craftsmanship in their clothing.

There were rare occasions when commoners were pushed so far that they rebelled against cruel and arrogant chiefs. Then dammed up emotions brought quick and direct results. This happened in the district of Kau on the island of Hawaii, a land where people grimly scraped together the necessities of life. A notorious chief who ruled this district regularly put to sea and commandeered the catch of fishermen. The fish he stole were essential for the families of the fishermen, and at last they had suffered enough. When once again the chief pulled alongside a canoe, the fishermen bent down, not to turn over their catch to him, but to reach for heavy rocks hidden in the bottom of their canoe. They hurled these into the chief's canoe, smashing out the bottom. Then they quickly paddled away, leaving the chief and his men to drown.

The people of ancient Hawaii lived under the menacing shadow of the priesthood. The kahunas, or priests, were men of tremendous power. Their presence struck fear into the heart of every commoner, because they dealt in the unknown—the supernatural. A kahuna might make it known he was praying a person to death and that person might die of fright. Many kahunas served a single powerful god while others specialized in prescribing medicine and performing rites over sick people or in conducting a whole variety of ceremonies. All events of importance in life required rituals which they alone could perform. The kahunas were dreaded, but the necessity of their services was not questioned.

Every ranking chief had a kahuna as a close and powerful advisor. The advice of the gods was essential in making decisions, and priests alone could communicate with the gods and relay their pleasure to the chief. It was essential for a chief to know if the gods looked with favor on a planned ocean voyage, whether or not he should wage war on a neighbor, or whether the time was right to conclude a peace treaty. If the issue to be decided was vital, human sacrifices helped assure the god of the importance of the occasion. The corpses of the victims were stretched out atop the heiau and then elaborate rituals were conducted before the kahuna received the answer from the gods and relayed it to the chief.

Important ceremonies were held at the heiau, a massive pile of fitted gray boulders, standing ten feet or more high. Atop these platforms were several houses—one where animal sacrifices were roasted, another which served as a drum house, and another which was a dwelling house of a god. Towering above all these was a high framework of poles. This was the oracle tower where offerings of food were placed. When the time had come the kahuna would climb to the top and commune with the god. The awesome effect of the ceremonies was deepened by the great carved images of the gods. These overbearing, fierce images evoked a feeling of dark apprehension. In this setting the kahunas performed intricate rituals before hushed audiences who sometimes squatted for hours beneath the walls in frightened reverence.

Gods were numerous. Commoners acknowledged those worshipped by their chief but often venerated many other deities as well. Each group of craftsmen had its own god, as did each household. All of them were important and deserved proper attention through prayers and offerings. If a god was neglected, a man had no reason to complain if the god, in turn, gave no assistance. Fishermen, for example, threw a stone on a pile by the shore after returning safely from the sea—as a mark of thanks to their god. Most gods were represented by crude images. They received their power, or mana, from prayers and offerings, certainly not from the expert way in which they had been carved.

Commoners formed the mass of the population, and from them came the taxes which supported the chiefs. These taxes might amount to two-thirds of what a commoner produced, and were paid in food, kapa (bark cloth), mats, and any sort of labor required by a chief. And with the right to till the land and to fish came the obligation for each man to serve his chief in time of war. In such an emergency the king ordered his chiefs to provide a given number of soldiers for a coming campaign. Chiefs in turn drafted the commoners who were under obligation to them.

The strenuous tasks of producing food, clothing, and shelter were best carried out through cooperative efforts. At planting time or when the fish were running, the whole village would turn out, but usually it was the family that worked together. In addition to the mother, father, and their children, the family unit might include assorted nieces, nephews, cousins, and in-laws. Children who were the offspring of earlier unions were also happily included in the family unit. Such affairs were a normal part of life. For commoners there was no "marriage," no ceremony which solemnized the union of a man and woman. A union was a matter of mutual agreement and convenience. All the children in a family group, no matter what their real relationship, were treated alike and were called son or daughter.

Often the first girl born to a couple was given to the mother's parents, and if the child was a boy he might be given to the father's parents. Grandparents were more likely to have the time to educate children, and through this instruction a certain continuity of custom was passed along. The custom was practical, since the young father and mother had all they could do to provide the necessities of life for their children, their parents, and themselves.

On a typical day a father and an older boy might follow the path to their taro patch. They started off in the early morning with their digging sticks over their shoulders to spend the day cultivating and weeding the plants, which were as much an agricultural staple for the Hawaiians as white potatoes later were for the Irish. Their patch might be along a stream where taro plants grew in watery terraces. The plants might grow two or three feet high, and the broad green leaves were cooked into a kind of spinach. The most important part was the corm, or thick stem, which grew below the ground in the same fashion as do beets. This corm was baked or steamed in earth ovens and then pounded into a gray paste called poi. Near the fields of taro might be patches of sweet potatoes and yams. Field work normally was the province of men.

While the father and boy might labor in the taro patch, other boys from the family might be fishing from the small family canoe. They likely would have set out before the first rays of the sun touched the mountain tips behind the village, carrying lines, hooks, and bait packed in large hollowed gourds. Perhaps the time of year was not right, but the boys nevertheless might paddle to an area where fishing had usually been good in season. They played out their lines, woven of strong olona fiber, into the deep water. Some of the hooks they used might have been carved from wood or precious ivory, others from human or animal bone. They were all prized possessions which had been fashioned by skilled craftsmen. The currents might periodically have carried the canoe away from the favored fishing grounds. Then they would paddle back, using landmarks as their guides.

The women of the family were probably busy at home. One young girl might have walked half a mile to a stream, carrying back fresh water in a hollowed gourd. In the shade of the workhouse her mother might be pounding the bark of the paper mulberry bush into kapa cloth. The strips of bark had alternately been pounded, soaked, and bleached in the sun, and now it was time for the final beating process. She wielded a four-sided wooden club with geometric designs carved into the four faces. Each blow of the club left a pattern in the kapa similar to a water mark. The anvil she pounded against was a partially hollowed section of log, and the rhythmic sounds of her work echoed far. Later the cloth would be spread in the sun to dry, and if there was time it would be decorated with colorful designs.

The mother might go about her chores in the workhouse, a place without walls but with a high peaked roof as protection against sun and rain. Nearby might be a thatched lean-to which was the cookhouse. Close to this could have been the stone-lined pit called an imu, which was the oven. The largest building probably was a rectangular sleeping house which had a high peaked roof and one door so low that even children had to stoop to enter. The last dwelling likely was somewhat smaller than the sleeping house, which could be used only by the women during their menstrual period, a time when they were "unclean" and must remain isolated from men. The sleeping house and house for women had been built over low platforms of level rocks. Plaited mats were spread on the rocks to form comfortable surfaces on which to sit and sleep. All the buildings were made of a framework of poles lashed together and then thatched over with tufts of light brown pili grass. In these four dwellings the family group lived comfortably.

The young children ran and wrestled in the dusty pathways by the houses. Boys boastfully imitated their elders. They rolled stones along the ground for distance or accuracy, and pitched bamboo shafts which they imagined to be spears. Soon after they learned to walk, girls and boys took to the water, and they became as much at home there as on land. As the women went about their chores, they teased and scolded the youngsters. Children were not a nuisance, but a delight to be enjoyed and indulged as long as possible.

In the hot sun of midafternoon the boys hauled their canoe ashore and headed home. They ran all the way, because they had good news. They had caught an abundance of fish during a season when fishing was not good. The family god had clearly given his help, and so a portion of one of the fish was cut off and placed before the image of the god. Now the father and another boy returned from the fields bearing both taro and yams. There was food enough for a feast, and the men immediately began to prepare the imu. When the wood had turned to bright coals, the fish, yams, and taro, wrapped in ti leaves, were placed among the coals and red hot rocks. Banana leaves were spread over the rocks and the food was left to steam. One fish was not put in the imu, but was passed among the men and eaten raw, the head and entrails all happily devoured. It was strictly kapu for women to eat with men, and so they waited patiently until the men were full.

By the time the evening meal was done the sun had disappeared below the horizon and the village houses lay in near darkness. Now the family members would normally have drifted off to the sleeping house and lain down on their mats, but this had been a successful day and the grandfather was moved to recite the story of Umi.

The family gathered within the sleeping house and reclined on mats. The women pulled kapa capes over their shoulders as protection against the evening chill. In the middle of the floor was a small hissing candle made of a string of kukui nuts set in a stone dish. The candle cast a dim flickering light, and the smoke which arose permeated the thatched walls of the house with a heavy oily smell. The story of Umi was a serious drama.

"Long, long ago a peaceful man by the name of Liloa ruled as king of the whole island of Hawaii. One day he traveled to the district of Hamakua, and as he walked along through the countryside he chanced on a woman washing herself in a stream. The beautiful woman was a commoner by the name of Akahi. She had just finished her menstrual period and was bathing herself before returning home to her husband.

"Akahi was at first frightened by the sudden appearance of the king. She feared some kapu had been broken and that she would be killed in punishment. But Liloa had no thoughts of punishment. He was enamored by the lovely Akahi and quieted her fears. The young woman was soon captivated by the king, and he was consumed with desire for the beautiful woman. By the edge of the stream Liloa's longings were gratified. At last he arose. Liloa instructed Akahi about the child she might have and presented her with items of his wearing apparel.

" 'If you have a child,' " Liloa said, " 'and it is a girl, name her after your family. If it is a boy, name him for me.' "

"A child, indeed, was born, and since it was a boy Akahi named him Umi. The husband, thinking he was the father, raised him as he would a son of his own, without chiefly training or special care. In fact, as the boy grew older the husband of Akahi often beat him, because the child gave food and kapa to other children.

"One day when the boy was receiving yet another beating Akahi informed her husband that Umi was not his son, but was really the son of the king Liloa. To prove the truth of her words, Akahi brought forth the helmet, the ivory neck pendant, and the loin cloth which had been given her by Liloa. Her husband was very frightened, because he had been beating a boy destined to become a chief of high rank.

"Soon after this Umi left his home to visit his real father. The boy was approximately ten years old, and with him went another youth whom Umi had adopted as his son. As the two traveled along, Umi wearing his helmet and ivory pendant, they met another boy whom Umi adopted as a second son. When they came to Waipio Valley, where Liloa lived, Umi approached the house of his father alone. He leaned against the crossed kapu sticks at the main entrance, and the guardian spirit of the ancestors caused the sticks to fall. Then he climbed the enclosure wall and entered the king's presence through the side door. Once within the house, Umi ran to the king and seated himself on his lap. The retainers surrounding the king shouted that the boy had broken the kapus and deserved death.

"Liloa asked Umi, 'Whose child are you?' Umi answered, 'Yours! I am Umi-a-Liloa.'

"Liloa recognized the helmet and the pendant and wept. Then the happy king issued a proclamation that he now had a new son. Umi soon became his favorite, and as time passed he grew into a strong and skilled warrior.

"Liloa also had a son by the name of Hakau who had been born by a chieftess of high rank. Hakau became jealous of the popular Umi. He beat him and taunted him with the reminder that his mother had been a commoner. When Liloa promised Hakau that he should inherit his kingdom when he died, the boy became less concerned about Umi. To Umi the old king entrusted the care of his war god.

"At the death of Liloa, Hakau became king and for a time ruled well. But at last he returned to his evil ways, seeking only personal pleasure and mistreating the chiefs, priests, and common people. Hakau's jealousy of Umi grew, because the young man was both handsome and kind. At last the persecution became unbearable, so Umi and his two adopted sons fled from Hakau and settled near Hilo. Here he took four wives, but he always hid his true identity. The god which Liloa had entrusted to his care had been hidden away in a cave. In spite of all misfortunes Umi never failed to bring the proper offerings before the god.

"One day two venerable men arrived in Hilo searching for Umi. They were priests of Hakau and they were seeking the lost son of Liloa. The abuse of Hakau had become unbearable, and when Umi identified himself the priests offered the kingdom to him. The priests inquired as to the size of the army Umi could raise, but realizing it was not large enough they decided on gaining their objective by trickery.

"At last Umi and the two priests agreed on the strategy they would follow, and the priests returned to Waipio Valley. The suspicious Hakau questioned them concerning their travels and asked if they had seen the missing Umi. To Hakau's surprise, the priests reported they had not only seen Umi, but that he was planning a revolt against the king. Hakau became worried. The priests advised him to send as many people as possible to the mountains to hunt the birds which supplied the red and yellow feathers necessary to decorate the god named Kauila Akua. Hakau did not wish to do this, because it was equivalent to a declaration of war, but at last he consented, and on the day prescribed by the priests he ordered his retainers to scour the mountains for the feathers. Now Hakau was left nearly unguarded, and Umi and his followers slipped into Waipio Valley and killed him. The only blood spilled was that of the king.

"Umi was king and made his adopted sons chiefs. He married his half-sister, the daughter of Liloa, so his heirs would be of the highest rank possible. Several chiefs on Hawaii, however, were not satisfied with the new king, and they thought they had the strength to overthrow him. In a succession of battles Umi met and annihilated these chiefs. Now his rule was secure over the whole island. He moved his capitol from the pleasant but damp valley of Waipio to the warm climate of Kailua in the district of Kona. Here he set an example for his people by working with his hands, both as a farmer and as a fisherman. Umi was a just ruler who cared for the old and fatherless. Because he prohibited murder and thievery, rulers of other islands brought their favorite daughters to him as wives.

"The king became the father of many children by women of chiefly rank and by women who were commoners. He had so many children, in fact, that later generations repeated the saying that no commoner could declare Umi-a-Liloa was not his ancestor. If a Hawaiian said such a foolish thing, it showed he was ignorant of his ancestry."

Umi was a real and famous man who ruled as king of the island of Hawaii. His story was retold over generations and became embellished just as the tales of King Arthur and the knights of the round table were embellished. The heroic Umi, who lived as a commoner and rose through adversity to his rightful position as king, must have been a favorite tale for most Hawaiians.

War hung as a black threat over the heads of commoners, because battles were total affairs with no quarter given the men, women, and children caught in the ebb and flow of fighting. To many chiefs, however, war was a favorite pastime. During intervals of peace, chiefs kept their warriors in training by waging sham battles, and as soon as the troops had been rested and provisioned they started off on another campaign.

On the field of combat the armies drew up in groups or companies led by warrior chiefs. As the armies faced each other, kahunas leaped to the fore, shouting obscenities and ridicule toward the enemy lines. The first attack would probably be a shower of stones, cast from slings. Then a champion might step forward and challenge an enemy to single combat. When the encounter was over, another shower of stones would signal the beginning of a free-for-all battle. As the armies moved closer, short spears were thrown and then began a series of individual contests with clubs and daggers. The chiefs, easily distinguished by their colorful capes and helmets, rallied and encouraged their soldiers. When one army was routed, the victors pursued and killed as many of the enemy as possible.

Some women followed their men into battle, but most noncombatants either lay hidden in the caves which honeycombed many areas of the Islands or else tried to reach a place of refuge. Each island had at least one such place of refuge. Their boundaries were marked by white kapa flags. All those within these boundaries were protected by a strong kapu respected by chief and commoner alike. In times of peace these enclosures were the one place where a person would be secure from the wrath of a personal enemy. Before a refugee could return home he had to perform such rites as the kahunas decreed, for the compounds of refuge were controlled by the priesthood. When a person returned home it was unlikely he would be bothered by an old enemy, because the fact that he had been able to reach a place of safety was proof that he was strongly protected by his god.

Wars might rage, but everyone could look forward to the makahiki season, which was the time when war was kapu and all labor ceased. A curious looking image of Lono heralded the beginning of the season as he was paraded around an island. Lono was symbolized by a small carved head at the top of a long pole. Below this image was a cross spar from which billowed two great sheets of kapa.

This time of entertainment could not begin until the required taxes of foods, kapa, and animals had been piled before the altars and counted. The promise of good times to come helped minimize the heavy taxes extracted from the people. The kahunas who carried the high pole with Lono's head at the top were fed by chiefs as they progressed around an island. When the necessary ceremonies were completed, the long awaited sporting contests began. Wrestling, boxing, foot races, rolling round stones, spear throwing, and sledding down runways paved with smooth stones were some of the sports avidly followed. The people cheered their favorites wildly, and some wagered house and family on the outcome of a contest.

By the middle 1700s, some 300 years after the reign of Umi, the Islands had long been isolated from the rest of Polynesia. The memory of those places in the south remained, but travel there had long ceased. In the course of hundreds of years of isolation Hawaii had become a formalized, feudal society. If the kapu system provided a sense of order for the people, the rituals of the system were undoubtedly burdensome and had lost much of their meaning. Generation after generation followed the same customs when a child was born, farmed or fished in the same way, prepared their food in the same way with the same implements, lived in the same kinds of houses which had been built with the same kinds of tools, worshipped their gods in the same way, fought with the same weapons, and mourned their dead in the same fashion. The mores and material culture of Hawaii had become ossified.

On a January morning in 1778 an Islander on Oahu saw strange shapes on the horizon. The shapes were distant, unclear, misty through ocean spray, but the excitement created must have been great. Those strange objects were Western sailing ships, and no one aboard or ashore could have guessed what momentous changes their presence would bring to the Islands of Hawaii.

Chapter Three

"THUS FELL OUR GREAT AND EXCELLENT COMMANDER!"

THOSE TWO STRANGE SHIPS on the horizon were under the command of Captain James Cook. He had sailed from Plymouth, England, in 1776, voyaging by way of the Cape of Good Hope, across the Indian Ocean to Tasmania, stopping at New Zealand, the Cook and Friendly Islands, and finally Tahiti. After bestowing gifts of cattle, goats, sheep, horses, and a variety of vegetable seeds on the islanders, Cook ordered his ships to sail north. The serious business of the expedition lay somewhere in the far north, away from the warm, cheerful islands through which they had passed.

Cook's mission was to find the long sought Northwest Passage, that waterway which supposedly linked the Atlantic and Pacific Oceans above the North American continent. If such a passage were found, the Pacific Ocean could be reached much more quickly from Europe, and the tedious, dangerous voyages around Africa or South America would be a thing of the past. The Earl of Sandwich, First Lord of the British Admiralty, instructed Cook to make every effort to find the passage. Parliament added a special incentive: to the crew of the English ship which should make the discovery would go a fortune of 20,000 pounds.

The two ships James Cook commanded had been slow, solid Whitby colliers, vessels he thoroughly knew from his years in the merchant navy. The flagship, *Resolution,* was a 100 foot long bark while her companion ship, *Discovery,* was 90 feet in length. In January 1778 the ships plunged through the sea, making north from Tahiti. One day the crew of the *Resolution* was mildly interested to learn that the lookout had sighted land birds. Then turtles were seen scurrying away from the bows of the ships. When currents grew stronger the old hands believed land was near. If the winds were blowing right, they would smell the rich odor of earth before they sighted land.

At daybreak on January 18 land was sighted, and what a land it was.

It was the Hawaiian island of Oahu, a majestic and massive shape, a faint blue-purple color through the mist. The sailors hung on the rail longing to put their feet again on dry land. The Hawaiians gathered along the northern shores of Oahu and looked in amazement at the strange, distant shapes floating along on the ocean. Adverse winds pushed the two ships away to the north.

Northwest lay the island of Kauai, and the *Resolution* and her consort ship, *Discovery,* were able to move close to the island by dark. During the night a Hawaiian fisherman by the name of Moapu, together with his companions, squatted in their canoe going about their routine nightly work. Suddenly they looked up to behold the silhouettes of James Cook's two ships as they glided by with lights ablaze. The Hawaiians dropped their fishing lines in terror and raced for shore to tell the chiefs the incredible news. Next morning curious Hawaiians paddled out in their canoes to see for themselves. They would not venture aboard, but they came alongside and tied pigs, fish, and sweet potatoes to a rope the English dropped. In return they were paid with bits of metal.

Waimea Bay seemed to suit Cook's needs, and the anchor chains of the two ships rattled through the hawse holes downward into the sandy ocean bottom. Before them the Waimea River languidly emptied over a sandbar into the sea, and along the river banks were crowded the grass thatched houses of the Hawaiians. More houses covered the hillsides and stretched along the shoreline. Behind the village were gently rising mountains, which disappeared into clouds in the distance. Here in the high mountains the Waimea River had its beginning, twisting through thousand-foot-deep canyons where cliffs of stone, earth, ash, and lava rock were as colorful as a Hawaiian rainbow.

The Islanders who crowded the shore were a shrieking mob. Some said the sails were giant sting rays. Others said the masts were trees moving about on the sea. A kahuna pronounced these unearthly shapes to be the heiaus of the god Lono. At last the ruling chief ordered a party of men aboard the ships to investigate. What they saw nearly drove them wild. They thought the tri-cornered hats of the English were three-cornered heads. The clothes appeared to be loose skin with pockets. The ranking chief who boarded the *Resolution* was presented a knife by Captain Cook. Deeply impressed, the chief announced that forthwith his daughter's name would be Changed-into-a-dagger.

The Hawaiians gave the best descriptive names they could to the mysterious things they saw. The sailor who raised the flag was called Ku-of-the-colored-flag, after an image which stood outside one of their heiaus. A man smoking a pipe was called Lono-of-the-volcanic-fire. When they saw the hide of a bull, they believed these haoles, or foreigners, had killed Ku-long-dog, a legendary man-eating dog. The Hawaiians supposed James Cook had come from the most distant, romantic place they could imagine, their ancient Polynesian home somewhere far to the south.

Supplies of food, fresh water, and wood were needed, so Captain Cook ordered Lieutenant John Williamson ashore to explore. A group of Hawaiians rushed into the surf to greet the English long boat, and when a Hawaiian grabbed the boat hook, the young lieutenant drew a pistol and shot him dead. Later the same day Cook waded ashore, dressed simply in a white shirt, breeches, and a cocked hat. He walked unarmed among the Islanders, who honored him as a high kapu chief. They fell to the ground as he approached, offering gifts of food, mats, and kapa cloth. Never before had he received such a welcome. These plentiful new lands, Cook decided, should be honored by a fine name. He decided to call them the Sandwich Islands after his patron, the Earl of Sandwich.

The Hawaiians excitedly discussed the great wealth of the foreigners. Some wanted to help themselves to the quantities of iron they saw aboard the ships, but a high priest counseled against it. The priest was undecided if the foreigners were gods or simply men. Finally he decided on a test. The haoles, or newcomers, should be offered women; if they accepted, they would certainly not be gods, but only mortals. The English promptly failed this test of divinity, but many Hawaiians were still uncertain.

The swarms of willing women distressed Cook, who knew that many of his crew were infected with venereal diseases. He ordered the known cases to stay aboard ship, but it did little good when women swam out to the ships. There can be little doubt that Cook's crew introduced syphilis and gonorrhea into Hawaii. The pay book of the *Resolution* lists the names of sixty-six men out of a crew of 112 who were treated for venereal diseases before the ship reached Hawaii. A year after Cook's first visit the diseases had spread through all the Islands, and shortly thereafter venereal diseases became a major reason for the sharp decrease in the Hawaiian birth rate.

Cook liked the cheerful Hawaiians just as he liked most Polynesians. He could speak a little Tahitian, and he was astonished to discover the language of these people was a variation of the language spoken 2,000 miles to the south. The Islanders and the English got on well. After two weeks of resting his crew and taking provisions aboard, Cook visited the small neighbor island of Niihau and then sailed away to search for the Northwest Passage. When the English ships had disappeared, messengers were dispatched to the other Hawaiian Islands to spread the news about the wonderful white men. The messengers described the sound of their talk as the twittering of birds. Their feet were covered, they blew smoke from their mouths like volcanoes, and their pockets were doors behind which treasures were kept. Many Islanders believed Cook was the powerful god called Lono. Now, with his departure, they had time to ponder.

In late November of 1778 Cook returned to the Hawaiian Islands. During the ten months he had been gone he had sailed through Bering Strait and pushed into the Arctic Ocean in quest of the Northwest Passage. For days fog had lain on the ships like heavy white shrouds. When they neared the shore at night, they heard the howling of wolves. Snow had to be shoveled from the decks every few hours, and the rigging sagged with the weight of ice. Finally the ships came to an impenetrable wall of ice, and Cook turned back. Pumps had to be manned day and night, and supplies were moved to avoid damage by salt water. The quarters of the crew were damp, and they thought with longing of the warm Islands of Hawaii. Cook was a tired, disappointed man as he sailed south.

Maui was the first Hawaiian island Cook sighted on his return, and he slowly searched the coastline for a suitable anchorage. As soon as his two ships were sighted, word of his coming spread through Maui. Canoe loads of men, women, and children put out to sea to gape at the ships, and some even dared to climb aboard the great tower of Lono. At night the canoe loads of Islanders paddled back to shore. The coast of Maui was rocky and exposed and offered no safe anchorage, so the English turned southeast toward the island called Hawaii. Along this coast Cook was accompanied by the usual gallery of Islanders, many of whom traded fresh provisions for pieces of iron. The two vessels passed the rich green slopes and the steep valleys which open onto the sea along the Hamakua coast. High up and distant loomed Mauna Kea, its peak covered with snow. Farther on they passed the broad v-shaped bay at Hilo, and beyond they saw the black lava fields which streak the districts of Puna and Kau. At last Cook rounded South Point and sailed the smooth waters of the Kona Coast.

The ships tacked first toward land and then to sea, moving with painful slowness. There was every reason for caution. Coming down from the north a seaman had been killed aboard the *Discovery* when dilapidated rigging was carried away. Rounding South Point the *Resolution* was endangered when three rotten sails were blown to shreds in a high wind. The search for an anchorage might be slow, but life aboard ship was no longer lonesome. David Samwell, the surgeon on the *Discovery,* reported many women tried to climb aboard when they were off Maui, but Cook had forbidden their coming into the ships. For this lack of hospitality the surgeon noted that the women "scolded us very smartly." As they sailed along the coast of Hawaii, orders must have been changed, for many women were then keeping the men company.

The commander of the two ships, James Cook, was a man of fifty years, one of the distinguished persons of his time. He was austere, modest, a man of simple habits. He stood over six feet, was spare of build, and somewhat bent. His complexion was dark, his eyes brown, his eyebrows shaggy, and his gaze intense. He tied his brown hair behind in the fashion of the times. He was a cautious, reflective man who might sit through a meal without saying a word to his fellow officers. Those who served under him had great confidence in him, and their affection for him was genuine. In fact, James Cook was respected even by his country's enemies: both France and the American colonies, then at war with Great Britain, ordered their navies to treat Cook as a neutral.

James Cook came from the humblest of beginnings. He was one of nine children born to a day laborer on a Yorkshire farm. His home had been a two-room house with walls of clay, and the education he received was meager. At thirteen he was apprenticed to a shopkeeper at a nearby seaside village, but he was quickly drawn to the sea. He studied astronomy, mathematics, and navigation. He won promotion to mate in the collier fleet and was in line for his own command when he volunteered for the Royal Navy.

Volunteers aboard His Majesty's vessels were rare, because the harsh conditions of life at sea made early death a likely possibility. Cook went in as a common seaman but quickly rose to sailing master. To advance beyond this was most difficult, for commissions in the Royal Navy were largely reserved for the sons of titled families, and Cook had none of the necessary connections. The only way for Cook was to prove his worth again and again. This he did, and at the age of forty the commission at last came.

This was James Cook's third expedition into the Pacific. After his second voyage he had been given the rank of captain at Greenwich Hospital, an easy post ashore. At least he could spend time with his wife and children. The Royal Society had unanimously elected him a member, and that august body awarded him the Copley gold medal for a paper he presented to them on the prevention of scurvy. He was internationally famous; life was comfortable and safe. Then one evening as he sat at dinner with Lord Sandwich, he learned that the admiralty planned to send another expedition into the Pacific. James Cook volunteered to lead it. Before the Copley medal could be struck and presented to him, he had sailed away.

Cook had the choice of many volunteers to man his ships. Among those he chose was young William Bligh, who went as sailing master on the *Resolution*. Later, at the age of twenty-nine, Bligh would gain fame as the captain of the *Bounty* and still later would become a vice admiral. George Vancouver was there as a midshipman. He would become one of the most renowned of Pacific explorers. James Burney was along too. He also rose to the rank of vice admiral and became a distinguished authority on the history of Pacific exploration.

James Cook had that magic combination of perception, patience, and determination which makes exceptional leaders. He observed that fresh fruits and vegetables could prevent scurvy during the long months at sea. On one occasion his crew refused to eat the greens he prescribed. Cook did not hesitate to use the cat-o'-nine-tails to change their minds. Sailors who suffered from scurvy were not as effective as healthy sailors, and they endangered the ship and the expedition, a situation Cook never tolerated.

In Hawaii James Cook would face a series of unfortunate happenings, different from anything he had faced before. At other Pacific islands he had been hailed as a visiting high chief. In Hawaii Cook was considered to be the god Lono. The masts and sails of his ships looked like the high pole and kapa cloth sheets of Lono, and both of Cook's visits occurred during the makahiki season.

At some ancient time Lono had been a mortal man, living at Kealakekua Bay on the island of Hawaii. One day, in a jealous rage, Lono killed his wife. He suffered great anguish because of this deed and thereafter spent his time traveling from island to island taking on all comers in boxing and wrestling matches. One day Lono sailed away in his strange canoe and was not seen again. Eventually the Hawaiians deified him.

After seven weeks of searching the coasts of Maui and Hawaii, Captain Cook saw a bay which he thought would be a safe port for his ships. He sent William Bligh off to determine if it was indeed a safe place and, receiving a favorable reply, ordered his vessels toward the anchorage. For the Hawaiians the selection of Kealakekua Bay was further evidence that a god had returned, because the last time Lono had been seen was when he sailed from that bay. The Hawaiians rushed out to greet Cook as the returning Lono.

From hundreds of canoes, from the shore line and a nearby cliff, the Hawaiians shouted and sang out greetings to the visitors. Cook wrote in his journal, "I have nowhere in this sea seen such a number of people assembled in one place; besides those in the canoes, all the shore of the bay was covered with people, and hundreds were swimming about the ship like shoals of fish." The curious, admiring Hawaiians in fact climbed on deck and up the rigging in such numbers that the ships were in danger of heeling over, and chiefs were told to order some of their people overboard. Lieutenant James King, a young officer in whom Cook had much confidence, estimated there were at least 10,000 Hawaiians surrounding the ship or watching from shore.

Soon a small, solemn old man by the name of Koa climbed aboard. Koa was hardly an imposing figure. He had small reddened eyes, and his face was covered with scaly blotches. Once he had been a warrior, but now he was an important kahuna. In the captain's cabin Koa presented Cook with a small pig, two coconuts, and a piece of red cloth which he ceremoniously wrapped about the captain's shoulders. Cook realized Koa was a man of importance, and he invited him to stay aboard for dinner.

Later in the afternoon a channel through the clutter of surrounding canoes was cleared, and Koa, together with a young chief by the name of Palea, escorted James Cook and Lieutenant King to a heiau which stood above the high tide mark at the head of Kealakekua Bay. As Cook walked by, the people prostrated themselves. Up the narrow steps of the fourteen-foot-high heiau Koa and Palea led Cook and King. The heiau was twenty feet wide and forty feet long. A wooden fence surrounded the top of the heiau, and human skulls, reminders of grim sacrifices, adorned many of the stakes.

In an elaborate ceremony conducted by Koa, the captain was invited to join the priest upon the shaky wooden framework of the oracle tower. After Koa communed with the gods, the two climbed down. Long, solemn chantings and prayers followed, and a putrid pig was uncovered as an offering to the gods. Finally, as evening shadows lengthened across the bay, Lieutenant King and Captain Cook were seated and offered fresh roasted pork and the narcotic drink called awa. In the honored tradition of the Hawaiians, Koa chewed the food first and then tried to feed Cook. The captain politely refused.

The Hawaiians heaped gifts of all kinds on the English, and the weary sailors accepted all the offerings. Many women came aboard the ships, and David Samwell reported, "We live now in the greatest Luxury, and as to the Choice & number of fine women there is hardly one among us that may not vie with the grand Turk himself." In return for their favors the sailors gave the women scraps of iron, scissors, beads, and mirrors.

Kalaniopuu, the king of the island of Hawaii, now made his appearance. He had been in the Hana district of Maui, one of his favorite battlegrounds, when Cook's vessels appeared. As a young man Kalaniopuu had been a famous warrior and athlete. Once he had been cut off from his troops and cornered by a group of enemy soldiers who closed in for the kill. They little knew the fierceness and strength of Kalaniopuu. He killed six of the enemy, and the survivors ran. He was a renowned wrestler and an expert in the art of breaking men's bones with his hands. Those days of prowess were long past, and Samwell described the king as he appeared at

Kealakekua Bay: "He seems to be about 60 years of age, is very tall & thin, seemingly much Emaciated by Debaucheries, tottering as he walks along, his Skin is very scurfy and his Eyes sore with drinking Ava. . . ."

Kalaniopuu presented the captain with large supplies of food. In addition he brought gifts of feather capes, helmets, kapa cloth, feather leis, and wooden bowls. The Hawaiians were friendly and helpful, gladly trading great quantities of salt, vegetables, and pigs for pieces of metal. Good relations seemed assured, and now repairs on the ships were earnestly pushed ahead. There was much to be done. In addition to the rigging, masts, and sails, the seams of the *Resolution* badly needed caulking. While sailing down from the north, as much as three feet of water had filled her well.

Every day hundreds of Hawaiians swam or paddled out to the ships. They so crowded the decks that the sailors could not work, and the Hawaiians were chased overboard. They did not mind. They simply swam about the ships until they were able to climb aboard again. Now and then the natives stole objects made of metal. It was annoying but not serious.

The English were eager to make exact celestial observations, and they could best do this by setting up an observatory on shore. The young chief, Palea, had become a trusted friend, and he offered to tear down some houses near the shore where an unobstructed view of the heavens was possible. Instead the English chose a sweet potato field which was near the heiau. Chiefs obligingly set up kapu sticks around the field so Hawaiians would not enter and bother the English.

The warm sun, friendly people, and ample supplies found at Kealakekua Bay were all the English could have hoped for. The landscape which they viewed from the decks of their vessels was somewhat less pleasing. The English ships were anchored bow-to-shore, and off their port lay the village of Kaawaloa behind fingers of lava which sank gently into the sea. Off the bow was a 500-foot barren cliff which rose straight up from the sea. The high face of this cliff was pitted with small and inaccessible caves where the bones of chiefs were secretly buried. To starboard the gray, rocky shoreline was somewhat relieved by a strip of sandy beach, and next rose the heiau where Cook and Koa had communed with the gods. The green fronds of scattered coconut trees brightened the shore, beyond which scrub growth and pili grass grew among a multitude of black lava boulders. Along the shore stood the thatched homes of thousands of Hawaiians.

High above all this loomed the lordly snow-covered mountain of Mauna Loa. The forests of tall trees on the high slopes and the mountain peak itself were a challenge to a corporal of marines, one John Ledyard. The young marine was an inquisitive man. The first thing people noticed about Ledyard was the back of his hands, which were heavily tattooed, a souvenir of his stay in the southern islands. He had been born in Connecticut and orphaned at an early age. Although he had enrolled at Dartmouth College, he had soon run off to sea. His travels landed him in England, where he joined the British marines and shortly thereafter was one of those who volunteered to sail with Cook. At Kealakekua Bay the restless John Ledyard, with two companions, set out for the top of Mauna Loa, a mountain more than 13,000 feet high.

Off the three men trudged, through the dry lowlands. The first night was spent in the flea-infested hut of a Hawaiian farmer. The next day they pushed on into the cool air of the mountainside, through stands of sandalwood and forests of great koa trees. They passed the huts of Hawaiian craftsmen who fashioned trunks of koa trees into rough canoes high on the mountainsides before hauling them down to the seashore. At night Ledyard and his companions slept beneath the trunk of a fallen tree. In the chill mountain air they pushed on again, but their way was blocked by masses of tangled undergrowth. They gave up and turned back.

Many adventures lay ahead for John Ledyard. When the expedition finally returned to England, Ledyard had become a sergeant, but he refused to fight against the American colonies in their war for independence. On a voyage to America he deserted. Then he wrote an account of Cook's third Pacific voyage, which appeared two years before the official admiralty publication. He was among the first to promote fur trade in the Pacific Northwest. He became a friend of Thomas Jefferson and eventually walked over much of Europe and Russia. John Ledyard died in Cairo at the age of thirty-eight, and his remains were covered over with desert sand.

Less than two weeks after anchoring at Kealakekua Bay, William Watman died. Watman had been on Cook's second voyage, and like his captain he had given up a berth at Greenwich Hospital to sail once more into the Pacific. Captain Cook was fond of the veteran sailor who served as quarter gunner aboard the *Resolution,* and an impressive ceremony was ordered. A guard of marines, with muskets reversed, marched ahead of the flag-covered coffin, keeping step to a funeral march played on a fife. Watman was buried near the heiau, and Cook himself read the Christian burial service, the first ever spoken in Hawaii. To some Islanders the death of William Watman was proof that the haoles, or foreigners, were mortals after all.

The ceremonies surrounding the burial service deeply impressed the Hawaiians. They wanted to do the right thing according to their customs by making the sacrifice of a pig at the grave, but the English would not allow it. At night, after the English had departed, a group of elders quietly climbed the stone base of the heiau and sat about Watman's grave. They killed a pig, threw its entrails into a small fire, and placed the warm carcass over the grave of the sailor.

The tropic sun soon thawed the Arctic cold from the bones of the Englishmen, and James Cook began to plan for another voyage to find the elusive Northwest Passage. The ships had taken on quantities of vegetables, firewood, salt, and pork. Slowly the battered vessels were patched. If there was a slight change in attitude on the part of the Hawaiians, the Englishmen were too busy to notice it.

There indeed had been a change in attitude, and it came partially because so many kapus had been violated. Breaking a kapu was an offense which lay heavily on the conscience of a Hawaiian. Not only would he suffer mental anguish but, if his offense became known to the priests, the transgressor was often speedily strangled or clubbed to death. The observatory camp near the heiau had been protected by kapu sticks, but the English constantly urged women to break the kapu and join the men in the forbidden enclosure. Chiefs viewed this urging with distress. One day the wooden fence atop the heiau was torn down and packed off to the ships as firewood. True, the Hawaiians granted permission, but they could hardly say no to a god. There was also the constant drain of food supplies. James Cook was known for provisioning his ships heavily, and the provisions which went into the vessels meant privation for the Islanders.

Time had strengthened the conviction of some Hawaiians that the English were mere human beings and not gods. Since the haoles provisioned their ships so heavily, the Hawaiians theorized they had left their own country because of a famine. They politely stroked the full stomachs of the English sailors and urged them to leave. They should come again at the next harvest time when there would be ample food. Others listened to the animated story of a woman who frequented the ships. As she lay with a sailor, she had dug her fingernails into his back, and he had cried out in pain. Old traditions proclaimed that gods did not lie with mortal women, much less did they know pain. Perhaps Cook was a god, but his men certainly were not.

If James Cook sensed the feelings of the natives, he calculated that his two ships would sail before trouble began. Cook undoubtedly pondered these things, perhaps in the quiet of his spacious cabin aboard the *Resolution*. Here, in solitude, the captain could see the calm water of the bay through seven great windows which opened astern. In this room he sat in a chair with a high straight back before a wide table and kept his journal. If Cook did not thoroughly understand the feelings of the Islanders, he very well understood the importance of his latest discovery. In his journal he recorded his thoughts concerning the island of Hawaii—"a discovery which, though the last, seemed in many respects to be the most important. . . ."

On February 4, 1779, four weeks after arriving at Kealakekua Bay, James Cook ordered his ships to up anchor. The Hawaiians were pleased. As a farewell gift the haoles were given a last generous supply of pigs, fruits, and vegetables. The English, however, still had unfilled water kegs, so the old priest, Koa, who had changed his name to Britannee to honor the visitors, sailed with Cook for several days to point out an inlet where fresh water could be found. After completing his task Koa and other visiting Hawaiians sailed off in their canoes. The *Resolution* and *Discovery* set their course toward Kohala, the northern tip of Hawaii.

Today you can stand on the Kohala hills and look down on the sea where the two ships sailed. A point of land juts out here which shields the sea from the wind. Beyond this point the ocean abruptly changes from quiet water to white-capped violence. When the English sailed into this sea, they ran into these winds, and during the night the foremast of the *Resolution* split. By the morning's light grim officers tried to estimate the damage. Support strips had been fastened, splint-like, around the foremast at Nootka Sound in British Columbia, and it had been considered seaworthy, but now the mast endangered the ship. To avoid disaster a quick decision was needed. Cook knew of only the one harbor within reasonable sailing distance. It had taken him seven weeks to find Kealakekua Bay in the first place, and this was certainly not the time for further searching. The order was given to come about and return to Kealakekua Bay.

When the two vessels again reached the familiar bay, it was deserted. A boat was sent ashore and the returning sailors reported that King Kalaniopuu had placed a kapu on the bay. Such a kapu was not uncommon in ancient Hawaii. After a section of land or a lagoon had been used excessively, chiefs often put areas off limits to allow plants or sea life to again grow undisturbed for a time.

The Englishmen were uneasy, but they had work to do. The foremast of the *Resolution* was unstepped and floated ashore where it could be worked on. To make the best use of their time, an observatory was again set up in the sweet potato patch. The next day the king came down to the bay and greeted the English in a friendly way, but somehow the mood of the people had changed. Somehow the warmth of the Hawaiians had disappeared. An incident erupted when chiefs ordered commoners not to help a party of Englishmen who had gone ashore for water. The six marines who protected the workers on shore were ordered to load their rifles with ball instead of grapeshot.

Cook and his trusted officer, James King, settled the dispute between the watering party and the Islanders. No sooner was this accomplished than the rattle of musket shots was heard from the direction of the *Discovery*. Cook looked up to see a canoe load of natives paddling furiously away from the ship toward shore. Obviously the Hawaiians had stolen something and were trying to escape. Cook, King, and a marine ran across the rocks and sand in an attempt to catch the thieves as they reached shore.

The three Englishmen were too late to intercept the Islanders, so they plunged inland after them. They kept up the pursuit through the undergrowth for some three miles before they realized that the Hawaiians from whom they asked information along the way were misleading them. When they returned to the beach, disheveled and winded, Cook learned that the master of the *Discovery* had decided to come ashore and seize the canoe the thieves had used. It turned out that the canoe belonged to chief Palea, the friend of the English. When Palea demanded his canoe, a fight broke out, and the chief was hit on the head with an oar. The Hawaiians attacked the English, who were forced to take cover behind some boulders in the surf. Fortunately Palea restored order, and the combatants supposedly parted as friends.

At dawn the next morning a German seaman, Henry Zimmerman, was standing watch aboard the *Discovery*. By the first dim light he saw that the cutter, which had been tied to a buoy a dozen yards from the bow, was gone. It seemed impossible, but the Hawaiians had succeeded in stealing her during the night.

At six o'clock Captain Charles Clerke, who was in command of the *Discovery*, was rowed over to Cook's ship bearing the bad news. Cook was furious. The cutter was the best boat the two ships carried. He ordered the bay blockaded so no canoes could enter or leave. He went to his cabin, loaded a double-barreled gun, and ordered his six-oared pinnace to carry him to the village of Kaawaloa at the northern tip of the bay. With Cook went Lieutenant of Marines Molesworth Phillips and a guard of nine marines.

Cook's mission was to see King Kalaniopuu. He planned to use a strategy which had worked in similar crises in the South Pacific: he would invite Kalaniopuu aboard his ship, and once there he would hold him hostage until his worried subjects returned the cutter. It had worked before, and he thought it would work again.

At seven o'clock James Cook and his marines waded ashore across the slippery black lava rock which stretched out into the sea. The pinnace and another boat, which had helped carry the marines, waited just off shore. Cook considered himself a friend of the Hawaiians. He did not fear them, nor had they anything to fear from him.

Some thirty yards from the sea was the thatched home of Kalaniopuu.

The king was just rising when Molesworth Phillips looked in at the door of the king's house. Cook entered and sat by the aged king, talking about the lost cutter. The captain decided the king knew nothing of the theft, but he still wished to carry through his plan, and he invited the king to spend the day aboard his ship. Kalaniopuu was most pleased. On his way to the royal house Cook had walked along with one of the king's sons and had invited him aboard also. The eager boy was already waiting in one of the English boats.

While Kalaniopuu and Cook were talking, a crowd of men and women gathered outside the royal house. The captain and the king left the house and started through the crowd toward the water's edge. The king's wives and some of his chiefs, however, did not think the old man should go. They loudly wept and pleaded with him to stay. Finally, near the shore, they forced the king to sit down.

The crowd had quickly grown, and it pressed forward. Lieutenant Phillips asked Cook if he might draw his men up along the water, where they could level their long black muskets and where no enemies would be at their backs. Cook thought it unnecessary, but he granted permission. At that instant the sound of firing echoed across the bay, and the Hawaiians became alarmed. Cook now knew he could not bring the king with him. He started for the pinnace alone just as a runner burst into the excited crowd and shouted that the Englishmen had killed a high-ranking chief who had tried to leave the bay in his canoe.

This was a declaration of war. Women and children disappeared. Men put on armor of protective woven mats and grasped spears, daggers, stones, and clubs. A warrior came at Cook, threatening him with an upraised dagger. Cook jerked up his gun and pulled the trigger. The barrel, containing small shot, pelted the mat armor of the warrior, who triumphantly turned to show the others he was unharmed. The timid were now emboldened to attack the man they had long believed to be a god. One Englishman estimated there were between 22,000 and 32,000 armed Hawaiians on the beach at Kaawaloa early that Sunday morning.

Cook retreated toward the ocean's edge. Molesworth Phillips was nearby. Another warrior attacked Cook with a dagger. Cook hastily fired, missed his assailant, but killed the man next to him. Phillips knocked down one attacker and shot still another. The marines had now lined up on the shore, and they fired a volley into the crowd. The men in the boats also opened fire. Cook had backed to the water and was standing knee-deep in surf. He turned to wave the boats in and called for a cease fire. When he turned his back, he was hit a furious blow on the head with a club. As he fell another warrior stabbed him in the back. An hour after coming ashore Cook was dead.

Phillips fired his last shot and, although badly wounded by a dagger thrust, drew his sword and fought off the Hawaiians in the surf. At last he turned and swam for a boat. No sooner had Phillips been hauled aboard than he saw an injured marine flounder in the sea and disappear. He jumped into the water again and pulled the man aboard. Later David Samwell reported that the marines had fired a volley, dropped their muskets, and run. Four of the nine were killed by the Hawaiians, while the others struggled toward safety aboard the boats. The sailors pulled at the oars to escape the shower of stones hurled by the Islanders. Lieutenant King described what happened when Cook was hit:

"On seeing him fall, the islanders set up a great shout, and his body was immediately dragged on shore, and surrounded by the enemy, who snatching the daggers out of each other's hands, showed a savage eagerness to have a share in his destruction.

"Thus fell our great and excellent Commander!"

The sailors aboard the *Resolution* saw the battle on shore and fired two cannons in the direction of the Hawaiians, who finally retreated from the beach. The boats could now have landed to recover the bodies of the dead, but Lieutenant Williamson, who was in command of one of the boats, refused to go in. This enraged Molesworth Phillips, who threatened to kill Williamson on the spot as a coward; on two later occasions Phillips challenged him to a duel, but Williamson refused. William Bligh's opinion was that the reluctant lieutenant should have been hanged from the yardarm. (Years later John Williamson was court martialed and cashiered from the Royal Navy. It happened in 1797, after the British had won the battle of Camperdown. The charge then brought against Williamson would have sounded familiar to many who had been at Kealakekua Bay: he was convicted of "disobedience to signals and in not rendering all assistance possible." He was never allowed to serve again aboard one of His Majesty's ships.)

The Englishmen were stunned and demoralized by James Cook's death. Nearly everyone on board the two ships had a great affection for their captain. His death seemed unreal and unnecessary. Seaman Zimmerman wrote, "Everyone on the ship was silent and depressed; we all felt we had lost a father." Zimmerman also noted that if Cook had gone ashore without armed men, all would have ended well, "but unfortunately he was too angry to do this." Samwell lamented, ". . . in every situation he stood unrivaled and alone; on him all eyes were turned; he was our leading star, which, at its setting, left us involved in darkness and despair."

Charles Clerke now succeeded to command of the expedition. Clerke was weak with tuberculosis, which he had contracted while serving time in a debtors' prison near London for the obligations of a relative. He would live six months more, dying at the age of thirty-eight, long before the two ships returned to England. Lieutenant Gore was promoted to captain of the *Discovery* and Lieutenant King to command of the *Resolution*.

The officers decided on two objectives. The mast and some of the sails of the *Resolution* were on shore, guarded by a small garrison of six marines, and men and equipment must be made safe against attack. The second objective was to recover the bodies of Cook and the four marines and retrieve the cutter from the Hawaiians.

No sooner had these decisions been made than the sound of musketry was heard on shore. William Bligh and the marines under his command were stationed atop the heiau, and they were firing at Hawaiians who tried to attack them up the narrow stairway. When reinforcements were rushed ashore, a truce was reached. The sails, the mast, and the instruments from the observatory were taken out to the *Resolution*. James King now tried to convince the Hawaiians to return the bodies of the five fallen men.

That night two nervous sentries aboard the *Resolution* heard the sound of paddles quietly dipped into the sea. They fired into the darkness, narrowly missing two Hawaiians who called out for permission to come aboard. When this was granted, they climbed on deck carrying a small bundle wrapped in kapa. They solemnly opened the bundle, and by the flickering light of a lantern, the English looked with horror at a heap of bloody flesh which had been cut from Cook's body.

The English were appalled by this treatment of Cook's body, and some accused the Hawaiians of being cannibals. Cook's remains however, had been given the honors befitting the highest chiefs. The Hawaiians traditionally scraped the flesh from the bones of great men. The bones were then tied together and buried secretly so they could not be desecrated later. If the dead person had been held in great affection, his bones might be kept in the home for a period of time. Because Cook was greatly esteemed, parts of his body were distributed among the high chiefs. His head went to the king. His scalp had gone to a high-ranking chief. The treatment that horrified the English was in fact an honor bestowed by the Hawaiians.

During the next several days the English took brutal revenge. The official journal of the voyage gives no details, but it appears the officers lost control of their men, who ran amok in an orgy of destruction and bloodshed. One attack took place on February 17 when an undetermined number of Islanders were killed and their village burned. More men were killed during the next several days. After one foray the heads of two Hawaiians were stuck on the bows of English long boats. King, who finished Cook's journal and who was ill during this time, later wrote a vague apology and concluded by saying, "Had I been present myself, I might probably have been the means of saving their little society from destruction."

One result of the bloodshed was that the Hawaiians were frightened into returning additional remnants of Cook's body to the English. On one occasion a chief dressed in a ceremonial red feather cloak returned the hands, skull, arms, and leg bones of the captain.

In the fading evening light of February 21, 1779, the remains of Captain James Cook, R.N., were sewed into a hammock, and after burial services were read by Captain Clerke, the hammock was slid off into the waters of the bay. The British flag was flown half up, and a ten-gun salute was fired. Many of the sailors and marines who lined the railings of the two ships wept openly. No Hawaiians crowded about the ships to watch the ceremonies, for the king had placed a kapu on the bay. The next morning the English sailed, stopping at the islands to the north, where the girlfriends of the sailors finally departed from the ships.

Captain Clerke made another attempt to find the Northwest Passage, but once again an impenetrable ice pack forced the ships to turn about. Clerke died of tuberculosis before they reached the Russian settlement of Petropavlovsk in Siberia. He had asked to be buried ashore, not in the frozen waters of the Arctic, and his remains were interred near this tiny settlement. From here reports were sent to the admiralty concerning the expedition. They were carried by dogsled and horse across Russia, reaching England six months later. When the *Resolution* and *Discovery* reached home, the war with the American colonies was going badly, and there was little interest in their explorations. The ships' crews were dispersed to various war duties. The *Resolution* was converted into an armed transport, and the *Discovery* became a convict ship where men were imprisoned until they could be shipped off to Botany Bay in Australia.

The government did take notice of Mrs. Cook, that patient and obscure woman who so rarely saw her husband. They voted her a pension of 200 pounds a year and half the profits from the sale of her husband's books. A coat of arms, which included a map of the Pacific Ocean, was bestowed on the family, but the six children of James and Elizabeth Cook died young, without issue, and there was no one to wear the family crest. Mrs. Cook survived them all, living to the age of ninety-three. She lived amid the collection of things her husband had gathered on his voyages, and she observed the anniversary of his death by fasting and reading from the Bible he had carried with him on his last trip into the Pacific.

Chapter Four

"ENJOY QUIETLY
WHAT I HAVE MADE RIGHT . . ."

WHEN THE ENGLISH DEPARTED, the Hawaiian chiefs returned to their own struggles for power. The Island chain had long been divided into four centers of power, which were the four largest islands. On the island of Hawaii, Kalaniopuu held unchallenged sway, and during much of his reign he was also able to hold the Hana district of east Maui. The rest of Maui, together with the small islands of Kahoolawe and Lanai, were ruled by the wily Kahekili. Oahu was controlled by an old warrior king while Kauai and its little neighbor, Niihau, were embroiled in a series of civil wars. The unfortunate island of Molokai, lying between Oahu and Maui, was periodically overrun by one or the other of its powerful neighbors.

In about 1775 Kalaniopuu launched another invasion of Maui. His army swept up the rocky mountain side at Kaupo, looting and killing the inhabitants. King Kahekili of Maui regrouped his forces, and the two armies locked in battle among the sweet potato patches which dotted the hillside. At last the warriors of Maui gained the upper hand and drove the invaders toward the seashore. Kalaniopuu suffered heavy losses before getting the remnant of his army off in canoes.

The only difference between this battle and hundreds of others which had been fought before was that it appears to have been the first action seen by a warrior from the island of Hawaii named Kamehameha. As the forces of the invaders were retreating, Kamehameha saw a companion warrior go down under enemy attack. The fallen warrior was Kamehameha's teacher in the arts of warfare. As the enemy prepared to dispatch him, Kamehameha led his men to the rescue. The bravery of Kamehameha was obvious to both armies, and the chiefs of Maui, in admiration, called him the "hard-shelled crab," a name he would bear through life.

The chiefs of Maui had marked their man well, for Kamehameha was destined to become Hawaii's most famous warrior-king. At the time of the battle at Kaupo, Kamehameha was a high-ranking chief, about nineteen years of age and a favorite of King Kalaniopuu. He was a brawny, proud, athletic youth whose fierceness was compounded by a savage, furrowed face. His paternity is not known, but some believed his father was none other than Kahekili, the king of Maui.

About three years later, when James Cook had returned to the Islands from the American northwest, Kamehameha was again on Maui with the forces which were battling in the Hana district. As Cook sailed by, a number of Hawaiians paddled out to board his ships. Among these was the warrior Kamehameha. Most of the Hawaiians returned to shore at dusk, but Kamehameha spent the night aboard the flagship, and when the sun rose the following morning, Cook's vessels and Kamehameha had disappeared. Kalaniopuu was distressed by the loss of his warrior, and he sent a canoe in pursuit. There was nothing to fear. James Cook had kept Kamehameha and several other Hawaiians aboard to help him find a suitable harbor on the island of Hawaii.

Later, when the Englishmen had safely anchored in Kealakekua Bay, Lieutenant James King noticed Kamehameha as he came aboard the *Discovery* with Kalaniopuu. King wrote the first description of the chief in his diary: "Kamehameha whose hair was now plastered over with a brown dirty sort of paste or powder, & which added to as savage a looking face as I ever saw, it however by no means seemed an emblem of his disposition, which was good natured & humorous, although his manner showed somewhat of an overbearing spirit, & he seemed to be the principal director of this interview."

The powerful weapons which the English displayed at Kealakekua Bay tremendously impressed the warriors of Kalaniopuu. If only they could get their hands on muskets and cannons, Kahekili and Maui would soon be conquered. With the guns, of course, they would need a white man as a teacher. Their choice was the personable Lieutenant King, a man many Hawaiians considered to be the son of Cook. Kalaniopuu approached James Cook and asked him to leave King behind. When Kalaniopuu made no headway with Cook, he talked to the lieutenant himself. The Hawaiians offered to hide him away in the hills until Cook had sailed. They promised that he would become a chief and a great man.

The Hawaiians failed to convince the visitors to give them weapons and an instructor, but their warlike ardor was not dampened. With the English gone, Kalaniopuu started preparations for another invasion of Maui. He assembled a vast fleet of canoes and sailed across the sixty-five miles to Maalaea Bay on Maui. His canoes lined the sandy beach for miles, and a picked corps of eight hundred warriors marched across the low sand hills of central Maui, hoping to push the defending forces into narrow Iao Valley. Kalaniopuu still was no match for Kahekili. The Maui king had shrewdly set a trap, and Kalaniopuu's forces were encircled and slaughtered before they reached Iao Valley. Of the eight hundred picked warriors only two escaped to carry word of the disaster to Kalaniopuu. On the following day Kalaniopuu and his chiefs again attacked Kahekili with a reserve force. Again Kahekili was victorious, and the king of Hawaii had to sue for peace. After many formal promises of friendship Kalaniopuu was allowed to return to the island of Hawaii. Soon afterward his stronghold in Hana was overwhelmed, ending completely his hold on Maui.

Kahekili was a ruthless, capable man. Neither Kalaniopuu nor Kamehameha ever brought him to heel. As a young man his favorite pastime had been diving from high cliffs into the sea. One half of Kahekili's body was heavily tattooed from head to foot, giving him a frightening appearance. His subjects believed he crept about at night listening for traitorous talk. After his bloody conquest of Oahu, Kahekili built a house of human bones and skulls which reminded the Oahuans of the fate which could so easily befall any of them.

Back on his home island Kalaniopuu attended to an important official act. He wanted his chiefs to know clearly who was to succeed him as ruler when he died. To make his wishes known he announced that a solemn meeting was to be held at the sacred heiau at Waipio Valley. In the beautiful setting of this valley Kalaniopuu announced that his son, Kiwalao, would succeed to the kingship of the island. Kamehameha, the famous warrior, was given custody of Kukailimoku, the powerful war god of the kings of the island of Hawaii, the god which generations before had been entrusted to Umi.

This war god was to play a great role in Hawaii's history during the next thirty years. The image of Kukailimoku was a bust which stood twenty-seven inches high. It was made of woven reeds over which were closely tied thousands of red and yellow feathers. The eyebrows and nostrils were of black feathers. A gaping mouth was inset with ninety-four dog teeth. A crest ran back from the forehead in the familiar helmet pattern. The large, glaring, almond-shaped eyes were of pearl shells. Kukailimoku was a grim figure. The image of the god was once lost but was discovered thirty years after Kamehameha's death in a cave on the island of Hawaii, where some faithful believer in the old religion had hidden it.

Kamehameha was a man of driving ambition who would never settle for less than absolute rule of the whole island. The mere fact that another had now been designated as king-apparent could not deter him. Kamehameha had respect and perhaps admiration for Kalaniopuu, but Kiwalao was simply an obstacle to overcome. After the pronouncements had been made at Waipio Valley, the old king discovered he had yet another task. A chief at Kau had revolted, and Kalaniopuu traveled south to battle the rebel. The uprising was put down, the rebel chief captured, and preparations were made to sacrifice him to the war god. Kiwalao was present as the representative of his father, and he was in the heiau about to perform the sacrifice when Kamehameha stepped forward and dispatched the rebel chief himself.

This was a breach of manners, an outright insult to Kiwalao, and Kamehameha was told by the old king to leave the royal court. Kamehameha retired to his lands in the north, carrying his war god with him. As for Kalaniopuu, he spent his remaining days enjoying his hula dancers. At last he died in 1782, and the way was open for a showdown between Kamehameha and Kiwalao.

The showdown was not long in coming. By the summer of 1782 the chiefs of Hawaii had chosen sides and a battle was fought. In the engagement Kiwalao was hit with a sling stone and then dispatched by a chief who cut his throat with a short dagger that had a shark's tooth blade. The issue was far from settled, however, for Kiwalao's half-brother, Keoua, successfully held out against Kamehameha. He was supported by Kahekili of Maui, who sent troops to help fan the flames of civil war. With a civil war keeping the island of Hawaii busy, Kahekili felt he could safely invade Oahu, and he soon subdued that island.

While the Hawaiians were involved with these struggles, events were happening in the distant offices of merchants which would soon bring many sailing vessels to the Islands. Before Cook's time only the Spanish could claim any knowledge of the central Pacific, for their galleons plied these latitudes voyaging between Mexico and the Philippine Islands. If the Spanish knew of the Hawaiian Islands, they kept the secret extremely well hidden. The seeds for the opening of the central Pacific were sown when Cook's men, on their homeward passage, discovered that the furs they had collected in the Pacific Northwest were in great demand in Canton. The profit was fantastic: a pelt could be bought for next to nothing in Northwest America and sold in Canton for $100. A fortune could be realized on a single voyage, and merchants in England and the United States were eager to take the risks to gain such profits. Hawaii was on the line of trade between the Northwest and Canton, and on this trying voyage few captains would dare ignore the opportunity to pause for rest and provisions. The first to come were Captains Portlock and Dixon in 1786. After that Western sailing ships soon became a common sight for Islanders.

The Hawaiians were fascinated by the marvelous things the haoles, or foreigners, possessed and they were eager to learn about the mysterious outside world. Large numbers of Islanders beseeched visiting captains to take them along. John Meares, who reached Hawaii in 1787 in command of an English trading vessel, described his experience on Kauai: "Presents were poured in upon us from the chiefs, who were prevented by the multitude from approaching the vessel, and the clamorous cry of 'Britannee, Britannee,' was for a long time vociferated from every part, and without ceasing: nor can their silent grief be described, when it was made known among them, that Kaiana, a prince of Atooi, [Kauai] was the only one selected to the envied honour of sailing with us."

It was no wonder Kaiana was the man Meares selected. The chief was a shrewd, winsome person, adept at judging men and capable of playing whatever role would benefit him. He certainly was an imposing figure, and on the way to China he endeared himself to the English captain. "Kaiana was about thirty-two years of age; he was near six feet five inches in stature, and the muscular form of his limbs was of an Herculean appearance. His carriage was replete with dignity, and having lived in the habit of receiving the respect due to superior rank in his own country, he possessed an air of distinction, which we will not suppose could suffer any diminution from his observation of European manners. He wore the dress of Europe with the habitual ease of its inhabitants."

Kaiana's voyage was full of adventure. He suffered a long, serious illness at sea. When he reached Canton he came across Winee, a woman who had been hired in Hawaii to serve as maid to a captain's wife. On the trip to China Winee became ill and was put ashore. Kaiana wanted her returned to Hawaii, and she was taken aboard, but she died and was buried at sea. Kaiana wailed loudly for his fellow Islander. Captain Nathaniel Portlock again saw the chief in Canton and reported the emotional greeting he received. Kaiana was so affected that "tears ran unheeded down his cheeks, and it was some time before he became calm and composed enough to utter the name of his old acquaintance. . . ." Kaiana must have charmed the English colony in Canton, because they presented him with enough money to buy a substantial supply of western goods and also to have his portrait painted. He sailed from there to the Pacific Northwest and then got passage with a Captain William Douglas back to the Hawaiian Islands. In December of 1788 Kaiana again saw the Islands of Hawaii on the horizon.

During his long travels Kaiana had fits of melancholy because he was so far from home. Once near the Islands, however, he became somber for quite another reason. He could not know what shifts in power had taken place during his travels, and he would be a doomed man if enemy factions now controlled Kauai. Captain Douglas was likewise concerned, since he had now joined the circle of those charmed by the Hawaiian chief. Douglas stopped first at the island of Hawaii, where he learned that Kaiana's enemies did indeed control Kauai.

Kamehameha quickly realized that the great warrior could be a valuable ally. He offered Kaiana land and a position of power on his island if he would stay. Kaiana accepted and brought ashore his possessions, which included saws, hatchets, knives, cloth of various kinds, carpets, bars of iron, and a considerable amount of China ware. More important, the chief carried back a supply of muskets and ammunition. Kaiana and Kamehameha now proceeded to explain the complicated political situation in the Islands to Douglas. They said Portlock and Dixon had supplied their enemies with guns and ammunition, and they needed the same to defend themselves. Douglas apparently accepted these statements at face value. Not only did he supply the chiefs with small arms, but he ordered his carpenter to build a sturdy platform on a double canoe on which he mounted a swivel gun.

Captain Douglas might not have been the most astute captain to visit Hawaii, but he could well have been the most long-suffering. He did every possible service for Kaiana, including bringing his family from Kauai to the island of Hawaii, yet it was his fate to be paid back with a series of harassments. At this time a popular pastime for the Hawaiians was to cut the anchor cables of visiting ships. If the ships drifted ashore, they could then be looted. Douglas' ship first had its cable cut at Kealakekua Bay, but the vessel did not drift ashore. Later, on Maui, a Hawaiian was caught attempting to do the same thing. Off Waikiki two cables were cut, and Douglas went ashore to discover that both anchors had been dragged into the hut of a chief. By bribing the chief with a pistol, a musket, and ammunition and at the same time threatening to burn down his village, the captain got his anchors back. By the time he arrived at Niihau Douglas had a different type of problem. Two sailors and the quartermaster deserted after their plan to set the ship afire had failed. Douglas got the two sailors back but not the quartermaster. Doubtless the captain was glad to see the Islands fall away beyond the horizon as he sailed for the Pacific Northwest.

In early 1790 two American trading vessels reached Hawaii. The first ship to arrive was the *Eleanora,* commanded by Simon Metcalfe. Following behind on a smaller vessel came his son, Thomas Metcalfe. When the *Eleanora* reached the north shore of the island of Hawaii, they had an immediate problem which the elder Metcalfe handled in a direct way. A chief by the name of Kameeiamoku came aboard with his retainers, and shortly Metcalfe caught the chief in the act of stealing. As punishment he hit the chief with a rope's end. Sailing on to Maui, Metcalfe lost his longboat one night. The boat, which was towed astern of the ship, had a Filipino seaman aboard as guard. The seaman had been asleep when the Hawaiians cut the towing rope and climbed aboard. The seaman awoke to stare into the faces of the Hawaiians. He drew his knife but was quickly overpowered and his body later offered as a sacrifice at a heiau. In the morning the Hawaiian women aboard the *Eleanora* sensed an ugly mood. They jumped overboard and swam to the beach.

Captain Simon Metcalfe at this time did not know exactly what had happened to his seaman and boat, although he was suspicious and his anger was rising. He refused to trade with the canoes which came out, and when the Hawaiians milled about the ship Metcalfe fired on them, killing or wounding three or four. That evening as the ship lay near shore, a Hawaiian swam out and tried to pry the copper plating off the bottom of the hull. He was captured, and Metcalfe swung a rope from the yardarm to hang him. His life was saved only by the intercession of several crew members. The next morning the *Eleanora* pulled in close to shore and fired on an armed group of Hawaiians who had gathered on shore. After they had been driven inland, a party of sailors landed and burned their village.

Metcalfe moved along the coast of Maui seeking news of his lost boat and hoping to procure fresh water. At one village not only was he able to fill his water casks but, according to a report published nearly two years later in a Boston newspaper, the captain bought a "small boy and a girl for two axes and a few beads." Metcalfe now started to sail away from Maui, but some Hawaiians overtook him in their canoe and said they knew the chief who had stolen his boat. The captain put about and the next day was visited by a chief who said he could recover both the longboat and the vanished seaman. The price agreed upon for producing the boat was one musket, eight charges of powder and shot, one bar of iron, and a piece of Bengal cloth. The same reward would be paid for the return of the seaman.

As they waited offshore a Hawaiian swam out and brought the thigh bones, all that remained of the missing sailor. Later the chief came aboard and received the reward promised him. Before long the chief again returned, bringing with him the keel of the long boat. The Hawaiians had broken it up for the metal it contained. The chief now asked for his second reward. According to the newspaper account, Captain Metcalfe said, "I will now give the reward they little expect."

Metcalfe planned a bloody revenge. All cannons were ordered to the starboard side of the ship. The Hawaiians were then told the port side of the ship was kapu, but trading canoes could approach the starboard side. Each of the seven large cannons were loaded with one hundred musket balls, about fifty nails, plus scraps of metal. Four quarter-deck guns were loaded with fifty musket balls each and the swivels with ten to twenty balls.

When the canoes had been coaxed in close, Metcalfe gave the order to fire a broadside. The newspaper account continued: "The attempt to describe the horrible scene that ensued is too much for my pen. The water alongside continued of a crimson colour, for at least ten minutes, some were sinking, others lying half out of their canoes, without arms or legs; while others lay in their canoes weltering in their blood."

The crew of the *Eleanora* wanted to finish off the wounded with boarding pikes, but somehow were restrained. An estimated 100 Hawaiians had been killed and many of the 200 or so who had been wounded died during the next few days. Later the Hawaiians dragged as many bodies as they could upon the beach at Olowalu. Because so many had been hit in the head, the Hawaiians called this the slaughter of "the spilled brains." It has gone down in history as the Olowalu Massacre.

Thomas Metcalfe, the eighteen-year-old son of Simon, had belatedly reached the Hawaiian Islands in the *Fair American*. By coincidence the young man had stopped in the northern part of the island of Hawaii, and chief Kameeiamoku came aboard his tiny ship, still smarting from the insult of being struck by the elder Metcalfe. The chief and his men waited their chance and then took quick revenge. All six members of the crew were thrown into the ocean, and only the mate survived.

The mate was Isaac Davis. When the attack began, he pulled a pistol from his belt and pointed it at the chief. He pulled the trigger, but it misfired. Davis was hurled into the sea. The Hawaiians pulled his clothes off and hit him with paddles as he struggled in the water. Then they pulled him across the outrigger booms of a canoe and jumped up and down on him. Davis, fortunately, was a husky, athletic man and somehow managed to survive. At last a chief took pity on him and gave him protection. When Kamehameha heard of the attack, made by a chief under his rule, he hurried north and severely reprimanded Kameeiamoku. He took the *Fair American* away from the chief and placed Isaac Davis under his personal protection.

While this commotion was taking place in the north, the elder Metcalfe had sailed from Maui to Kealakekua Bay, not knowing that his son had reached Hawaii, much less that he had been drowned in a bay a short distance away. The boatswain of the *Eleanora,* a round-faced, sad-eyed Englishman by the name of John Young, was sent ashore to inquire about provisions. Immediately Kamehameha realized he had a dangerous situation on his hands. If the captain of the *Eleanora* learned of the capture of the small ship and the killing of her crew by Kameeiamoku he could well seek revenge. Kamehameha, by this time, might also have heard of the elder Metcalfe's vengeance at Olowalu, which certainly would have added to his apprehension. Kamehameha wasted no time. He put a kapu on the *Eleanora,* so Hawaiians could not carry word of events to her captain. Then he took John Young captive, so word would not reach Metcalfe through the boatswain.

Captain Metcalfe waited several days for Young to return to the ship. He fired signal cannon and even sent a letter ashore asking the help of several white men living near Kealakekua. Finally Metcalfe sailed away, probably convinced that Young had deserted and still ignorant of the fate of his son. Some four years later Simon Metcalfe and another son were trading for furs off Queen Charlotte Islands in the Pacific Northwest. Their ship was crowded with Indians, who suddenly attacked the crew, killing both father and son.

In quick succession two white men had fallen into Kamehameha's hands. He could not have known what great assistance this pair of Englishmen would be to him, but it must have been clear soon that Davis and Young were different from the usual white derelicts who had deserted or had been dropped on the beach by passing captains. Davis was about thirty-six years old and John Young about forty-five when they came to Hawaii. They had little formal education, but they possessed an unusual degree of common sense and integrity. Early in their captivity the two unsuccessfully tried to escape, but before long they decided to cast their lot with Kamehameha, who made them important chiefs. In turn they gave the Hawaiian ruler long years of loyal service.

The wily Kahekili was now living at Waikiki on Oahu, and Kamehameha felt he had the strength to overcome Maui and yet maintain his position on the island of Hawaii. This time he was right. Without Kahekili's leadership the warriors of Maui were driven across the sand hills of Wailuku and into Iao Valley. John Young and Isaac Davis had mounted cannons on carriages, and the loud noise of these guns, echoing back and forth up the narrow valley, probably did more to demoralize than destroy the enemy. The slaughter was great, however, because the Iao River was blocked by the bodies of the dead, and the battle became known as the "damming of the waters."

Encamped on Molokai, which had also fallen to him, Kamehameha pondered a message he had received. Earlier he sent a messenger to a famous kahuna on Kauai asking what he must do to conquer all the Hawaiian Islands. Now the answer had come. Kamehameha must build a great heiau at Kawaihae for his war god, Kukailimoku.

At this time Kamehameha learned that his old enemy, Keoua, had invaded his lands on Hawaii, and he rushed back to the island of Hawaii.

The archenemies engaged in fierce fighting with neither army winning a decisive victory. Both armies fell back to respective strongholds, and in doing so Keoua was dealt a serious blow. As a division of Keoua's army marched south, they passed the crater of Kilauea. Suddenly that volcano erupted explosively, sending up clouds of heavy smoke, spewing forth stones, ash, and suffocating gases. Four hundred men, women, and children were asphyxiated or killed by falling rocks. It was a demoralizing loss for Keoua, because it clearly showed that the fire goddess, Pele, was on the side of Kamehameha.

With a truce in effect, Kamehameha decided to build the great heiau at Kawaihae. The site chosen was a hillside overlooking the sea, and here thousands of workers camped to labor on the project. Kahunas were everywhere, attending to the vital rituals which had to be followed as work progressed. Kamehameha himself carried stones to the building site. Work was interrupted when a fleet of Kahekili's boats appeared, but in a long naval battle off Waipio Valley the forces of Kamehameha drove off the invaders. Sometime during the summer of 1791 the heiau was completed at last.

The events which followed the completion of the heiau are not clear, but it appears that Kamehameha resorted to treachery to eliminate Keoua. Two chiefs were sent to Keoua inviting him to visit Kamehameha at Kawaihae. What the two emissaries told Keoua is not known. Strangely enough, Keoua agreed to come. There seems to have been much fatalism in Keoua's agreement to make the trip, because he selected as the companions for his canoe those chiefs who were suitable death companions for him.

As Keoua sailed into the bay, Kamehameha stood on the shore, clad in feather cape and helmet, greeting him from a distance. When Keoua stepped ashore, one of Kamehameha's warriors threw a spear at him and then rushed up and in a brief struggle killed him. The rest of the men in the canoe were slaughtered. The act could have been one of sudden violence on the part of an impetuous chief, but more likely it had been planned by Kamehameha. Keoua's body was taken to the new heiau as a fitting sacrifice. The whole island of Hawaii was now Kamehameha's, and he spent the next three years developing his ravaged land and trading with foreign ships.

It was during these few peaceful years that a stocky, stern bachelor sailor by the name of George Vancouver made three visits to Hawaii. Of all the captains who visited Hawaii, Vancouver probably made the greatest impression on Kamehameha. The English captain was thirty-five years old when he had been given command of a three-ship expedition into the Pacific. He had sailed in the Pacific twice before, on Cook's second and third expeditions. Vancouver's orders instructed him to return lands and property seized by the Spaniards in the American Northwest to British owners and to complete the charting of the Northwest coast, a job Cook had started.

His flagship was a three-masted, full rigged sloop of war, with a copper sheathed bottom, mounting ten four-pounders and ten swivel guns. He called the ship *Discovery,* the name borne by Cook's second ship. On the after part of the quarterdeck stood a strange little structure which must have irritated the captain of a man-of-war. It was a greenhouse built for the use of Archibald Menzies, a botanist, who served as ship's surgeon for most of the voyage. Vancouver noted in his journal that the greenhouse was "for the purpose of preserving such new or uncommon plants as he (Menzies) might deem worthy of a place amongst His Majesty's very valuable collection of exotics at Kew." Along with the *Discovery* went the *Chatham,* a slow two-masted ship, which constantly fell behind the flagship.

The two vessels departed from Falmouth on April 1, 1791, sailed around the Cape of Good Hope, proceeded to New Zealand and then to Tahiti. Aboard ship was a Hawaiian named "Towereroo" who had been carried to London in 1789 on a fur trader. In Tahiti Towereroo jumped ship after meeting an engaging young Tahitian maiden. Vancouver was a literal-minded man, and his orders were specific. Towereroo was to be returned to Hawaii, and so the desolate deserter was retrieved and Vancouver sailed north toward Hawaii.

In March, 1792, Vancouver anchored in the familiar bay at Kealakekua, and before long Kaiana came aboard the flagship. Kaiana immediately asked for guns and ammunition, but the Englishman would give him none. Then Kaiana requested passage for himself and his retinue to Kauai, an island he had every reason to avoid. Vancouver suspected that the chief was really looking for an opportunity to seize the *Discovery,* so he mustered his men on deck in a show of force, and Kaiana quickly departed. This experience, in the same bay where Captain Cook had met his death, made Vancouver doubly wary of the Hawaiians.

As Vancouver sailed up the Island chain, his ship came upon a small canoe, and he was surprised to be hailed by a Hawaiian who called out in broken English. It turned out that the Islander had traveled to the Pacific Northwest aboard a fur trader, and he wanted to serve the expedition as an interpreter. The Hawaiian, who preferred to be called Jack, was signed on by Vancouver. Jack more than earned his pay. As the *Discovery* anchored off Waikiki, Jack acted as an advance publicity man. He told the Hawaiians that the Englishmen were great warriors and not mere traders. The natives were impressed, and Vancouver easily obtained needed supplies.

At Waimea Bay, on Kauai, the nervous Vancouver was met with "distant civility" by the Hawaiians. On two walking expeditions up Waimea Valley, Vancouver was shocked by the "excessive wantonness" of the females. His party was "pestered . . . with the obscene importunities of the women." It was much more blatant than in Cook's day, and Vancouver caustically noted in his journal that their actions must have been the influence of "civilized" people.

The fears of the captain were hardly lessened when an illiterate chief produced four letters, which he considered to be in his praise. In reality the letters warned visiting captains to be most cautious in dealing with the Hawaiians. Vancouver told the chief that the letters were "much in his praise and favor and desired that he would not omit showing it to the commander of the next and every other vessel that might arrive at Kauai, which he promised to do." After a stop at Niihau, Vancouver sailed off for the northwest.

By October of 1792 Vancouver had peacefully concluded his mission with the Spaniards at Nootka Sound. Several days before his ships were to sail from the northwest for Hawaii, an English trading ship came to anchor nearby, and the captain asked Vancouver to return two young Hawaiian girls to their homes on Niihau. It is not clear whether the young ladies had gone along as a lark or if they had been kidnapped. The ages of the girls were about fourteen and eighteen. The two passengers considerably lightened the four-month trip to Hawaii, and George Vancouver developed a great affection for his two charges.

In mid-January, 1793, Vancouver sighted the island of Hawaii. He proceeded slowly down the west coast, and somewhere north of Kealakekua Bay Kamehameha came aboard ship. This was Vancouver's first visit with Kamehameha since Cook's ships had stopped here fourteen years earlier. Vancouver expected to see the same savage Hawaiian, but the captain wrote, "I was agreeably surprised in finding that his riper years had softened that stern ferocity which his younger years had exhibited and had changed his general deportment to an address characteristic of an open, cheerful and sensible mind; combined with great generosity and goodness of disposition." As favorable as this impression was, Vancouver still would not allow the Hawaiian king to stay aboard ship overnight.

Kaahumanu, who was about sixteen years old at the time and the favorite wife of Kamehameha, came aboard ship. She impressed Vancouver, who said she was "one of the finest women we had yet seen on any of the islands." The Englishman presented Kamehameha with a scarlet cloak which reached from his neck to the ground. It was adorned with lace, trimmed with colored gartering, and with blue ribbons to tie it down the front. Kamehameha proudly showed it off to his subjects.

At Kealakekua Bay the two ships put down their anchors in the sandy bottom. Now it was Kamehameha's turn to impress the Englishman. He came out in a fleet of eleven canoes which approached the *Discovery* in a *V* formation. Kamehameha was in the lead canoe, wearing the "most elegant feathered cloak I had yet seen, composed principally of beautiful bright yellow feathers and reaching from his shoulders to the ground on which it trailed. On his head he wore a very handsome helmet, and made altogether a very magnificent appearance." The canoes circled the *Discovery* once, and then ten canoes lined up under the stern of the flagship while Kamehameha's canoe came alongside and the king grandly stepped aboard. The Hawaiian formally asked, "Is Vancouver my friend?" Then he asked, "Is King George my friend?" After Vancouver had assured him, Kamehameha and Vancouver touched noses as a sign of the sincerity of their statements. Kamehameha presented the Englishman with four feathered helmets. Of more immediate value were the plentiful supplies of hogs and vegetables which the king ordered aboard.

Kaiana soon appeared aboard ship bearing presents of hogs, but the English had all the supplies they could handle. Kaiana complained because the gifts he received were not as numerous or valuable as those given the king. Kamehameha angrily told Kaiana he would do all the supplying of the English. Vancouver described Kaiana as a man of "the most turbulent and ambitious disposition with great activity of mind, and a thorough contempt of danger. Had his power been sufficient, or had his plots and designs been countenanced and adopted by Kamehameha, they must have proved fatal to many of the small trading vessels that have visited these islands."

Charmed as he was by the king, Vancouver remained uneasy about the Hawaiians in general. He worked out rules of conduct with Kamehameha to be followed by his men and by the Hawaiians. Only chiefs were allowed aboard ship. Vancouver's men would not wander about the countryside, and they would stay out of the heiaus. There was no attempt, however, to limit either the numbers or the hours of the boatloads of women who came to the two vessels. Aboard ship there was much grumbling, because the only men allowed ashore were those on duty. Vancouver visited the place where Captain Cook had been killed and later sat through a violent exhibition of mock warfare in which Kamehameha joined. Six spears were thrown simultaneously at the king. Three of these spears he caught in midair, two he parried, and one he sidestepped. To Vancouver the battle was a "riot-like engagement."

Vancouver rigged a set of sails on one of the king's largest canoes and also presented him with a Union Jack to fly from the mast. Kamehameha suggested that a swivel gun would look nice on the canoe, but Vancouver firmly said no. All the guns of the English belonged to King George, who had put a kapu on them. He did, however, have his men teach the Hawaiians the rudiments of military drill. As a parting gift Kamehameha gave Vancouver a yellow feather cloak, a present for King George. The gift was truly representative of Kamehameha, for it bore two spear holes from a recent battle.

Vancouver moved on to Lahaina, Maui, where he tried to get information about a tragedy which had happened the year before. A supply ship, *Daedalus,* which belonged to Vancouver's squadron, had stopped at Waimea on Oahu for fresh water. The commander of the ship and the ship's astronomer went ashore with two seamen. The unarmed party was attacked by the Hawaiians, and only one sailor escaped. Vancouver was determined to bring the culprits to justice. On Maui, Kahekili told the captain that the murders had been the acts of lawless men and had not been condoned by chiefs. In fact, three of the men who had taken part in the tragedy had already been executed.

Vancouver sailed on to Oahu, where he anchored at Waikiki. He learned that there were three men at large who supposedly had taken part in the murders, and Vancouver wanted to try them. The captain felt that "justice demanded exemplary punishment, in order to stop, or at least to check, such barbarous and unprovoked outrages in the future." Subsequently three tattooed Hawaiians were brought on board ship and tried. Everyone agreed they were the guilty ones, and at length Vancouver was convinced. With marines drawn up on deck, the wretches were tied hand and foot, placed in a canoe next to the ship, and a chief was directed to blow out their brains with a pistol. The English captain was somewhat shocked by the matter-of-fact way in which the chief did his job. Vancouver wanted the bodies of the three strung up on a tree on shore to serve as an example to the rest of the Hawaiians. Now it was the chief who was shocked. He explained to the Englishman that such an act was wrong and against their religion.

Vancouver was convinced he had ordered the execution of guilty men, but a Hawaiian historian later wrote that the chiefs of Oahu well knew who had really committed the crimes. They, however, were not about to turn the real culprits over to foreigners, and so they presented three innocent men to Vancouver. Kahekili himself might have been involved in the affair.

The English captain had one more chore to do before leaving the Hawaiian Islands. He wanted to return the two girls he had taken aboard at Nootka Sound to their homes on Niihau. At the familiar anchorage at Waimea, Kauai, Vancouver learned that Niihau was suffering from a severe drought, so he decided to settle the two young ladies on Kauai. During the voyage the girls had become accustomed to the dress and eating habits of the western world and, to be sure they could now live decently, Vancouver procured a tract of land for each of them. The Waimea chiefs gave solemn assurances that the two women would be well cared for, and then the ships departed for the northwest.

Nine months later George Vancouver was on his way back to Hawaii. At Hilo Bay Kamehameha came to meet him. The Hawaiian king wanted Vancouver to remain in Hilo, but the English captain thought it a dangerous place to anchor. So, accompanied by a number of chiefs, the ships sailed around South Point toward Kealakekua Bay. Some chiefs brought their women on the trip, but Kamehameha did not, and Vancouver learned that the king had had a falling out with his favorite, Kaahumanu. The reason was "that too great an intimacy had subsisted between her and Kaiana." Vancouver realized that the king was still very fond of Kaahumanu, and he offered to attempt a reconciliation. Kamehameha proudly refused.

At Kealakekua the English were quickly able to get the provisions they needed. A camp was set up on shore, and Archibald Menzies hiked to the top of Hualalai and Mauna Loa. More cattle and sheep were landed, and Vancouver was pleased to see that animals brought earlier had multiplied. The English captain ordered his carpenters to lay the keel for a thirty-six-foot vessel for Kamehameha, which was called the *Britannia*. Isaac Davis and John Young visited the *Discovery,* and the captain noted they were held in the "warmest affection" by the king and most of the Hawaiians.

It was clear to Vancouver that Kamehameha still missed Kaahumanu, and the Englishman again offered to try and reconcile the two. This time the king agreed, and Vancouver presented his plan. He would invite Kaahumanu and her father aboard ship to receive presents. Shortly Kamehameha would come aboard ship and walk into Vancouver's cabin, acting as though he did not know visitors were already there. The plan worked perfectly. When Kamehameha walked into the cabin, Vancouver immediately took the king's hand "and joining it with the queen's, their reconciliation was instantly completed. This was fully demonstrated by the tears that involuntarily stole down the cheeks of both as they embraced each other." To celebrate the reunion everyone had a glass of wine. Before leaving the ship the queen got Vancouver to extract a promise from Kamehameha that he would not beat her.

With Kamehameha's domestic problems solved, Vancouver got down to serious business. On his previous visit the English captain had discussed ceding the island of Hawaii to Great Britain. Now Vancouver pushed his proposal. Some Hawaiian chiefs had been cheated by unscrupulous traders who sold them inferior merchandise. Often firearms, purchased at high prices, burst on being fired for the first time. The Hawaiians were victimized, and they thought that by ceding their island to Great Britain they would have the protection of a strong power. Many Hawaiian chiefs had an honest basis for complaint, but much of the desire for cession was pinned to the hope that ties with Great Britain would bring not only arms but troops and ships which would help in the wars against their neighbors.

Kamehameha issued a call for all chiefs to gather at Kealakekua. Even Kameeiamoku, who had been responsible for the capture of Thomas Metcalfe's ship, was ordered to come. He was most reluctant, fearing reprisals from the English. On his way Kameeiamoku stopped frequently at heiaus to make sacrifices and to consult kahunas to see what was in store for him. In the end he decided on a show of force, and he swept into Kealakekua Bay with a fleet of canoes and a thousand retainers. He apologized for his action, admitting he had seized the younger Metcalfe's ship out of revenge.

That night Vancouver invited a number of chiefs to dinner. During the evening some chiefs poked fun at the nervous Kameeiamoku for his awkwardness and lack of table manners. After dinner bottles of wine and grog were passed, and Kameeiamoku drank more and faster than the others. Before long he was not only sick but couldn't walk. As his retainers carried Kameeiamoku out, the chief called out that Vancouver had poisoned him. One of Kameeiamoku's retainers fingered his knife and eyed George Vancouver, but Kamehameha laughed, as did the other chiefs. To prove that the chief had not been poisoned, they drank from his bottle.

On February 25, 1794, the chiefs gathered on board the *Discovery*. Kamehameha made a speech, saying that of all the nations he knew he would like most to be a subject of Great Britain. Several other chiefs made speeches, and then the king again spoke. He announced they were no longer people of Hawaii. Now they were people of Great Britain. Lieutenant Puget went ashore and raised the British flag, a salute was fired, and a copper plate, announcing the cession, was nailed to Kamehameha's house.

Vancouver had finished his business, and he made his farewells to Kamehameha. Jack, the Hawaiian interpreter, was put ashore, and the ships made ready to sail. Before departing, Vancouver had one last word of admonition. He warned the Hawaiian king about the many white men who had settled in the Islands and of their bad influence. Not all were bad, but the majority were, and Vancouver felt they should be sent away. After these last words the captain stopped at Kauai and, satisfied that the two girls he had settled there were getting along well, he sailed away. He traveled south, around the tip of South America, back to England.

The cession of Hawaii was never recognized by the British government. Vancouver retired to his country house. During most of this last voyage he had been under a surgeon's care. It is possible that the violent outbursts of temper which his fellow officers endured were due to a serious hyperthyroid condition, and he died before he could finish the editing of his journals. The *Discovery* met an ignominious end. It was beached and converted into a prison ship at Deptford. Little noted in England during his lifetime, George Vancouver, together with the Englishmen Davis and Young, helped create a feeling of good will for Great Britain in Hawaii which would last well into the nineteenth century.

In 1794 the shrewd old king, Kahekili, finally died. His domains had included the islands of Maui, Lanai, Molokai, and Oahu. A brother and son were to divide this kingdom, but soon they were at each other's throats, and by the end of the year the brother had been killed in a battle fought near Pearl Harbor. Kamehameha realized that this was his great opportunity. His armies were rested, and his supplies of arms and ammunition were substantial. His fleet crossed the channel to Maui, and soon the defenders there were overpowered. He sailed on to Molokai and quickly conquered that island.

While Kamehameha was resting and preparing his forces for the invasion of Oahu, the long-smoldering feud between Kaiana and the king came to a climax. Kaiana had not been included in a council of war, and the powerful chief feared that Kamehameha was plotting his death. Rather than risk this, Kaiana and some of his men deserted and sailed to Oahu, where he joined forces with the ruler. In the spring or summer of 1795 Kamehameha moved against Oahu. His great fleet of canoes landed at Waikiki and Waialae, the beaches on either side of Diamond Head. His men crossed the plains where the city of Honolulu now stands, pushing the enemy before them. At the mouth of Nuuanu Valley a stone fort had been built, and here Kaiana was said to be stationed. Kaiana was reported killed by a cannon ball, and the fort was overrun. Some enemy warriors were able to escape up the rugged mountain walls of the valley while others were pursued to the head of the valley, where they were forced over the pali, or cliff, and dashed to death on the rocks below. The king of Oahu wandered about in the mountains of Oahu for several months before he was captured and offered as a sacrifice to the war god, Kukailimoku.

Now only Kauai remained outside Kamehameha's authority, and he wasted no time in preparing his forces to make his conquest of the Islands complete. In the spring of 1796 he tried to transport his army to Kauai, but the wind and wild seas of the channel between Oahu and Kauai swamped many of his canoes. He had no choice but to turn back and await another opportunity. Then trouble on the island of Hawaii forced Kamehameha to turn his attention there. The brother of Kaiana had revolted, and

Kamehameha returned to dispose of this latest threat. The rebel army was beaten in a battle fought at Hilo, and the chief suffered a familiar fate. He was offered as a sacrifice to the gods.

Maui and Oahu were firmly under his rule, so Kamehameha spent the next six years on the island of Hawaii organizing and directing his government and trading with foreign ships. Then the king returned to Oahu determined to invade Kauai and bring this last island under his control. He built a fleet of special canoes designed to weather the stormy Kauai channel. Just as the attack was to be launched, an epidemic decimated Kamehameha's army. It is not known what the disease was, but it might have been cholera or typhoid. Kamehameha himself lay ill for some time. The invasion of Kauai had to be postponed again.

Finally, in 1810, Kauai did come under Kamehameha's control, but not through force of arms. Reluctantly Kaumualii, the king of Kauai, agreed to sail to Honolulu and meet with Kamehameha. At this meeting the Kauai king acknowledged Kamehameha as the supreme ruler of all the Islands, but Kaumualii would continue to directly govern Kauai. It was a happy solution for both. Kamehameha's ambition was fulfilled, and Kaumualii retained a great part of his independence. This meeting had been a practical matter for Kaumualii. He undoubtedly knew the strength of Kamehameha, and he could hardly count on providence to save the island from a third invasion attempt.

Ships of many nations dropped anchor in the Hawaiian Islands during the early years of the nineteenth century, and the desirability of the Islands was apparent to many a captain. Among those who benefited most from the Islands was the Russian American Company, which held a government monopoly on the fur trade in the Aleutian Islands and Alaska. The trade was indeed profitable, but the isolated Russians suffered severely from a shortage of food and other supplies. Ships bringing provisions from Russia sailed out of distant Baltic Sea ports, and time and cost involved were staggering. Some supplies were purchased from American and English trading vessels which roamed to the far north, but this source was neither sufficient nor dependable. It is likely that a solution flashed into the mind of Alexander Baranov, governor of the Russian American Company in Alaska, when he was visited by Captain Hugh Moore in 1792. Moore's ship limped into Prince William Sound for repairs. Included in Moore's crew were a number of Hawaiians, and the captain might have described the potentialities of Hawaii to the Russians. Perhaps the seeds were planted at this time, but nothing would happen for many years.

The first Russians did not come to Hawaii until the summer of 1804 when two ships under Ivan von Krusenstern sailed up from the south. The ships were seeking provisions, but they came at an unfortunate time. Kamehameha was on Oahu, where the epidemic had leveled his army, and the Hawaiians were hard pressed to feed themselves. Von Krusenstern soon sailed away to Alaska, but Urey Lisiansky, captain of the smaller of the two ships, stayed behind and turned to Kealakekua Bay. Lisiansky was also unsuccessful in gaining provisions, but he found there was no scarcity of women. He turned back about a hundred who swam out to his ship, and he noted in his journal that "It was with a degree of regret that I felt myself obliged to give a damp to their joy: . . . and this troop of nymphs were compelled to return with an affront offered to their charms, which they had never experienced before, perhaps from any European ship."

Lisiansky by-passed the plague ridden island of Oahu and sailed on to Kauai, where he met Kaumualii. The young king was delighted to learn of the epidemic which had laid his enemies low on Oahu. Kaumualii asserted he was ready for any invasion attempt. He had five Europeans in his employ, boasted three six-pounders, forty swivel guns, and quantities of muskets and ammunition. Kaumualii could speak bravely, but the haoles who worked for him were building a boat in which they could escape from the island if things went badly. According to Lisiansky, Kamehameha at this time employed some fifty whites and possessed vast supplies of arms.

Kamehameha heard of Alexander Baranov's interest in obtaining supplies from Hawaii, and he sent the Russian a letter saying he would be willing to supply them with a shipload of supplies a year. In 1807 he did provision a small ship headed for Sitka, and late the following year a Lieutenant Hagemeister sailed to Hawaii to obtain a load of salt to be used in preserving pelts. Aboard the Russian ship was a young passenger by the name of Archibald Campbell. Campbell was an Englishman who had first gone to sea at the age of thirteen. Eventually he sailed off to the Pacific Northwest, where he was shipwrecked. With other survivors he sailed through wintry seas in an open boat, suffering greatly from exposure. The young sailor's feet were severely frostbitten, and when he was rescued by the Russians both feet had to be amputated. Campbell was not quite twenty-one years of age.

When Campbell came ashore in Honolulu, he recorded in his journal that the Russians were interested in founding a colony in the Hawaiian Islands, but no attempt was made at that time. He noticed that the king's residence, which was close to the shore, was protected by a battery of sixteen carriage guns and that the British flag was flying. Campbell was a good sail-maker, and his services were appreciated by Kamehameha. Before long the king granted him sixty acres of land near Pearl Harbor, where one of his neighbors was William Stevenson, an escaped convict from Botany Bay who lived with a Hawaiian woman. Stevenson's distinction in Hawaiian history is that he introduced the art of distilling fermented ti roots to produce an alcoholic beverage called okoleheo. Kamehameha thought Stevenson spent too much time drinking, and he eventually appropriated his still. Campbell noted there was a general excess of drinking among the Hawaiians. Most chiefs had their own stills. Kaahumanu regularly took advantage of the time Kamehameha spent at a heiau to indulge with her women retainers, and she seldom stopped short of intoxication.

Baranov temporarily turned his energies toward establishing a supply station in California, where he founded a colony at Fort Ross. Because the California colony could not provide what he needed quickly enough, in 1814 Baranov again dispatched a ship to Hawaii for supplies. The desired cargo was obtained at Honolulu, but as the ship lay at anchor in Waimea Bay on Kauai a sudden storm drove the ship ashore. The vessel was a loss, but the cargo was salvaged, ending up under the questionable care of King Kaumualii. The captain went off to Alaska to report the disaster to Governor Baranov, and the crew of the vessel, many of whom were Aleutian Indians, moved ashore on Kauai.

Alexander Baranov was not only determined to recover the cargo, but now he also hoped to establish a colony or a trading post in Hawaii. The man who happened to be available for this mission was Georg Anton Scheffer, a German doctor who had worked with the Russian police until he signed on as surgeon aboard a Russian American Company vessel. During the voyage Scheffer quarreled with the officers, and when the ship reached Alaska in late 1814 the German doctor left her.

Baranov was not sure Scheffer was the man for the job, but there were few people to choose from, and before long the doctor was aboard an American trading ship headed for Hawaii. Scheffer's instructions said he should work his way into the confidence of King Kamehameha. Then, with the king's help, he was to retrieve the cargo left on Kauai or to receive payment for it in sandalwood. Next he was to work out some arrangement with Kamehameha by which the Russians could gain a monopoly on the sandalwood trade in the Islands. In October of 1815 Scheffer left for the Hawaiian Islands accompanied by two half-breed boys, one of whom was the son of Baranov by an Indian woman.

When Scheffer arrived at the island of Hawaii, he encountered immediate opposition. Several Americans who traveled aboard ship with him had gotten a bad impression of the doctor during the voyage, and they warned Kamehameha about the newcomer. John Young was suspicious of Scheffer's motives, and several visiting captains joined the chorus. Some warnings were motivated by sailors who were worried that their favorable trade arrangements might be upset by Scheffer, but apparently it was easy to dislike Scheffer, who was a dominating, autocratic man.

A keen judge of character, Kamehameha was cautious of this haole who first passed himself off as a naturalist. Scheffer could well have been discouraged, but he was not. He was a man of genuine ability and determination. He assured the king again and again that his presence would not bring trouble. Then the king became ill. Scheffer cared for him and Kamehameha recovered. During this illness the doctor had indeed gained the confidence of the king, and he was granted a tract of land on Oahu where the Russian American Company could construct buildings.

In the meantime Baranov was preparing to send Scheffer reinforcements should he need them. He instructed Lieutenant Podushkin, in command of the *Otkrytie,* to pick up Scheffer from the island of Oahu, then proceed to Kauai and retrieve the lost cargo. Podushkin was told that if he could not regain the cargo by peaceful means, he was to use force and conquer Kauai for Russia. If added force was needed, they could wait for the arrival of another Russian ship which would follow soon after.

When the *Otkrytie* arrived, Scheffer was ready to sail for Kauai. First the doctor appealed to Kamehameha, asking him to order Kaumualii to return the lost cargo, but such an order was not forthcoming. At this point unexpected support arrived when a Russian ship came from California. In May of 1816 Scheffer arrived at Waimea Bay on Kauai. Here he learned that Kaumualii had recently sent most of the cargo back to Baranov aboard a trading vessel. The first part of Scheffer's mission had been accomplished with ease. Kaumualii now implored the Russians to help him shake off the yoke of Kamehameha. Soon a grand plan took shape in the creative mind of Scheffer, one which would dwarf his original mission.

Kaumualii had recognized Kamehameha as supreme ruler in 1810, but the Kauai king certainly was never happy about the matter. He complained to every visitor who would listen, and he had beseeched earlier Russian visitors to Kauai for help. Now he boldly asked Scheffer for an alliance with Russia. The German doctor apparently had no orders to cover this situation, but he was not a man to allow an opportunity of this kind to pass. Outside of Kamehameha's cession to Great Britain, which had never been acknowledged by the English government, no other territory in the group had been claimed by a western power.

On June 2, 1816, Kaumualii and Scheffer reached an agreement. The King of Kauai pledged allegiance to Emperor Alexander I of Russia. Kaumualii promised to trade exclusively with the Russian American Company, to have the company establish factories on his island, to supply men to put up buildings, and to furnish provisions for Russian ships. In return for this Scheffer gave Kaumualii the protection of the Russian Empire and said that an armed ship would arrive when the first shipment of sandal-wood was ready. Scheffer bestowed on Kaumualii a silver medal and made him a line staff officer in the Russian navy.

Once the treaty was in hand, Scheffer vigorously went to work. He started construction of a house at Waimea and then sailed off to Honolulu to look after his trading station there. It was disturbing when the *Otkrytie* lost two masts in a storm and, after emergency repairs, sailed for Alaska. Scheffer purchased two American vessels which were in Hawaii to make up for the deficiency and promised the captains they should receive payment from Baranov in Alaska. The purchase of the ships pleased Kaumualii and undoubtedly made him feel his treasonous alliance had not been such a bad idea.

Another secret treaty was drawn up with the Kauai king in which Kaumualii promised Scheffer 500 men to be used in the conquest of Oahu. Scheffer said he would supply all the arms and ammunition necessary, and when victory was won each should have half of the island of Oahu. At the mouth of the Waimea River on Kauai, Scheffer built a stone fort, which he called Fort Elizabeth after the consort of Alexander I. Kaumualii presented to Scheffer the beautiful valley of Hanalei on the north shore of Kauai, and soon the Russian flag flew over two earthen forts raised at the entrance to the Hanalei River. To make his claims more secure, a whole-sale exchanging of Russian names for Hawaiian names now took place. Hanalei became Schefferthal. The Hanapepe River became the Don. Even some chiefs took Russian names.

The first crack in the walls of Scheffer's empire occurred when one of his ships returned from Oahu carrying all the men who had made up his Honolulu post. The Russians had begun to build a fort in Honolulu over which the Russian flag was flown. Enraged by this breech of sovereignty and also by the desecration of a heiau, the Hawaiians, aided by Americans, burned the Russian buildings. When the news reached the aging Kamehameha, who was on the island of Hawaii, he ordered that a force be assembled to drive the Russians out. Faced with this, the Russians closed down their Oahu operations and withdrew to Kauai.

Scheffer had made enemies of most of the American captains who visited Hawaii at this time, because he had cut off their trade on Kauai. On more than one occasion Americans had tried to tear down the Russian flags which flew on Kauai. These actions had been bothersome to Scheffer, but little more. Now a serious blow to his plans was to fall. Otto von Kotzebue, lieutenant in the Imperial Russian Navy, arrived in Hawaii in command of the ship *Rurick*. Georg Scheffer knew of the coming of this ship and had expected to receive supplies from her.

It was late November, 1816, when the *Rurick* hove in sight of the mountain of Mauna Loa on the island of Hawaii. As the ship moved down the coast toward Kealakekua, the Russians learned from Hawaiians who came aboard that five months earlier two ships of the Russian American Company had met with difficulties trading here and had threatened to come back with a strong force. This threat, added to Scheffer's activities, alarmed the Hawaiians, and when they received word that a Russian ship had arrived, Kamehameha stationed 400 armed men along the coast in anticipation of an attack. Von Kotzebue allayed the fears of the Hawaiians and went ashore to visit Kamehameha, a man, he wrote, "who had attracted the attention of all Europe, and who inspired me with the greatest confidence by his unreserved and friendly behavior."

As the Russian officer sat in Kamehameha's thatched house, the king recounted the evil actions of Scheffer. Von Kotzebue assured the king that the emperor of Russia had no intention of injuring or conquering the Islands. When Kamehameha heard this good news, he ordered the glasses to be filled, and a toast was drunk to the health of the emperor of Russia. Von Kotzebue now proceeded to Honolulu harbor, where his ship was the first to fire a salute to the fort which the Hawaiians had built in anticipation of a return by Scheffer. Von Kotzebue did not so much as bother to visit Kauai, sailing directly to Alaska.

It was now clear Scheffer had no official backing from the Russian government, and opposition to his grand plans stiffened. Soon word arrived that Baranov was not in sympathy with Scheffer's schemes. He had even refused to pay for the two ships Scheffer had earlier bought from American captains. On Kauai Scheffer returned to Waimea from Hanalei to find that the Russian flag was no longer flying there. On his return from a later trip the doctor found King Kaumualii had called together about 1,000 of his men. The Kauai king had either been warned by Kamehameha to dispose of Scheffer or he had seen for himself that his new ally could bring trouble. Scheffer was seized and told he must leave Waimea.

The doctor had no choice. He sailed to Hanalei, where he grandly claimed the whole island of Kauai for Russia. Here he hoped to make a stand, but a message soon came from Kaumualii ordering him to leave the island altogether or suffer the consequences. Scheffer fled aboard a leaky vessel which he was able to keep afloat only by manning the pumps around the clock. Five days later he arrived off Honolulu harbor.

The German doctor was anything but welcome in Honolulu. He flew the Russian flag upside down, as a distress signal, because the condition of his vessel was precarious. American captains in port were greatly annoyed. Finally he was told he could come ashore only on the condition that he go as a prisoner to the island of Hawaii, and this he would not do. Then a stroke of good fortune fell Scheffer's way. Captain Isaiah Lewis put into port. Scheffer had given Lewis medical treatment the previous year, and the captain was grateful. He agreed to carry Scheffer with him to Canton.

Georg Scheffer had been in Hawaii about eighteen months. Events had moved so fast and communications with Baranov and Russia were so slow that neither knew what was taking place until months after the events occurred. Not until October, 1816, did Baranov meet Captain Isaac Whittemore, who presented him with a claim for 200,000 piasters, the sum due him for the ship Scheffer had purchased. And it took additional months to get messages back to Hawaii. The directors of the Russian American Company in St. Petersburg had not received Scheffer's first report until after he had been run out of the Islands. Baranov, who seems to have had a real affection for Kamehameha, was annoyed by the actions of Scheffer. The Russian governor had authorized the use of force only in obtaining the lost cargo on Kauai. He did not wish to establish trading stations and plantations in the Hawaiian Islands except on a peaceful basis.

The directors of the Company in St. Petersburg thought well of Scheffer's reports. Before learning that the doctor's plan had failed, they sent messages of encouragement to Scheffer and ordered presents be sent to Kaumualii. The Russian government was less impressed with Kaumualii's cession of Kauai to Russia. Although the Company directors felt that Kaumualii's agreement with Scheffer should be accepted, Emperor Alexander I politely but firmly said no.

Georg Scheffer continued to urge the acquisition of the Hawaiian Islands as he made his way back to Russia, but without effect. For a moment the opportunity had been there, but now it was gone. If von Kotzebue had supported Scheffer, or at least had not denounced him, the result might have been different. If the Company directors had not been so distant, Scheffer might have received needed support. In the end, of course, Scheffer defeated himself, because he aroused antagonism instead of loyalty among those about him. What would have happened if Scheffer had been supported by Russia is one of the interesting points of speculation in Hawaiian history. As for Scheffer, his adventures finally took him to Brazil, where he bought a title from the emperor and became known as Count von Frankenthal. He tried to recruit German colonists to migrate to Brazil, and in 1836 he died in his adopted country.

By the time Scheffer left Hawaii, Kamehameha was an old man. He chose to live at Kailua, Kona, where he greatly enjoyed fishing in the calm, deep coastal waters. He had ruled well, encouraging the industry of his people and gaining a knowledge of western ways from foreigners who settled in the Islands. He did not allow haoles to buy land, although if they were industriously inclined they could use tracts of land during their lifetimes. Once the king had been a heavy drinker, but he soon concluded that this brought him no benefits. He had the will power to refrain from alcohol, and he issued a futile order that all Hawaiians do the same.

He was well aware that powerful chiefs would rebel if they thought they saw a chance of success. He made this difficult by keeping the most powerful chiefs with him, away from their subjects, who might support an uprising. He talked to the numerous foreign captains who came to Hawaii and had developed a rude concept of the positions of various world powers. All visiting ships were treated the same, no matter what their nationality. When he learned that foreign ports charged entrance fees, he did the same. Ships paid forty dollars to enter the outer harbor of Honolulu and sixty dollars to enter the inner harbor. He enjoyed bargaining with visiting captains, who found him a shrewd man. He could not read or write, but he knew the weights and measures necessary for trade, and during his life he had acquired a fortune in coin.

One day the great king fell ill. Many persons ministered to him, but no one could help. The chief kahuna proclaimed the king must build a heiau for his old war god, Kukailimoku. Kamehameha was too weak to visit the heiau, so his son went instead. A human sacrifice was suggested, but Kamehameha refused. Other kahunas came, but the king grew weaker. His faithful retainers hovered over him, trying to get him to take some nourishment. He could swallow only a mouthful of poi and a sip of water.

The end was near. A brother of Kamehameha bent over the king and asked him for his last commands. The king whispered, "Enjoy quietly what I have made right. . . ." He was dying. The white-haired John Young leaned over the king and kissed him. By two o'clock on the morning of May 8, 1819, Kamehameha was dead.

The kingdom was stunned. Some chiefs requested that they be buried with the king. Many persons knocked out their front teeth as a sign of grief. Others tattooed the date of his death on their bodies. The proper ancient ceremonies were performed, including the cleaning of the bones of the king. Then a chief by the name of Hoapili, who had been so designated by Kamehameha, had the honor of secretly burying the remains of the king. At night Hoapili carried away to the north the wicker basket containing the bones of Kamehameha. The remains of Hawaii's greatest king probably are buried somewhere in the Kohala district of the island of Hawaii, but the secret burial cave has never been found.

Chapter Five

TRAINING THEM FOR HEAVEN

Sᴇᴠᴇɴ ᴅᴀʏs ᴀꜰᴛᴇʀ ᴛʜᴇ ʙᴏɴᴇs ᴏꜰ Kᴀᴍᴇʜᴀᴍᴇʜᴀ had been laid away in a secret cave the ranking chiefs of the kingdom were summoned to Kailua. This solemn group gathered at the seashore in a great half circle, clothed in their feather cloaks and helmets. Liholiho, the favorite son of Kamehameha, wore a red and gold English uniform under his feather cloak. Together with Kaahumanu, he stood near the surf, amid the alii and facing a great mass of commoners. It was Kaahumanu who addressed the assemblage. She proclaimed Liholiho as the "Divine One" and said the will of Kamehameha was that Liholiho should possess the land, but that she and the new king would jointly rule the kingdom. Hawaii had a new king, officially known as Kamehameha II, and also a powerful queen regent.

The peaceful passing of power from the deceased king to his designated heir was a result of Kamehameha's planning. When Liholiho was five years old, he had been proclaimed the heir to the kingdom. Over the years he had gradually been given increasing amounts of royal power. Now he was twenty-one and was a familiar symbol of authority to the chiefs. The transition was made without shock. While some chiefs grumbled at Kaahumanu becoming queen regent, she was nonetheless respected for her high lineage and her practical experience in government affairs.

The new rulers faced great and immediate problems. The most urgent was the kapu system—a system which was terribly burdensome for those who strictly followed the rules. Adventuresome Hawaiians had secretly broken kapus for centuries, but when Captain Cook came, Islanders watched foreigners openly violate kapus and go unscathed. Those who sailed off to foreign lands broke kapus constantly and did not suffer for their transgressions. The old king had upheld the ancient system, and as long as he lived no one dared suggest that changes be made. But now Kamehameha I was dead. When word reached the Islands that the kapu system in Tahiti had been overturned, the pressure for change heightened. Kaahumanu and others pressed the king to make a clear move, but it was a very difficult thing for Liholiho to do since he had been brought up to respect the ancient beliefs.

In November of 1819 the king made a momentous decision. He ordered a feast to be prepared at Kailua. One table was set for men and another for women, as had always been the custom. When all the guests were seated, Liholiho walked around both tables and then suddenly sat down at the table for women and began to eat. He had broken the kapu which forbade men from eating with women, and it marked the demise of all the old rules. For two days before taking this drastic step Liholiho had reinforced himself with rum, but this fact in no way lessened the import of what he did. What had been done for so long in secret was now publicly sanctioned. When the king ordered that heiaus and religious images be destroyed throughout the kingdom, his subjects knew he was serious. With one symbolic act Liholiho had cut away the religious foundations of the nation and seriously eroded the social system.

There were many who were outraged by the king's action. Certainly many images were secreted away and honored in much the same manner as Umi had honored his war god generations earlier. Some chiefs and most of the kahunas strongly disagreed with Liholiho. A cousin of the king, the high chief to whom Kamehameha had entrusted his precious war god, Kukailimoku, came forth in open rebellion. In a battle south of Kailua the forces of Liholiho were victorious. The rebel chief was killed by musket fire as he crouched behind a stone wall, and his wife, who had fought by his side through the day, soon suffered a similiar fate. With them died open opposition to the change.

Two weeks before Liholiho had abolished the kapu system a ship bearing a Protestant missionary company eased out of Boston harbor bound for the Hawaiian Islands. These missionaries sailed in 1819, but the origins of their movement went back many years. New England missionary fervor had been reinforced by religious revivals in England. As early as 1793 a missionary company departed from England destined for India. Two years later the London Missionary Society was formed. By this time the inspirational sermons of English evangelists were being printed and circulated in New England. The theme of these sermons was a plea to observe the Biblical admonition: "Go ye into all the world, and preach the Gospel to every creature." In 1796 the London society had invaded the Pacific by dispatching a missionary ship to Tahiti.

On June 29, 1810, in a meeting at Bradford, Massachusetts, the American Board of Commissioners for Foreign Missions was founded. It was interdenominational, with Congregationalists as the dominating group. The attention of the American Board was quickly drawn to Hawaii by the reports of New England sailors who had visited the Islands and by the not infrequent appearance in New England of real live Hawaiian heathens who had signed aboard American ships during Pacific voyages.

Probably the first Hawaiian seen by Bostonians arrived one summer afternoon in 1790 when the *Columbia* came to anchor in the inner harbor after an absence of three years. The *Columbia* had the distinction of being the first American ship to circle the earth. Enroute a cargo of furs had been taken aboard in the Pacific Northwest and sold in Canton at great profit. It was the American beginning of the rich Pacific fur trade. The citizens of Boston crowded the dock and welcomed the *Columbia* with three huzzahs. After the commotion had subsided a Hawaiian stepped ashore, appareled in a bright red and yellow feather cloak and helmet. He proudly marched up the street to call on Governor Hancock. Several years later Hawaiians appeared in plays staged in Boston and New York depicting the tragedy of Captain Cook. The production in the latter city included a human sacrifice and ended with an earthquake and volcanic eruption.

The Hawaiian who stirred the emotions of religious New Englanders most deeply was Henry Obookiah. This young man had been a victim of wars which raged back and forth across the island of Hawaii. He had been fortunate enough to survive and at last escaped by signing aboard a visiting ship. In 1809 Obookiah reached New Haven. Missionary feeling was at a high pitch and his presence created intense interest. The Hawaiian lived for some years with different pious New England families, including President Dwight of Yale.

Obookiah showed more promise of becoming a sincere Christian than did most Hawaiians who came to New England, and because of this he was sent to school. His progress was excellent, and his mission-minded mentors visualized Henry Obookiah as the first Islander to return to Hawaii and preach the true religion. Obookiah would not fulfill their dream, for in February, 1818, while still a student at the Foreign Mission School in Cornwall, Connecticut, he died, a victim of typhus at the age of twenty-six.

In death Obookiah performed a greater service for the Mission than he ever could have in life. Stories of his piety and of his anguish for his unredeemed countrymen filled eyes with tears and made firm the resolve of the religious. Copies of the dramatic sermon preached at his funeral were widely circulated. Soon a little book appeared which bared the sad tale of Henry Obookiah's life. New religious fervor was inspired.

This deluge of feeling caused the American Board to organize a missionary company to go to Hawaii. Two young men, the Rev. Hiram Bingham, thirty years old, and Rev. Asa Thurston, thirty-two years old, were the ordained ministers in the group. Both had completed their theological training at Andover, Massachusetts, in September of 1819. Ten days later they were ordained at Goshen, Connecticut, by the Rev. Heman Humphrey, who later became president of Amherst College. His sermon, entitled *The Promised Land,* laid out the logic of the missionary endeavor: "Immense regions of the earth, which belong to the church, are still unsubdued. . . . The ultimate conquest and possession of all these is certain. . . . But for the lamentable and criminal apathy of the church, it might have been accomplished ages ago. . . . That as Christendom now possesses ample resources and ability, she is solemnly bound in the name of God, and with the least possible delay to set up her banners in every heathen land. . . ."

The Rev. Heman Humphrey then mused on the kind of reception he fervently hoped the missionaries would receive from the Hawaiians. "I can fancy that I see them, hastening down to the shore to welcome you as friends, and as the bearers of those 'glad tidings of great joy, which shall be unto all people'; that I behold them gathering around you by hundreds, and listening with silent amazement, while you talk to them of the babe of Bethlehem;—that I see them casting away their idols and exclaiming with one voice, Your Savior shall be our Savior. The news of your arrival spread from district to district and from island to island. Wherever you go, you are selected as messengers of salvation from that far land, where Obookiah became and died a Christian."

But Rev. Humphrey knew that this kind of reception was highly unlikely, and he so warned the two newly ordained ministers. "But, ah! my dear brethren, this after all may, perhaps be no more than a bright and lovely vision. . . . Satan is not yet bound, and he will not yield the empire of the Sandwich Islands without a struggle."

The American Board believed all members of the missionary company should be married before departing. To help things along the Board recommended suitable mates for the unattached men. Three men of the missionary company married in the five weeks prior to sailing, and all the rest, except for the Chamberlain family, had been recently wed. The little band gathered in Boston to organize themselves into a congregation. Then on the afternoon of October 23, 1819, they gathered with friends on the dock, sang a hymn, joined in prayer, and at last were rowed out to the ship *Thaddeus.* It was a tearful farewell, for the company fully expected to spend the rest of their lives in Hawaii.

In addition to the Binghams and Thurstons the company included five other men who were listed as assistants. Daniel Chamberlain was an agriculturalist; Dr. Thomas Holman, a physician; Samuel Whitney, a mechanic and schoolmaster; Samuel Ruggles, a catechist and schoolmaster; and Elisha Loomis, a printer and schoolmaster. All the men were by now married, and the Chamberlains were accompanied by their five children. Three

Hawaiians, all trained as teachers at the Foreign Mission School, were also aboard.

Another passenger on the *Thaddeus* was George Kaumualii, the son of King Kaumualii of Kauai. This young man had been a student at the Foreign Mission School but had not shown much evidence of being truly converted. George had left Kauai at an early age to go to school, but the money set aside for this education was soon squandered, and he was left to shift for himself. He joined the U. S. Navy and sailed to the Mediterranean with Stephen Decatur during his campaign against the Tripoli pirates. In the War of 1812 he was wounded in an engagement with a British vessel. Sometime after that he ended up at the mission school. If George did not prove a satisfactory Christian, he at least had other helpful attributes. He was a high-ranking chief, which would prove useful to the missionaries, and in addition he had learned to play the bass viol, a popular instrument in New England churches. His playing and strong voice would delight the Hawaiians.

The *Thaddeus* was bound for Hawaii via the Straits of Le Maire, and the voyage was a severe trial for the missionaries. Reverend and Mrs. Thurston and their baggage were jammed into a six-by-six-foot cabin and the others fared little better. No sooner had the ship reached the open sea than every member of the company except the Hawaiians became seasick. Several days passed before any of them were interested in moving from their bunks.

Private devotions were held morning and evening by the Thurstons in their cabin. On the Sabbath a private service was held in the cabin, and then at noon, weather permitting, a group service was held on deck. The passengers took advantage of such comforts as they could discover. Lucia Holman enjoyed time on deck, seated on a mattress spread out in a long boat. The active Chamberlain children must have brought pleasure as well as concern to the missionaries, for they were soon very much at home in the ship's rigging. The children were also adept at learning the language of their future home from the Hawaiians aboard.

On one occasion, when the ship lay becalmed in the Pacific, Thurston, Bingham, and two of the Hawaiians went over the side for a swim. They had no sooner climbed aboard again when a huge shark appeared. The incident caused Bingham to reflect piously on the reasons for their narrow escape. Three days before reaching Hawaii there was more excitement when Samuel Whitney fell overboard while helping crew members paint the ship. Someone had the presence of mind to throw a bench in his direction and Whitney clung to this until the *Thaddeus* could come about and pick him up. The bench remained a treasured piece of furniture in the Whitney household for many years.

Christmas and New Year were quietly observed aboard ship, and for both occasions Mr. Conant, an officer on the *Thaddeus,* composed hymns which reflected the hopes of the missionaries. The fifth stanza of the New Year hymn was at least partially prophetic.

> Soon may the heathen see the light,
> Which dawns to close the pagan night,
> And say with truth forever more,
> Hawaii's Idols are no more.

The depth of feeling of their common calling was the reason why the little company got along so well under the trying, crowded conditions of the long voyage. A consuming desire to accomplish their divine mission submerged personal differences. There was, however, one obvious exception to this unity. The forceful Hiram Bingham had been appointed the leader of the company, and he was very quickly at odds with Dr. and Mrs. Holman. As a matter of fact Bingham and Holman must have been eyeing each other with dislike about as quickly as the *Thaddeus* departed from Boston harbor. The first encounter took place when Bingham objected to the Holmans keeping the wine and fruit presented to Mrs. Holman as farewell gifts. Angry words followed. Everything, Bingham argued, was common property. Before long Bingham questioned the propriety with which Dr. Holman administered the supply of wine entrusted to his care for medical purposes. The opening rounds had been fired in what would become a bitter battle of accusation and counteraccusation.

On March 30, 1820, when the ship was 164 days out of Boston, the Hawaiian Islands were sighted. Neither crew nor missionaries knew what to expect from the Islanders; in preparation for the worst, cannons had been hoisted from beneath decks and placed in their carriages. The armorer's forge was set up, and boarding nettings were arranged. A party ventured ashore at the northern part of the island of Hawaii and brought back word that Kamehameha was dead and, more important, that the kapu system had been overthrown by his son. The joyous news of the end to the system of idol worship was proof that God had indeed prepared the way for the missionaries. Lucia Holman noted in her journal, "The most powerful obstacle which was anticipated could stand in the way of planting the standard of the cross upon these shores (abolishment of idolatry) is done away—and not by any human means either, but 'it is truly the Lord's doings and marvellous to our eyes.' " By April 4 the missionaries had sailed south to Kailua, where they presented themselves to Liholiho. The gifts they laid before the illiterate king included a huge Bible. After the presents had been given, they said they wanted to teach Christianity to the people.

What the missionaries saw about them tempered the pleasure of once more being on dry land. The size of their task was truly apparent for the first time, and it was disheartening. Rev. Hiram Bingham wrote, ". . . the appearance of destitution, degradation and barbarism, among the chattering, and almost naked savages, whose heads and feet, and much of their sunburnt swarthy skins, were bare, was appalling. Some of our number, with gushing tears, turned away from the spectacle. Others with firmer nerve continued their gaze, but were ready to exclaim, 'Can these be human beings! How dark and comfortless their state of mind and heart! How imminent the danger to the immortal soul, shrouded in this deep pagan gloom! Can such beings be civilized? Can they be Christianized? Can we throw ourselves upon these rude shores, and take up our abode, for life, among such a people for the purpose of training them for heaven?' "

In spite of their doubts the little missionary company requested permission of Liholiho to stay, permission which was not immediately granted. Some chiefs suggested the presence of such a large group of Americans would arouse the hostility of British or French representatives in the Islands. Others felt the missionaries had come for some political purpose. After four days of deliberation Liholiho agreed to let the missionaries stay for a year on a trial basis. When the missionaries asked to establish a station at Honolulu as well as Kailua, four more days of deliberation went by before they received a favorable reply. Liholiho requested that the doctor remain in Kailua, and the company voted that the Thurstons should remain with Dr. and Mrs. Holman, who had become somewhat estranged from the others.

The remainder of the company, which came ashore at Oahu, was granted the right to use a plot of land about half a mile from the village of Honolulu, along the path which led to Waikiki. The land between the mountains and the sea, where the city of Honolulu now stands, was then a hot, arid plain with only a few scattered trees. The wind often blew clouds of dust over the three thatched houses which Boki, governor of Oahu, had built for the newcomers. The missionaries went to work with great determination and energy. No chore was too great. No obstacle lessened their resolve.

On Christmas Day 1820 a ship arrived in Honolulu bringing a supply of lumber to supplement that carried on the *Thaddeus*. The missionaries asked Liholiho for permission to put up a permanent building, but the king took his time in granting approval, reluctant to allow anyone to have a better house than he. In the end it was probably the charming and quiet Lucy Thurston who convinced the king to grant permission. By August of 1821 Daniel Chamberlain and his family moved into the comparative luxury of a fourteen-by-fourteen-foot room. During the next few years the missionary houses, made of wood and of coral blocks, were enlarged, and many families of later companies lived there at various times.

Water had to be carried from Nuuanu Stream, something less than a mile away, until a well was dug on the premises. Even then the brackish water had to be filtered through a block of coral before it was usable. The chinaware which had been brought in barrels from New England had been smashed enroute, and only through the kindness of visiting merchant sailors was it replaced. Life was primitive and was not made easier by the fact that the missionaries themselves seemed unable to realize that the layers of clothing they wore in New England were hardly suitable to tropical Hawaii.

It was quickly apparent to the missionaries that the commoners and lesser chiefs would never embrace Christianity until the high chiefs had set an example through their conversion. The first major targets were King Lihiliho, Queen Regent Kaahumanu, and several high chiefs. Progress was slow. Liholiho knew Christianity meant he would have to give up four of his five women as well as rum drinking. He had no intention of foregoing either, but told Bingham he might consent later, perhaps in five years. Kaahumanu treated the missionaries with a great haughtiness. When they called on the queen regent, she customarily beckoned them into her presence with a motion of her little finger.

Then Kaahumanu fell ill and was nursed back to health with missionary help. Her haughtiness melted, and soon she became the unfailing friend of the missionaries. In April 1824 she publicly announced her intention to follow the laws of God. Even the missionaries had no idea how important this conversion would be. Soon many prominent chiefs became converts, and before long the missionaries were preaching to audiences which numbered in the thousands. But there was no wholesale acceptance of Hawaiians into the church. Standards for membership were exceedingly severe. A lengthy probation period was necessary to qualify for full church membership. No person was admitted who had not fully demonstrated that his conversion had resulted in a changed way of life. So strict were the missionaries' rules that during their first seventeen years in the Islands only some 1,300 Hawaiians were admitted into the church.

The missionaries believed that if the Hawaiians could only read the gospel for themselves, a great amount of time-consuming work would have been accomplished. But there was a monumental problem. The Hawaiians had not developed a written language. Very early the missionaries had tried to teach the Islanders to read and write English, but progress was painfully slow, and the missionaries decided they must reduce the Hawaiian language to written form.

The final puzzle of the language was not solved until six years later, with much help coming from Rev. William Ellis, an Englishman who had served as a missionary in Tahiti and who was familiar with the Tahitian language. The missionaries, however, did not wait for these refinements before publishing. A little over a year after their arrival they had made enough progress to publish a simple spelling book and a reading book in Hawaiian. Kaahumanu had shown the first flicker of interest in the missionaries when she saw these books.

Now began one of the most successful educational programs ever undertaken anywhere. Once the chiefs had shown an interest in reading and writing, the great mass of Hawaiians eagerly followed. The missionaries placed no limits on their time or energy, and they were rewarded with the unlimited enthusiasm of the Hawaiians. In 1824 some 2,000 students were attending school. In 1828 there were 37,000, and by 1831 about 52,000 pupils, approximately two fifths of the entire population, were attending some 1,100 schools. Reading and writing had become exciting new adventures for the Hawaiians. Fad though it was, the results were nonetheless beneficial.

Initially most of the pupils were adults. More often than not they sat on mats in thatched schoolhouses. Occasionally conditions were somewhat better. In one schoolhouse on Kauai surfboards were used to make seats and writing tables. In about ten years a majority of the adult Hawaiians had learned to read.

The need for ministers and teachers quickly became critical, and other missionary companies arrived from New England to fill the breach. At no time, however, was their number adequate to handle the chores which needed to be accomplished, and so in 1831 a high school was founded above the village of Lahaina on Maui. The school was called Lahainaluna, and its purpose was to train young men to become assistant ministers and teachers. A number of Hawaiians were successfully trained to become teachers, but the missionaries were extremely cautious in granting the Islanders authority as ministers. Not until 1849 was a Hawaiian ordained to preach and conduct affairs in a small parish, although several men had been licensed to preach a few years earlier.

Examinations in reading and writing were given four times a year, and the Hawaiians quickly made these festive occasions. The Rev. Reuben Tinker described an examination which took place in Honolulu in 1831: "The shell horn blowing early for examinations of the schools, in the meeting house. About 2,000 scholars present, some wrapped in large quantity of native cloth, with wreaths of evergreen about their heads and hanging toward their feet—others dressed in calico and silk with large necklaces of braided hair and wreaths of red and yellow and green feathers very beautiful and expensive.

"It was a pleasant occasion, in which they seemed interested and happy. . . . They read in various books, and 450 in four rows wrote the same sentence at the same time on slates. They perform with some ceremony."

Tinker went on to explain that a teacher stood at the head of the group and called out orders like a drill sergeant. First the rows of students were ordered to sit up straight. Then, at the order, they jumped to their feet. Next they presented slates, resting them on their arms. The next order was to bring chalk up, and then the sentence to be written was cried out by the sergeant-teacher. Rev. Tinker reported that most of the students wrote their sentences correctly. It was apparent to Rev. Reuben Tinker that many of the Hawaiians valued the festivities above their newly won knowledge.

In Kailua the Thurstons and Holmans at first shared a one-room thatched hut which was also inhabited by a variety of vermin. Outside it was hot and dusty. Water was scarce. An added irritant were the curious Hawaiians who followed them everywhere and stared into their hut when they sought refuge there. Tom and Lucia Holman were miserable. Four months after their arrival they had had enough. The Holmans sailed for Lahaina, with the permission of Liholiho, but without bothering to ask for the consent of the missionaries. Before the Holmans departed from Kailua, Reverend Bingham had decided the doctor was not what he wanted, and he wrote to the American Board asking for a man "with the *heart* of a *missionary* & the *skill* of a physician."

Lahaina was something of an improvement over Kailua, but the Holmans were there only a month when the doctor was summoned to Honolulu to nurse a stricken crew which had just arrived from Manila. Meeting Bingham face to face again further strained this relationship. When the crew had recuperated, the Holmans sailed for Kauai, where Mercy Whitney and Nancy Ruggles were expectant mothers. The Holmans stayed seven months on Kauai, and the doctor delivered not only the Whitney and Ruggles babies but also his own first-born child. By now the running battle between Thomas Holman and Hiram Bingham had deteriorated to the point where Holman had been excommunicated from the church and Lucia had been suspended.

Thomas and Lucia Holman returned to Honolulu only briefly. On October 2, 1821, they boarded a whaler for their return to the United States. They sailed by way of China, and Lucia Holman likely became the first American woman to sail around the world. Five years later Dr. Holman died at the age of thirty-three, but Lucia lived almost to her ninety-third birthday.

Lucia and Thomas Holman were not imbued with the intense zeal which inspired the other members of the first missionary company. Holman was strong-willed, independent, a vocal man who would not accept the authoritarian rule of Hiram Bingham. Unpleasant though the affair was, it did little damage to the missionary cause, although Bingham was sufficiently aroused to spend valuable time writing an exhaustive 115-page account of his relations with Thomas Holman to the mission board in New England.

Seldom in history has such a small group of people as Hawaii's Protestant missionaries caused so much heated debate. Their activities are still a subject which often brings forth extreme emotions. Some glorify the missionaries, calling them the saviors of the Islands. Others accuse the missionaries of being deceitful, of exploiting the Hawaiians to enrich themselves under the guise of Christianity.

There are no easy generalizations, because the Protestant missionaries were individuals, differing from each other in outlook and zeal. They labored under strict discipline, but they also believed that each man had a direct and personal relationship with his God. If some viewed salvation for the human soul as coming from a fierce Old Testament Jehovah, others believed just as strongly that salvation came more readily through the compassionate, forgiving Christ of the New Testament. If some missionaries had a weakness for power or for material possessions, others sought to heal and strengthen this Hawaiian race which was disjointed and living in a world out of context.

Most missionaries did what they considered to be good for the Hawaiians. The most important good, of course, was to save their souls. After that they taught them crafts, warned against the evils of drink, against the degradation of prostitution, and tried to show them that many merchant sailors exploited them. They taught them to read and write—a giant step toward bridging the gap between ancient Hawaii and the nineteenth-century world.

The great damage the missionaries did was an unintentional one, a harm they would have been hard pressed to understand. Christianity was a Western religion, and to be a Christian one had to have the conscience of a Western man. The Hawaiians were Polynesians, and the concept of Christian sin missed the Polynesian mind. So missionaries attempted to destroy the old Hawaiian standards and substitute Western ideals of right and wrong. Only when this had been done would the concept of sin be realized and the need for a Christ become apparent.

The missionaries preached endlessly about how depraved and stupid the Hawaiians had been. The Islanders were told they must feel great shame for what they had been, for their unenlightened parents and hero ancestors. It was a long, humiliating experience, one that only a few were willing to endure during the early years of the mission. Most missionaries through the middle 1800s would have said that it was necessary and right to do it this way, that a soul saved was worth any price and that the Hawaiians should willingly pay this price for eternal life. And the Hawaiians did pay an enormously high price. The price was the loss of a sense of their own worth and self-respect. Eventually the missionaries proudly proclaimed Hawaii a Christian nation. What they did not say was that the Hawaiians had lost that vital sense of worth and self-respect—that they were a maimed race destined to an unhappy fate.

Late in 1823 Liholiho decided to visit England. His reasons for making the trip are obscure, but he did wish to reaffirm his close ties with Great Britain, particularly in the face of the growing numbers of Americans in his kingdom. Liholiho considered himself to be under the protection of Great Britain, and he might well have thought such protection would soon be needed. Perhaps the king believed a visit to England would enhance his prestige. He well knew that he was constantly being measured against his illustrious father, and a visit with the king of England would add to his stature.

Liholiho began to choose the persons to accompany him. Kamamalu, his half-sister and favorite wife, was chosen, as was Boki, governor of Oahu, and his wife Liliha. The son of John Young went, and a Frenchman by the name of Jean Rives. Rives was secretary and interpreter. He was just under five feet tall, an unattractive man with tobacco-stained teeth. Rives had come to Hawaii at the beginning of the nineteenth century and eventually became a confidant and drinking companion of Liholiho. Through his Hawaiian wife he had acquired the use of extensive lands. Rev. William Ellis was originally selected as interpreter, but the captain of the whaler, *L'Aigle,* refused to accept Ellis as a passenger. The captain, whose name was Valentine Starbuck, readily accepted Rives, and their close relationship later appeared to be a conspiracy.

On November 27, 1823, the king and queen together with a company of twelve boarded *L'Aigle.* It was a scene of great emotion. Queen Kamamalu chanted of her great love for Hawaii and for her ancestors. The shore was crowded with people who wept as the party was rowed out to the sailing vessel.

L'Aigle put into Rio de Janeiro, and the Hawaiian delegation was grandly entertained by the British consul general and by Emperor Dom Pedro, the same man from whom the adventurer Georg Scheffer, now known as Count von Frankenthal, had bought his title. Indeed, Scheffer might well have attended the official functions honoring the Hawaiians if he had not been on one of his frequent business trips to Germany. In Rio John Rives succeeded in leaving behind his enemy, John Young. While Young was ashore, Rives sent him a note saying he was not to return to the ship. Before Young knew what had happened, the vessel sailed. Later Young caught up with the party in London.

Liholiho expected to pay his expenses with $25,000 he carried in great locked chests and which were placed under Starbuck's care. When the chests were opened at the Bank of England, only $10,000 was counted out. Captain Starbuck reported $3,000 had been spent in Rio de Janeiro, but there was no explanation for the disappearance of the rest of the money. Suspicion fell heavily in the direction of Rives and Starbuck, but no money was recovered and no legal action was brought against the two.

The British government had no advance notice of the coming of the King of Hawaii, but once his presence was known they reacted nobly. The party was put up at Osborne's, a most respectable hotel. It was very cold in London that summer, and the clothes missionary wives had sewn were not enough to keep the royal party warm. They were supplied with appropriate clothes by their hosts. Mr. George Canning, Secretary of State for Foreign Affairs, held a reception in their honor. They attended Westminister Abbey, where the king stared at the elaborate ceiling through the service and the queen leaped in fright at the first booming sounds of the organ. They sat in the royal box at Covent Garden Theatre and at Drury Lane Theatre. Crowds cheered their coming and going, and their pictures appeared in many store windows. At last a date was set for an audience with King George IV.

The Hawaiians enjoyed this exciting new world enormously, and considering their excitement they stayed remarkably free of trouble. On one occasion, however, they did come very close. It happened when several chiefs were wandering through the streets of London and chanced upon a fish market. Before them lay a delicious, familiar sight in the form of a gray mullet. The impulsive Hawaiians grabbed the fish and ran back to their hotel. The fish was devoured raw, washed down with twenty bottles of wine. It was an orgy of homesickness.

On June 10 one of the chiefs fell ill. Within nine days every person in the party had been stricken with the measles. The Hawaiians had no immunity to this Western disease, and to them it was a serious infection. The best doctors came to attend them. Slowly all the Hawaiians improved, with the exception of Queen Kamamalu. She grew steadily worse, and on July 4 Liholiho was told there was no hope for her recovery.

The king had been ill also but was recovering. Now he was taken to the queen's room in a wheelchair and was lifted onto her bed where he embraced her. The two wept. At six o'clock in the evening of July 8, 1824, Kamamalu died. Liliha took charge of the queen's body. She dressed the dead queen in the traditional long Hawaiian skirt, or pa'u, and found flowers for her hair. Then the body was carried to Liholiho's room. The death of Kamamalu drained the will to live from Liholiho, and he declined. Six days later, at four in the morning, the grief-stricken king turned to Boki and said, "I die in the morning of my days, alas! for I shall see my country no more."

Liholiho had not lived to meet George IV, but finally, on September 11, the survivors of the Hawaiian delegation were presented to the English monarch. The details of the meeting are not recorded, but apparently King George said he would protect Hawaii from foreign nations. As for internal affairs, the Hawaiians must manage as best they could.

The English had been generous and gracious hosts. They had paid all the bills for the Hawaiian delegation during their stay in England, and now they provided a warship to carry the bodies of the deceased king and queen back to Hawaii, together with the surviving company. *H.M.S. Blonde,* a forty-six-gun man-of-war, was ordered to make the trip. The vessel was under the command of Lord Byron, a cousin of the famous poet, and inheritor of his title. In late September the shores of England fell behind.

News of the death of Kamamalu and Liholiho preceded the *Blonde* to Hawaii via an American whaling ship. When, in early May of 1825, the English warship reached Honolulu harbor, it was met by a weeping, black-garbed group of missionaries and Hawaiian royalty. Five days after the *Blonde* arrived the two huge, triple caskets of lead, mahogany, and oak were rowed ashore. The caskets were covered with crimson velvet.

A sad procession wound its way between double rows of Hawaiian guards, many of whom were dressed in parts of Russian uniforms, to the great thatched church now somberly draped with bolts of black cloth. First, twelve Hawaiian warrior chiefs, in feather cloaks and helmets, marched with lowered kahilis, the feathered emblems of royalty. Then came the smartly uniformed marine contingent from the *Blonde,* advancing with measured tread, muskets reversed, heads bowed. The band from the British vessel proceeded next, playing a dirge. Then followed the chaplain and surgeon of the *Blonde* together with two American missionaries. Then came the caskets, on two black draped carts, each drawn by forty chiefs. Behind walked Kauikeaouli, the twelve-year-old heir to the throne, splendidly dressed in a Windsor uniform presented to him several days earlier by Lord Byron. On his left was Richard Charlton, the newly arrived British consul for Hawaii, and on his right was Lord Byron. Then came a parade of chiefs in order of their rank. Next were the foreigners and the captains of ships which were in port. Finally one hundred sailors from the *Blonde,* in white uniforms with black handkerchiefs, marched two by two.

The procession stopped before Honolulu's only church, a thatched building seventy feet long and twenty-five feet wide. The door of the church was too narrow to admit the great coffins, so services were held at the entrance. Here the chaplain of the *Blonde* read burial services. A missionary said a prayer and another addressed the assembled crowd in Hawaiian. Then the caskets were placed in a thatched house until a permanent mausoleum of stone was completed.

Lord Byron was annoyed by the missionaries, particularly by Hiram Bingham, but he diplomatically hid his feelings. Bingham was present during the Englishman's first audience with the Hawaiian rulers, and the minister had suggested that prayers would be in order. Then followed, according to one account, "a long dull grace." With the funeral ceremonies decently past, the English announced they intended to give a public showing of lantern slides. The announced time for the show was a Saturday evening, but although excitement over the event was great, very few people came. Some missionaries considered the timing as bad and advised the Hawaiians not to go. After all, the next day was the Sabbath and the faithful were expected to appear in church five times that day. Anything which might cause their attention to wander must be avoided.

The account of the voyage of the *Blonde* to Hawaii refers to Bingham as the inflexible leader of the missionaries. "This man is, we have no doubt, truly zealous in the cause of religion; but we cannot forbear to remark, that he has in a manner thrust himself into all the political affairs of the island, and acts as secretary of state, as governor of the young princes, director of consciences, comptroller of amusements, etc."

His work completed, Lord Byron upped anchor and departed from Honolulu. With him sailed Kaahumanu and two missionaries who went as far as Hilo Bay. In his honor Kaahumanu renamed the bay Byron Bay. Before sailing for home Byron visited Kealakekua Bay to honor the memory of James Cook. Near the spot where the English captain was killed he erected a ten-foot cross of English oak and posted a copper plate.

The strongest opposition to the missionaries came from haoles, not Hawaiians. Many haoles longed for the good old days when there were no missionaries to teach the Hawaiians that sexual freedom, work on the Sabbath, and drinking were grievous sins. In the old days the haoles had not been harassed by the sensitive consciences of clergymen. Sailors who returned to the islands and found that missionaries had changed things were often disposed to violence. Once Hiram Bingham was attacked by a mob of infuriated sailors, and the home of Reverend Richards in Lahaina was the target of the cannons of a British whaling vessel.

The missionaries were repeatedly shocked by the events which happened about them. One shock came in 1825 when Oliver Holmes died while intoxicated. Holmes had been a long-time resident, and Bingham had early reported that the singing of hymns drew tears from his eyes. Like other haoles who early helped the missionaries, Holmes found their restrictions more than he could abide. Two missionaries were nevertheless invited to join the funeral procession, but they discovered to their sorrow that the procession was made up of godless foreigners parading with their mistresses or prostitutes. As an added insult flags atop the grogshops were flown at half mast in honor of their late good customer. Elisha Loomis noted the event in his journal and added, "From this account you may form some idea of the state of society here."

Another shocking event had occurred earlier when a ship's captain strode through the dusty lanes of Honolulu, stalking a rival captain. In his belt were two pistols. When he sighted his rival he opened fire without warning, seriously injuring his enemy. The wounded captain had succeeded in luring away the mistress of the gun-carrying captain, and that was the reason for the shooting. The captain who had done the shooting was anything but repentant, and apparently many haoles in Honolulu sympathized with the direct way he had settled his grievance.

The two extremes—sailors and missionaries—met when the chiefs called a meeting to establish a set of laws for the kingdom. No violence took place, but the gap which separated the two groups was evident when the missionary-instructed chiefs suggested the Ten Commandments be made the law of the land and sailors and other haoles demanded that boatloads of women be allowed to accommodate visiting ships.

The missionaries gained their greatest single success when the powerful and portly regent, Kaahumanu, was converted. No one in the Hawaiian kingdom was her equal in authority, and her acceptance of Christianity gave the new religion official sanction. Kaahumanu was not baptized until December, 1825, but her sympathy for the missionaries had been of aid earlier.

Kaahumanu had become a wife to Kamehameha when she was about sixteen. George Vancouver said she was the loveliest girl he had seen in Hawaii. Her skin was fair and smooth, without blemish. Her warrior-king husband kept a close watch on her, and when he discovered she was having an affair with a nineteen-year-old chief, the king quickly executed the culprit, even though he was a relative and loved friend. In full womanhood Kaahumanu stood six feet tall and grew very portly, a mark of prestige among Hawaiian royalty. As a convert to Christianity she lavished great affection on the missionary women, often fondling a wife in her ample lap like a child.

Kaahumanu was a great help to Kamehameha in keeping ambitious chiefs in line. She was related to many high-ranking chiefs, and these blood ties helped prevent rebellion. Three years after Kamehameha died Kaahumanu brought Kaumualii, who had so long ruled Kauai, to Honolulu and announced to that rather frightened man that he was to be her husband. In 1832 Kaahumanu became ill and retired to her house in Manoa Valley. The missionaries comforted her, but there was no saving her life. Before she died Hiram Bingham rushed to her a copy of the New Testament, in Hawaiian, which had just come from the presses. It was bound in leather with her name stamped in gold on the cover. It brought her pleasure in her last moments. She died in June at the age of sixty-four. Hawaii had lost a wise woman, a protector of the people.

The Protestant missionaries were making progress with the Hawaiians, but new problems suddenly appeared in the form of three Catholic priests and several lay people who arrived in Honolulu in 1827. They had come to Hawaii through a set of circumstances which began with Liholiho's visit to England. Jean Rives, the man who had gone along as the king's translator, was the originator of the problem, and as a consistent enemy of the missionaries he would have been pleased by the considerable vexation he caused the Protestants. After the death of Liholiho Governor Boki fired Rives, and the Frenchman returned to his native land. As a farewell gesture Rives stole the watch of the late king.

In France Jean Rives was able to drum up support for a commercial scheme he had devised. He planned to use his former extensive lands in Hawaii as a base for a permanent French agricultural colony, which would be supplemented with a trading station. An important part of the expedition was a company of Catholic priests who would spread their religion among the Hawaiians. The expedition sailed aboard two ships, but Rives, who started the whole undertaking, never reached Hawaii. In Lower California, where his vessel stopped, Rives learned that his activities in London had been so badly thought of in Hawaii that it would be dangerous for him to return to the Islands. He remained on the West Coast and finally died of cholera in Mexico some years later. Without Rives' supposed connections the agricultural colony did not materialize, and the priests had difficulties in obtaining supplies.

The three priests were Alexis Bachelot, who was named Apostolic Prefect, Abraham Armand, and Patrick Short. With them were an agriculturalist, a choir brother, and two lay brothers. The three priests had been sent out by the young, zealous order of the Congregation of the Sacred Hearts of Jesus and Mary. No sooner had the Catholic missionaries landed than Kaahumanu ordered them to leave on the same ship on which they had arrived. Her command, however, could not be carried out. The captain of the ship on which they came was furious at not finding Rives in Honolulu, since he was to receive payment from Rives for the cargo he had carried to the Islands. In a fit of anger he sailed away, leaving the little Catholic colony behind.

The Catholics had learned on the West Coast that they would not be welcomed in the Islands. On arrival the priests made no formal request to stay and even declined an invitation to meet with Kaahumanu. For the first several months they remained behind the enclosure which surrounded their three huts, spending much of their time learning the Hawaiian language. Five months after landing, Governor Boki granted them a small parcel of land on which a chapel was built. Here the company lived in peace for over a year.

The presence of the Catholic missionaries soon became a serious issue. Governor Boki played a major role in creating this situation. He had become the antagonist of Kaahumanu, and one way he could annoy her was to help the Catholics. Kaahumanu saw in the images and rituals of the Catholic Church a resemblance to ancient idolatrous ways, and she even envisioned a return of the restrictive kapu system. Kaahumanu thought the two religious factions might split the nation and eventually bring civil war. When the priests actively sought converts, she was alarmed.

About the middle of 1829 an order was read through the streets of Honolulu forbidding Hawaiians to attend Catholic services. In January of 1830 Kaahumanu personally forbade the priests to teach the Catholic religion. The priests refused to obey her order, and no attempt was made to enforce it. Then in April, 1831, a letter was delivered to the two remaining priests, Fathers Bachelot and Short, ordering them to leave Hawaii within three months. When it became apparent that the priests had no intention of complying with the order, a Hawaiian brig carried the pair to California. The two priests had left against their will but suffered no violence. They were landed at San Pedro and continued their missionary efforts in California. There is no record of what happened to Armand.

The Protestant missionaries were delighted to see the two Catholic priests depart, and they undoubtedly encouraged the chiefs to come to the decision to oust them. The Protestant missionaries, however, played no part in the persecution of the Catholics which took place before Bachelot and Short departed. These persecutions, in addition to prohibiting persons from practicing Catholicism, took the form of periodic imprisonment and hard labor for those who remained adamant. Some Protestant missionaries attempted to halt the imprisonments and sentences of hard labor while others ignored the whole situation.

In 1835 Brother Columba Murphy was ordered to visit Honolulu to determine whether a mission could again be started. Murphy was optimistic about the possibilities of success, and the next year a young priest by the name of Arsenius Walsh arrived in Honolulu. He was ordered to leave, but before he could depart a French warship dropped anchor in Honolulu harbor. Three weeks earlier a United States man-of-war had arrived, and the following month a British warship put into port.

To all of these foreign captains the Hawaiian government's order to expel Walsh appeared to be more than a question of religious toleration. The broader questions concerned what right the Hawaiian government had to expel any foreigner and what rights a resident foreigner had to transfer land and buildings to a second person. In a series of discussions with the captains it was agreed that the Hawaiian government still owned all the land and that foreigners could use the land only at the king's pleasure. The king, however, did not have the right to destroy the houses or other property of foreigners.

Father Walsh and the French colony saw hope for their cause in the French warship in the harbor. They went aboard and gave their version of the expulsion of Bachelot and Short to Captain A. N. Vaillant and asked his help in establishing their own mission. The captain approached the king in connection with the two lay brothers who still remained, since they were French citizens, and it was agreed they could remain peacefully in Honolulu in possession of their property.

The case of Arsenius Walsh was a different matter. He was a British citizen, and although the French espoused the Catholic cause, they could not legally impose Walsh on the Hawaiian government. The captain of the British man-of-war entered a plea for fellow citizen Walsh, but all the Hawaiians would allow was that the priest could remain in the Islands as long as he obeyed the laws and did not attempt to spread his religion.

In April of 1837 Fathers Bachelot and Short reappeared on the scene. They came ashore, Short attempting to disguise himself with a long beard and broad-rimmed hat. The two were immediately recognized and once again ordered to leave. The British and French captains intervened, and finally Bachelot and Short were escorted back to their old quarters in Honolulu by the two captains. In November of 1837 more priests arrived. Feelings ran high. Affairs were clearly heading toward a climax.

Word had filtered back to France that Catholic priests had been refused permission to land in Hawaii, and that nation decided it must teach Hawaii to respect both France and the Catholic religion.Captain C. P. T. Laplace, in command of the frigate *L'Artémise,* was given the job of setting things right in Hawaii. He arrived in Honolulu on July 9, 1839, and the next day issued an ultimatum to the king. His list of demands included freedom of worship for Catholics and the grant of a parcel of land from the government for a church. He also decreed that the Roman Catholic church in Hawaii be ministered by French priests and that the government deposit $20,000 with the French as a guarantee that the conditions would be carried out.

The government had little choice, for Captain Laplace said that if his demands were not met, war would follow immediately. The king was at Lahaina at the time, so the governor of Oahu signed the document on his behalf. The $20,000 was borrowed from Honolulu merchants. Five days after the first document was signed Laplace appeared with another list of demands. Among the items forced on the government this time was one stating that French citizens could only be tried by a jury of foreigners proposed by the French Consul and accepted by the Hawaiian government. Another provision stated that there would be no prohibition of French wines and brandies. This last demand made ineffectual a Hawaiian law of the year before which had greatly restricted the sale of liquor.

Again Hawaii had felt the harsh demands of foreign powers. Those who reflected on these recent happenings must have wondered just how much sovereignty the little kingdom possessed. The answer was distressingly clear and simple: Hawaii had only as much sovereignty as the major powers wished to grant it.

Chapter Six

"THE DEVIL IS BUSILY ENGAGED . . ."

THE THIRTEEN American colonies were impoverished by the War of the Revolution. The plight of the New England merchant marine in particular was a solemn reminder of the price of independence. Nantucket probably had been hardest hit. At the beginning of the war a fleet of 150 ships called Nantucket Island home port. By the war's end 149 had been destroyed or captured.

In prewar days the bulk of American trade had been across the Atlantic with England. During the war a profitable, although limited, trade had been carried on with France. Some people thought it might grow, but Americans had never acquired a taste for French goods, and the hope was soon abandoned. So, in spite of bitter feelings, a certain amount of trade with England was resumed. As New England shipyards sent more vessels down the ways, the need for new commercial outlets became pressing. Some ships sailed the northern seas to St. Petersburg, but this trade with Russia occupied only a small part of the merchant marine.

Other American ships ventured across the Atlantic Ocean, around the Cape of Good Hope, and on to Canton, China. These voyages brought some profit, but the traders faced a major problem in finding items which would be acceptable to the Chinese as payment for their tea, chinaware, and silk. The Chinese wanted Spanish gold pieces above all else, but the United States was desperately low on hard cash. The Chinese merchants valued such delicacies as edible birds' nests, sharks' fins, and a variety of sea slug, found on South Pacific reefs, known as *bêche-de-mer*. These delicacies were all made into soups. Another favored oddity was a root called ginseng, which was dried and brewed into tea. The Chinese firmly believed this tea restored virility. The time spent in collecting these items made trade difficult and slow.

American merchants noted in the journals of James Cook's last voyage and also in John Ledyard's narrative that Cantonese merchants placed a very high value on sea otter pelts. In 1787 Bostonians fitted out the *Columbia* and the *Lady Washington,* both less than one hundred feet in length, to investigate the feasibility of using the sea otter as a trade commodity. The two pioneer vessels voyaged around South America, then north to Vancouver Island, where they secured a cargo of furs. From the Pacific Northwest the ships sailed to Hawaii and then to Canton, where the furs were traded to Chinese for tea and other goods. The venture was not a great commercial success, but it offered promise.

The British had found their way to Canton long before the Americans, and they too sailed to the American Northwest for cargoes of furs which they carried to China. The English were keen competitors, but problems at home, including the continuing war with France, forced England to concentrate her energies in Europe. American vessels now dominated this particular portion of the China trade.

By 1810 Yankee merchants had discovered a new, accessible medium of exchange which was welcomed by the Chinese. It was sandalwood, and it was available in quantity in the Hawaiian Islands. The Chinese carved delicate boxes and sacred objects from the wood, and its heavy fragrance made it desirable as incense. Oil distilled from the wood went into medicines, perfumes, and cosmetics.

Optimism ran high. Pacific trade could be speeded up, and greater profits would soon follow. It was not yet to be, for America's long smoldering dispute with England erupted into the War of 1812. New Englanders vividly remembered the economic carnage of the American Revolution, and they were unalterably opposed to this new encounter. Feelings were vehement, and talk of secession from the Union was common in the northern seaboard states. Yankee ships continued to trade with the enemy through Quebec and, since the British profited by this trade, they allowed New England ports to remain open while all other East Coast ports were blockaded. Not until seven months before the end of the war did the British finally see fit to blockade New England Ports also.

New England merchants feared for the safety of their ships in the Pacific, so they dispatched a letter-of-marque vessel to warn American ships that a war was on, to capture any enemy vessels en route, and in the process make a profit by carrying a cargo of furs to Canton. Many American ships sailed for the safety of neutral ports on learning of the war and remained there until peace came at last.

In October, 1812, the forty-six-gun frigate *U.S.S. Essex* slipped from Delaware Bay bound for the South Pacific. Captain David Porter, in command of the ship, carried orders to protect American vessels and destroy or capture British whalers and merchant ships. Porter's unexpected appearance caused consternation among the confident British and, more important, he inflicted considerable damage on the enemy merchant navy.

After a year at sea Porter decided his crew needed rest and provisions, and his ships badly wanted repairs, so he made for Taiohae Bay in the Marquesas Islands. There he constructed a fort on shore, ran up the American flag, and formally took possession of the island group for the United States, an act which was never recognized by Congress.

With the *Essex* again in seaworthy condition, Porter departed from Taiohae Bay, leaving behind three captured British ships under the command of a young lieutenant of marines by the name of John M. Gamble. The handful of men Gamble commanded included many British merchant sailors, who after their capture had agreed to serve as loyal crew members aboard prize ships. When the first good opportunity came, most of these sailors mutinied and escaped in one of the ships.

The Marquesans saw that the forces of their unwelcomed visitors were weak, and they succeeded in killing or wounding several of the remaining men. John Gamble, who had been wounded by a pistol ball in his encounter with the mutineers, set the second ship afire and escaped the avenging Marquesans by putting to sea in the remaining vessel. His crew consisted of eight men, only two of whom were fit for sea duty. Without chart or compass Gamble somehow navigated his ship north to the Hawaiian Islands in the short time of seventeen days. His vessel, which was really an armed merchantman, was the first United States ship under military command to reach Hawaii. At Oahu the twenty-four-year-old marine signed on additional crew and set sail for the island of Hawaii to visit King Kamehameha.

Ill fortune continued to shadow Gamble. Before Oahu had dropped from the horizon, he was overtaken by a British man-of-war and taken prisoner. Lieutenant Gamble did get to visit the aging Kamehameha, although not in the way he planned. He met the king in the company of his British captors and listened in anger as John Young explained to the British officers what routes American vessels usually followed near Hawaii, so they would be able to intercept them.

A peace treaty was signed at Ghent on Christmas Eve, 1814, and the unpopular war was over. As word of the treaty traveled around the world, New England merchant ships emerged from neutral ports to pick up the threads of trade they had dropped three years earlier. By now sea otter and seals had become somewhat scarce, but trade with the Russian settlements in Alaska was brisk, and Hawaiian sandalwood offered the medium of exchange needed in China.

Kamehameha I had quickly noticed the eagerness with which foreign merchant sailors sought out sandalwood. To gain the greatest money from the wood, the king made the business a government monopoly, and so all trade had to go through him. Realizing that the forests would soon be depleted, he enforced conservation rules which protected the young trees.

After 1819, with the old king dead, the rules were ignored, and individual chiefs exploited the forests as fast as they could.

Sandalwood is something less than a noble looking tree, especially viewed amidst the many strong, tall trees of ancient Hawaiian forests. It is a rather shaggy, stunted tree with narrow stiff leaves and a reddish blossom. The heartwood is straight-grained, an attractive yellow-brown to orange in color. The wood is so dense that it barely floats. The Hawaiians used powdered sandalwood as a perfume, often sprinkling it between layers of newly manufactured kapa cloth.

The merchant sailors measured sandalwood by the picul, a measure common in China, the equal of 133⅓ pounds. The value of a picul was approximately $10. With free access to the sandalwood forests, the chiefs ordered commoners by the thousands into the mountains to cut the valuable trees. Farms went untended while these orders were carried out, and on at least one occasion the Islands were seriously close to famine as a result.

To the chiefs this wood represented a buying power they had never known before. The eager traders were willing to bring any luxury to Hawaii if sandalwood could be exchanged for it. Fancy New England winter clothes, billiard tables, carriages, and sailing ships were gladly traded for wood. In a few years all the accessible sandalwood had been cut, but the demand continued. As an inducement to keep searching and cutting, the merchants offered easy credit to the chiefs. They supplied goods immediately against wood which would be cut and delivered in the future. The chiefs gladly accepted, and soon they were hopelessly in debt. The quality of sandalwood also deteriorated, since much of it came from remote areas where growing conditions were poor. By 1829 the sandalwood forests had been depleted, and the trade was close to its end. The debts of the chiefs remained a grim reality, but their ability to pay had all but disappeared. It would require years of prodding and the appearance of U. S. warships on three occasions before payment was finally made in full.

Every New England boy with adventure in his heart longed to sail to Hawaii and to the Pacific beyond. Distant place names were household words in the harbor towns. Tales of high danger and of peoples with unfathomable customs filled many an evening. Vessels often sailed for the Pacific with teen-aged boys as crew, commanded by captains and officers still in their twenties.

A voyage to the Pacific meant stormy days navigating the Straits of Magellan, perhaps an encounter with the treacherous Indians of the Pacific Northwest, and then the warm, hospitable Islands of Hawaii where many a young man lost his virginity to a smiling, carefree girl. Beyond Hawaii there were monotonous days on the vast Pacific, but then came the exotic port of Canton, a place so strange that those who lived prosaic lives ashore could never really comprehend what it was like.

Reaching Canton was not easy. Starting at Macao, some sixty miles from Canton, the advance to the city was a formalized ritual designed for the protection and prestige of the dozen or so merchants who had each paid substantial sums of money to win a trading franchise. After vessels had been measured to determine the customs duties to be paid, after assurances had been given that crews would behave well, and after the cargo had been ferried off in junks, the vessels were at last allowed to move to Canton and anchor before designated trading houses.

The city of Canton was off limits to visiting sailors. The only dry land they could tread was a small space before the warehouse of the merchants their captain dealt with. Curious seamen could see little ashore, but the Chinese population which lived aboard junks did their best to present their wares to the ships. An assortment of junks crowded about each visiting vessel, their owners hawking every kind of merchandise and pleasure. There were barber boats, bird boats, flower boats, floating brothels, and gambling boats.

James Hunnewell, a young man from Massachusetts, was among those familiar with the Canton trade. A descendant of early settlers in the Bay State, Hunnewell had made up his mind to become a sailor while still a child. At the age of fifteen, weighing all of ninety pounds, he won the consent of his parents to go to sea. Later Hunnewell recalled, "My mother, father and other friends told me all the frightful stories they could think of to try to deter me from going to sea. The effect of these frightful stories on me was this, that instead of deterring me they increased my desire to go, and to encounter its dangers and hardships."

James Hunnewell had served as second officer aboard the missionary ship, *Thaddeus*. He was the man in command of the longboat sent ashore at the north of Hawaii, and he carried back the joyous news that the kapu system had been overthrown. He had been in Hawaii three years earlier. The vessel he then served on was sold to chiefs, and the young man was assigned the job of staying in the Islands to collect the value of the ship as well as the merchandise she carried. All trade was done by barter, except for a small amount of cash which came from an English vessel. Hunnewell took a great amount of sandalwood as payment, and he sailed to Canton with this cargo, where he sold it for additional profit. When he finally made his way back to Boston, he was twenty-four years old.

James Hunnewell married soon after he returned to New England, but just weeks later he sailed off aboard the *Thaddeus*. After depositing the missionaries in the Islands, the ship traveled to California, then returned to Hawaii, where it too was sold to chiefs. Once again Hunnewell was left to collect payment. At this time the young man decided that Honolulu needed a general merchandise store, and he made up his mind to come back "to commence a new and independent commission business."

After six months at home James Hunnewell was offered the job of taking out the *Missionary Packet,* a vessel to be used by the missionaries for inter-island transportation. Hunnewell received no wages, but he was allowed to carry out some forty or fifty barrels of his own merchandise. The contents of the barrels represented the captain's savings and his hopes.

The *Missionary Packet* was not meant for the open sea. Fully loaded the deck stood a scant foot above the sea. Waves quickly carried away the sideboards, and for a good part of the voyage the decks were awash. His crewmen were either alcoholic or lazy; however, after an endurance test of nine months and one day he reached Honolulu. Hunnewell wasted no time in self-pity. He opened a store near the waterfront, offering the assortment of merchandise which came from his forty or fifty barrels.

The young merchant exchanged furs and sandalwood for goods from Canton. He imported those New England goods which were in demand and would bring profit. Two years later he hired a young sailor as an assistant. Business was an unglamorous cycle of keeping books, checking inventories, and collecting accounts. James Hunnewell did these things well. He was a shrewd trader, and his profits were great.

Four years after he came he was ready to return to his patient wife. His assistant would gradually buy out his business. Hunnewell had increased an original investment of some $3,000 to approximately $67,000. With his fortune, he settled on a farm in Massachusetts, although he continued to be active in Pacific trade. The company he founded became known as C. Brewer & Co. Ltd., and is now considered the oldest American corporation west of the Mississippi River.

1819 might stand as the most momentous year in Hawaii's history. In that year Kamehameha I died and with him the ancient kapus. That year a band of determined missionaries sailed for Hawaii. In 1819 rich whaling grounds were discovered off the coasts of Japan.

Captain Joseph Allen of Nantucket was the first to take whales in the Japan grounds. In late 1820 his ship, heavily laden with oil, put in at Honolulu for supplies. The news of the great abundance of whales in those seas spread through Honolulu's waterfront with great speed. A scant two years later some sixty whalers visited Honolulu. Between 1820 and 1830 the yearly average ran between sixty and eighty vessels.

Whale ships were different from other vessels. They were built like floating warehouses to carry enough supplies for months at sea and to store away cargoes of oil and bone. Whalers were also factories where blubber was rendered out in trypots on deck. Smoke soon blackened their sails, making them identifiable far away. Whalers stood high in the water and looked like shoe boxes, which led sailors to wonder if they were not built by the mile and sawed off to the desired length.

Life for the crew was so wretched that a Calvinist missionary might have been moved to consider it an approximation of hell. The crew existed in the forecastle, a small triangular shaped dungeon with a low overhead deck. Bunks lined the perimeter, each so closely atop the other that sitting up was impossible. A chest was allowed each crewman, the only sitting and storage space. Ventilation, when there was any, came through the companionway. In southern seas the forecastle was a sweat box and in northern seas an ice box. It was dark, cramped, and heavy with the odors of tobacco, whale oil, mildew, sweat, and food. At mess time a wooden tub was carried to the forecastle or on deck if the weather was good. The usual fare was a mixture of salted beef, potatoes, rice, or beans, and the sailors ladled out their portions. If supplies were low or if the captain was economizing, the stronger ate and the weaker did not. The officers were often brutal men who enjoyed the iron hold they had on men at sea. In time a seaman could almost grow used to a kick or a fist, but the cat-o'-nine-tails was something different, and it was always available as a quick solution to problems.

A sailor's reward for enduring these cruelties certainly did not come in the form of high wages. A man signed on a whaler for a lay, which was a percentage of the profits that would come from the voyage, and a one one-hundredth would satisfy most hands. After a four-year voyage a seaman might walk away from his ship with as little as $100 for his labors. A financially successful voyage could be made more profitable for captain and owners if crew members would desert after most of the whale killing had been accomplished. Any ruthless captain could persecute crew members to the point where they would jump ship at the next port they touched. With desertion a sailor's pay would revert to the ship, and if a new hand were needed he would receive only a fraction of what was due the deserter.

Some captains did not thrive on brutality, and there were even a handful who mixed Christianity with their business. One such man was Captain Charles W. Gelett. He visited Hawaii many times, regularly signing on Hawaiians to supplement the crews he brought out from New England. Captain Gelett posted a notice on the binnacle which read, "No Swearing Allowed Aboard This Ship." The officers and crew voted unanimously to refrain from hunting whales on the Sabbath, and instead services were conducted on that day. Furthermore, no liquor was allowed aboard except for medicinal purposes. This strange behavior did not jinx Captain Gelett's ships. He did well for himself and his owners.

In the 1820s and 1830s the crews who manned American whalers were mostly professional sailors from New England. After that young Yankees showed less inclination to go whaling, preferring to migrate westward or seek employment in New England's growing commercial and industrial complex. Although fewer New Englanders were willing to sail, the number of whalers setting forth was increasing. Crews were picked up where they could be found and included blacks, American Indians, white renegades, and liberal numbers of Hawaiians.

This new activity in the Pacific meant wealth for the merchants of the Islands, because Hawaii was the only reasonable place in the Pacific to go for supplies. Here whalers usually came twice a year, to take on provisions, make repairs, trans-ship casks of oil, and recruit Hawaiians to replace the dead and deserted. As one successful season followed another, more and more ships were sent around the Horn. At each stop in the Islands the crew and owners of a whaler spent an average of between $700 and $800. Quickly it became the most lucrative and dependable business the islands had ever known.

Theophilus H. Davies was a Honolulu businessman during the whaling years, and he remembered how those who could prosper from the visiting vessels would crowd the docks to welcome the captains. The butcher, sail-maker, and coppersmith "smile and bow and shake hands with a hungry joy." There was always a collection of unsavory characters on hand to help the crewmen spend their money at a rapid rate. "Then the crimps get hold of poor Jack, and give him cash in advance at frightful premiums, and minister to his wants and fancies. Then the harpies pounce on him and poor Jack is held in bondage of sin for six weeks and finds his 'lay' has been spent, and he has to get a heavy advance against the next season."

The ports of Honolulu and Lahaina, and to a lesser degree Hilo, became boisterous places during the months when whaling ships were in port. Davies recalled, "Troops of Hawaiian maidens come from country homes to Honolulu . . . and few of them ever return. . . ." Shops and dance halls were open every night and money flowed freely. The exploitation of the crews troubled the conscience of Theophilus Davies, who stated that the respectable merchants did not take the wages of the sailors, but they supplied silks, satins, perfumes, and brandy to those who did. The missionaries were shocked by what was happening. Rev. Lorrin Andrews wrote to a fellow clergyman about the situation at Lahaina: ". . . the Devil is busily engaged in Lahaina as you may judge from the fact that 97 whale ships have anchored here since the first of July."

Most whale men ashore were not inclined to act like sober, law-abiding citizens. They had lived through the mental and physical bullying of a voyage, and that was reason enough to celebrate. On shore the police were the symbol of authority, and sailors were apt to rid themselves of smoldering hates against authority by looking for trouble. In 1852 events boiled to a climax in Honolulu. It had been a successful season in the Japan grounds, and so many vessels crowded Honolulu harbor that only a narrow passage remained for those captains wishing to thread their way to sea.

A stream of some 3,000 sailors spilled from these ships into the dusty streets of Honolulu. The Honolulu police were lenient toward sailors, partly because they spent a great deal of money and partly because the police could not handle any major discipline problems. In late 1852, however, things became wilder than usual, and the police made numerous arrests for drunkenness, wild horseback riding, and general disorderliness. Transgressors were locked up in the fort located near the waterfront.

On the evening of November 8 an incident took place which suddenly threatened order in the entire town. A sailor named Henry Burns was arrested for drunkenness and disorderly conduct and was carted off to the fort and packed into a cell with eight or ten other culprits. Seaman Burns was still not ready to calm down. He began to tear up the brick floor of the cell and hurl the bricks at the cell door.

George Sherman, a guard, came to stop the furor, but Burns paid no attention to orders. The jailer then opened the cell door and with the help of at least two soldiers began to clamp the prisoners in irons. At some point Sherman hit Burns with his club and with that single blow to the temple killed him. The news of Burns's death spread quickly, and the next morning sailors began to gather before the fort, talking in small groups about the brutality of the police. Before long they came forward with an ultimatum. They wanted the guilty jailer turned over to them for punishment.

William Parke, the bewhiskered marshal of the kingdom of Hawaii, waited behind the closed gates of the fort. He quickly replied that the jailer would not be turned over to the sailors. He told the sailors that Sherman would be properly tried and would be punished if found guilty. Parke now mustered some seventy-five of his best soldiers and a force of constables and prepared to march out and disperse the gang of seamen.

At that point a messenger arrived at the fort with orders from the governor of Oahu telling Parke to keep his forces within the fort. The governor believed serious trouble could still be avoided if the government did not become too aggressive. Parke cooled his heels during the day while the sailors milled about in the dusty street which separated the fort from the docks. The next day Henry Burns was buried in Nuuanu Valley cemetery. Many sailors attended the rites, and emotions boiled close to the surface.

A rumor now spread among the seamen that fellow sailors confined in the marine hospital in Honolulu were being mistreated, and a crowd marched off to find out for themselves. William Ladd, a Honolulu merchant who also ran the hospital, was forewarned of their coming. He hastily gathered hospital documents and cash before departing. The sailors roamed through the hospital and, finding nothing amiss, headed back to town.

By evening the mood of the mob demanded violence. Some sailors carried firearms, and the rest raided woodpiles for clubs. Honolulu residents believed the town was going to be burned to the ground. The American Commissioner and the American Consulate tried to get groups of seamen to listen to reason, but little attention was paid them. The U. S. Consulate ordered handbills printed and distributed among the sailors. They declared: "Justice shall be done. I request you to go on board your ships quietly at sundown, and those on shore not to join, assemble or gather in very large numbers. My countrymen, listen to me. Remember that you represent a country of law and order, and don't refuse to obey the laws here."

Handbills had no more effect than personal entreaties. The sailors again marched to the fort and demanded that Sherman be handed over to them. Failing to accomplish their goal a second time, they attacked a three-story building nearby which housed the police department and the offices of the harbor master and harbor pilot. They drove out the few police officers who were there and seized the arms and ammunition. Then they piled the broken furniture in the middle of the floor and set it afire. The wooden building and two adjoining shops went up in flames. When the fire department arrived, sailors cut the hoses and formed a ring around the burning building to prevent firemen from extinguishing the blaze.

The three-story building was located close to the docks and ships. Prevailing winds normally blew from the town toward the docks, but fortunately that night their direction was reversed. Even so one ship did catch fire, but the blaze was quickly brought under control. If the flames had got hold among the ships, loaded with thousands of casks of whale oil, the whole closely packed fleet as well as the town would have ended up as charred ruins.

The fire was enough excitement for some sailors, but many others continued to roam the town unopposed, breaking into bars, driving off the proprietors, and consuming liquor supplies. Someone suggested Dr. Gerrit Judd, a prominent cabinet member, was a suitable person on whom they could release their vengeance, since he was an important man in the government. They set off through the dark streets toward his home. The walk was a long one, and most of the fifty or so men who set out fell by the wayside. When the remnants reached Judd's home, they were satisfied to stand at the fence and hurl threats at him. Another crowd set out for

Rev. Richard Armstrong's home in lower Manoa Valley, but it too disintegrated along the way.

The next morning William Parke had become sufficiently disgusted with his inactive role to resign as marshal. The resignation aroused the king, who asked Parke what he would suggest. The marshal replied he would advise calling a meeting with the governor of Oahu and the foreign citizens. The king agreed.

Affairs now moved to a fast conclusion. Martial law was declared. A company of foreign residents, some two hundred strong, was organized. They joined with the Hawaiian militia in clearing the town. There was little opposition from the sailors. Days and nights of roaming the streets, accompanied by the liberal consumption of alcohol, had taken their toll. Some 200 seamen were locked up in the fort, and the remainder were ordered aboard ship and told to stay there. The whole experience was vivid enough for the foreign company to remain as an organized unit, calling themselves the Hawaiian Guards, a company which was soon reinforced by a cavalry unit.

Six weeks after the riots jailer George Sherman was brought to trial. The jury returned a verdict of guilty of manslaughter, and Sherman was sentenced to five years in prison at hard labor.

On May 2, 1843, a young seaman joined the many sailors who roamed the dusty streets of Lahaina. In his pocket he might have carried as much as $20, the sum he had been paid when he left the whaler *Charles and Henry*. This twenty-four-year-old man was not markedly different from the thousands of others who came ashore each year. But a close look would have revealed a sensitive face and sad eyes, and a short conversation would have disclosed an inquiring, creative mind. His name was Herman Melville.

Two years earlier Melville had signed aboard the New Bedford whaler *Acushnet* as an ordinary seaman. He had experienced the hazards of rounding the Horn, had survived forecastle life and the dangers and thrills of the whale hunt. In the summer of 1842 the *Acushnet* put into Taiohae Bay in the Marquesas Islands, the same anchorage used by Captain David Porter twenty-nine years earlier. To Melville the presence of land meant a place where he could escape the horrors of the ship. He and a shipmate, Tobias Green, deserted just before the *Acushnet* sailed. In a bid to catch the deserters, the wily captain put to sea for a day and then returned, hoping to find the two seamen sunning themselves on the beach.

Melville and Green had other ideas. By the time the *Acushnet* reappeared, the pair was struggling over sharp ridges and through precipitous canyons toward the valley home of a tribe called the Taipi. For nearly a month the two men stayed with these cannibal people. Melville's experiences among them would become the basis for his first novel, *Typee*.

Melville escaped the Marquesas by signing aboard a visiting Australian whaling barque. This second experience on a whaler was worse than the first. Mutiny was averted only when the captain became seriously ill and the ship shifted course to Tahiti for medical aid. Here Melville and several others were confined in a stockade on shore, and to their delight they were left behind when the whaler finally sailed. In November 1842 Melville was again aboard a whaler. This time it was the *Charles and Henry,* whose captain agreed to discharge the young sailor at Lahaina.

Lahaina offered few employment possibilities for a discharged sailor, so after sixteen days there Melville left for Honolulu. It was lucky he did, for shortly after he departed the *Acushnet* came to anchor and the ship's captain filed an affidavit with the United States Vice Commercial Agent stating that Herman Melville had deserted ship in the Marquesas. The *Acushnet* moved on to Honolulu, but Melville was lucky again, because the ship remained only overnight and he went undetected. The *Acushnet* would one day gain a kind of fame as the prototype for a whaling ship in a novel called *Moby Dick*.

Herman Melville certainly did not like Hawaii, but it seems probable that once here he either had to sign on as a seaman or buy passage home. Signing aboard another whaler would have been abhorrent, and Melville did not have the money to buy passage home. Perhaps to earn this money he sought work in Honolulu. His first job was setting up pins in a bowling alley.

The man who offered Herman Melville a better job was Isaac Montgomery, an Englishman. Montgomery had come to Hawaii five years earlier and had a store of his own by the time Melville arrived in town. Montgomery sent supplies to merchants in Australia and, like his contemporaries, was inclined to look for a fast profit.

When Melville arrived the Islands were under the control of Lord George Paulet, an English naval captain, who arbitrarily annexed the kingdom, hoping for approval by his government. The approval never came, but during Paulet's brief rule the Englishmen in Hawaii tried to gain concessions which they could not hope to extract from the American-dominated Hawaiian monarchy. Isaac Montgomery was not backward in making requests. He applied for a liquor license for his "House of Entertainment" on the road to Waikiki. He also applied for a license as an auctioneer and attempted to gain title to Honolulu lands which he said rightly belonged to his wife. Montgomery's wife was the daughter of Nathan Winship, a New England merchant, and Montgomery stated that the property had been granted Winship by Kamehameha I.

Isaac Montgomery deplored the American missionaries—in this Montgomery and Melville agreed. Melville had lived with the still primitive Marquesans, he had seen what had happened in Tahiti, and if he had any doubts in his mind about the corrupting influence of white men on Polynesians, they disappeared in Hawaii. He believed that the untouched savage was greatly superior to the poor wrecks he found in Hawaii, where missionaries had been working for over twenty years.

When Melville returned to the United States, his anger was still intense, and later he wrote an appendix to *Typee* in which he described the missionaries in Hawaii as "a junto of ignorant and designing Methodist elders." The Hawaiian king, he believed, had fallen under the influence of foreigners, and his closest adviser, Dr. Judd, was "a sanctimonious apothecary-adventurer." In the appendix Melville noted that during his stay in Honolulu he "was in the confidence of an Englishman who was much employed by his lordship" (Paulet). It is possible Isaac Montgomery was that Englishman. Certainly Montgomery and his friends applauded Melville's sentiments when they appeared in print.

Herman Melville and Isaac Montgomery signed a contract which was supposed to last a year. Melville was to be a general clerk and bookkeeper. He was to receive board, lodging, and laundry, with an annual wage of $150. The agreement was short-lived, for about six weeks after it was signed the warship *United States* dropped anchor in Honolulu harbor. Melville visited with some of the sailors who came ashore, and on August 17, 1843, he gave up his clerking job by signing aboard as an ordinary seaman. He was anxious to escape the south seas. Perhaps he had come to the conclusion that it would be quicker to return home as a sailor on a U. S. warship than to save money and buy his passage.

Isaac Montgomery lived out his life in Hawaii. He was a rather successful businessman, at one time operating a salt works near Pearl Harbor which produced quality salt used in the Islands as well as by the Russians in Alaska. He seriously ran afoul of the law in 1855 when he was accused and sentenced for stealing cattle and selling stolen goods. Less than three years later, Montgomery died. He bequeathed a fortune of from $20,000 to $30,000 to the Catholic Church. It may have been his final protest against the American Protestant domination of Hawaii.

One of the commercial houses which attracted patronage from visiting whaling ships as well as missionaries was the firm of Ladd and Company. The company was founded in Boston, a place where news of the exploits of the Hawaiian mission caused real excitement. Apparently inspired by these tales, William Ladd, Peter Brinsmade, and William Hooper each put up $2,000 and formed a partnership in 1832. After Ladd and Brinsmade had selected suitable wives, following the practice of the missionaries, they sailed forth with a cargo of merchandise. Their purpose was commerce, but they had a missionary-like dedication.

In the early nineteenth century devout men believed Christianity, Commerce, and Civilization attracted each other. If any of these conditions existed, the other two could not be far behind. Christianity had arrived in Hawaii with the missionaries. Now Commerce would help enlighten the Islands through the firm of Ladd and Company. Two days after their arrival in the summer of 1833 they had rented store space in Honolulu. Their no-nonsense attitude should have been fair warning to competitors.

Peter Brinsmade, at twenty-eight, was the oldest of the three. He was a man of eloquence and he assumed the role of spokesman. Brinsmade had studied for the ministry at Andover Theological Seminary and at Yale Divinity School. These were impressive credentials, and with the deep religious interest of the other two partners, they gained the favor of the missionaries who wanted strong backing in the commercial community. There was no formal agreement between the missionaries and Ladd and Company, but favoritism in dealing with the new company was obvious, and other merchants in town were resentful. They sneeringly called the partners "the pious traders." In just one year the pious traders had built one of the largest mercantile houses in Honolulu. A branch store was opened on Kauai, and a leaky old ship called the *Velocity* was purchased to transport goods among the Islands.

The ambitions of the partners did not end with a successful mercantile business. A scant two years after their arrival they had won the right to lease a thousand acres in the Koloa district on Kauai. The rental was $300 per year, and the lease ran for fifty years. William Hooper, the unmarried partner, was sent off to Kauai to grow sugar cane and build a mill to grind the cane.

Hooper knew nothing about sugar cane or mills, but he made up for his deficiencies by sheer tenacity. He built a dam to insure a regular water supply and printed his own scrip with which he paid his workers. The scrip was redeemable only at his store, so he was assured of double profit. Laborers were paid 12½ cents a day plus a meal of fish and poi. A makeshift mill was constructed where trypots from whaleships were used as boiling tubs. The rollers which pressed juice from the cane were of wood. He got twelve acres of sugar planted, forty-five acres of taro set out, 2,000 banana trees, and 5,000 coffee trees planted. At the end of two years two tons of poor quality sugar and 2,700 gallons of molasses were his reward. These were sent to Honolulu to be sold through the Ladd and Company store.

Finding workers for his plantation was the most distressing problem Hooper faced. The Hawaiian chiefs had promised him laborers, but when men occasionally did show up they displayed little interest in working. The main reason was that Hooper had been instructed to pay the chiefs, who in turn were supposed to pay the workers. Laborers oftentimes did not see their wages. An appeal to the king partially cleared up the situation.

By 1837 Hooper had constructed a more efficient mill, and some of the local chiefs who had bedeviled him in the past were now growing cane which Hooper milled in return for a percentage of the crop. A section of land was subleased to raise mulberry bushes, hoping for the development of a silk industry. Cotton was considered another commercial possibility, and Hawaiians were encouraged to cultivate this new crop. The labor situation had improved somewhat, but it still vexed Hooper. In 1838 he wrote to his partners, "No galley slave looks forward to the day when he is to be made free with half so much satisfaction as I do when I shall bid final adieu to intercourse with the Hawaiians! Gracious Anticipations!"

In the same year that Hooper's new sugar mill was constructed the company experienced its first financial crisis. A severe economic recession in the United States forced East Coast merchants to withdraw credit the company had counted on being available. Brinsmade hurried to the East Coast, rekindled faith in the Hawaii enterprise, and things again flowed along smoothly.

By now missionary activity on Kauai rasped William Hooper's overworked, sensitive nerves. Some missionaries on Kauai were growing sugar cane, and others were seriously considering it. Hooper did not approve, although he carefully kept his views from the Kauai missionaries. To his partners in Honolulu, however, he expressed himself with bitter vehemence. Hawaii had become a theocracy, Hooper believed, and with the obvious hope of eventual revenge he foresaw the collapse of the missionary efforts. ". . . when it does burst, not a vestige of its fabric will be found —happy day for true Christianity."

The commercial enterprises of the missionaries continued to incense Hooper, whose letters to his partners became more impassioned. "That the Missionaries may not think that I am privately slandering them I request that you read to any of them, that you please, all that I have written and tell them farther, that there were once on earth a parcel of Missionaries who 'for their Journey' took no pen, ink or paper, 'nothing save a staff only! no script, no bread, no money in their purse' and these very men accomplished more than all the Missionaries which the Am. Board have or ever will send out, unless a different course is pursued." There is no evidence that these sentiments ever were relayed to the missionaries.

By July, 1841, the plantation at Koloa represented an investment in excess of $31,000. Two years earlier Ladd and Company had shown their continuing interest in expansion when they sought and were granted the right to lease any acreage on Kauai not in use and which they could develop. To be granted such generous rights was remarkable, because the government had established a very strict policy against allowing foreigners the right to lease land.

In about 1840 Ladd and Company had considered selling their holdings to some outside interest who would have the capital to develop more fully the great potential of these lands. The idea of some unknown outsiders invading Hawaii and holding such power greatly concerned some officials, notably Rev. William Richards, a prominent adviser to the king. With a sell-out as a threat, a secret agreement was entered into between Ladd and Company and the government on November 24, 1841, which granted the company fantastic additional rights. The contract stated the company now had "the full right and privilege of occupying for the purpose of manufacturing agricultural productions, any now unoccupied and unimproved localities on the several island of the Sandwich Islands, suitable for the manufacture of sugar, indigo, flour, raw silk, Kukui oil, or any other productions of the country."

The government would receive 50 cents per acre a year rent on all lands used and $10 a year for any mills which would be constructed. Leases were to be drawn to run for one hundred years. The agreement had been drawn up secretly at Lahaina between Richards and Brinsmade.

One stipulation had to be met before Ladd and Company could exercise these rights. The United States, France, and Great Britain would first have to recognize Hawaii as an independent nation. Although this appeared to be a big undertaking in light of the strained relations between Hawaii, France, and Great Britain, it would not be the reason why the grand project finally failed.

To succeed in this mammoth undertaking the company needed enough capital to develop the vast lands now open to them. The eloquent Peter Brinsmade went off to the United States to raise money. He talked to Secretary of State Daniel Webster and visited the financial centers of Boston and New York. It was of no avail, so he continued to Europe where he again encountered apathy on the part of British and French investors. He was advised that venture capital was available in Belgium, and so he hurried there.

At last Brinsmade struck a solid rock of interest, and he settled down to serious discussions with the Belgian Company of Colonization. At this point Rev. William Richards unexpectedly appeared on the scene. With Richards came Timothy Haalilio, secretary to the king of Hawaii. They had come to Europe to seek official recognition of Hawaii as an independent nation by Great Britain and France. Brinsmade saw their presence as an opportunity to further his goals. William Richards held the power of attorney for the king, and Brinsmade now talked him into making Kamehameha III an official party to the proposed Belgian contract, thus adding stature to the company and to the negotiations under way.

While Brinsmade was involved in negotiations, the diverse operations of Ladd and Company in Hawaii were slipping badly. The company had expanded while suffering from undercapitalization. Operating funds had to be secured by mortgaging land to the government and private parties. Their financial woes mounted when Koloa plantation lost money. A rumor spread through Honolulu that a contract with the Belgian Company of Colonization would bring many Catholic immigrants to Hawaii. The influential missionary forces could hardly approve.

At this strategic moment several loans of Ladd and Company were called, some people thought through the efforts of ex-missionary Dr. Gerrit Judd, who had now entered government service. It was a greater strain than the house of Ladd and Company could stand, and it collapsed. In April, 1845, the assets of the company went at auction for $3,600. Much of it, reputedly, went at prices far below market value. The government contended that the failure of Ladd and Company meant their agreement was no longer valid. Ladd and Company filed a suit for $378,000 claiming the government had deliberately ruined the company. A solution was sought through arbitration and, as proceedings dragged on, the company finally withdrew. The case was the sensation of Hawaii, with persons lining up in support of one side or the other. It was one of the bitterest battles of accusation and counteraccusation in Hawaii's history.

How had Ladd and Company been able to secure such great land concessions in the first place? There were numerous reasons. The three partners had established reputations for getting difficult jobs done quickly. The success of their Honolulu store and Hooper's ability to overcome obstacles on Kauai were impressive. Another important reason for the government's generous offer was the fact that the partners had been successful in getting the Hawaiians to work the land and share in the profits. Chiefs on Kauai, who had ridiculed Hooper in the beginning, were themselves planting sugar cane a few years later. The Hawaiian government and the missionaries were concerned by the fact that foreigners were principally benefiting from the development of lands. With the three partners leading the way it seemed possible the Hawaiians could be drawn into the commercial growth of the Islands. No other company had offered such a hope before.

By the time Ladd and Company reached the financial abyss, they had lost missionary and government support. The reason for this change can only be surmised. It was a time of intense feeling against Catholicism, and unfortunately the only source of financing seemed to be Catholic Belgium. This was also a time when the missionaries were starting their own commercial enterprises, and Ladd and Company could have been viewed by some as a potential competitor.

Peter Brinsmade had made slow but real progress in working out plans with the Belgian Company of Colonization, but somehow the consummation of his plans always eluded him. During the many months of negotiations Brinsmade's personal finances evaporated, and he had to borrow from Reverend Richards for living expenses. The three partners went their separate ways, each man pursuing commercial ventures in Hawaii. But clearly the intensity of feeling had run so high that the Islands could hardly be a happy place for the losers in this battle. Eventually they all drifted away to the mainland.

At the time Ladd and Company was organizing its Honolulu store, David Douglas disembarked from a ship at Hilo. It was January, 1834, and his arrival was the realization of a cherished dream. David Douglas was thirty-four, small of stature, and somewhat handsome in a Grecian way. His one handicap was poor eyesight. Like the missionaries and the pious partners, Douglas was driven by an all-consuming passion. For him it was the study of botany.

Douglas had been launched on his career at the age of eleven when he was apprenticed to work in the Earl of Mansfield's gardens in Scone, Scotland. At eighteen he moved to the Horticultural Society of London. Traveling was the best way for him to discover new species of plants, and Douglas soon had crossed the Atlantic Ocean and tramped through upper Canada, across much of the Eastern United States and California. His interests then shifted to the Columbia River region and British Columbia.

Throughout his travels David Douglas was unconcerned about his personal safety or the hardships he had to face. The scientific instruments he customarily carried weighed some sixty pounds, which precluded his carrying much in the way of personal comforts. His one constant companion was a dog—a little terrier he had brought from Scotland. Today botany books list dozens of plants named after Douglas. The best known is the Douglas Fir, a tree the botanist, ironically, was not the first to discover.

During his stay in California Douglas unwittingly was party to a discovery which, when found again some twenty years later, would electrify a good portion of the world. Douglas had shipped a number of sapling pine trees to England from California, and when the trees arrived in London it was discovered that the earth in which the roots were packed contained small flakes of gold. The discovery was duly noted but caused little concern at the time.

The first visit of Douglas to Hawaii happened by necessity, not choice. He had been in Monterey, California, waiting for passage back to the Columbia River. Transportation was infrequent along the Pacific coast, and Douglas found that the quickest way to the Northwest would be to journey to Hawaii and board a ship there for the Columbia. Once in Honolulu, Douglas was fascinated by the botanical specimens which surrounded him. The Islands were a treasure house where a few families of plants had developed many species. His stay was marred by an attack of rheumatic fever, but this did not prevent him from collecting a variety of curious specimens, as well as a pair of live Sandwich Island geese, which were safely shipped to the Zoological Society in London.

Fifteen months later Douglas returned to Hawaii. He stayed in Honolulu only until he could find passage for the island of Hawaii, where he arrived on January 2, 1834. In Hilo he hired John Honolii as interpreter and guide and a group of porters to carry his baggage. Honolii was one of the Islanders who had returned to Hawaii with the first company of missionaries aboard the *Thaddeus*. His missionary training had not been forgotten. Each Sunday Honolii would round up as many persons as he could and preach to them both morning and evening.

It was the worst time of year for mountain climbing, but such minor matters did not concern Douglas, who started off for the summit of Mauna Kea. Some inner urgency would not allow him to waste time or heed danger, and he strode on far ahead of his porters. Rains reduced the trails to muddy ruts. In crossing one stream John Honolii nearly drowned. When Douglas reached the snow-covered summit of the mountain, the dry air caused the skin to peel from his hands and face. He marched down the mountain collecting specimens, returning with nearly fifty species of ferns, together with other plants, seeds, mosses, and lichens. The amount of food his porters ate astounded Douglas. To a friend he wrote, ". . . the quantity of Poe [sic] which a native will consume in a week, nearly equals his own weight!" The porters each received two dollars for their work.

The botanist's next goal was the active volcanic crater of Kilauea. There he pitched his tent at the edge and contemplated the "lake of liquid" which lay below him. His thoughts, however, might well have been on the great mountain which loomed behind him. This was the peak of Mauna Loa, the last real climbing challenge on the island of Hawaii. The ascent of the. mountain was painful and slow. Rain poured down day and night, and they plowed through knee-deep morasses of mud. At night there was little shelter and no dry wood for fires. Atop the mountain the brightness of the snow inflamed Douglas' already weak eyes.

Douglas was exhausted after having conquered the two highest mountain peaks in the Pacific in quick succession, but he had no time for rest and started to classify his collections. He had gathered some 2,000 specimens of ferns, among which were ninety that would be new to science. In early April, 1834, he arrived in Honolulu, only to discover that he would have to wait until July before a ship would be going to England. He decided to spend his time in classifying plants on Oahu into zones according to their elevation above sea level.

In the midst of this chore Douglas became acquainted with Rev. John Diell, chaplain of the Seamen's Mission, who was interested in visiting the island of Hawaii. There was still a considerable length of time before the arrival of his ship, so Douglas decided to accompany the minister to Hawaii. The party consisted of Douglas, Reverend and Mrs. Diell, their child, and a black servant simply known as John. Their vessel stopped at Lahaina, Maui, where Diell decided to detour to Molokai before rejoining Douglas in Hilo. Somehow John missed the ship to Molokai and so proceeded to Hawaii with David Douglas.

The vessel carrying Douglas and John paused near the northern tip of Hawaii, and the impatient botanist decided to walk to Hilo instead of waiting for the ship to continue. The distance was about 100 miles on a trail around the slopes of Mauna Kea which was frequently used by the Hawaiians. The pair had not tramped far before John fell behind, footsore and tired, attempting to keep up with David Douglas. The botanist could not wait. He left John to find his own way to Hilo and pushed on, accompanied only by his terrier.

Douglas spent that night at the house of a hospitable rancher and continued on his way early the next morning. Soon he came to the large thatched home of Ned Gurney, an Englishman who lived at the upper reaches of the forests on the eastern slope of Mauna Kea. Gurney had married a Hawaiian woman and made a living hunting wild cattle. He was one of many who had escaped the Botany Bay penal colony in Australia and who now lived in the Hawaiian Islands. Gurney later reported Douglas had stayed for breakfast and that he had suggested the botanist join a group of Hawaiians who were expected through before long. Douglas refused and Gurney said he accompanied him down the trail for about a mile. Before turning back Gurney said he warned him of three deep pits he had dug farther along the trail which had been carefully camouflaged to trap wild cattle.

Two or three hours later the party of Hawaiians passed by a water hole on the trail. They noticed a torn piece of cloth by one of the pits and, looking in, saw that a wild bull had fallen into the hole. From the soft earth beneath the bull protruded the foot and shoulder of a man. The

Hawaiians ran back to Gurney's house. Ned Gurney hurried to the scene and shot the bull. The body of David Douglas was pulled from the earth and lifted out of the pit.

Gurney wrapped the body in a bullock hide and hired two Hawaiians to carry it to the seacoast village of Laupahoehoe. It was dark when the shattered remains of David Douglas were sent on from there to Hilo. A single Hawaiian in an outrigger canoe navigated the rough coastal waters southward through the night. At dawn he reached Hilo.

Rev. John Diell had arrived in Hilo two days earlier and, on hearing that the body of a haole had been brought in a canoe, he ran to the shore together with Rev. Joseph Goodrich. The two clergymen stared at the mangled remains of David Douglas, grotesquely enveloped in a bullock hide. An amateurish examination of the body revealed a badly gashed head, a broken cheek bone, broken ribs, and a multitude of severe bruises. Diell and Goodrich were in a state of shock. They did what seemed essential. One man was hired to build a coffin and another to dig a grave.

The news shocked Hilo, and among the curious persons who came to look at the body of Douglas was an American by the name of Hall. Hall, like Ned Gurney, made a living hunting wild cattle, and it was his opinion that a bull could not have inflicted such wounds as Douglas suffered. Hall suggested that David Douglas had been murdered. The two clergymen realized they too were suspicious. It was decided the body should be examined by a doctor. Since there were none in Hilo, the ministers decided to ship the remains to Honolulu. Diell and Goodrich disemboweled the corpse, filled the cavity with salt, packed the body in a coffin of salt, and enclosed the whole in a box of brine.

The two clergymen then wrote a letter to Richard Charlton, British Consul in Honolulu, telling of the death of Douglas and expressing suspicions that Ned Gurney might have been the murderer. After the letter had been sent, Gurney arrived in Hilo, bringing the terrier of Douglas, some money Douglas had in his pockets, and other possessions of the botanist. The two missionaries at first were somewhat relieved at Gurney's arrival, but then an informant said Douglas had been carrying a certain amount of gold with him and this was missing. Hall journeyed back to the pit where Douglas had died. He said the blunt horns of the dead bull could not have caused the lacerations which covered the body of the botanist. He cut off the head of the bull as evidence and carried it back to Hilo. Subsequently the head was sent to Honolulu, but it is not known if it arrived by the time the autopsy had been performed.

Drs. Gerrit Judd and T. C. R. Rooke made the examination in Honolulu. The efforts of the amateur embalmers in Hilo had not been too successful, and the body was in poor condition. Two physicians from aboard a visiting British warship were called in as consultants. The verdict of the four medical men was that David Douglas had, indeed, died from wounds inflicted by a wild bull.

An English naval officer read final services over the remains of Douglas, which were buried in the cemetery next to Kawaiahao Church on August 4, 1834. Years later a visiting Englishman believed the grave of the famous botanist was not properly marked, and he ordered a headstone carved and placed over the grave. This was duly done, but in time the exact location of the grave was lost. Eventually the wording on the headstone became indistinct, and to protect it from further deterioration it was embedded in the wall of the vestibule of the church, where it still remains. One hundred years after his death residents of Scots ancestry on the island of Hawaii erected a stone cairn with a bronze plaque among a grove of newly planted Douglas fir trees near the spot where the botanist was killed.

The report of the four doctors concerning the cause of Douglas' death carried much weight, but it did not end speculation. Over the years stories periodically came to light, most of them pointing the finger of guilt at Ned Gurney. The evidence was always nebulous. As for Gurney, some said he left Hawaii soon after the incident, others said he later was drawn to the California gold fields, and still others said he spent the rest of his years in Hawaii.

There is a mystery within a mystery in the death of David Douglas. John, the servant of Reverend Diell, was never seen again after Douglas abandoned him on the trail from Kohala to Hilo. His disappearance deepens the mystery which surrounds the death of the famous botanist.

By 1840 Honolulu had become a busy frontier town. On June 6 of that year the first issue of a Honolulu newspaper appeared, called the *Polynesian,* edited by James Jackson Jarves. In the first issue the prospering firm of Ladd and Company purchased two large ads, more space than any other company had bought. One ad listed sixty-seven diverse items of merchandise which had just been received. Included were window glass, olive oil, fancy biscuits, shovels, Irish linen, and silk umbrellas.

Jarves printed news from the United States and Great Britain as well as local happenings. There were optimistic stories about Hawaii's cotton and silk industries. Much space was devoted to the injustice of the recent treaty France had forced on the Hawaiian kingdom, and the Opium War between England and China was well covered. Lawlessness was deplored by the editor, who proclaimed that "Thieves and topers are becoming plentiful in Honolulu as swine in the streets." The June 27 issue carried on the front page the poem, "Old Ironsides" by Oliver Wendell Holmes.

Honolulu also had flashes of rather fashionable social life. Late in

1840 Hannah Holmes, the eldest of the beautiful daughters of Oliver Holmes, entertained sixty officers of the American exploring expedition under Commodore Wilkes, then visiting Honolulu. Hannah Holmes's large living room was decorated with flags from many nations. Tents had been pitched on surrounding lawns as protection against possible rain. The guests began arriving at 5 P.M. and before long the *Polynesian* reported there were "several little flirtations going on" between officers and Island belles. Two long tables provided room for the 200 guests to sit and enjoy a great variety of food, including even baked dog for the daring. The governor of Oahu came, and many complimentary toasts were drunk.

At eight o'clock the music began in the living room, the signal for waltzes, cotillions, and reels. At ten, Hannah summoned her guests outside to watch the exciting ascension of a great balloon filled with hot air. At midnight proper young ladies began to depart, and an hour later the party finally ended, "with unbounded expressions of mutual good will."

By 1840 about 600 foreigners lived in Honolulu. The business community now included twenty retail shops, four wholesale stores, two hotels, twelve boarding houses and grog shops for sailors, seven bowling alleys, four blacksmith shops, three vegetable markets, one bath house, fourteen ship carpenters, three physicians, three tailors, two sail-makers, one printer, and two cigar-makers.

This commercial complex was beyond the comprehension or interest of most Hawaiians. They were mainly spectators in the hectic buying and selling phenomena which unfolded before them. Many found it desirable to retreat and live the rural life, where the basic needs could be gathered from a patch of land and the sea. Then too, the Hawaiian population had declined frightfully. New diseases had ravaged them, enforced labor in cutting sandalwood had weakened them, and the population had further been thinned by the departure of many young Hawaiians who went to sea, often for years at a time.

Sailing captains had early discovered that Islanders were superb seamen. They signed them aboard by the thousands. There was an empathy between Hawaiians and the sea, and a shrewd captain quickly saw this. For three years, starting with 1845, nearly 2,000 Hawaiians a year sailed off as seamen aboard visiting ships. Feats of heroism among these Islanders were commonplace. The logs of sailing vessels become monotonous in reporting their deeds. Most often they were episodes in which amphibious Islanders saved shipmates from drowning.

The promise of adventure roused Hawaiians more than the prospect of pay, as was proved when Captain Hypolito Bouchard came to Hawaii in 1818. Bouchard was a Frenchman who claimed he sailed in the service of a group of South American nations, but he could accurately be described as a pirate. Before he left he signed some eighty Islanders aboard his two ships. Bouchard proceeded to the coast of California, where he attacked Spanish settlements. At Monterey the captain armed his Hawaiians with pikes. They formed the first attack wave, and when the Spaniards saw the naked Islanders coming at them, they fled to the hills.

The standard of values of these traveling Hawaiians was hard for Yankees to comprehend. Richard H. Dana, author of *Two Years Before the Mast,* came across many Hawaiians in California. At San Diego he encountered a group of them living on the beach. The Islanders were offered $15 a month wages to sign on, but to the surprise of Dana they were uninterested. They had sufficient money in their pockets for the needs of the moment, and they apparently enjoyed the warm climate and their freedom.

One important Hawaiian chief tried his best to turn the new commercial techniques to his benefit. His name was Boki, one of those who had accompanied Kamehameha II to England. Perhaps the major reason for Boki's drive for financial success was the pressure of debts. He was an extravagant man, and his creditors pushed him for payment.

In 1827 Boki opened a retail store in Honolulu, and later the same year the Blonde Hotel started operations in the same two-story building. The hotel was named for the ship on which Boki had returned from Great Britain, and the building was the place where Lord Byron had stayed while in Honolulu. A year later Boki sent off a trading vessel to the Russian settlement in Alaska and dispatched two brigs which visited Manila and Canton. He opened a saloon in Honolulu and made an attempt to operate a sugar plantation in Manoa Valley. This frenzy of activity produced little income.

In 1829 the Hawaiian government was more or less forced to accept responsibility for the debts chiefs had incurred in taking goods against the promise of payment in sandalwood which they could not provide. The debt amounted to $48,000, and as governor of Oahu, Boki became responsible for raising one quarter of the total. This new debt was doubly irksome, since it was owed to American merchants, and the chief was pro-British and loudly anti-American. Boki's prospects were bleak.

In November, 1829, the *Sophia* arrived from Sydney. Aboard were two men who confided to Boki that the captain had discovered islands rich in sandalwood. The captain had tried to keep the location a secret, but the two men had taken bearings and knew where the islands were. Boki bought the locations of the sandalwood islands from the two and frantically outfitted two brigs and recruited some 500 men. The bitter rivalry between Boki and Kaahumanu speeded the chief's departure. He said, in fact, that he had no intention of coming back as long as the queen regent was around.

The expedition was hastily organized and poorly run. The two vessels succeeded in reaching Rotuma, north of Fiji. Boki then sailed for Eromanga in the New Hebrides, instructing the captain of the second ship, who stayed behind to retrieve an anchor caught in the reef, to meet him there. When the second vessel reached the rendezvous, Boki and his ship were not to be found. The chief, crew, and ship had vanished without a trace. The sailors aboard Boki's vessel had commonly sat on kegs of gunpowder as they smoked their pipes. Perhaps Boki and his companions had disappeared in a tremendous explosion, although some people in Honolulu suspected the chief had simply gotten tired of the troubles he faced in Hawaii and had sailed off to a remote Pacific island.

The second ship limped back to Honolulu about nine months after its departure. The survivors told of battling the natives of Eromanga and of an unknown disease which killed scores of Hawaiians. At last the ship turned for Honolulu, leaving the seriously sick behind. As the vessel made its slow progress northward, starvation and disease ravaged the crew. The dead and sick alike were thrown overboard. Of the 500 or so persons who had sailed away, only twenty returned.

The disaster had a profound effect on Islanders. Soon a phrase became popular—"it will happen when Boki comes back"—meaning some task was impossible.

The twenty years between 1820 and 1840 forged the direction Hawaii's business community would take for the next 100 years. It is amazing that so many basic rules were laid down so early and followed so closely for so long. The early merchandise firms, which imported and sold hundreds of different items, set the pattern for the powerful houses which dominated Hawaii's wholesale trade and much retail trade until after World War II. The operation of Koloa plantation, started by Ladd and Company and destined to become Hawaii's first successful sugar plantation, served as a guide for running a profitable sugar operation. Plantations would establish their own retail stores, where workers bought on credit against future paychecks, and would purchase equipment and services through large merchandise firms in Honolulu, which in turn marketed the sugar and molasses of the plantations. In time it all became complicated and distressingly ingrown, but it also proved to be extremely profitable.

Chapter Seven

HYSTERIA IN HONOLULU
RIVALED THAT IN CALIFORNIA

IN 1840 CALIFORNIA bore few of the scars of civilization. Its population was small and spread thinly over a vast territory. Raising cattle was the only significant occupation, and the huge ranches were far apart and nearly self-sufficient. The few purchases which were necessary were often barter transactions. California was under Mexican rule until 1846, and the high tariffs the Mexicans imposed were a further complication.

Those New England merchant ships which bothered to trade in California normally sailed around South America to Hawaii and unloaded the bulk of their goods in the Islands before proceeding to California. In California they did such trading along the coast as they could and took aboard cargoes of hides, horses, and lumber. Vessels often returned to Hawaii before sailing for home port. Most California stores had trading arrangements with Island firms, and often they were branches of Honolulu companies.

Californians were an independent breed, and relations with the Mexican government were never amiable. The Mexicans were involved with more immediate problems and paid small attention to their distant territory. The less Californians had to do with Mexico the better, and those who thought about it considered Honolulu, not Mexico City, as the closest oasis of civilization.

Thomas O. Larkin, the prominent American merchant and United States Consul in California, was one of those with close Island ties. When Larkin married the widow of Captain Holmes of Hilo, the ceremony was performed by John C. Jones, United States Consul to Hawaii, aboard a vessel off the California coast. Larkin was the California agent for the *Polynesian,* and when he needed printed stationery his orders were filled by the newspaper office in Honolulu.

One of the chief concerns of the Larkins was the proper education of their children. California offered practically nothing, so the Larkins, together with other well known California families, sent their offspring to the Islands for their early education. The Larkin boys were sent to Hawaii when they were six or seven years old and stayed for several years before continuing their schooling in New England. Among the native Californians who came to school in Honolulu were Ronualdo Pacheco and Pedro Carrillo. Both later became politically prominent men in their state.

The children from California went to Oahu Charity School, which had been opened in 1833. The funds for its operation came through public subscription. Many of the pupils had Hawaiian mothers and haole fathers. The school was truly cosmopolitan, for in addition to part Hawaiians, native Californians, and the children of Yankee California traders, it also enrolled children from the Russian settlements in Alaska.

William Heath Davis was one of the Islanders who became important in California trade. He had been born in Honolulu in 1822 and named after his father, a Boston captain and trader who roamed through the Pacific. The elder Davis was one of those involved in a sandalwood monopoly agreement with Kamehameha I. The mother of young Davis was none other than the remarkable Hannah Holmes.

The elder Davis died in 1822, and sometime thereafter Hannah Holmes, who preferred to use her maiden name, had set up housekeeping with John C. Jones. Jones was a merchant as well as American consul for the Hawaiian Islands. Whatever standards Jones personally followed, he had strict ideas about the upbringing of Hannah's two sons. At the age of five the older boy, Robert, was sent off to New England for schooling. William received a more practical sort of education. When he was nine the lad sailed with Jones on a voyage to Alaska and California. They returned to the Islands with a cargo of hides below and horses tethered on deck. The horses were in much demand in Hawaii, and the hides were transshipped to Boston.

At the age of sixteen William Davis abruptly left Hawaii and moved to California, where he was employed by Nathan Spear, a prosperous merchant who was married to a sister of Hannah. The reason for the quick departure of William might be traced to a one-sentence item in the *Sandwich Island Gazette* of January 27, 1838. The item read, "Married on Friday evening, January 21st by Rev. Lowell Smith. Mr. William H. Davis to Kaimiaina." Davis did not arrive in California with a wife, and he does not mention her in his later writings. Who Kaimiaina was and what became of her are a mystery.

In San Francisco Davis served his apprenticeship in Nathan Spear's store. His employer had only words of praise for the young man's industry and intelligence. Before long Davis was riding through central California taking orders for merchandise from the rancheros and publicizing the new mill which Spear had installed to grind grain. On these rounds Davis bought cattle, tallow, and hides from the rancheros.

When William Heath Davis sailed away from Hawaii in 1838, he apparently had decided to turn his back on the Islands, and during his long life in California there is no evidence that he ever changed his mind. Davis wanted financial success and respectability. In 1838 his chances of financial success were probably as good in Hawaii as in California, but his chances of gaining community respect in the Islands was indeed remote. His mother was not the kind of person proper ladies would invite into their parlors. His father and his mother's father had caused much solemn head-shaking among the missionaries. His dilemma might have reached a climax with his involvement with Kaimiaina, and he fled. His desire to put Hawaii behind him was shown by the fact that years later he listed his residency in California as dating from 1831, the year he first touched that coast as a boy of nine.

The turn of family affairs in Honolulu following Davis' departure hardly made him homesick for the Islands. John C. Jones deserted Hannah and married the daughter of a former governor of California. Hannah was constantly at odds with the missionaries and often with the courts of law. Her expensive clothes and involvement with numerous men made her a delectable subject for Honolulu gossip mongers. As Davis heard of one episode after another, he undoubtedly was happy to be far away.

Pre-gold rush California suited Davis well. He was an agreeable young man, adept at conducting business on a personal basis. He joined in the hunting, horse racing, and cockfighting which the Californians loved. Seven years after coming he had saved enough money to buy into a merchandise firm as a partner. He learned the tricks of evading the ruinous Mexican tariffs, which often ran from 80 to 100 percent of the value of the merchandise. Davis was an expert at smuggling goods ashore and in bribing customs officials.

In the mid 1840s Americans were descending on California in substantial numbers, and this meant increased business for merchants. Davis bought rum at $1 a gallon in Honolulu, and it was snapped up at $3 to $4 a gallon in San Francisco. Not all the newcomers could be trusted, of course. On one occasion William Davis advanced Colonel John Fremont $6,000 worth of provisions on credit. Fremont promised to pay within six months, but full payment was never received. Bad debts, however, were rare and Davis was becoming a wealthy man.

In 1847 William Davis married Maria Jésus Estudillo, the daughter of a distinguished California family. The wedding was a great three-day festival. Davis was now linked to one of the first families of California. By the time he was twenty-five years old, William Heath Davis had achieved his goals of wealth and prestige.

In December, 1838, a small, lean man came ashore from the Hudson's Bay Company bark, *Columbia*. Hawaii was not this man's destination, but in Honolulu harbor he would be able to find a ship to carry him on. His goal was California, and his mind was full of a grand scheme for founding a little kingdom there.

The man was Johann August Sutter. During the four years before his arrival in Hawaii, Sutter had tried his hand at a number of enterprises, most of which ended in failure. These failures did not shake his firm conviction that greatness would eventually be his.

Johann Sutter was born in a German village near the Swiss border, where his father was foreman in a paper mill. Such work did not please Sutter, so he moved to Aarburg in Switzerland and he worked as a clerk. At the age of twenty-three he married Annette Bubeld; the day after the ceremony was performed, she presented him with a son. Sutter went into the dry goods business, but debts were a nagging problem. When his mother-in-law sold the building which was both his store and home, he was ruined. After four years in business Sutter ended up with debts of 50,000 francs and assets of 15,000. He had to choose one of two alternatives. He could either go to debtors' prison or he could flee.

Sutter had no intention of going to prison. He bade farewell to his wife and five children, secretly gathered a few possessions, and departed for France. From there he sailed to America to seek his fortune. His efforts to make that fortune went badly, and as he turned from one endeavor to another, he moved westward. At last he ended up at Fort Vancouver, the Hudson's Bay Company post in the Pacific Northwest.

As he moved westward, Sutter exchanged the humble facts of his earlier life for a collection of inventions which were calculated to turn him into a man of consequence. His father was no longer a mill foreman, but became a Lutheran clergyman. Sutter claimed he had been a captain in the elite Swiss guard. He said he had come to America with a fortune but had lost it during a recent business recession. His performance must have been convincing, because in the Northwest he was given letters of introduction to leading citizens in Hawaii, including one addressed to U. S. Consul John C. Jones.

Johann Sutter led a very agreeable life in Honolulu, and he later recalled that Kamehameha III had offered him the command of the Hawaiian military forces. If the offer was indeed made, Sutter had enough sense to refuse it. In Honolulu he was confident enough of his new identity to put it down in writing. The occasion grew out of an article which appeared in a magazine called the *Hawaiian Spectator*. The article stated that a Mr. Gray had been attacked in the Northwest by a group of Sioux Indians led by a Frenchman. Sutter, who had recently been there, claimed to know the true circumstances and proceeded to explain them in a letter published in the *Sandwich Island Gazette*. The details of the attack on Mr. Gray now seem unimportant, but the letter is interesting because Sutter identifies himself to readers by saying, ". . . I was formerly an officer of the Swiss guard in the French service. . . ."

Pleasant as Hawaii was, Johann Sutter's dream lay in California, and he now found a way of getting there. A group of Hawaiian merchants had chartered a ship which was to trade with the Russian colonies in Alaska and then proceed to California. Sutter took on the job of handling trading details in return for free passage for himself, his supplies, and his troop of followers.

Prior to departing Sutter spent his time enlisting recruits and buying tools and an arsenal of weapons, including two brass cannons. One store allowed him over $3,000 credit. It was a debt which was not paid until ten years later when one of the partners confronted Sutter in California. On April 20, 1839, Sutter sailed off with his supplies, eight Hawaiian men, and two Hawaiian women. Two or three haoles also accompanied him. Sutter later wrote that he agreed to pay the Hawaiians $10 a month and to return them to the Islands at the end of three years.

By July Sutter had finished his trading chores and was in California. By this time he realized the importance of letters of introduction, and so he presented a sheaf of them to California's Governor Mariano Vallejo. One letter was from John C. Jones describing Sutter as a "Swiss gentleman of the first class among men of honor, talent, and estimation." It took just two or three days for Sutter to receive a grant of land from the governor.

Sutter's party disembarked at San Francisco, and Nathan Spear agreed to allow his valuable new employee, William Heath Davis, to guide the party up the Sacramento River to their future home. During his first years, when Sutter was struggling to establish his colony, the Hawaiians were his stalwart helpers. They put up the first buildings at Sutter's fort and ran his farm. Some of the Hawaiians who came with Sutter navigated his boats along the Sacramento and American Rivers.

Honolulu was the first town outside California to hear the momentous news that gold had been discovered in the raceway at Sutter's sawmill. Soon the hysteria in Honolulu rivaled that in California. The *Polynesian* of June 24. 1848, gave the discovery good play. The story rated the top of page two, which was valuable space, since the whole of the front page was regularly devoted to advertising and ponderous essays on world affairs. The first paragraph of the story read:

> The only item of interest they contain (the newspapers from California) is the tidings of the fearful ravages of a terrible fever which has nearly depopulated all the seaport towns and caused a general rush to the interior. It is not exactly the yellow fever, but a fever for a yellow substance called gold. An exceedingly rich gold mine had been discovered in the Sacramento Valley, and all classes and sexes have deserted their occupations and rushed *en masse* to the mines to make their fortunes.

The article went on to say that a Mr. Gray, the super cargo aboard the *Louise,* had brought two pounds of gold with him, and "knowing ones here pronounce it worth its weight in gold." In spite of the flippant tone of the article, Islanders knew something important had happened, because the story mentioned that anything usable in the mines was selling at very high prices and that laborers could not be found for $15 a day. The article concluded with the observation that "this new resource will enable the California traders to pay the large amounts already due our merchants." From Hawaii news of the discovery of gold was carried by sailing vessel to the Pacific Northwest.

There was no mention of the gold rush in the next issue of the *Polynesian,* undoubtedly because no ships had arrived from California during the interval, but the issue of July 8 noted that gold fever had reached across the Pacific to Hawaii. "The California *alias* gold fever is beginning to rage with unprecedented fury among the denizens of our town. One after another comes to request us to announce 'their intention to depart from this Kingdom.' . . . In the emergency of the occasion, creditors will do well to watch their interests closely, for it is impossible to tell who will go next. If the fever continues to rage we intend putting up a bulletin at our office door on which to post the names of those who intend departing the Kingdom."

Fortunately for Island merchants, a law had been passed earlier in the year requiring every person who was leaving Hawaii permanently to publish a notice of intention two weeks before departure. Passports were not granted until such a notice was printed. In spite of this law many persons simply booked passage and left without worrying about passports.

The July 8 issue of the *Polynesian* carried the names of four persons who intended to depart, and a week later the names of twenty-four persons were listed. Each issue of the newspaper carried more details of the fabulous gold fields of California along with more names of persons who had decided to go and try their luck. "Nearly all the inhabitants of California are engaged in digging for gold. Immense quantities are found. Single pieces weighing five ounces have been taken from the earth." In the months of June and July fifteen ships had departed from Hawaii for California. Space aboard vessels was at a premium. The *Polynesian* printed a dialogue to show how independent ship owners were and how desperate some gold seekers were to get to California:

> *Stranger*. —How much do you ask Mr.————, for a cabin passage to California?
>
> *Ship-owner*. —One hundred dollars cash down, in advance. But I can't take you—all full in the cabin.
>
> *Stranger*. —Well, suppose I go in the hold, how much will you ask then?
>
> *Ship-owner*. —Eighty dollars; but I can't take you. Hold is full.
>
> *Stranger*. —But can't I go in the forepeak?—What is the price of a passage there?
>
> *Ship-owner*. —Eighty dollars, but I can't take you. Full, fore-and-aft.
>
> *Stranger*. —Well, can't I go aloft somewhere? and suppose I do, what will you charge?
>
> *Ship-owner*. —We charge eighty dollars to go any where; but can't carry you aloft. Got to carry provisions there.
>
> *Stranger*. —It is a hard case, isn't it? But as I want to go tolerably bad, what will you charge to *tow* me?
>
> The ship-owner retreated suddenly, and didn't make his appearance again, till the vessel had sailed.

This dialogue only slightly exaggerated the facts. The prices the ship-owner had quoted for cabin and hold passage were accurate. In addition deck space went for $40 and cargo went at a rate of $40 a ton.

Among those who announced their intention to leave Hawaii were the three partners of Ladd and Company. William Hooper was the first to go, departing in late 1848, and he apparently went into business in San Francisco. William Ladd, who had earlier opened a merchandise business in San Francisco, left in February, 1849. Peter Brinsmade arrived in San Francisco several months later. Brinsmade worked as a surveyor and at one time was involved in San Francisco politics. Eventually Ladd and Brinsmade returned to New England.

Some men were so deranged with gold fever that they were willing to run any risks to reach California. The *Polynesian* reported, "One man *started* in a whale boat, thinking, probably that the 'gold region' was a magnet of sufficient attractive power to direct his course to *the* place." Another publication, *The Friend,* wrote of "three seamen belonging to the 'E.

Freith', took a ship's boat, and started, as is supposed for California. They supplied themselves with a compass, watch, clothing, bread, water, etc. Up to this date, nothing has been heard from them, except a boat under sail was reported the following day off Diamond Head. Serious fears may be entertained respecting their fate. . . ."

The editor of the *Polynesian* commented, "The little city of Honolulu has probably never before witnessed such an excitement as the gold fever has created." He noted that many well known and successful men were leaving the Islands as well as many undesirables. He expressed fears about the future of California, where so many people fought over gold and where there was no law and order. The editor concluded by offering a challenge to his fellow Islanders. "With our present limited export we cannot supply half the wants of California. Shall we sit idle and allow others to outstrip us and secure the market which is now ours?"

Honolulu merchants were certainly not sitting idly by. Warehouses and stores were emptied of all merchandise which could be sold in the gold fields. Supplies normally reserved for whaling vessels disappeared. Boots, shovels, and flour were in particular demand. By September Islanders were sending their old clothes to California to be sold. Honolulu was booming and the ever increasing columns of newspaper advertising reflected the urgency and optimism of Honolulu citizens. Dr. Colburn opened an office and boldly proclaimed, "DENTISTRY!" Five hotels regularly ran ads. A "California Lunch and Eating House" opened. A bakery advertised for three skilled workers at a time when wages had zoomed to $10 a day.

The Honolulu press continued to paint a glowing picture of what was happening in California. "There are no poor men in California," stated the September 23 *Polynesian*. There were also occasional tales of lawlessness which somewhat balanced the picture. In October, 1848, a specific sad example had Islanders talking. It was the story of John von Pfister, who had recently gone off to the gold fields. Von Pfister was knifed to death by a drunken renegade somewhere on the south bank of the American River. He was a well known Honolulu businessman, and his murder was a touch of cold reality for those who thought of California only as a land of fast wealth.

San Francisco eating houses lured customers by posting such signs as "Potatoes to-day" or "Potatoes at every meal." In the first years no one in California could take time to grow potatoes, and Hawaii was the logical place to come. A fertile area on Maui called Kula was an ideal place to grow potatoes, and farmers flocked there, buying land from the government at $3 an acre. In late 1849 a former California gold seeker was moved to write that "California is yonder in Kula—. There is the gold without the fatigue and sickness of the mining country." Kula became known as Nu Kalifornia. Another potato-growing area was at Waimea on the island of Hawaii, and the prosperity excited Rev. Lorenzo Lyons. "Some never had so much cash before—never had any before! Many natives growing rich." A barrel of potatoes was bringing $4 to $5.

Hawaii's hope for supplying agricultural staples to California vanished as quickly as it came. By the end of 1851 potatoes were arriving in California from Oregon and other places at prices Hawaii could not match. Trading vessels began to supply California without the usual stop at Hawaii. Ships went directly there from East Coast U. S. ports, from the Pacific Northwest, Chile, and Peru. Even New Zealand joined in the California trade, stopping at Hawaii to take on supplies and to learn the latest in West Coast trading conditions. The strong influence Island merchants had had in California quickly melted away. As early as 1852 Island businessmen were aware of the turnabout when aggressive San Francisco merchants bought big ads in Honolulu newspapers offering their wares in competition with local stores. Hawaii was no longer the hub of trade in the North Pacific, but the mainland coast, from Washington to California, was alive with new economic growth, and Hawaii's business community hoped to share in the prosperity.

Californians journeyed to Hawaii during the winter months to escape the cold and rains of mountain camps. Boarding houses charged what they could get, and when Californians came ashore in large numbers, prices more than tripled from the usual $3 a week. The newcomers greatly enlivened Honolulu. Henry Lyman was a schoolboy then, and he later recalled being fascinated by the Californians who attended services at Bethel Chapel. Some had long hair, bushy beards, and mustaches. They wore Panama hats and some were arrayed in brilliant sashes of Chinese silk.

Most Islanders viewed Californians with caution. One of the reasons was that rumors periodically reached Hawaii that filibustering gangs on the coast considered the Islands an easy mark. Some Californians believed the Hawaiian king could be bought out if not frightened from his throne. They were encouraged by one San Francisco newspaper which felt such an attempt should be made. In 1851 a filibustering gang did show up in Honolulu, headed by Samuel Brannan. Brannan had seen Hawaii five years earlier, when he arrived in charge of a party of Mormons who were bound from New York to California. During that first visit to Honolulu, Brannan preached each day aboard ship—the first Mormon sermons heard in the Islands.

Mormonism offered little profit for Brannan, and he soon turned to more promising fields. During the gold rush he made a quick fortune in California real estate. But a fortune was not enough. Like Johann Sutter he wanted a little kingdom of his own, and he thought that his wish might be easily accomplished in Hawaii. Brannan set out for the Islands with a gang of twenty-four armed men. Enroute U. S. mail bags apparently were rifled in an attempt to see if news of his intentions was being carried aboard the same ship. For Brannan and his gang much of the voyage to Hawaii was passed in an alcoholic haze.

Stories of Sam Brannan's gang reached Hawaii ahead of his arrival, and William C. Parke, marshal of the kingdom, was waiting. When Brannan and his men stepped ashore, they were closely watched. On the afternoon they arrived one of the gang raced his horse through the town and was arrested. He pulled a pistol on the policeman but was knocked down before any damage was done. When Brannan came to claim his man, Parke informed him that his plan was known and that the carrying of weapons was prohibited. After one half-hearted attempt to see the king, Brannan and his cohorts drifted back to the mainland.

In California William Heath Davis prospered greatly. His place of business was at the corner of Montgomery and Clay streets, which then bordered the bay. In 1849 as many as twenty ships a day were anchored before his store, and he sold goods as fast as they came into his possession. Much of the merchandise he sold was carried to San Francisco in his own ship.

With his profits Davis bought property and constructed buildings. He put up the tallest structure in town, a four-story brick building which he rented to the U. S. Customs Service for $3,000 a month. Rentals from other properties raised his income to $10,000 a month. He was elected a member of the town council and to the board of school trustees. William Heath Davis was a prosperous, famous man.

Prosperity was short-lived. One of the fires which periodically swept the town destroyed his brick building together with much other property. His total losses were estimated at $750,000.

As he pondered over the ashes, William Davis came to an unfortunate conclusion. Instead of returning to the merchandise business, which he knew so well, he decided to regain his wealth quickly through real estate. This he planned to do by founding a new city. Others had done it and the successful ones had profited enormously. The site Davis chose was where the present city of San Diego now stands. Davis moved his family to this desolate spot, constructed buildings and roads, and marked off lots he hoped to sell. To accommodate ships he constructed a wharf. The location was superb, but Davis was too early. Immigrants to California were not ready to settle in his embryonic village. In an attempt to hold on until success came, Davis sold off his valuable San Francisco real estate. But success continued to elude him, and Davis was forced to give up.

William Davis took his family northward to the ranch of his father-in-law in San Leandro, but he was destined to suffer more disappointment. Squatters settled on the land, and there were too many to be forced off. There was no organized law enforcement body to help him, and the courts were of little assistance. His lands shrank and problems multiplied. The final blow came in 1868 when a severe earthquake damaged every building on the ranch. Davis gave up and moved his family to nearby Oakland where he attempted to make a living in insurance and real estate. His heart was not in it, and the children had to go to work to support the family. For nearly twenty years William Davis lived in Oakland. Once he had been renowned, but now he was forgotten.

Davis began to reminisce about his happier days of success and fame. He made notes about how things were then, and in doing this he launched himself on his final career. Davis drew from a retentive memory, and the things he wrote interested those about him. Soon his articles appeared in San Francisco newspapers and readers were delighted. Davis left his family in Oakland and moved to a humble apartment in San Francisco.

His articles became the basis for a book which brought him a certain amount of fame and a small amount of cash. Davis was encouraged, and he began work on what he called his "great manuscript." Over the years the manuscript swelled to more than two million words, a work so huge that no publisher would accept it. Fate once more decreed against Davis. In 1906 the San Francisco earthquake leveled much of the city. Davis was visiting his family in Oakland at the time of the disaster, and when he succeeded in returning to San Francisco, his manuscript had disappeared from the ruins of his apartment. It was never found. William Heath Davis lived for three years more, but he did not have the heart to continue his writing, and when he died much intimate detail from California's history was lost forever.

Among the native Hawaiians who went off to California was the adventurous William Kanui. Kanui had served in the U. S. Navy and had seen action against the Tripoli pirates in the Mediterranean. He had been a farm hand, a livery man, and had worked in the Brooklyn Navy yards. Samuel F. B. Morse, the famous inventor and artist, included him in a group portrait. Kanui was among those who attended the missionary school at Cornwall, Connecticut, and he sailed back to Hawaii aboard the *Thaddeus* with the first missionary company.

Lured to the gold fields, William Kanui tried his luck in the Sugar Loaf hill area in Modoc County. He came away with about $6,000, which he promptly lost when the bank he deposited it in failed. He turned to other occupations, including running an eating house at Sutter's fort and working as a bootblack and junk dealer in San Francisco. His missionary training stayed with him, and he was a Bible class teacher and staunch member of the Bethel church. For a while Kanui lived at Indian Creek, which was a colony of devout Hawaiians, some of whom did missionary work among the California Indians. Eventually he returned to Honolulu and taught school. He died in 1864 and was buried next to Kawaiahao Church, a fitting resting place for a member of the first missionary company.

Westerners had a slang name for a Hawaiian—Kanaka—and the place names where Islanders gathered in the gold fields sometimes included this word. There was a Kanaka Creek in Sonoma County and a Kanaka Glade in Mendocino County. Places along several rivers became known as Kanaka Bar. Hawaiians had also settled at a place called Verona, and they made a living by catching salmon in the Sacramento River. These Hawaiians intermarried with California Indians and whites, but the Verona colony nevertheless maintained its Hawaiian identity into the late nineteenth century.

In February, 1852, the *Emily Bourne* sailed from San Francisco for Hawaii. She was a small brig, commanded by John Mount Thain. He came to the Islands to buy provisions which could be sold in California. The voyage probably was little different from hundreds of others, but it is set apart by the fact that a Scottish gentleman, whom we know only as John, sailed as super cargo on the voyage and kept a journal of the trials of the *Emily Bourne*.

In the remarkably fast time of ten days, the Hawaiian Islands were raised, but then the winds turned hostile and six more days passed before they were able to drop anchor outside Honolulu harbor. John roamed through Honolulu. After one excursion he noted, "This morning I carried on a brilliant conversation with a young lady sitting down to an occupation both quite proper and necessary in itself. Yet so far as I know before, universally held to be performed in private. She did not commence talking until she had squatted and then of her own free will and accord."

After two days in Honolulu, Captain Thain decided that John should go to Waimea, on the island of Hawaii, where he might be able to buy fowls and potatoes at lower prices. The *Emily Bourne* remained in Honolulu harbor to secure a new mainsail and to smoke the rats out of the ship. John was aware that Thain had another reason for staying. He wrote in his journal that "the Captain did a bit of smuggling in brandy." Smuggling was a very profitable sideline for captains in the early 1850s.

Waimea, John's destination on the island of Hawaii, was an area about ten miles up country from the landing at Kawaihae. He had little success in finding provisions at Waimea, so he decided to try Waipio Valley, some sixty miles around the rugged northern coast of Hawaii. John started out in a whale boat with a crew of Hawaiians, who were a casual lot, and when they lay on the edge of breakers, with only cliffs and boulders looming ahead, John "began to feel decidedly uncomfortable."

The surf at Waipio Valley was running high, and John was not eager to go through it in the whale boat. Two canoes were inward-bound at the same time, and when one came alongside and offered to take John through the surf for fifty cents, he felt it was a good bargain. Ashore John hired a Chilean to round up all the fowls he could buy, but two days of searching produced only two dozen turkeys. After several attempts to get through the breakers in the whale boat, John gave up and hired two canoes, one to carry him and another to carry the turkeys. The Hawaiian crew took the whale boat to sea, and beyond the breakers John and his cargo transferred from the canoes for the return to Kawaihae.

John described the experience of going through the surf: "Off we went—slap came one right on my chest and through it we went—then another, oh the green monster! How he curled and roared—lost sight of the Bow Paddle—slap on my breast, whack on the crown of my hat, then bang over me. Up went the canoe in the air and down she came on the other side with a crack that made me look down to my feet expecting to see her split in two like a dry bean husk. You might have heard the report a mile off—but we were safe outside and I gave vent to a hearty roar of laughter."

At Kawaihae John learned that the *Emily Bourne* had had a close call at Honolulu because of Captain Thain's brandy-smuggling attempt. The captain had been arrested but was soon released for lack of evidence. On his release Thain sailed immediately, and wisely so, for soon divers discovered casks of brandy on the ocean floor close to the place where the *Emily Bourne* had been moored. Thain had tried a smuggling technique familiar to the Honolulu police. Captains would weigh down casks of liquor and drop them overboard. After the ships departed, accomplices on shore would send divers to locate the casks and under cover of darkness haul them up. In this way delivery of the liquor took place after captains departed. Some believed it reduced the chances of being caught and of paying the high penalty of having their vessels confiscated.

After his close call Thain was a nervous man. He ordered the weapons aboard ship to be "burnished and ready for action." Because of his fear of being pursued, he could hardly give ample attention to collecting the provisions he had hoped to carry back to California. After a quick search along the coast of Hawaii, Thain decided he had better leave the Islands while he still could, and he headed for San Francisco. As the Islands faded in the blue mist, John felt a touch of regret. He wrote in his journal, "its little Highland looking burns and fern covered glens, its deep dark ruts and long white tails of falling water, its waving palms, its musical coral reefs and its curly ended roaring surfs will not soon be forgotten."

John Ricord was a vagabond who wanted success and wanted it fast. He was not very different from many other adventurers who came to the Islands, but he is set apart from the rest because he arrived in Hawaii at an extremely opportune time.

John Ricord was born in New Jersey of a Dutch Calvinist mother and a French Catholic father who separated because of their religious differences. Ricord studied law in the office of an uncle in New York and was admitted to the bar in that state. But the urge to seek success elsewhere was strong, and he started off on a series of travels which would continue as long as he lived. In 1836 he was in the Republic of Texas, where he became private secretary to President David Burnet and then to his successor, Sam Houston. When Ricord learned that his father, who lived in the West Indies, had died, he hurried there to settle his estate. Next he set himself up in Florida and while there was admitted to practice before the Supreme Court of the United States.

Florida did not suit John Ricord, and he decided to try New Orleans, but enroute he met Dr. Marcus Whitman, who persuaded Ricord to join his party of settlers who were following the Oregon Trail to the Northwest. Toward the end of 1843 the party reached their destination. John Ricord paused for several months to do some legal work and then set off once again, this time bound for the Hawaiian Islands.

Ricord arrived at exactly the right moment. The Islands were nearly bare of lawyers at a time when the government was involved in bitter litigation with Ladd and Company. Ricord did not hurry ashore. He stayed aboard ship for two extra days to mend his tattered clothing, but word that a lawyer was in port reached Dr. Judd, then minister of foreign affairs. Judd was ill and overworked, and a bright lawyer would be a tremendous help. He immediately sent for Ricord and without government authorization hired him. Nine days after arriving in Honolulu, Ricord had sworn allegiance to Kamehameha III and had been named attorney general for the kingdom. The quick success Ricord coveted was now his.

Ricord worked with intelligence and dedication. He served the government well in the Ladd and Company case and also in other legal entanglements. He wrote statutes which were vital in organizing the government into three branches. He was indeed industrious, but he was also officious, and he used his position as a weapon. In Texas, in Florida, and in the Pacific Northwest he had made enemies quickly, and in Honolulu he added to the list. Archibald Gillespie, a lieutenant in the U. S. Marines, stopped in Honolulu on his way to California, and he wrote a letter to the Secretary of the Navy in which he reported on John Ricord. "The Americans generally are constantly in expectations of some unjustifiable attack from the Attorney General John Ricord, who is without doubt one of the veriest knaves who ever escaped from civilized society to become a Kanaka."

Dr. Gerrit P. Judd was very much Ricord's benefactor, but both men were proud, ambitious, and stubborn. It was not possible for the two to live peacefully together for any length of time. Ricord speeded the disaffection by falling in love with Judd's oldest daughter, Elizabeth, who was just fifteen years old. Elizabeth declined his proposal of marriage, and Ricord became abusive. Creating problems for Elizabeth was the fastest possible way for John Ricord to make an enemy of Gerrit Judd. As the situation worsened Ricord actively attacked Judd and at one point accused him of defrauding the kingdom of $23,000.

John Ricord was never one to hesitate about moving on, and he departed in August, 1847, for California. During his three and a half years in the Islands he had performed a real service for the government, but he failed dismally in dealing with fellow human beings.

In California Ricord practiced law, tried quicksilver mining, coal mining, and ranching. William T. Sherman, who later became a famous Civil War general, was then a young soldier in California, and he watched Ricord unsuccessfully try to gain the confidence of his commanding officer through flattery. Sherman also reported that Ricord resorted to trickery in an attempt to establish a mine claim. Again he was unsuccessful. When the gold rush struck, John Ricord apparently forgot his mining and ranching endeavors. Thomas O. Larkin saw him in the fields "digging and washing over his ounce and a half per day."

By the beginning of 1849 Ricord joined forces with Honolulu merchant Isaac Montgomery in opening a store close to Sutter's fort. Ricord took his merchandise to the miners at their diggings by mule train. The merchandise was mostly whiskey, which he sold at $20 a shot. By 1851 he was ready to head for the East Coast. En route he stopped in Nicaragua where Ricord found himself in the midst of a revolution. Along with other foreigners, he was imprisoned, and when he was released he discovered that most of his money had been stolen.

After a series of South American adventures, Ricord ended up in Tahiti, where he remained for about three years as a clerk in the office of the United States consul. At some time he visited Australia and Thailand before finally returning to visit his mother in New Jersey. Soon he was off again, this time to Liberia, where he hoped to receive a U. S. government post. It did not materialize, so he went on to Paris to visit two uncles, both prominent medical doctors. In Paris John Ricord's wanderings came to an end, for in 1861 he died. He was forty-eight years old.

John Ricord was impatient, intelligent, arrogant, immature. He was an easy man to dislike, but there was one rather touching side of the man's character. Elizabeth Judd refused Ricord's marriage proposal, but his affection for her seems to have been genuine. Years later, when Elizabeth married, Ricord was moved to write a poem in which he bemoaned ". . . those strange mistakes" which a person in love makes. John Ricord never married, and when he corresponded with Honolulu friends through the years, he often asked that his best wishes be given to Elizabeth.

In three or four years the California gold rush produced changes which otherwise would have taken decades. California achieved statehood in 1850, and the United States was suddenly a powerful and close neighbor of the Hawaiian kingdom. San Francisco was comparatively close— about fourteen days away. East Coast ports were eighty days from Hawaii, and it took even longer to reach European harbors. If Hawaiian royalty emotionally allied itself with Great Britain, economic reality and fast communications allied Hawaii with the United States. The destiny of the Islands was becoming firmly entwined with the destiny of the United States.

Chapter Eight

"O WHERE IS HONOR
WHERE IS JUSTICE"

T HE CONSULS OF the United States, France, and England who served in Hawaii during the first half of the nineteenth century were monumental troublemakers. When we view their antics from the distance of our time, they appear as incredible comics, but in their day, when the tiny kingdom could barely stand on wobbly legs, these foreign representatives nearly destroyed the government. The combination of Polynesian culture and missionary influence seemed to madden these men. They were arbitrary, threatening, meddling, self-seeking.

The chief offender was Richard Charlton, Consul of Great Britain to the Sandwich, Society, and Friendly Islands. The reports of James Cook and George Vancouver had spurred interest in the Islands, and both the Board of Trade and the admiralty thought a British representative in the Pacific would benefit the merchants who roamed the Pacific. Richard Charlton arrived in Honolulu in April, 1825, and his first official act was to express the sympathy of the British royal family to the Hawaiian government on the death of Liholiho and his queen in London.

The selection of Richard Charlton was a convenient one for the British. He was a sea captain who had been to the Pacific and Hawaii before. He had planned on returning to Hawaii to continue his trading activities. In addition to his personal business, he would act as consul for the sum of 200 pounds a year. The prestige of consul and the right to engage in business undoubtedly sounded like a profitable combination.

Richard Charlton was the prototype of the English captain of his day. He had gone to sea as a cabin boy and had survived the merchant navy's gauntlet of miseries, rising at last to command his own brig. By the time he reached Hawaii, Charlton was a hard-drinking, hard-swearing man. He had not been in Honolulu long before he aligned himself with those merchants who believed that the missionary influence was harmful to business. Consul Charlton's temper rose as missionary influence increased. He graphically described to several chiefs how he planned to hang chiefs or perhaps cut off their heads. To Lord Aberdeen, Secretary of State for Foreign Affairs, Charlton wrote that the king and chiefs "cannot be dealt with as civilized people."

His first serious misadventure took place in October, 1829. One of his cows had repeatedly broken into the field of a nearby Hawaiian farmer and damaged his crops. The exasperated farmer took down his musket and killed the beast with a barrage of seven musket balls. John C. Jones brought Charlton the news, and the two rode off to the farmer's house. Charlton pulled the culprit from his house, threw a rope over his neck, tied the other end to his pommel, and set off at a brisk pace for town. When the man could no longer run as fast as the horse cantered, he was dragged along in the dust. A passing Hawaiian cut the noose, but it was too late, and the farmer soon died.

By 1836 Charlton's constant stream of letters to the British foreign office brought a warship to investigate his deluge of charges. The captain of the vessel, with accompanying threats from Charlton, forced a new treaty on the Hawaiian monarchy. This final act of Charlton's was too much, and Kamehameha III addressed a letter to the King of Great Britain asking that the consul be removed. In requesting the recall, Kamehameha listed three cases where Charlton had either threatened individuals or the kingdom as a whole. The fourth grievance was the case of the Hawaiian farmer. A final reason was proof to Charlton that the missionaries indeed controlled the king. "This too is one great thing of his. Although he may perhaps be married to his own wife according to the laws of Great Britain yet his child by a Hawaiian mother is living with us here on these Islands, and he gives full support to such shameful things."

Richard Charlton was so involved in angry situations that it would appear he had little time left for business or consular activities. He was the defendant in two slander suits, one verdict costing him $3,450 and costs. His sheep and cattle continued to roam onto the property of others, and even his dog was a source of trouble. On two occasions the victims of Charlton's dog tried to persuade the police to fine the owner the $5 the law allowed. In addition Charlton found time to horsewhip the editor of the *Polynesian,* accost the Minister of Foreign Affairs as he walked home one noon, and to upbraid the chief of police.

Richard Charlton's most celebrated legal battle involved his claim to a waterfront lot which adjoined the fort of Honolulu. His claim was based on a document signed by a governor of Oahu and by Boki. By the time Charlton got around to pressing for the property, both the men who had signed the document were dead. The battle went on for years. The ex-missionaries, Judd and Richards, who were then influential people in the government, claimed that the governor of Oahu had no right to grant land in the first place, and when this tack failed they claimed the documents were forged. Finally it was agreed a decision should be rendered in England, and all the documents were sent there. At last Charlton won his case—in London.

The frustrations of Richard Charlton brought on one of the most anxious moments in the whole history of the monarchy. By late 1842 Charlton decided he was going to present his grievances directly to his superiors in London. Before departing he could not resist hurling one last threat. On September 26, 1842, he wrote to the Hawaiian king. "Your Majesty's Government has more than once insulted the British flag, but must not suppose it will be passed over in silence. Justice, though tardy, will reach you; and it is you, not your advisers, that will be punished." On his way to London Richard Charlton very likely met Lord George Paulet at Mazatlan, in Mexico. Paulet was captain of the frigate *H.B.M. Carysfort,* a vessel of the British squadron assigned to the Pacific station.

With the British consul out of the way, the agent for the Hudson's Bay Company in Hawaii brought suit against Charlton on behalf of a South American firm which sought $10,000 in damages. Charlton's property was attached, and soon the jury announced a verdict in favor of the South American company. A report on these happenings was sent to the British consul in Tepic, Mexico, by Alexander Simpson, who was a cohort of Charlton's and whom Charlton had appointed acting consul in his absence. Simpson asked the Tepic consul to use his influence in getting a warship to sail to Honolulu.

Rear Admiral Richard Thomas, commander of the British Pacific squadron, had periodically heard about discrimination against his countrymen in Hawaii. Now he acted. On January 17, 1843, he wrote Captain Paulet ordering him to proceed to the Sandwich Islands for the purpose of "watching over and protecting the interests of British Subjects." Paulet sailed with all haste, arriving before the port of Honolulu on the afternoon of February 10.

The commander of the *Carysfort* was a handsome, affable man of thirty-nine with blue eyes, curly, short, chestnut colored hair, and a fair complexion. Captain Lord George Paulet belonged to one of the oldest and most distinguished families in England. One of his ancestors had fought with the Duke of Gloucester against France in 1380 and another Paulet had been Lord Treasurer to Edward VI and became the first Marquis of Winchester. The frigate George Paulet commanded was sixth rated, the lowest ranked vessel in the British Navy. It carried only twenty-six guns, but to the residents of Honolulu it looked formidable enough.

As soon as the *Carysfort* appeared, Alexander Simpson went out to the vessel to confer with Paulet. It was evident that the captain was not in a friendly mood since he did not fire the traditional salute to the Hawaiian flag when he arrived. The fears of Honolulu citizens increased when they learned that neither the U. S. nor French consuls who had gone out to the ship were received as representatives of their countries. The two consuls had rejected Simpson as the representative of Great Britain, so Paulet now refused to acknowledge them.

The king was in Lahaina, and while he awaited his return Paulet conferred only with Simpson. The snub of the U. S. and French consuls aroused the apprehension of the citizens of the two countries. When Kamehameha III returned, he was greeted by a large number of people, including some 300 soldiers. It was obvious the kingdom was headed for another crisis.

Before the king arrived, Americans were relieved by the appearance of the U. S. sloop of war *Boston*. The emotion the sight of this vessel aroused in the hearts of Americans was expressed in the journal of merchant William Paty:

> *Hurra! hurra! hurra! for the Stars and Stripes. hurra! for our gallant Navy. hurra! for our glorious country. Oh ye Yankees who live at home at ease how little can you imagine the stirring thrill of joy and pride that agitates the bosom of your countrymen who, roaming far away in foreign lands, and in midst of trouble, difficulty and danger, hears the cry of Sail O and the next moment sees the Stars & Stripes floating over the brave hearts and powerful batteries of an American Ship of War. There may be readers who will smile in derision at this but I feel assured that they will not be from among the number of Americans who were resident at Honolulu in February 1843.*

A letter from Paulet awaited the king, demanding an immediate audience with the ruler. When the king advised Paulet that Dr. Judd would act as his representative, another letter was immediately sent declining to deal with the doctor. The second letter included a list of six demands on the Hawaiian government, including the removal of the attachment on Charlton's property and the recognition of Simpson as the British consul. And, Captain Paulet concluded, if these demands were not met by 4 P.M. the next day, he would "take coercive steps." In his journal Rev. Cochran Forbes asked the question, "O where is honor where is justice."

Lord George Paulet wrote Captain Long of the *Boston* telling him specifically what he meant by "coercive steps." He said he intended to "make an immediate attack upon this town at 4 P.M. tomorrow (Saturday) in the event of the demand now forwarded by me to the King of these Islands, not being complied with by that time." The next morning news of Paulet's threat spread through town, and near panic seized Honolulu. The Hawaiians streamed from the town, seeking protection in the upper reaches of the valleys behind Honolulu. Mrs. Gorham Nye recorded what the Americans were doing "while the Lord hauled his frigate opposite the Fort, guns all on the broadside—ready to fire!" Mrs. Nye, as well as all other Americans, had been offered protection aboard the *Boston* by Captain Long. She filled a trunk with her valuables "supposing the houses would be plundered and the town set on fire."

William Paty wrote that "the streets were crowded with carts containing Money Chests, Book Safes, Trunks, Personal Clothing & all hastening toward the Wharfs to be placed on board of the Ships . . . for safety." The English residents of the town were taken off to an English ship which had earlier been towed outside Honolulu harbor. Many people were still waiting on the wharfs to be rowed out to ships in the harbor when word swept through the community that the demands of Paulet would be met "under protest."

Emboldened by success, Alexander Simpson decided to press for more concessions. With Paulet's backing, Simpson demanded compensation for an assortment of damages which totaled over $100,000—a staggering sum for the near bankrupted monarchy. After three days of conferences the king and Judd decided that what Paulet and Simpson really wanted was the cession of the Hawaiian kingdom to Great Britain. Privately the king and Judd talked to the American and French consuls, hoping to find some alternative course of action. It was suggested the Islands might be ceded to France or jointly to France and the United States, but such action was deemed impractical.

Frantic discussions produced nothing, and on the morning of February 25, 1843, it was agreed the kingdom should be provisionally ceded to Great Britain. The king and others hoped the foreign office in London would reverse the course of events and hand the nation back to the king. For Kamehameha III it was a time of heartbreak. The situation drove him to the edge of madness.

Captain Paulet wasted no time in officially taking possession of the Islands. At 2:30 in the afternoon the band and marines from the *Carysfort* marched the six blocks from the British consular office to the fort. This procession was led by the triumphant Alexander Simpson together with British officers in dress uniforms. Within the fort Hawaiian infantry formed three sides of a square and British marines the fourth. The square faced a balcony where the king, many chiefs, and British officers joined Paulet and Simpson.

In his report to the Secretary of the Admiralty, Paulet reported there were many spectators present, "principally Natives." After the deed of cession had been read, an officer of the king hauled down the Hawaiian flag and Lieutenant Frere hoisted the Union Jack while the band played "God Save the Queen." A twenty-one gun salute was fired from the fort and was answered by the *Carysfort*. In a postscript to this report, Lord Paulet noted this second cession of Hawaii took place exactly forty-nine years after Captain George Vancouver had accepted the Islands for Great Britain from Kamehameha I.

What Paulet did not mention in his official report was the speech made by Kamehameha III during the cession ceremonies. It was an eloquent lament by a bewildered man:

"Where are you, Chiefs, people and commons from my ancestors, and people from foreign lands!

"Hear ye! I make known to you that I am in perplexity by reason of difficulties into which I have been brought without cause; therefore, I have given away the life of our land, hear ye! But my rule over you, my people, and your privileges will continue, for I have hope that the life of the land will be restored when my conduct is justified."

When this speech was published, along with the official cession papers, Paulet was annoyed. A public notice was printed stating that the speech was not "official." Captain Paulet believed the king had given the speech so the chiefs would not accuse him of giving up too easily.

Lord George Paulet decided that a Commission should take the place of the Privy Council as the governing body of the kingdom. In addition to Paulet the members of the Commission were Lieutenant Frere, Dr. Judd, and Duncan Mackay. Mackay soon resigned, pleading ill health, and Judd resigned on May 11. It was futile for the two to remain as members, since Lord George Paulet ran things as he wished.

Immediately after the flag was raised over the fort in Honolulu, men were dispatched to Hawaii, Maui, and Kauai to raise the Union Jack in those places also. A high chief named Leleiohoku went to Kauai, and another named Paki went to Hawaii. Paulet immediately established the Queen's Native Infantry regiment, numbering 130 men, and an artillery company of thirty-four men as a defense against a possible French invasion. The troops were drilled by a marine sergeant from the *Carysfort*. Paulet also appropriated the three schooners which belonged to the government and gave them the solid British names of *Victoria, Albert,* and *Adelaide* in place of their Hawaiian names.

The American missionaries had hoped the U. S. would eventually annex the Islands, but they were not greatly upset over the British takeover; their real fear was that Catholic France would annex Hawaii. Protestant England was immeasurably safer. George Paulet was polite and even friendly. He called on the missionaries, attended church, and visited the Royal school, and in return the children were invited aboard the *Carysfort*.

Missionary indifference changed to hostility when Lord George revised the laws on fornication. The missionaries had preached against the sin of fornication, and a law of the kingdom specified a fine of $15 for each person convicted of this crime. Paulet abolished the law. The missionaries were horrified and began to lament the degradation which Paulet was causing.

While Paulet changed laws to suit his fancy, those who hoped to reestablish the monarchy were doing their best to gain support from England, France, and the U. S. On the day prior to the cession the king wrote a letter to Queen Victoria which would have touched the heart of that lady if it had ever come to her attention. "With trouble and distress we inform you, Most kind Queen, of the Great Misfortune that has befallen our Nation. . . . Oh Queen, He has given out orders that he will punish us if we do not accede to his demands in nineteen hours."

Dr. Judd worked endlessly and effectively on behalf of the monarchy. He secretly drew up documents to be sent to the United States, England, and France explaining what had happened. He wrote these at night using the underground crypt of the royal mausoleum as his office and the coffin of Kaahumanu as a desk. A canoe was sent to Lahaina to bring the king, who secretly sailed to Waikiki, where he was met by Judd with the documents. After signing the documents the king returned to Lahaina aboard a schooner. Paulet heard of the king's visit to Waikiki and that Judd had met him there, but Judd insisted the meeting was unimportant.

How were these documents to be put into the hands of the respective governments? A twenty-three-year-old American, James Fowle Baldwin Marshall, was selected as the courier. Paulet would not have allowed Marshall to depart if he had known his mission, so to get passage James Marshall claimed he had to make a business trip for Ladd & Company. On March 11, 1843, he sailed for San Blas, Mexico. His only fellow passenger was Alexander Simpson, who was bound for London with dispatches from Captain Paulet. The secret title James Marshall carried was "Envoy Extraordinary and Minister Plenipotentiary to the Court of St. James."

In Mexico the two men parted. Simpson traveled overland, eventually arriving in London via Havana. Marshall also traveled overland, heading for New Orleans and then Washington, D. C., where he delivered his first set of dispatches. Then he dashed off to England and reached London just a week after a very surprised Alexander Simpson arrived. In London James Marshall presented his case to Under Secretary Addington, supported in his statements by officials of the Hudson's Bay Company and reinforced by Richards, Haalilio, and Brinsmade, who had come over from the continent to help. After presenting their case the Hawaiians could only wait and hope that the government would decide that the Paulet takeover was unacceptable.

In Honolulu Captain Paulet was leading a pleasant life. The official hours the commission kept were 10 A.M. until 2 P.M. Paulet established residence on shore and rode about on a horse which he named Carysfort. The streets of Honolulu seemed bare to him, and he ordered that trees be planted to enhance the appearance of the town. The antagonism of the missionaries bothered him little. He was lionized by the English community, and even some of the Americans thought he ruled the Islands well. Women found the handsome, outgoing captain to be a very attractive man, and Paulet did what he could to encourage their interest.

In her account of the raising of the British flag at the fort, Dr. Judd's wife reported that the band played not only "God Save the Queen" but also "Isle of Beauty, Fare Thee Well." The latter, Mrs. Judd observed, "was played by the request of some lady friends of Lord George, and regarded by us as a refined cruelty, which could only emanate from a woman." When Paulet was publicly seen in the company of a beautiful Hawaiian girl, the conservative part of Honolulu's population was further outraged. The young lady's name was Kamalo-o-Leleiohoku, and she was said to be a great-granddaughter of Kamehameha I.

Paulet's takeover of Hawaii did not receive the general approval of his countrymen. The *London Times* of June 15, 1843, stated in a lead article that "the view which has been taken of this treaty of cession in this country is not favorable to its confirmation." In the same month the British minister to the United States wrote to the U. S. Secretary of State, telling him that "the occupation of the Sandwich Islands was an act entirely unauthorized by Her Majesty's Government."

Tension was high and time dragged. Every captain who arrived in Honolulu was questioned for news, but there was no definite word whether London had accepted or rejected the cession of the Islands. At last, on July 26, 1843, the British frigate *Dublin* hove into sight. It carried the red and white flag of Rear Admiral Richard Thomas, commander of the Pacific squadron. He immediately asked for an audience with the king, and a meeting was arranged for the next morning.

The Hawaiian government was bruised by Paulet's actions and desperately needed a champion. Admiral Thomas proved to be that hero. He quickly made it known that the official feeling of the British government was that the Islands should be returned to the Hawaiian monarchy. All he asked in return was that certain rights of Englishmen in Hawaii be guaranteed. The monarchy had won another reprieve.

July 31 was set as the day when the kingdom would formally be re-

turned to Kamehameha III. A plain to the east of Honolulu was designated as the place where this historic event should take place. Marines
from the *Carysfort* and the *Dublin* were ordered onto the plain at 8 A.M.
in dress uniform. Admiral Thomas arrived in a carriage, followed by the
king on horseback. As the king entered the grounds, he was given a salute
of twenty-one guns. Every Hawaiian and American who could come was
there.

After the salute was fired, the English flag officer pulled down the
Union Jack and the Hawaiian flag was raised. As this was done the *Carysfort* fired a twenty-one gun salute, followed by the *Dublin*. Then came a
twenty-one gun salute from two American warships and finally the same
salute from the fort and from the batteries atop Punchbowl, the crater behind Honolulu. The place where the ceremonies took place became known
as Thomas Square.

Emotions ran high. As the king returned to town he was enthusiastically cheered. He pardoned those men who had joined the British infantry
and artillery companies, and in the afternoon he attended a thanksgiving
service at Kawaiahao church. Judd read a communication from Admiral
Thomas, restoring the kingdom, and Kamehameha III made a short speech
in which he is said to have spoken the famous sentence, "The life of the
land is preserved in righteousness," words which are the official motto of
the State of Hawaii.

Kamehameha III also proclaimed an act of grace. "Anxious to express our Gratitude to God, and to give the fullest proof of our attachment
to the English Nation," the proclamation decreed that no subjects should
be punished for any act committed to the injury of the government between February 25 and July 31. A second provision freed all prisoners "of
every description, from Hawaii to Niihau." The last provision declared a
suspension of all government business for ten days so "that all persons
may be free to enjoy themselves in the festivities and rejoicings appropriate to the occasion."

For many years July 31 was the foremost national holiday in Hawaii.
It became traditional to have great parades and for the king to give luaus
attended by thousands of guests.

A Honolulu resident, Edwin O. Hall, was moved to celebrate the
happenings in song. By July 31 he had written the words for three stanzas
to the tune of "God Save the Queen." It was called the Restoration Anthem.

> Hail! to our rightful King!
> We joyful honors bring
>   This day to thee!
> Long live your Majesty!
> Long reign this dynasty!

> And for posterity
>   The sceptre be!
>
> Hail! to thy worthy name!
> Worthy his Country's Fame
>   *Thomas,* the brave!
> Long shall thy virtues be,
> Shrined in our memory
> Who came to set us free,
>   Quick o'er the wave!
>
> Hail! to our Heavenly King!
> To Thee our thanks we bring,
>   Worthy of all!
> Loud we thine honors raise!
> Loud is our song of praise!
> Smile on our future days,
>   Sovereign of all!

The poetry may have lacked refinement, but the sentiments were what the people felt, and the anthem was enormously popular. The children at the Royal School copied the verses as a penmanship exercise and were often called upon to sing the stanzas. The anthem was sung at the great luau the king gave on August 4 and at the numerous parties which enlivened Honolulu.

Rear Admiral Richard Thomas did not look the way a hero is supposed to look. He was a short, plump man with a fringe of hair circling a round head. His eyes were the most noticeable thing about him, large and rather sad. When he restored the kingdom, Thomas was sixty-seven years old, and fifty-three of those years had been spent in the Royal Navy.

The admiral decided to remain in Honolulu until the new British consul arrived, and to make his stay more pleasant he moved into a waterfront cottage. Early rising residents saw the admiral set off on his regular morning walks. Thomas recommended these walks as healthful exercise, and soon a number of Honoluluans were following his example. He was the prize catch for Island hostesses, and he responded with graciousness even though some occasions were a hardship upon him. One such occasion was a formal dinner given by the Judds. As usual, no liquor was served, a practice which did not take into consideration the habits of Admiral Thomas, who nevertheless gamely remained at the table for three hours.

At last the new British consul arrived, and Admiral Richard Thomas made ready to depart. It was February, 1844, and Thomas had been in the Islands for more than six months. His popularity was undiminished. When it was known that he was leaving, there was a new outpouring of affection. Kamehameha III wrote a letter saying, "In moments of great tribulation to me and my Subjects, it was you, Admiral, who flew to our aid, and who taking a just view of the friendship of Your Sovereign for us, anticipated the gracious intentions of Her Majesty touching the restoration of our Islands. . . ."

The missionaries sent a joint letter, astonishing because of its unstinting praise: "You found our community in disorder and confusion: you leave us in peace and tranquility. You found us cast down and disheartened; you leave us cheerful and happy in our work, with prospects of success as bright as they have ever been." Twenty businessmen joined in another letter: ". . . we tender to you the warmest assurances of our respect and esteem. . . . May the Smiles of Heaven rest upon you."

The departure of Admiral Thomas moved Edwin O. Hall to write an additional two verses which could be sung following stanza two of his original Restoration Anthem. The final stanza went:

> Farewell! May friendships smile
> Thy lonely hours beguile,
>   While yet you roam;
> May each propitious breeze
> Safe waft thee o'er the seas,
> To friends as warm as these,
>   And thine own home.

Hawaii's great hero was not forgotten. In 1847 the minister of foreign affairs wrote to Thomas, "I am further ordered by the King to request of you, as a favor, that you will be pleased to sit for your Portrait, in full uniform, to be of good size from the middle upwards. . . ." A year and a half later the minister acknowledged the receipt of the portrait: ". . . I was present when the High Chiefs and many others cheered the likeness of the generous and grave Restorer of the Hawaiian Crown with an enthusiasm and prolonged repitition [sic] that could not have been surpassed even if the much respected and beloved original had stood before us."

Admiral Richard Thomas retired from the navy to his home at Stonehouse, Plymouth, and was visited there by Dr. Judd together with Prince Alexander and Prince Lot in 1850. The two young men had been assigned the Restoration Anthem as a penmanship exercise at the Royal School in 1843. They were so moved by seeing the old admiral that Prince Alexander reported they sang the anthem in the railway carriage on their return to London. Rev. William Alexander wrote to the minister of foreign affairs after visiting Stonehouse and planting some mango seeds at the admiral's home: "I intend to tell my children that the trees which will, I hope, spring from these seeds, are to be a perpetual memorial to the man who poured the 'balm of Gilead' on the wounds of a poor & injured nation. . . ."

At the age of eighty-one, Admiral Richard Thomas died, and news of his death reached Hawaii in December, 1857. The *Polynesian* ran a broad black border around the story. The king ordered "that the Court go into mourning, and all officers of his Majesty's Government wear crape on the left arm for fifteen days."

What happened to the players in this drama? Admiral Thomas gained the rank of full admiral before he retired from the navy. Richard Charlton, who had gone to England to present his case to the government in 1842, returned to Honolulu in the middle of 1844 to claim his waterfront property. After selling his land Charlton departed, and the *Polynesian* regretted that it had to allude again to his career. The story of his departure began, "This man [Charlton] left these islands, we trust for ever, on the morning of Thursday, the 19th inst." Richard Charlton died in Plymouth, England, eight years later.

Alexander Simpson, the man who had carried the Paulet dispatches to London, was disappointed with the actions of his government. He felt Great Britain could have held the Hawaiian Islands and that his government made a bad mistake by not supporting Paulet. Simpson retired to Scotland and wrote a book denouncing government shortsightedness.

The story of George Paulet is a longer one. The handsome officer departed from Honolulu harbor on August 25, just one month after Admiral Thomas had arrived. Much to everyone's surprise, his vessel reappeared in Honolulu harbor about a year later. The jovial captain bore no ill feelings toward Islanders, and he thought they bore none toward him. Ashore Paulet was greeted by a crowd of old friends. He requested an audience with the king, but Judd apparently created obstacles, and the two did not meet. The *Polynesian* noted, sarcastically, "We have not learned as yet the occasion of this visit, but presume the Right Honorable Lord will feel gratified in witnessing for himself the prosperity of the country and its rapid advance since his departure."

Captain Paulet could not restrain himself from one amusing act before departing from Hawaii. Again the *Polynesian* reported the story: "Our good towns-people were suddenly startled from their slumbers at mid-night Monday last, by the report of a heavy broadside, and the rapid and successive firing of guns by divisions and single pieces. . . . It was discovered to proceed from the Carysfort, and considerable excitement ensued, as it was supposed she had opened fire upon the fort. . . . The next morning we were informed that it was done to show how quick the crew could be beat to quarters from their hammocks, and engage in a mock combat." After this little amusement Lord George Paulet departed from Hawaii for the last time.

Kamalo-o-Leleiohoku, Paulet's paramour, was left behind when the captain sailed in 1843, and it is not known whether the two met again when Paulet returned in 1844. It would, however, seem very possible that Paulet became aware that he was the father of a child born to Kamalo. The child was given the name Hanakaulani—flower of heaven. Hanakaulani grew into a handsome, aristocratic lady, standing nearly six feet tall, with slender face, fine dark hair, and large Hawaiian eyes. The stories she told her children about George Paulet would one day move a daughter to seek out the Paulet family in England.

The seizure of Hawaii in no way hurt Paulet's career. The motivation for his action was undoubtedly the fear that France would annex Hawaii before England could, since the French had just taken over the Society Islands and rumors of the day indicated that the French were interested not only in Hawaii but also California. The British government had annexed New Zealand in 1840, again in order to beat the French. Sir Thomas Raffles had appropriated territory without the approval of the British government and had earned praise for his actions. Paulet had ample precedent for his action. What made the case of Hawaii different was the special relationship the Island kingdom had with England, as well as the keen interest which the United States showed in Hawaiian affairs.

By 1854 Lord George was in command of a seventy-eight-gun vessel which took part in the first bombardment of Sebastopol during the Crimean War. In 1867 he retired from the navy with the rank of full admiral, and twelve years later he died at the age of seventy-six. Over the years Paulet corresponded with the Hawaiian minister of foreign affairs, and he always expressed an interest in the royal family and often said he hoped to return to Hawaii.

The new British consul for Hawaii was General William Miller, a slender man of fifty. He was a bachelor but was accompanied to Hawaii by a niece and a male secretary named Robert C. Wyllie. Miller was paid the respectable sum of 800 pounds a year to devote full time to consular affairs.

The new consul was a distinguished soldier who had served in the field train of the royal artillery when the Duke of Wellington defeated Napoleon in the Peninsular War. He joined the British army in the United States during the latter part of the War of 1812 and was with the expedition which burned Washington, D. C. Later he was at New Orleans when the British were defeated by the Americans. In 1817 Miller went to South America and joined the revolutionary forces which were battling the Spanish in Chile and Peru. He served under Generals Bolivar and Santa Cruz and was wounded several times. Santa Cruz appointed William Miller a Grand Marshal of Peru, and when Santa Cruz fell from power in 1839, Miller was banished from the country.

From South America Miller traveled to Boston, where he visited his good friend William H. Prescott, the famous historian. In November, 1840, Prescott reported on Miller to a mutual friend: "We have, by the bye, General Miller of Peru passing the winter here. I see him often. He is a noble fellow, but in the turn of the wheel has been thrown out of power and is now waiting for some favorable change in Peru. . . ."

Miller gave Prescott valuable help in his *History of the Conquest of Peru,* help which was acknowledged in footnotes. Later, when the United States was on the brink of war with Mexico, Miller sent Prescott a note saying "that the United States may come off second best if they go to war with that country." When the United States won handily, Miller admitted his mistake. "I confess frankly that my Predictions have turned out totally erroneous."

General Miller's predictions of disaster for the United States might have been based on wishful thinking, for the general did not have much use for Americans. There were, however, several exceptions to this rule. Miller admired William Prescott and George Washington, and portraits of these two men hung in the sitting room of his cottage in Honolulu.

Miller had taken over the residence of his predecessor, Richard Charlton, and he turned it into an immaculately kept English cottage. The road which ran before his home came to be called Miller Street. He established a hospital for British seamen which he called Little Greenwich. Eventually he acquired some thirty acres of land near the mouth of Manoa Valley. The country home he constructed there was named Little Britain.

General Miller was a willful man who took his duties as a representative of the Queen of England very seriously. Compromise was not part of his nature. He insisted on spelling Oahu as "Woahoo," because that was the way Captain Cook had spelled it. Before long many persons in the government believed Miller supported everyone and everything the government opposed. At one meeting in May, 1847, twenty-seven resolutions were passed by the Privy Council aimed at Miller's recall, the council contending that Miller had no respect for the laws or officers of the Hawaiian kingdom. The requests were nevertheless rejected.

The gap between Miller and the Hawaiian government was not so great that it could not be bridged, but it took an emergency to bring the two together. In 1849 a French admiral was in Honolulu making demands on the government. Consul Miller offered the king the sanctuary of the British consulate if hostilities occurred. This act of consideration seemed to ease the tensions between Miller and the government. By 1854 the consul and the king were on such good terms that Miller presented to the admiring king all his South American uniforms and medals.

William Miller was jealous of American influence in the Islands, and he feared that the kingdom would be pushed into the hands of the United States. His fears were well founded. In 1851 the king and Privy Council agreed that the kingdom should be ceded to the United States in the event of either seizure by France or invasion by gangs from California. Miller appeared before the council and urged against that cession. When the king asked Miller if he could guarantee that Great Britain would protect Hawaii, Miller replied that he could not. So the United States was the only remaining hope.

General Miller used what resources he could to thwart the growing influence of the United States, but there was little substantial he could accomplish when Americans held influential positions in the government and when Yankee businessmen multiplied and prospered. In an effort to steer the kingdom away from the U.S., Miller pointed to the American blacks and said that annexation would reduce the Hawaiians to a state of slavery. His arguments were of no avail.

The British consul's depreciation of the United States did little to endear him to American residents. In his dispatches to the Secretary of State, U. S. commercial agent David Gregg referred to Miller quite often. On May 29, 1855, he wrote, "The health of Gen. Miller continues to be feeble. His mind is evidently very much imparied by the peculiar disease under which he labors—a softening of the brain accompanied by moral insanity—and his sudden death would not at any time create surprise."

Some five years passed before ill health finally forced William Miller to resign as British consul. He returned to Lima, Peru, where the government had reinstated his rank as a Grand Marshal and where he was once again recognized as a leader in the wars of independence. General William Miller died toward the end of October, 1861, aboard a British storeship at anchor off Callao. The Hawaiian consul in Peru reported that after his death the physicians of the president of Peru were sent on board ship to embalm the body, in the course of which they counted twenty-two battle scars and extracted two musket balls from the body of the old soldier.

In his will General Miller left the sum of 1,000 pounds to either William Prescott or to Sir John Bowring toward the publication of his biography. Prescott had been dead for two years, and there is no record that Bowring, who acted as Hawaiian envoy in Europe for a time and became best known as a writer of hymns, ever undertook the task.

The official title of John C. Jones in Hawaii was United States Agent for Commerce and Seamen, although he performed the duties of a consul. Like the British and French representatives, Jones considered himself above the laws of the country. By 1839 he had so often irritated and challenged the government that Kamehameha III sent him a letter which, among other things, charged him with bigamy. In closing the king stated, ". . . I refuse any longer to know you as consul from the United States of America. Respect for the government of your country as well as respect for my own compels me to do this." In a letter to the President of the United States the King made essentially the same points. When John C. Jones finally left the Islands, few persons mourned his departure.

Peter Brinsmade assumed Jones's responsibilities and in 1844 received the official title of United States Consul. Brinsmade was having deep troubles of his own in connection with Ladd & Company affairs, and he lasted only six months. From the appointment of Brinsmade as consul until the last consular appointment was made in 1892, twenty-three different men held this position or its equivalent. The average length of time a consul remained in the Islands was just over two years.

There were several reasons for this constant turnover. The position was an appointive one, and as administrations changed in Washington, D. C., so did the consuls. The Hawaii post was also much sought after, because it was so lucrative. In those years consuls were compensated through fees and not by fixed salary. For a period of time Honolulu was second only to Liverpool in the number of visiting American vessels, and consuls collected fees from every ship which came into port. The consul received $1 from every American seaman who left ship in the Islands and $1 when he shipped out. In addition the ship paid him 50 cents for each sailor left or signed on. Whaling vessels often paid their crews a portion of their wages in Hawaii, and this had to be done at the office of the consul. Crews were paid a lay, or a percentage of the catch, and the consul supplied the latest prices that whale oil was selling for on the East Coast, which was the basis on which the crew was paid. For performing this service the consul received 2½ percent of each seaman's wages.

There was yet another reason why Hawaii held such charm for U. S. consuls. From some time in the late 1840s until about the time of the American Civil War, a properly scheming consul could make enough of a fortune in a few years to retire for life. The key to this quick wealth lay in the control the consuls had over the United States hospitals for seamen. In Hawaii hospitals were located in Honolulu, at Lahaina, and for a short period at Hilo.

The need for such hospitals had become apparent as the number of American vessels coming to Hawaii increased. More sick sailors were put ashore with no provision for their care. Often they were destitute and turned to the U. S. consul for help. As long as the number of sick was relatively small, they were cared for in private homes and public boarding houses. The boarding houses were crude places, usually connected with saloons, and something better was needed. The need for hospitals was genuine, but the method of administration was an open invitation to corruption.

The U. S. consul had complete control over the hospitals. He appointed the physician as well as the hospital manager. The U. S. government paid the hospital a flat rate per day for each patient. The consul had the right to land or to refuse to land U. S. sailors, so the flow of patients was also within his power. In 1854 the hospital at Honolulu was paid 62½ cents per patient per day. David Gregg, who was conducting a quiet investigation of the situation, reported to Secretary of State W. S. Marcy that the hospitals could be run at a profit if the rate had been 37½ cents per day.

In addition to this daily rate each seaman was periodically supplied with a shirt, underclothes, trousers, socks, and stockings, and every four months he received a hat, a pair of shoes, and a handkerchief. On being discharged from the hospital, sailors usually received a heavy pea jacket, a pair of trousers, one or two woolen shirts, a mattress and pillow, a pair of blankets, a pot, a pan, and a knife. Without doubt many a sailor had never been so well clothed in his life. The government, of course, paid for the clothes, and Gregg quotes one witness who believed the government was charged between 200 and 300 percent more than the current retail prices in Honolulu.

The U. S. consul was in an all-powerful position. He could be most selective in choosing the physician and the manager for the hospital. For a number of years the most important consideration was the amount of the kickback a consul could get from the two men he appointed. In early dispatches Gregg was inclined to believe such kickbacks were in the form of "presents" without any agreement as to percentages, but in later dispatches he cites the case of one hospital manager who paid ten percent to the consul on board and lodging bills and twenty percent on bills for clothing. One physician declared he had paid the U. S. consul twenty percent of his income from medicines and treatment.

It was to the obvious advantage of the consul to keep the hospital as full as possible. During some seasons there was a dearth of American seamen, and some consuls were not adverse to filling the hospitals with destitutes off the streets of Honolulu and Lahaina regardless of their nationality. An easier means was to get discharged seamen to sign blank forms which would later be filled in by the doctor certifying that they were still bonafide patients. When a sailor was discharged from the hospital, he received a modest sum—from $24 to $36—to help him return to America. From this sum the sailor had to pay the consul $1.

David Gregg believed that one consul, Benjamin F. Angel, was among the most adept at making money. Angel received his commission as consul on May 24, 1853, and stayed until August 2, 1854. Gregg reported to the Secretary of State that Angel at one time even held title to the hospital lot and building. He engaged his brother-in-law as manager and received bids from those interested in filling the position of physician.

Consul Angel's money-making abilities extended beyond the hospital. Gregg reported that the captain of the *U.S.S. Susquehanna* was suspicious of Angel after he saw the enormous bill charged for putting coal aboard his vessel. In one dispatch Gregg states that Angel certified a cargo of German-caught whale oil as being American so that U. S. customs duties could be avoided. The fee for having done this was $200.

Things were bad at Honolulu, but Gregg thought the situation in Lahaina even worse. The Lahaina hospital practiced at least one refinement which somehow missed Honolulu: Lahaina seamen were sent out to work while they were supposedly patients in the hospital, and their wages went to the hospital. David Gregg's investigation was frustrating. Many persons who knew what was going on would tell Gregg what was happening but would not sign affidavits.

The cost of hospital care in Hawaii did not go unnoticed in Washington, D. C., although it took a long time before anything was done about it. In 1852 the Federal auditor's office sent a letter to Secretary of State Daniel Webster, pointing out that the cost of caring for seamen at Lahaina had increased from $6,000 a quarter to over $20,000 a quarter. Expenses per patient at Lahaina were averaging $110.06 while at Honolulu the costs were $62.37 per patient. The auditor wondered if it would be possible to transport the sick at Lahaina to Honolulu or even to California or Oregon.

On May 10, 1859, Lewis Cass, Secretary of State, wrote to Isaac Toucy, Secretary of the Navy, concerning the alarming situation in Hawaii. Each year the cost of maintaining the hospitals in Hawaii rose substantially. In fact, the Hawaii operation apparently was costing more than all the hospitals for seamen in the rest of the world combined. A warship, the *Levant,* was to leave soon for the Pacific, and Cass suggested that the captain of the vessel, Commander W. E. Hunt, investigate the hospital situation in the Islands. James W. Borden, then U. S. Commissioner in Honolulu, could assist him.

Hunt and Borden duly completed their investigation and wrote their report. In August, 1860, the *Levant* departed Honolulu for Panama, where the report was to be sent on to Washington. Weeks passed and no word was received in Hawaii concerning the *Levant*'s arrival at the isthmus. Island newspapers became alarmed over the possible fate of the vessel, and at last it could only be assumed the *Levant* was lost. Later a section of a mast was washed ashore on the island of Hawaii and tentatively identified as belonging to the vanished ship.

Apparently no complete copy of the Hunt-Borden report had been left in Honolulu, but somehow the gist of the findings did reach the mainland and were printed in the *Boston Commercial Bulletin* in late 1860. The article was reprinted in a Honolulu newspaper. It outlined some of the ways the U. S. government had been defrauded. Those who were implicated let out screams of protest, and there were charges and countercharges, threats of violence, and shouting confrontations. The secretary for the Hunt-Borden investigation came forward and stated that the article contained the essentials of the report.

In 1861 the clouds of the impending Civil War in the United States made such matters as hospital scandals unimportant. Apparently no further investigations were made by the U. S. government. Probably the great amount of newspaper publicity which the affair received did much to cure at least the obvious ills of the system.

Of the three major powers interested in Hawaii, France was the most prone to use force against the Island kingdom. Perhaps the French realized they had virtually no friends within the kingdom while Great Britain, their traditional enemy and chief competitor in the Pacific, not only held the favor of the royal family but could count upon a fair number of supporters among Island inhabitants. In 1849 there were just a dozen French citizens living in Hawaii, and for many years even the French consul was a British citizen of French descent. Another irritant was Protestant dominance at a time when France considered itself the champion of the Catholic faith. It was easy for the French to believe they were discriminated against in Hawaii.

Many French warships came to Honolulu harbor and made demands on the kingdom, but the most distressing visit of all was that of Rear Admiral Legoarant de Tromelin in the summer of 1849. Admiral de Tromelin commanded the French Pacific fleet. When he arrived, the king, Gerrit Judd, and John Young were on the island of Hawaii. They had hurried back to Honolulu before they knew of the admiral's arrival, because John Young's wife had suddenly died. In the midst of the funeral rites the admiral demanded an audience with the king, and before Kamehameha III had time to reply he received a list of ten demands from the admiral.

Some of the demands were predictable. The admiral wanted a reduction on the brandy tariff, and he wanted Catholics to have as much control of the public educational system as Protestants. The admiral also demanded that the Hawaiian boys from Lahainaluna, who had prankishly dipped their hands in Catholic holy water, be punished. To agree to these demands would have meant that foreign powers had the right to interfere in the smallest internal matters of the kingdom, and the king was not willing to allow this. Rear Admiral Legoarant de Tromelin decided to teach Hawaii a lesson.

On August 25, 1849, a curious crowd watched an armed force come ashore. The Frenchmen proceeded to the fort, which faced the harbor. They spiked the cannons and pushed them off the walls, smashed muskets, broke swords and bayonets and threw them into the well, and dumped kegs of powder into the sea. The house of the governor of Oahu, which was within the fort, was reduced to a windowless skeleton filled with debris which had once been its furnishings.

The royal yacht, called the *Kamehameha III,* was stolen, and perhaps this upset the king the most. The schooner was close to his heart. It had been built four years earlier in Baltimore and had cost $10,000. A French crew sailed the vessel off to Tahiti. It was never returned. Later, the Hawaiian government asked for $100,060 in damages from France, but their demands were denied.

The admiral remained for several days to savor his victory and then sailed off. The French consul, who had brought the admiral to Hawaii through a series of distorted letters, realized he had better depart while he could. He loaded his furniture aboard and sailed away with de Tromelin.

Ten days before Christmas, 1854, Kamehameha III died. From Punchbowl forty-one minute guns announced his death. Criers ran through the streets calling out the news. So, in his forty-first year, passed the man who ruled Hawaii longer than any other monarch. His funeral was a pageant, a mournful spectacle which combined the pomp of England with the warmth of the Hawaiian spirit.

The thirty years during which Kamehameha III was king were restless, unsettled times. Hawaii was gingerly feeling its way in a strange new world, and Kamehameha III epitomized the hesitant nation. Just before reaching his majority and assuming actual control of the kingdom, he had rebelled against the regent, Kinau, because she, with the support of the chiefs, had refused to buy him the yacht he so desperately wanted. In his resentment he threw off all the missionary restraints and for nearly two years lived the kind of life he wanted. Then he repented and reformed.

During his years as ruler he alternately swung between the extremes of embracing the mores of his ancestors and being a pious, closely controlled Christian. At one time Kamehameha III owned three distilleries and at least one public house but later he forbade the manufacture of all alcoholic beverages in his domains. As a young man he broke the law against fornication, and when Kaahumanu reminded him of the penalty he voluntarily sentenced himself to labor at building the stone walls of a cattle pen.

In his youth he deeply loved his half-sister, Nahienaena. Many chiefs in addition to the king favored the marriage, but the missionaries protested loudly. The word of God, they said, forbade such a union. The king did not marry Nahienaena, but he did have a child by her. The infant died, and the mother lived only briefly. The king proclaimed the day of his half-sister's death a national day of mourning. For the missionaries the fate of Nahienaena and her child was proof that God would not allow such things to go unpunished.

The earthly kingdom of Kamehameha III was threatened by the British, French, and Americans, and the missionaries threatened his soul with eternal damnation. Threatened in this life and for all eternity and hemmed in by restrictions he found unnecessary, Kamehameha III must have prayed that some avenging Hawaiian god would sweep these intruders forever from his Islands.

The avenging god did not appear, and alcohol served as a substitute. As often as he could the king escaped from Honolulu and went to Lahaina, where he felt free of the pressures which were such a burden to him. For a time the seaside village of Lahaina was actually the capital of the Islands.

In December, 1850, F. Gerstaecker stopped in Honolulu on a journey around the world. He noted that "if Kamehameha I had conquered the whole group, with the war-club in his hand, and the battle cry on his lips, Kamehameha III for his part, was entirely conquered by the spirit—partly that of religion through the missionaries, and partly that of cognac through the French—but conquered he was. . . ." Gerstaecker nevertheless found the king a pleasant fellow, and he expressed an opinion concerning his excessive drinking. "Kamehameha III does his best to kill himself with strong drinks, and I really believe a great part of the cause lies in the restless talk and tedious warning of the missionaries, in opposition to the old chieftain's pride. . . . What I heard of the king in Honolulu was all in his favor; he is, if left to himself, a kind, friendly man, only, of course, distrustful toward strangers—and he has just cause for it. In spite of his drinking, he is strong and active yet, being an excellent horseman, and a very good hand in the noble art of self-defense, possessing at the same time most extraordinary strength of muscles."

There was truth in the comments of traveler Gerstaecker, but the appraisal leaves out the substantial accomplishments which took place during the reign of Kamehameha III. Many of these achievements were in the area of social legislation, and while they were often initiated by Westerners, they would not have materialized if Kamehameha III had not been a rather liberal king willing to make changes which he believed would benefit his people. The first step along this road took place in 1839 when a Bill of Rights was enacted which gave protection to the people and their property and stated that "nothing whatever shall be taken from any individual, except by express provision of the law." The following year Hawaii had its first constitution, changing the form of the government from an absolute monarchy to a constitutional monarchy. This document established a legislature, consisting of a house of nobles and an elected representative body, which allowed commoners a voice in the government for the first time. A court system was also established.

One of the most significant changes concerned land ownership. The total mass of the Islands is small, and steep mountains reduce the usable land to a fraction of the total. Thus land in Hawaii has always been precious. In ancient times the land belonged to the king, who dealt out parcels for the use of those chiefs who supported him. The beginning of land reform started in 1845 when a land commission was established. Three years later the Great Mahele, or division of lands, took place. In a somewhat complicated exchange of titles, the land was divided among the king, the chiefs, the government, and the common people. This whole transaction involved some 4,030,000 acres of land. Commoners received only about 30,000 acres of this, so the redistribution did not make them great property owners. But the achievement should not be underrated. A pattern of land ownership had been established which made it possible for commoners to own land for the first time. The Great Mahele was a boon for the haoles, because it made it possible for sugar planters to gain title to land, which speeded the development of that industry.

Now it was a December morning in 1854, and the king was dead. William Parke, marshal of the kingdom, and Abner Paki, a high-ranking chief, were in charge of the funeral. As the chiefs descended on Honolulu from the neighbor islands to attend the rites, each of them, some 2,000 in all, were supplied with appropriate black clothing. The king's palace was likewise draped in black.

The funeral services had been set for January 6, but heavy rains made streets quagmires, and the services were delayed until January 10. On that day the subjects of the late king lined the streets and spread grass before the funeral car so it could more easily pass. The Hawaiian cavalry, infantry, and artillery, all draped in black, were followed by the band with muffled drums. The black charger of the late king was led before the funeral car, its trappings empty, and this sight caused the crowds to wail aloud. Kamehameha III had been a gentle and unassuming king, deeply concerned for the welfare of his people. His good traits were the best traits of his people.

The funeral had been a costly affair, totaling some $28,000, and the chore of paying the bills fell to William Parke. During the two weeks following the funeral, Parke went about Honolulu protected by a guard of soldiers and paid the bills from a wheelbarrow loaded with coins.

The haole who wielded the greatest power in the government was Gerrit Parmele Judd. He was born in a village south of Utica, in central New York state. The family was Calvinist, and for some 175 years they had been staunch New Englanders. Judd's father made a sufficient living, although the family was far from wealthy. Fear of God and nought else was their ruling principle.

Young Judd, like his father, wanted to become a doctor and attended Fairfield Medical College, where he obtained a good medical education. Gerrit Judd was a heavy-boned, squarely built man with a rather handsome face and intense eyes. His countenance was stern, if not downright forbidding. He chewed tobacco and in later years easily put on weight.

Judd was of a serious turn of mind, interested in questions of morality and religion. When he heard the noted evangelist Rev. Charles G. Finney, he experienced a religious illumination which remained a driving force for the rest of his life. He was moved to apply to the American Board of Commissioners for Foreign Missions for appointment as a physician. A year later he was accepted for the Hawaii mission with the understanding that he would eventually preach the Gospel as well as heal the sick.

Dr. Judd now had to solve the same problem others had earlier faced: he needed a wife before departing. His choice was Laura Fish, a lady who had undergone many hardships during her young life and who had likewise experienced a religious awakening. An uncle of Judd's did the proposing, and a month later Laura and Gerrit were married. Less than six weeks later they were on their way to Hawaii.

In Honolulu the Judds set up housekeeping with Reverend and Mrs. Bingham. Dust blew through the clapboards of the frame house in which they shared quarters. What medical fees Dr. Judd earned went into the common treasury which supported the entire mission. Laura Judd wore second-hand clothes sent out by mainland supporters. By 1831 Judd had studied enough theology to be allowed to preach. A year later the mission decided physicians need not be ordained ministers, and medicine again took first place in Judd's thoughts. Four years after coming to Hawaii the Judds left the Binghams and moved into a cottage of their own.

Hard work was a part of Judd's religion. En route to Hawaii he and his wife had studied Hawaiian, and by the time they reached the Islands they could speak the language fairly well. They also gained the respect of royalty. When Kamehameha III defied his advisors and returned to the ways of his ancestors, Kinau, the distressed regent, came to the Judds for consolation. The relationship became so close that their first daughter was named Elizabeth Kinau.

There was no chore the doctor would not attempt. He constructed buildings, he preached, practiced medicine, spearheaded temperance drives, and cultivated twenty-two acres of land which the king had given him near the entrance of Manoa Valley. Children were arriving periodically, and Laura spent her time taking care of them and keeping a journal which is one of the most interesting of missionary chronicles.

In late 1840 Lieutenant Charles Wilkes arrived in Hawaii in command of a U. S. exploring expedition. Judd accompanied the group to the island of Hawaii to act as doctor, interpreter, and manager of the Hawaiians they would hire. The doctor spent several months with Wilkes, and when the work was completed the naval officer surprised Gerrit Judd with a gift of $700. Many of the missionaries were annoyed with Judd for, first, abandoning his medical duties for several months and, second, for personally accepting the $700 which they felt should go into the communal treasury.

The argument raged so hot in Honolulu that the matter was referred to mission headquarters in Boston. In a burst of indignation Judd declared he would turn the money over to the mission, and the mission decided he could keep the funds after all. By the time these angry decisions were reached the whole matter had become academic, because Judd had resigned from the mission. On May 10, 1842, he had been appointed President of the Treasury Board of the kingdom.

The government badly needed assistance. Soon a French captain came to Honolulu making demands, and shortly after that Lord George Paulet showed up. As Judd accepted other cabinet positions, his power grew. He was tough, enormously hard-working, and possessed deeply ingrained ideas of right and wrong. His admirers thought he held the kingdom together. His detractors claimed he placed letters before the king which were signed without being read. They ridiculed his pretensions and called him King Judd.

Gerrit Judd got the king to sign a temperance pledge and bought him a billiard table to keep him home and out of trouble in town. He set up the kingdom's first system of keeping fiscal accounts and reduced the national debt. His very presence probably scared some persons about him into remaining honest. In the course of all this Judd came to verbal blows with nearly every prominent citizen in Honolulu. In 1848 his enemies attempted to impeach him on the grounds of his financial dealings. They were unsuccessful.

Judd's government posts brought him into contact with many kinds of people, and his former missionary associates thought he had become too secular. The businessmen in town considered him too stern and rigid. The result was that he lost friends from both sides. No matter what kind of devil he might have been considered in the community, he was a hero in his own home. He was warmly reassured by his wife and eight children.

The charges against Judd became nearly continuous. In 1853 a petition was presented to the king demanding his dismissal on the grounds that Judd was pushing too hard for annexation to the United States. At last, by the end of 1853, Gerrit Judd was overcome by a host of enemies, and he resigned. To the end he was stubborn and hostile to all those who disagreed with him.

Out of government employ, Judd needed substantial income to support his large family. He attempted many things, including practicing medicine, farming lands on windward Oahu, selling life insurance, raising sugar cane on Maui, and collecting guano from distant atolls. In all of these things he enjoyed only minor success.

On July 12, 1873, Gerrit P. Judd died. He was buried in a cemetery near his home, and on his headstone are the words "Hawaii's Friend." If helping to maintain the monarchy was being "Hawaii's Friend," the epitaph is true, because Judd did much to shore up the kingdom.

Chapter Nine

"THEY WILL EAT US UP . . ."

Davia Malo was a different kind of Hawaiian. Physically he was tall, slim, and dark. He was unusually intelligent, sensitive, intense, and possessed of great nervous energy. By birth he was a commoner, although his father had been a warrior of Kamehameha I. Young Malo's agile mind retained the complex genealogies of the high chiefs, and he soon became a popular court fixture on the island of Hawaii. A chiefess, much his elder, claimed the young man as her husband. During these early years he was apparently content with the drinking, dancing, and general frivolity of court life.

In the 1820s David Malo went to Lahaina. His first wife had died, and he again married an older chiefess. Together with Princess Nahienaena and others, he attended a nonmissionary school. Malo was an exceptional scholar, and in September 1831 he was among the students selected to make up the first class at the mission school at Lahainaluna. When Kaahumanu visited Lahaina, she urged Malo to get a good education so that eventually he could assume a high government position.

David Malo quickly learned to read and write Hawaiian, and he gained a fair knowledge of English. He read every Hawaiian book and pamphlet printed by the school press. In 1832 Kaahumanu died and Malo was grieved. He wrote a song of lamentation which began with references to ancient Hawaiian mythology:

> . . . her spirit glides away to the far regions
> beyond Kahiki. She flies; averting her eyes,
> she fades away in the wild mists of the
> northland, the deep, dark, mysterious north.

Near the conclusion of the poem Malo describes her departure in the light of Christianity, the consuming passion of Kaahumanu's later years:

> . . . She sings praise-psalms of joy in the
> paradise of glory, in the everlasting day time

of the Lord. He is our Lord, the everlasting
Lord, He indeed, in truth.

The teachers and missionaries at Lahainaluna tried to make the best
use of their talented pupil. Malo worked closely with the school principal,
Rev. Lorrin Andrews, in writing Hawaiian history, mythology, and custom. He wrote a biography of Kamehameha I, but subsequently the manuscript was lost. He helped translate parts of the Bible into Hawaiian.

David Malo became a devout Christian and warmly applauded the
work of the missionaries. But other haoles perplexed Malo. He saw whaling captains threaten missionaries who tried to stop boatloads of women
from going out to the vessels. At one time Reverend Richards reported
such a case to the mission board in New England, and a story on the incident appeared in the *Missionary Herald*. The captain named in the article
was considered a respectable New England family man, and when he
learned that his activities in Lahaina had appeared in print on the East
Coast, he was wild with indignation. He demanded the monarchy punish
Reverend Richards. By continuing the affair the captain had little to gain
except added publicity, and so the case was dropped. Malo tried to practice Christian principles in daily life, and he quickly discovered that nominally Christian sailors seldom did the same. He was firmly convinced that
the nonmissionary haoles would destroy the Hawaiians.

In 1837 Malo wrote a letter to Kinau, who was then queen regent:

> *You must think. This is the Reason. If a big wave comes in large
> fishes will come from the dark ocean which you never saw be-
> fore, and when they see the small fishes they will eat them up;
> such also is the case with large animals, they will prey on the
> smaller ones; the Ships of the whitemen have come, and smart
> people have arrived from the Great Countries which you have
> never seen before, they know our people are few in number and
> living in a small country; they will eat us up, such has always
> been the case with large countries, the small ones have been
> gobbled up.*

David Malo was labeled a radical, and the chiefs and most missionaries would have liked to ignore him, but he was too popular, too bright,
and too sincere a Christian to be put aside. He was a successful businessman, growing and grinding sugar cane. The molasses he produced was in
demand throughout the kingdom because of its superior quality. He grew
cotton and wove cloth, from which he made his own clothes. In 1841 he
was appointed the first superintendent of schools for the kingdom, a job he
held until 1845. He was elected a member of the first house of representa-

tives in 1842. A year later the missionaries licensed him to preach, the second Hawaiian to receive this privilege.

All of this success, however, did not change David Malo's ideals. He still believed the nation was being taken away from the Hawaiians. In 1845 a petition reached the king which bore the signatures of many Hawaiians, but the thoughts were clearly those of David Malo:

> . . . if this kingdom is to be ours, what is the good of filling the land with foreigners? . . . the native man is palsied like a man long ailing in his back. . . . If a good thing, let the coming of foreigners into this country be delayed for ten more years perhaps, and let there be given to us lands with the understanding that they are to be cultivated and have cattle raised upon them, and so perhaps we shall lose our present palsy, and it will be good perhaps to encourage foreigners to enter the country.

The king sent an investigating commission to Lahaina, which quickly determined that David Malo was the man behind the petition. Somehow Malo was persuaded to stop creating trouble.

In mid-1848 word reached Honolulu that David Malo and others were plotting to overthrow the government. There were numerous rumors. The English flag would be run up. The fort would be seized by force. Henry Swinton, sheriff of Lahaina, kept the government informed about Malo's activities. Swinton believed there was "more mischief in him than people dream of," but he did not believe Malo would do anything dangerous.

The situation was serious enough for the king to tour Maui, giving speeches explaining that foreigners would be in the government only until there were enough trained Hawaiians to fill the positions. The furor quickly died. The earlier rumors of revolt were undoubtedly exaggerations. Laura Judd had an explanation for Malo's discontent: "Now Malo expected some good position under the new organization, and was disappointed in not getting it. The chiefs were afraid of his *radicalism,* for he was good and talented and conscientious. . . ."

David Malo's attempts to keep Hawaii for the Hawaiians had failed. He turned his thoughts to religion, and in 1852 he was the second man of Hawaiian ancestry to become an ordained minister. He was given charge of a tiny coral rock church at Keokea on Maui. At the time of his ordination the *Polynesian* reported he was "of feeble health."

David Malo had a heavy cross to bear. His second wife had died, and he had married a third time, a young woman named Rebecca. Rebecca bore him a daughter, but she was far from being the ideal wife for a Christian minister. She disappeared for days at a time with strangers, and she wore flowers in her hat. Malo beat her and prayed for hours with her, but Rebecca's changes of heart were only temporary.

Thirteen months after he was ordained, David Malo lay down to die. He would neither eat nor drink, and the faithful from his congregation gathered at his side to pray. He asked to be taken to Lahaina and was carried there in a canoe. He asked that his body be buried on a hill behind the town, because he believed that the cemetery lands in Lahaina would some day be coveted by haoles and then his bones would be disturbed. In October, 1853, David Malo died and, as he requested, was buried on a hill high above Lahaina.

In reporting his death Rev. William Alexander wrote, "I do not know what disease he had; he seems to have had a general failure of vitality, a wearing out of the machine."

Most missionaries quickly became convinced that liquor was one of the worst enemies of the Hawaiians. Many missionaries were not teetotalers when they arrived in the Islands. They often enjoyed a glass of wine or rum, but when they saw the debilitating effect liquor had on Hawaiians, most missionaries became abstainers.

Kamehameha I had consumed a substantial amount of rum in his day, but when he saw that alcohol was subverting the entire nation, he gave up drinking and eventually enacted a prohibition law. A good portion of the adult life of Kamehameha II was spent in a drunken languor, and during his short reign there were no restraints placed on liquor consumption. Drunkenness among chiefs and commoners reached epidemic proportions.

After Kamehameha II died Kaahumanu wielded great authority, and following her conversion to Christianity she was a powerful temperance advocate. Both Kamehameha III and IV sporadically advocated temperance, but their support was often half-hearted. One of the favorite demands of the French warships which came into Honolulu harbor was that brandy be allowed to enter the kingdom duty-free, and this made laws on liquor control useless.

The temperance movement which began in the United States in the 1820s and continued into the 1830s had its effect on Hawaii. During these years many a captain came to port preaching as well as practicing abstinence. In 1843 Rev. Samuel C. Damon began publishing *The Temperance Advocate and Seamen's Friend*. During its early years this monthly paper dwelled heavily on the pitfalls awaiting those who indulged, giving many examples. Later the title was shortened to *The Friend,* and it devoted more of its columns to other happenings in the community.

Honolulu's business community recognized the problem and gave the temperance cause a boost in the 1850s when a club was formed called the

Dashaways. The name came from the pledge members took—that they would dash away liquor from their lips. Its membership included many of the most prominent of Honolulu's business world.

A lesser evil, but still an evil in missionary eyes, was the circus. By 1850 the population of California was great enough to attract entertainers from the East. Winter weather in California sometimes caused circus groups to try their luck in the Islands. It must have been a profitable adventure, because from 1851 on nearly every winter brought at least one circus company to Hawaii.

A circus in the 1850s was relatively small and simple. It might consist of acrobats, trained ponies and riders, perhaps a black-faced comic, and a strong man. The performances were often bawdy affairs, and if the audience included seamen the chances of a riot were substantially increased.

On November 23, 1857, Professor Risley and his circus arrived from the Columbia River region. Nearly a year had passed since Honolulu had seen a circus, and the rush for tickets was overwhelming, but the *Advertiser* added it was "not greater than the performance merited." The circus advertised that within their tricolored tent "The strictest decorum observed." The sensation of the show was Monsieur Devani, "the India-Rubber man." Honolulu newspapers were fascinated with him. His act produced "astonishment and admiration," and the circus promoters were happy to supply all the details the newspapers would print.

As the weeks passed, Devani continued to be the major attraction. He was "a complete prodigy—a human puzzle. . . . While traveling with Prof. Risley in Europe, the medical fraternity of both London and Paris solicited the privileges of a private examination of M. Devani's physical construction, which was readily granted, and the result was that they declared he set all the laws of nature at defiance—made, as he was, like other men—and they could not account for his extraordinary performances."

Richard Risley Carlisle, known professionally as Professor Risley, had performed for Queen Victoria in the course of his career as a very successful circus entrepreneur. Risley was an all around athlete, excelling in skating, wrestling, jumping, hammer throwing, marksmanship, and together with his two sons, pioneered circus acrobatics. The professor was also a betting man. Once he lost $30,000 on the outcome of a single game of billiards. When he was in Honolulu, Risley's popularity was fading. He later left the circus world for the theater, which proved disastrous for him. Sixteen years after his Honolulu appearance the professor died in a lunatic asylum in Philadelphia.

On December 14, 1860, a renowned visitor, Prince Albert, came to

Honolulu. Seldom had visiting nobility caused so much excitement. The *Advertiser* reported two weeks after his arrival that "The natives . . . are all wonder and astonishment." Prince Albert was the first elephant to visit the Hawaiian Islands.

Prince Albert belonged to the Dan Rice circus, which had come from a successful season in California. A day after the elephant arrived an ecstatic reporter wrote: "Have you never seen an Elephant?—now is your time. Do you ever want to see one?—now is your time; or forever after hold your peace." The circus could not perform until December 21, because heavy rains turned Honolulu into a morass. When the show did open, the tent could not accommodate the crowds. Some 1,000 men, women, and children stood outside to catch a glimpse of the elephant. The newspaper ad for the circus carried a large illustration of an elephant, and a news story on December 20 described the show as having "some of the most renowned actors in the world. Besides these there is the celebrated elephant ALBERT, which is the first animal of the kind which has ever been brought to these islands." Prince Albert was a star.

The *Polynesian* became sentimental about the whole thing. They noted that the circus would be "long remembered; and as of old, mothers marked the age of their children from the death of Kamehameha or the war on Kauai, so the year of the Elephant will hereafter be noted as an epoch to date from." Two days after the circus had sailed, a reporter wrote of the nostalgia felt by many Honoluluans. The place where the circus had stood, "whence their antics and gambols made the town vocal with human notes of exclamation, stands lonely and forlorn."

Occasionally theatrical groups came to Honolulu, and in 1855 Edwin Booth arrived with several fellow actors. Booth was only twenty-one and practically unknown at the time, although his father was the famous Shakespearean actor, Junius Brutus Booth. A younger brother, John Wilkes Booth, also an actor, later became infamous as the assassin of Abraham Lincoln.

Booth came to Honolulu on his return from Australia, where he had been part of a touring company. They had struggled through two weeks in Sydney and had tried their luck at Melbourne, but business was very poor. As their ship stopped at Honolulu harbor, they spotted the Royal Hawaiian Theatre and decided to give the town a try. Pooling their funds, the company came up with $50, enough to rent the theater for one month. The only woman in the group was Laura Keene, and after an argument with Booth she climbed aboard the vessel on which they had arrived and sailed off for San Francisco. The actors did not have enough money to rent rooms, so they slung hammocks in the theater.

The Hawaiians liked *Hamlet* the best. They sat in the pit watching and listening with great intensity, and between acts they excitedly discussed their interpretations of the happenings. The overall favorite in Honolulu was *Richard the Third*. Kamehameha IV came to the performance, but he could not be seen publicly since the official period of mourning for the late king had not yet passed. The king therefore sat in the wings in an armchair, and when a scene called for a throne, the king graciously surrendered his chair for use on stage. After the performance the king patted Booth on the shoulder and told him that he had seen his father play *Richard the Third* in New York.

The little group of players had to improvise all the way. Laura Keene had departed in anger, and the best substitute Booth could recruit to play the part of Lady Anne in *Richard the Third* was an unattractive man whose only theater experience was as a stage hand. Another problem was putting up posters around town. Booth claimed he was reduced to doing this himself, because the Hawaiian boys who were hired ate the poi, which was used as paste, and threw away the posters. It would seem more likely that Booth put up the posters out of sheer economic necessity, although the story about poi made an amusing tale in later years.

Edwin Booth and his fellow actors spent thirty-nine days in Honolulu. The plays they performed were mostly Shakespeare, and they were well received, although the financial rewards were small. When Booth landed in San Francisco he had $10 in his pockets.

On September 13, 1859, the inter-island sailing vessel *Maria* came to rest at its pier in Honolulu harbor. It was a routine occurrence, but the news the ship brought shocked Honolulu to its foundations. The king had shot and seriously wounded his personal secretary at Lahaina.

Henry A. Neilson was the victim. He was a handsome man with dark hair, heavy eyebrows, and large eyes. He was an Eastern gentleman, well spoken and with gracious manners, who came from a distinguished and successful New York family. His father was a respected physician, and E. H. Harriman, later a railroad tycoon, was a nephew.

Henry Neilson left New York to seek his fortune and by 1849 was engaged in trade in California. He went on a voyage to Canton, China, and on his return he stopped at Honolulu to dispose of some merchandise. When he arrived economic conditions in the Islands were so poor that he had difficulty in selling his goods. Eventually he became the Hawaiian representative of the New York Board of Underwriters.

In letters home Neilson told of his visit to the island of Maui, of reading Herman Melville's *Typee,* of his bout with smallpox, his concern for a girlfriend who had not written, and of hearing the famous Kate

Hayes sing in Honolulu. He described Queen Emma as being "rather short, and not remarkably beautiful,—but still good looking." In March, 1855, he proudly announced to his family that he had been named private secretary to the king. His salary was to be $2,000 a year, but since he would take his meals at the palace this was "as good as 4 or $500 more."

Henry Neilson performed few official acts. His real job was to serve as companion to the king, and the two often traveled through the Islands, expeditions which were mainly good-time jaunts. The same month in which he received his appointment Neilson wrote home requesting a number of things, including a ring with the family coat of arms and a large reproduction of the coat of arms for hanging on the wall. By the end of the year he sent home a daguerreotype of himself in full uniform.

In the middle of 1856 Neilson reported an accident. He and the king were testing new pistols which a salesman was trying to sell the king. The king stepped forward to fire, and Neilson stood behind, his pistol in his right hand. The muzzle of Neilson's gun pointed into the calf of his leg, and for some reason the gun discharged. The ball went down through the calf and was extracted in the area of the ankle. No bones were broken, and after two weeks in bed Neilson was able to hobble about.

Some respectable citizens of Honolulu felt that Henry Neilson and others were a poor moral influence on the king. Neilson not only had a mistress, but he brought her to official functions. On one occasion a Honolulu housewife stopped Neilson on the street and expressed the hope that he would soon return home. Hawaii, she told him, was a bad place for unmarried men.

Events went gaily along until September, 1859. At that time Kamehameha IV was at Lahaina with Neilson and others. The group had been making a "progress" through the Islands and, as usual, having a good time. In spite of this display of comradeship, the king had long been suspicious that Henry Neilson was having an affair with his queen. This suspicion seems to have been nurtured in the king's mind by a woman who traveled as a member of the royal party.

The night before the violence occurred, the king drank heavily and the next morning continued imbibing aboard his schooner off Lahaina. When his supply ran low, a case of liquor was sent to the schooner by canoe. The king stayed aboard until about 11 P.M. when he came ashore to the cottages and buildings which were scattered beneath a coconut grove and which made up the royal residence at Lahaina.

Neilson's version of the incidents which then happened so quickly was written to his brother some six weeks later. Neilson said he first saw the king on the veranda of the governor's house, where he was attended by his physician and several other persons. Neilson observed that the king was "in an apparently half delirious state." Neilson remained with the group for a short period and then went back to his own quarters. Before going to bed, however, he went out on the steps, and while he was there he reported that he saw one of the king's servants "being taken to prison for refusing to get him his pistols." Another servant promptly did the king's bidding.

A moment later the king appeared on the veranda, and his private secretary turned to meet him. Neilson did not notice that the king carried two pistols and

> *. . . when within three or four feet of me, without speaking he fired from a dueling pistol straight at my body. The ball struck me fair on the lower part of my chest, just where the short ribs join the breast bone, and where there is a good deal of cartilage, it then passed towards the right side, struck a rib about midway which it followed, and just managed to drop out a few inches below the right arm pit, passing as the physicians tell me, in a most miraculous manner, through the only part of that portion of the body, where a fraction on either side could have hardly failed to prove fatal.*
>
> *To return to the King—I made some exclamation, and turned into the hall, as I knew the doctor was on the seaboard side of the house, I felt myself bleeding rapidly but found the doctor who immediately assisted me to a small house near by, and calling another physician they did the best they could that night for me.*

Earlier in this letter to his brother Neilson had stated that the reason for the king's action was ". . . totally unfounded jealous suspicions of his Queen."

The tragedy was the talk of Honolulu. Later vessels from Lahaina added a few facts and a multitude of rumors, but the newspapers remained silent. Kamehameha IV was enormously distraught and stated that he wanted to abdicate. He requested a special meeting of the cabinet, which was already in a state of extreme emotion. At first it was decided that an official proclamation should announce what had happened, but this idea was subsequently overruled. Robert Wyllie, minister of foreign affairs, wrote to the king telling him that any declaration would only "exaggerate what has occurred."

Minister Wyllie sent a barrage of letters to the king, using every persuasive technique he could to keep him from abdicating. On September 24 he wrote, "I pray you, in God's name, for the sake of your pure and virtuous Queen and Your hopeful son the Prince of Hawaii, as well as of Your whole People, to banish for ever, such an idea from your thoughts—*without any further hesitation or consultation*—to turn your mind to business of State. . . ." Three days later David Gregg, then a member of the cabinet, was dispatched to Lahaina to tell the king that the cabinet would not accept his abdication. Again Wyllie wrote the king. "I believe all my Colleagues concur with me in a desire to disuade you from your purpose of self-immolation."

The king did what he could for Henry Neilson. He provided the best doctors the kingdom offered and paid all the bills. Tension was heightened by the fact that reports on Neilson's condition varied from day to day. One day the doctor reported the patient was improving, and next day Neilson's condition was called critical.

On October 1, 1859, the *Polynesian* finally broke silence with a one-sentence statement: "We are authorized to state, for the purpose of allaying any anxiety that may exist in the public mind, that the rumors in regard to His Majesty's abdication are, we are happy to say, without foundation." Twelve days later the king wrote a private letter to Neilson:

> *I shall commence by an honest statement to you, that the act committed by me was premeditated, founded upon suspicions long harrowed up and extending through a length of time, though facts could not sustain me in my suspicions, I felt they were well founded, and consequently acted in the manner I did."*
>
> *To say that I regret the sad occurance [sic] were too little, that I sorrow sincerely for the injuries I have unrighteously conferred, would hardly be justice even, but believe Sir, I would be thankful indeed if anything I may say in this letter, could fully convey to your mind the feelings of self reproach and sorrow which I assure you I feel night and day.*

On March 31, 1860, the *Polynesian* carried a story saying that Neilson had been brought to Honolulu at the suggestion of the king. "We are glad to learn that Mr. Neilson is not worse for the fatigue of the journey, but as his strength is yet feeble, his many friends will consult his interest by delaying their visits for a few days." The months rolled on and public interest turned to other things. Neilson remained bedridden, cared for by the king's doctors, and for a time he lived in the king's beach cottage. For nearly two years his condition did not change.

Then, on February 3, 1862, Wyllie wrote a letter to the king, who was on Hawaii. "It is my duty, altho a painful one, to inform Your Majesty that Mr. Neilson is rapidly sinking, and in the opinion of Dr. Hillebrand cannot live many days." Wyllie commented that tuberculosis was the cause of his decline, a remark which Kamehameha IV could hardly have believed. Robert Wyllie closed by noting that Neilson's "stomach has lost its powers of digestion, it rejects every thing, and the bowels are affected with Diarheea [sic]." The next day Wyllie again wrote. "I have just seen Neilson. The hand of death is upon him . . ."

It took Henry A. Neilson two and a half years to die. At about seven o'clock on the morning of September 12, 1862, his suffering ended. The next day a terse three-sentence item appeared in the *Advertiser* under the general heading of Notes of the Week: "Yesterday morning Mr. Henry A. Neilson died in this city. In former years he was well known, but for two years and a half has been confined to his room by the unfortunate occurrence which is familiar to all. His funeral will be held at 4 P.M. today."

Simple funeral rites were held over the remains of Neilson at the cemetery in Nuuanu Valley. It was a cold, overcast day with northerly winds, and only a few persons watched as his remains were lowered into a grave which would go unmarked.

Kamehameha IV had not recovered from the tragedy, nor would he ever. He and his queen had always felt a close alliance with England, and, as with numerous other monarchs before him, tragedy swept him toward the church. At the invitation of the king and queen, the English Episcopal church came to Hawaii. In late 1863 Kamehameha IV died. He had lived out his life racked by the injustice he had committed against Neilson and by the tragic, early death of his only son.

Four years after Sam Brannan had preached the first Mormon sermon in Hawaii, a group of young Mormon missionaries arrived in Honolulu. There were ten men in all, and after finding a place to lodge they climbed a hill behind Honolulu, and each man added a rock to a pile which formed a crude altar. One of the elders, George Q. Cannon, later wrote, "We then sang a hymn, and each one, in his turn, expressed his desires." The young men divided in pairs and set off to begin their work in the Islands.

Disappointment was close at hand. Most of the Mormons believed they had been sent to Hawaii to convert Caucasians, but Caucasians were few in number and uninterested. In three months half of the missionaries had given up and left. Elder Cannon thought their conduct disgraceful.

George Cannon was one of two sent to Maui. He and his companion were desperately poor. They boarded with a Hawaiian family in Lahaina for $4 a month. During this time Cannon realized that if the Mormons were going to succeed, it would have to be among the Hawaiians. Very soon the two missionaries could not afford the $4 a month, and they lived upon the charity of the Hawaiians.

George Cannon studied the Hawaiian language and decided to have a close look at Maui as well. He borrowed a valise from his companion and

Kamehameha I was not considered a handsome man, but few doubted his courage or dedication to the Hawaiians. This portrait of the King was painted by Louis Choris, a draftsman aboard Captain von Kotzebue's expedition, after he had sketched Kamehameha I in 1816.

Captain James Cook was a revered man when he died in 1779. This engraving, made from a drawing by John Webber, shows Cook being carried up to heaven after his death at Kealakekua Bay.

Hanakaulani, the aristocratic wife of Owen Holt, was the grand lady of the Holt estate at Makaha on Oahu. She brought up the Holt children partly as English gentry and partly as Hawaiian alii. Owen and Hanakaulani were not sure whether they should identify with their English or their Hawaiian heritages.

Sugar cane was the crop which brought economic stability to Hawaii. The accomplishment took back-breaking work. A sufficient labor force was a constant concern of the planters, and in the late 1880's the major source of this labor was Japan. Here a Japanese field hand is loading cane for transportation to the mill.

Lord George Paulet, captain of *HBM Carysfort*, seized the Kingdom of Hawaii for Great Britain in 1843. Paulet was a son of one of England's most distinguished families. During his stay in the Islands he purportedly fathered Hanakaulani by a Hawaiian woman of chiefly rank.

Major Henry Neilson, left, aide and companion of Kamehameha IV, died about a year after he was shot by the King, who suspected him of having an affair with the Queen. It took all the persuasive ability of the Cabinet to convince the grieving King not to abdicate. Neilson came from a well-known New York family. The man on the right remains unidentified.

In the early years, sugar cane was carried to the mills in carts drawn by oxen. Eventually tracks were laid through fields, and cane was transported in small railroad cars. Ways to improve growing, harvesting, and milling cane were constantly sought by the planters. The above photo was taken at Lihue, on Kauai.

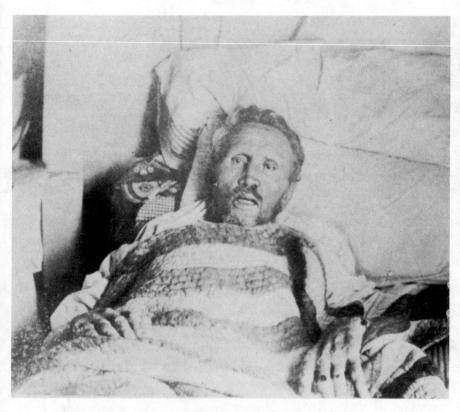

This photograph of Father Damien was purportedly taken a day before he died of leprosy at Kalapapa on Molokai. Clinical evidence of leprosy first became evident in his left foot, and the effects of the disease are apparent in his bloated hands in this photograph.

Robert W. Irwin was Consul General of Hawaii in Japan when an emigration convention was signed between the two countries in 1886. The convention opened the door for a massive migration of Japanese into Hawaii, which was arranged by Irwin. The Hawaiian Consul was paid for his work on a per-head basis and profited greatly. Irwin's wife was the daughter of a successful Japanese businessman.

Robert Louis Stevenson and King Kalakaua became friends during the writer's stay in Hawaii. Stevenson sympathized with the plight of the monarchy and at one time considered writing a pamphlet in its defense. As Stevenson departed from Honolulu, Kalakaua, accompanied by members of the Royal Hawaiian Band, bade him farewell at dockside.

Sanford Ballard Dole sits behind his desk, with Lorrin A. Thurston beside him. Thurston, a grandson of the pioneer missionary Asa Thurston, was the firebrand of the revolution of 1893. When Queen Liliuokalani was deposed, however, the more restrained Dole was chosen to serve as President of the new Republic of Hawaii.

LEFT: Robert Wilcox, a part-Hawaiian who had attended a military school in Italy, wanted to establish a strong monarchy. After the monarchy was overthrown, Wilcox made a futile attempt to restore it. A man of great personal ambition, he achieved his greatest victory when he was elected the first Delegate to the United States Congress after Hawaii became a Territory.

BELOW: Queen Liliuokalani was a strong-willed woman and the last ruler of the kingdom of Hawaii. In attempting to maintain control of the kingdom, she provoked the powerful business interests of Honolulu and was overthrown in a revolution which resulted in just one man being wounded.

Joaquin Miller was hiking in Manoa Valley during the insurrection of 1895. Soldiers of the Republic escorted the strange looking man to their headquarters in the King's bungalow, next to Iolani Palace, where Miller was identified and then posed in the doorway with soldiers. Joaquin Miller was a California poet who briefly visited Hawaii.

ABOVE: During the Spanish-American War the United States realized that Hawaii was a vital base when fighting a war in the Pacific. Here troops sit on the railing of a ship in Honolulu harbor, pausing before continuing on to the Philippine Islands. Once the value of the Islands was understood by officials in Washington, Hawaii was quickly annexed.

BELOW: The cruiser *USS Charleston* was a familiar sight in Hawaiian waters in the late nineteenth century. Kalakaua went to California aboard this ship in 1890, and the following year his body was carried back to the Islands in the same vessel. On the return voyage the superstructure of the warship was draped in black to let Islanders know the King was dead before the vessel actually docked.

Jack London visited Hawaii several times. Here he stands bedecked in leis aboard the *Snark* on his arrival in 1907. Behind Jack is his wife, Charmian. Like other writers, before and after, London became a controversial figure in Hawaii.

ABOVE: When the German firm of H. Hackfeld and Company was taken over by American interests during World War I, the German name of the company was chiseled off the main entrance of the head office in Honolulu. The new owners of the company renamed it American Factors, Limited.

BELOW: Shirley Temple was one of many celebrities who arrived in Honolulu by ship in the 1930's. Boat day was an important happening, and photographs of well known persons who arrived were sent to newspapers and magazines across the country. Behind Shirley Temple is Duke Kahanamoku, Hawaii's Olympic swimming star.

To begin his second tour of Army duty in Hawaii, George S. Patton sailed to the Islands in his own yacht, learning navigation on the way. Patton was an enthusiastic polo player and captained the Army team. During World War II, Patton talked with General Eisenhower about his wish to retire to Hawaii.

Sergeant Tadao Beppu stands before the main entrance to the Vatican in Rome when he served in the infantry during World War II. Tadao was one of the young men who upset the established Republican power structure after the war. He became Speaker of the State House of Representatives.

started walking. He found food and shelter from hospitable Hawaiians as he went. It was very primitive. Poi, in particular, was a trial for Cannon. The gray paste-like substance revolted him, yet he was determined to overcome this problem too. He later wrote: "I asked the Lord to make it sweet to me. My prayer was heard and answered; the next time I tasted it, I ate a bowlful, and I positively like it."

The persons least happy to see George Cannon were ministers of other denominations. The clergyman at Wailuku preached against Mormonism on a Sunday when Cannon was in the audience. The young man stayed after the service and argued with the minister. In the Kula district he listened to Reverend Green attack the newcomers, using as his text the words from St. Paul's epistle to the Galatians: "But though we, or an angel from heaven, preach any other gospel unto you than that which we have preached unto you, let him be accursed." When the sermon was over, but before the congregation had been dismissed, Cannon stood up and presented his views. The congregation dispersed in confusion.

Word spread that a new religion was being preached, and curious Hawaiians came to look and listen, which supplied George Cannon with an audience for the first time, and there were several converts. When Protestant and Catholic clergy realized they were actually losing a few members, they put pressure on the fallen, who often returned to the true religion.

The first great success for George Cannon came at the village of Keanae, a small point of land which juts out from the mountainous north shore of Maui. Cannon's fellow missionary on Maui had been working on the residents of this village in advance of Cannon's coming, and he had done his work well. George Cannon arrived on a Wednesday, and by Monday he had baptized more than 130 persons. Apparently neither Protestant nor Catholic ministers were at Keanae when this great conversion took place, but once they heard of the happenings there they descended on the village and preached the evils of Mormonism. Cannon reported that one "French priest had said that we ought to be driven out of the place and off the island. . . ."

Less than two months after coming to the Islands Cannon started to translate the Book of Mormon into Hawaiian. It was a great task, since the young man was simultaneously trying to learn Hawaiian. In three years, with considerable help from Islanders, the task was done. A printing press, type, and paper were ordered, but when they arrived Cannon had completed his service and was in California. The equipment was sent there, and the California mission appointed Cannon to supervise the printing of the Book of Mormon in Hawaiian. In 1855 the job was done.

The Protestants and Catholics vocally opposed the Mormons, and the government, while not persecuting them in any way, did hinder their work by refusing to grant elders the right to perform marriages. The reason given was that Mormons believed in polygamy, although there is no evidence that this doctrine was ever preached in Hawaii. The greatest harm the Mormons suffered during these early years did not come from outsiders, but rather from opportunists within their own ranks.

John Hyde, Jr., was a great annoyance. Hyde had been sent from Salt Lake City to Hawaii as a Mormon missionary in 1856. Somewhere enroute John Hyde had a change of heart, and in October, 1856, he lectured on the evils of Mormonism to a packed house at the Bethel chapel. A Honolulu newspaper reported that "At the close of the lecture, a member of the Mormon community had the impudence to get up before the assembly and charge the lecturer with horse-stealing, which, whether the charge was true or not, was deemed altogether out of place. . . ." The man who made the charge then sent a letter to the editor of the newspaper saying Hyde had "charged a whole community with dishonesty, in their absence, which in any other cause but that of Mormonism, would be considered mean and cowardly."

The Mormons wanted to escape this harassment, and they decided to establish a gathering place where the faithful could work and follow their beliefs without interference. Such a colony would be in keeping with the instructions of President Brigham Young, who had expressed the hope that Salt Lake City would eventually be the gathering place for all Mormons. Until that could be accomplished he advised the Hawaiians to "obtain a fitting island or portion of an island where the brethren can collect in peace and sustain themselves unmolested." A Mormon elder, Francis A. Hammond, founded a congregation on the small island of Lanai, across a narrow channel from the town of Lahaina. In 1853 Hammond rode into the interior of Lanai, to an upland plateau called Palawai, an area which had once been a volcanic crater. The area had possibilities, and it was decided Palawai would become the gathering place for the faithful.

A Hawaiian chief on Lanai generously allowed them to live on the land without cost, and the Mormons came with their possessions. Livestock was loaded aboard a scow which rowers in three whaleboats pulled to the island at night to avoid the intense heat of the sun. They planted sweet potatoes, corn, beans, and melons. Elder Green laid out the streets for a town, and by the end of 1854 fifteen houses had been built.

In 1856 the Mormons opened an English-language school where classes were conducted six hours a day. Some twenty children were students during the day, and a like number of adults came at night to study English. Half interest in a small vessel was purchased to carry produce to market and bring supplies to the island. Insects and drought, however, made Lanai something less than a farmer's paradise. During the annual general conference of October, 1857, it was decided that another location should be sought.

No move was made, however, for in 1858 missionaries were called back to Utah because of the threat of war between the Mormons and the United States. The colony on Lanai was left under the care of Kelehune, who soon began raising money to purchase 10,000 acres on the island. When he used the money for his own purposes, he was excommunicated. With the missionaries gone, the Mormon church in Hawaii declined.

By 1861 Mormon influence in the Islands had nearly disappeared. On July 4 of that year Walter Murray Gibson arrived in Honolulu. With him were his daughter, Talula, and two men, H. B. Eddy and C. O. Cummings. Gibson presented himself as a man of literary accomplishments and gave lectures on Malaysia in the Fort Street church. Neither he nor his entourage revealed that they were of the Mormon persuasion.

Gibson moved quickly to build a reputation for himself. He sent H. B. Eddy to the offices of the *Advertiser* with a handful of old newspaper clippings which described Gibson as a very distinguished man. Eddy identified himself as the son of a Massachusetts clergyman and correspondent for an East Coast newspaper. The initial reaction to Gibson was favorable, but as the weeks passed some Honolulu citizens became suspicious of him. One reason was that Gibson stayed on in Honolulu, although he had early stated that his real destination lay farther on in the Pacific. Another was Gibson's southern accent; the American Civil War had just begun, and some believed Gibson's real reason for being in Hawaii was to outfit a Confederate privateer.

The *Advertiser* voiced its doubts about Gibson in print. One story declared that Gibson's party was "concealing the real object of their mission." After two months in Honolulu Gibson and his followers departed for Lahaina. His activities were mysterious, and the government watched him closely. Some of the people in official positions in Honolulu became alarmed. The U. S. Commissioner wrote to the Hawaiian foreign minister, "Walter M. Gibson is an enemy to your Government." David Gregg wrote to the king, "Let him be watched. . . . Mr. Gibson is a pirate;—Mr. Gibson is a Mormon;—Mr. Gibson is a secessionist."

At Lahaina Gibson designed and flew a flag of his own, which brought new speculations. The flag included eight stars, and first reports described it as the Confederate emblem. In October, 1861, it was confirmed that Walter Murray Gibson was a Mormon. In that month the Mormons held a conference on Maui, and Gibson revealed to the faithful few that he carried a commission from the church. He had letters from President Young and a very impressive certificate with seals and colored ribbons. He also displayed a gold watch which had been given him by Brigham Young. Having established his right to lead the Mormons, Gibson moved to Lanai, which he called the Hawaiian Zion. He gave himself the title of Chief President of the Islands of the Sea, and of the Hawaiian Islands for the Church of Latter-Day Saints.

Walter Murray Gibson indeed was a baptized Mormon. His romance with the religion was the latest event in a life which had been full of adventure and intrigue. The Mormon phase of it had begun when Gibson became acquainted with Dr. John M. Bernhisel, the Mormon representative in Washington, D. C. at the time when war seemed likely between the United States and the Mormons in Utah. Gibson came up with the idea of removing the Mormons to New Guinea and thus eliminating the problem. Dr. Bernhisel and Gibson succeeded in getting an audience with President Buchanan and presented their plan. The plan was considered but rejected because of the cost.

Gibson still had hopes of selling his idea to Brigham Young. He spent the fall and winter months of 1859 in Salt Lake City and the January 15, 1860, issue of the *Deseret News* recorded the fact that "Walter Murray Gibson and Talula Lucy Gibson were baptized by Heber C. Kimball at 7:30 P.M. in City Creek. . . ." Gibson lectured on the Pacific and proved to be an enormously popular speaker. Such great crowds came to hear him that the only place large enough to hold the audiences was the Mormon Tabernacle, and President Young granted special permission for its use. Gibson's descriptions of the Pacific were so moving that many Mormons would undoubtedly have followed him there if official sanction had been given.

Walter M. Gibson apparently became something of a problem, and Brigham Young sent the new convert to New York to do missionary work. Being a Mormon missionary on the East Coast at that particular time was trying if not dangerous. It was not the kind of situation which offered much chance of success, and it certainly was not what Gibson wanted. Soon he was back in Salt Lake City, but he was not given much time to disrupt things there. Three weeks after his return he was sent forth as an elder to do missionary work in the Pacific. President Young had sized up his disciple. He wrote "If Brother Gibson would magnify his calling he would do more good than he ever anticipated doing."

Walter Murray Gibson said he was born on January 16, 1822, aboard a storm-tossed vessel in the Bay of Biscay. His parents were poor farmers who lived in the hinterland of South Carolina. Gibson taught school as a very young man, and at the age of seventeen he married a neighborhood girl who was even younger. After four years of poverty and hardship his young wife died, leaving Gibson with three children. The widower found lodgings for his children and set out to seek his fortune.

As a child Gibson had heard tales of an uncle who had gone to India and become a very successful merchant. The stories caught the imagination of the boy, and he wanted to win success for himself. He went to sea and before long became master of his own small vessel. He tried his luck in South America, and on at least one occasion attempted gun-running. He went to the California gold fields and then headed for the Dutch East Indies.

Gibson easily envisioned himself as a powerful white ruler in the Indies. He made an amateur attempt at revolution against the Dutch in early 1852. He wrote a letter to the Sultan of Djambi which not only promised "powder, bullets, guns, muskets," but also implied the United States would assist in the uprising. The letter was intercepted by Dutch intelligence, and Gibson was promptly arrested. He was tried and sentenced to stand for half an hour under the gallows, spend twelve years in prison, and then be banished. Two weeks after Gibson was sentenced he escaped, probably with the knowledge of the Dutch, who could see no profit in feeding a prisoner for twelve long years. They profited in another way. By escaping Gibson forfeited his ship to the Dutch.

Back in the United States Gibson protested loudly to the U. S. government, presenting a very convincing case and demanding damages of $100,000. His case was pressed by Secretary of State Marcy with the Dutch government. Considerable feeling was generated as notes flew back and forth between the two nations.

In presenting his case Walter Murray Gibson, of course, denied attempting to start any sort of revolt in the Dutch East Indies. The affair suddenly became embarrassing for the U. S. when a letter written by Gibson to the Governor of Netherlands India was added to the evidence. In the letter, written after his arrest, Gibson admitted his guilt. The letter read in part, "I remember to have indulged in bravadoes that I would become a potentate in the East and this to Europeans and natives, who I cannot suppose to have attached any importance to what I said, than as a vain glorious boast; but I must ever add in extenuation that this was after a plentiful indulgence in wine."

"I have been too often led away in life by some high colored romantic idea."

Secretary Marcy wrote to the President of the United States in January, 1855, suggesting the matter be dropped.

Gibson continued to be led away by highly romantic ideas. He traveled to England, because he somehow believed another baby had been born aboard the same vessel at about the same time he was born. The parents of this child were English nobility and, of course, Gibson was convinced that somehow the two infants had been switched. In England Gibson gazed at portraits of his supposed noble parents, and he found the resemblance to himself striking. Before leaving England he visited Nathaniel Hawthorne, who wrote a glowing account of the young adventurer. Back in the United States Walter M. Gibson became acquainted with Dr. Bernhisel and his Mormon adventure began.

In November, 1861, Gibson was on the island of Lanai, the leader of the Mormons in Hawaii. He had great enthusiasm, and some thirty Hawaiian men and women toiled beside him at Palawai. Momentarily contented, Gibson wrote in his diary, "I would fill this lovely crater with corn and wine and oil and babies and love and health and brotherly rejoicing and sisters kisses and the memory of me for evermore."

The immediate, urgent need was money—money to buy land on Lanai. And Gibson was the man who knew how to raise money. The church became his fund-raising instrument. Church offices were sold. The position of apostle went for $150 while a simple meritorious certificate could be bought for 50 cents. The faithful were implored to give to the very limit. The Hawaiians became his "red-skinned brothers and sisters," and they were urged to give not only all the cash they could, but also anything else which had value. Goats, horses, turkeys, chickens, kapa, and furniture were collected by Gibson's men and sold for whatever they would bring. As the money came in, Gibson bought land.

In May, 1862, Gibson believed he had found what he wanted and reported his contentment in his diary.

> *I say this is my heaven, my shelter from the sad storms of life.*
> *My heart is full of song, of the song of the valley, of the hills, of*
> *the sea, and of my sweet child Talula more than all. Oh I do*
> *think this is something of the peace and sweets of what is called*
> *a better world. For is not that better world all within us, and*
> *may it not be here? . . . I have had happiness on Lanai. My*
> *pulse has beaten time with the melodies. I run and rejoice in my*
> *strength. I stretch out my limbs for sleep and it comes without*
> *coaxing.*

Lanai was the scene of great activity. The Hawaiians were taught handicrafts, wells were dug to add to the water supply, girls were taught the proper care of children and how to organize a home. Gibson's two male followers, Eddy and Cummings, concluded they were not going to become rich and powerful following this kind of life, so they drifted off to further adventure in the South Pacific. As Gibson gained power the Mormon religion was of less use to him, and he paid less and less attention to religious matters. This neglect concerned some of the faithful, and eight Hawaiians joined in writing a letter to Brigham Young in December, 1863. Brigham Young sent out a committee to investigate. On April 2, 1864, the committee arrived on Lanai.

Two public meetings were held to discuss the situation. At the first Gibson arrived late, and as he walked to the front of the meeting room the Hawaiian congregation rose in deference to him. It was a calculated demonstration of the power he held over his followers. The Hawaiians were not moved by the pleas of the committee members. At the second meeting Gibson announced he was not accountable to these intruders, and he once again displayed the certificates he had brought from Salt Lake City.

One day Talula Gibson took two of the visiting committee members riding. They came upon a large boulder enclosed with a fence of poles, and the two visitors dismounted to look inside. Talula asked them not to enter, but her plea was ignored. A chamber had been cut into the boulder and inside was a Book of Mormon. They learned that Gibson had proclaimed the boulder would be the cornerstone of a great temple and that anyone who went within the fence would be struck dead. If the Hawaiians saw some emerge unharmed, Talula feared their faith would be shaken.

During their six days on Lanai, the committee members were unable to convince the Hawaiians that Gibson should be cast out. They returned to Lahaina and there voted to excommunicate Walter Murray Gibson. They declared that those who were true to the church must leave Lanai. Eventually a new gathering place would be chosen. Not only did the investigators fail to dislodge Gibson, but they also failed to obtain title to the lands on Lanai which Gibson had bought with Mormon contributions. Title to the land was in Gibson's name, not in the name of the church, and Gibson must have enjoyed this triumph over the committee. Years later Gibson wrote a newspaper article in which he stated, "Our temporary connexion with the Mormon Community for a political object, of which we shall give a history at our convenience, is well-known and has never been denied."

The Hawaiian settlers at Palawai dwindled away because Gibson no longer made an effort to practice Mormonism and because of a constant shortage of water. Gibson was faced with the problem of repopulating his domain. In 1868 he decided sturdy New England farmers were what he needed, and he traveled to New York City to find them. He described his wonderful lands on Lanai to a reporter from the *New York Times* who quoted him as saying, "A sugar field in the Islands is worth many gold mines." Thirty-two New England farmers did come to Lanai, but they found a dry and unpromising land, and most of them quickly left in disgust.

In the later 1860s J. M. Lydgate and Dr. William Hillebrand visited Lanai on a botanical trip. They spent several days at the Gibson ranch, which they described as a primitive place. The best fare Gibson could offer his guests was roast mutton, boiled rice, molasses, and coffee. If the dinner was not particularly memorable, the entertainment which followed was. Walter Gibson reminisced of his days in the Dutch Indies and his guests were fascinated. During the course of their stay Hillebrand discovered a "striking and rather showy plant" a very rare lobelia, which he named *Cyanea Gibsonii* in honor of his host.

A primitive life and an ever dwindling number of subjects was not the world Walter Gibson wanted. He turned his attention to Honolulu, where eventually he would become one of the most powerful, controversial men in Hawaii's history. His years on Lanai were only a prelude.

Royal scandal, the excitement of the circus, and tales of the strange beliefs of Mormons might entertain or shock Hawaii's residents, but they did not provide a livelihood. During the 1840s most businessmen made a living by supplying the varied needs of whaling ships. If the season was good, officers and crews would have money to spend. If the catch was poor, the ships would be few, only limited supplies would be bought, and crews would have little to spend in the grog shops. The cornerstone of Hawaii's economy rested on a very unsure foundation. If whaling grounds in the Western Pacific became barren, Hawaii's economy would collapse.

It appeared to some of the more farsighted businessmen that the most desirable base for their economy would be agricultural products which could be exported. If some staple could be grown which would be in demand in foreign countries, Hawaii could have a dependable economic base. Cotton was grown and silk culture was seriously attempted. Coffee and cattle ranching provided a living for a few. None of these endeavors were sufficiently profitable to serve as the cornerstone of the economy.

By the middle 1840s it was beginning to appear that sugar offered the greatest opportunity for success. In the '40s Koloa plantation, started by Ladd & Company, continued to be the best example for others to follow. After Ladd & Company collapsed Dr. R. W. Wood acquired the plantation, and it continued as a profitable operation. In 1846 there were eleven plantations in the Islands, most of them consisting of small acreage. The cane grown was obtained locally, descended from the varieties carried to Hawaii by the Polynesians. A mill usually consisted of two vertical stone or wooden rollers turned by horse or bullock power. Cane stalks were hand-fed through the rollers one at a time, and so much juice remained in the crushed cane that it would not burn. The juice was boiled in try pots obtained from whaling vessels. The equipment was frequently moved to the areas where cane was easily accessible. The process was wasteful and the sugar was of low quality.

The sugar was sold wherever a market could be found. Australia, the East Coast of the United States, and a small market on the West Coast provided the main outlets. When the California gold rush quickly turned that area into a well populated state, Hawaiian sugar had a vastly increased market. During the early and middle 1840s the export of sugar seldom exceeded 200 tons. In 1849 some 325 tons of sugar was exported and in the following year over 370 tons. Export figures hovered around these new high marks, except for the year 1851, when severe competition in California and inferior Hawaiian sugar reduced exports to a ruinous ten tons. One bad year was enough to close down several plantations.

The sudden increased demand for sugar emphasized some of the painful problems which the industry had long faced. One problem was a lack of capital. Sugar plantations required large outlays for equipment and for the wages of laborers. It took approximately eighteen months for a crop of cane to mature, and additional months passed before the sugar was sold and the proceeds returned to the plantation. Long-term financing was a necessity. Capital was scarce and interest rates were usually 9 percent or more.

The California gold rush heightened another problem for the planters. Laborers by the hundreds departed for the gold fields at a time when many sugar men wanted to expand, and several plantations closed because labor was not available. Up to the gold rush days Hawaiians had provided the great majority of plantation labor, but now demands were greater and the Hawaiian population was fast declining. Beginning in 1852 a few workers from the Orient were imported, although Hawaiians continued to supply the bulk of plantation labor until well into the 1870s.

A third problem concerned high United States tariffs, a substantial obstacle along the road to fortune. There had been discussions about a treaty with the United States which would allow the goods of each country to enter the other duty-free, and this idea was pushed with new enthusiasm. The United States, however, had little to gain by such an agreement and was unresponsive. To many Hawaiians such an intimate agreement with the U.S. seemed to be a dangerous step along the road to annexation.

These problems did not prevent the planters from attempting to improve methods of growing and refining sugar. Perhaps the single most valuable advance occurred in late 1850 or early 1851. At that time a description of a centrifugal machine which would separate molasses from sugar reached Honolulu. David M. Weston, a skilled mechanic, began manufacturing the parts and building the machine from the written description. The machine was then tested on a Maui plantation. The results were sensational. Prior to this time molasses had been separated from sugar crystals by drilling a hole in the bottom of the sugar keg and allowing the molasses to drain out slowly. The process not only took weeks but did nothing to improve the quality of the sugar. In minutes the centrifugal did extremely well what had taken weeks to do poorly before. There was a great saving in time, and the higher quality sugar commanded better prices.

Among the successful merchants who entered the sugar-growing business was Boston merchant Henry A. Peirce. Peirce had made his fortune once in Hawaii, but in 1849 he returned on a trading voyage. On visiting Kauai he observed that the land around Nawiliwili Bay was ideally suited for raising sugar cane, and so he organized H. A. Peirce & Company with a total capital of $16,000. Peirce put up half the sum and William L. Lee, the first supreme court justice in Hawaii, and Charles R. Bishop, the man who would become Hawaii's foremost banker and the financial savior of sugar, each put up $4,000.

H. A. Peirce & Company changed its name to The Lihue Plantation ten years later, and under that name it became one of the most profitable and famous plantations in Hawaii. Its success was partially due to the tenacity of its early owners, partially to its excellent location, and partially to imaginative plantation management. But in the beginning profit and fame were far distant. The first crop, harvested in 1853, totaled between one fourth to one third of what was expected. Much of the 1854 crop rotted because of continuous storms. During these first years James F. B. Marshall, the man who carried the dispatches to England during the Paulet affair, was manager and part owner of the plantation. Other well known investors included W. C. Parke, marshal of the kingdom, and E. O. Hall, the patriotic songwriter.

In 1854 William Harrison Rice bought an interest in the plantation and became manager. Rice had come to Hawaii as a missionary-teacher and had taught agricultural courses at Punahou School. Rice was worried about the future of his family, because a constant cough reminded him that his health was poor and because the New England board had withdrawn financial aid to the Hawaiian mission. He went to work at Lihue for $400 a year plus house, firewood, ground for pasture, and garden for an orchard. In 1856 Rice spent $7,000 on an irrigation ditch which brought water over a ten-mile course to the fields. The experiment was a great success, and other plantations soon began digging irrigations ditches.

One of the best things which happened to The Lihue Plantation took place on November 8, 1858, when a young German immigrant was hired at a wage of $20 a month. His name was Paul Isenberg and he had traveled halfway around the world to manage a cattle ranch and farm owned by a German trading firm in Honolulu. Isenberg was a big man physically, and to the German merchants who had brought him to the Islands he looked like a big lazy ox. They refused to hire him, and so he found a job at Lihue.

Four years later Isenberg was manager of the plantation. He was just twenty-five years old, but he had shown a great capacity for hard work, and under his leadership additional lands were brought under cultivation. Three years after becoming manager he had saved enough money to buy an interest in the plantation. During the evenings he studied bookkeeping and became proficient in Hawaiian. He sent for a younger brother who became a master at boiling sugar and who, in turn, passed his knowledge on to another younger brother.

Paul Isenberg went to Scotland to buy the best sugar mill equipment. Additional irrigation ditches were dug, and the cane from neighboring plantations was ground at the Lihue mill. Isenberg, son of a Lutheran minister, had a Lutheran church built at Lihue, where he installed Rev. Hans Isenberg as minister. He brought a man trained in the Prussian forest service to Kauai and reforested 5,300 acres of mountainside behind the plantation.

In 1878 Paul Isenberg returned to Germany and made his home in Bremen. He kept close watch on his business interests in the Islands and returned every two years for extended visits. In 1898 he was elected president of the large Honolulu merchandising and factoring firm of H. Hackfeld & Co. When Paul Isenberg died in 1902, his personal estate amounted to $7,000,000. By that time Lihue Plantation was one of the largest, most modern and prosperous plantations in the world.

By 1860 sugar was the leading agricultural crop, and it promised to become the bulwark of the economy. The extent of the financial rewards was still uncertain, but hopes were high. The great day for sugar lay just ahead, and a catastrophe made that day a sudden reality. The catastrophe was the American Civil War, which created a tremendous demand for sugar in the Northern states. In Hawaii that cornerstone of the economy had at last been found.

Chapter Ten

"HONOLULU HAS NOT BEEN
THE SAME SINCE"

T HE OUTBREAK OF the American Civil War was announced in the *Polynesian* on May 11, 1861. The attack on Fort Sumter and its subsequent surrender were reprinted just as they had appeared in San Francisco newspapers. The newspaper noted: "The storm so long pending has at last burst over the land, and the Lexington of the second revolution has been inaugurated in blood."

During the first months of the war battle reports were often contradictory and generally confusing. The newspapers printed what reports came to their hands, but beyond the fact that the two armies were in combat, little was known. By the end of August it was reported that the Confederates had been the victors at the first battle of Bull Run.

By November, 1861, the reporting had improved. One reason for this was the completion of the transcontinental telegraph line which placed San Francisco in rapid communication with the East Coast. The telegraph meant that events in the East would reach Hawaii, via San Francisco newspapers, some two weeks faster than previously. A Honolulu newspaper called the telegraph line "the most important event in modern history."

The feeling with which U.S. citizens in Hawaii greeted the war could hardly have been exceeded by their most enthusiastic mainland cousins. Far from home, small in number, the American citizens in Hawaii were moved to let all know their great devotion to their country in its time of peril. The United States was new, less than 100 years old, and they believed they were the founders and makers of the country. Many of their grandfathers had fought in the War of Independence, and they remembered this with pride. They believed the United States had been eminently blessed by God, and these beliefs were demonstrated by unashamed emotion and fierce pride.

Most of the Americans in Hawaii came from New England, and their sympathies lay with the Union. In early June, 1861, they cheered a Union naval vessel which arrived in Honolulu. The ship's crew hung a banner over the doorway of their favorite bar which read "No secession! What our fathers fought for we will maintain—the Union!" On July 4 a giant flagpole, 175 feet tall, was raised in Honolulu, and a silk American flag was pulled up by the women who had sewn it. Union sympathizers wore red, white, and blue rosettes or neckties. H. W. Severance, a merchant, advertised "UNION BUNTING! . . . very superior quality . . ."

In Hilo Thomas Spencer woke up his neighbors early on July 4 with a noisy display of patriotism. He had organized Spencer's Invincibles, a company of eighty infantry men. They paraded in Hilo, and later their leader spread a feast for the neighbors he had awakened. In December, 1861, Spencer petitioned the monarchy to allow him to transport his troops to the North to fight, but the kingdom had declared its neutrality and forbade Spencer to leave the Islands, because a breach of neutrality could give Confederate privateers a reason to prey on Hawaiian registered ships. The decision reduced Thomas Spencer to tears.

In late Summer of 1861 a young lady visitor to Honolulu hung a Confederate flag from her veranda. A newspaper reported that the daughter of a neighbor entered the premises and "pulled down the emblem of rebellion." The newspaper account went on to editorialize, "All honor to her, whoever she was; she had the blood and spirits of '76 flowing in her veins." Later, the newspaper happily noted the Confederate flag had been confiscated when the young lady returned to San Francisco.

Many Islanders volunteered for military service with the Union. One was Henry Hoolulu Pitman, the son of a prominent Hilo merchant. Henry's mother was Hawaiian, and probably because of this the twenty-year-old youth ended up in a black regiment. Private Pitman was captured and placed in a prison camp. He died of "lung fever" February 27, 1863, and was buried at Mt. Auburn Cemetery, near Boston.

Some of the Islanders who enlisted were attending schools on the East Coast at the beginning of the war. Nathaniel B. Emerson, the son of a missionary, was at Williams College. He enlisted in the First Regiment of Massachusetts Volunteer Infantry. Emerson was wounded twice at Fredericksburg and once at Chancellorsville. He recovered in time to see action at Gettysburg, where an exploding shell ripped off the back of his cap. His enlistment had expired, but he remained with his regiment throughout the Richmond campaign. Nathaniel Emerson went back to school, earned his M.D. degree, and returned to Hawaii, where he became known as a physician, translator of Hawaiian lore, and historian.

Confederate sympathizers in Hawaii were a small minority, and they could ill afford to make a public display of their feelings. Curtis Perry Ward was among these. Ward came to Hawaii from Kentucky in 1852 and became a successful businessman. He married a part Hawaiian woman and built a home in downtown Honolulu which he called "Dixie." His beach home in Waikiki was named "Sunny South"; fifteen years after the Civil War had ended, he built another home called "Old Plantation." The sentiments of Ward were well known, but he could say little. Yet every night he had the satisfaction of going to sleep under the Confederate flag, for the Rebel banner formed the under part of the canopy above his bed.

Now and then familiar names appeared in the newspapers—names oldtimers remembered. In early 1863 it was reported that Abbott Brinsmade, the only son of Peter Brinsmade, had lost a hand in battle. Abbott Brinsmade was a captain in the Confederate army, and his wife, a native of New Orleans, had been arrested as a spy in New York, although she was not convicted. The end of 1861 brought news of Captain Charles Wilkes, the man who had spent time in Hawaii with his exploring expedition twenty years earlier. Wilkes was in command of the *San Jacinto* when it overtook the British mail steamer *Trent*. Two southerners, Senators James Mason and John Slidell, were taken off the vessel. The captain's action made him an instant hero in the North, but the seizure brought a fierce denunciation of the Union by Britain. In the end the senators were released. The dispute is remembered as the Trent affair.

At the beginning of the Civil War whaling fleets were beginning to shrink, because whale oil was being displaced by petroleum. The war speeded the dissolution of the whalers. Some ships were transferred to military service and others were laid up to await the war's end. The vessels which did put to sea numbered about half the prewar fleet. And, as in the American Revolution and the War of 1812, the whalers which dared to venture out suffered heavily. Confederate privateers destroyed them by the dozens.

Honolulu businessmen who made livings by supplying the whalers had to look elsewhere for income. Some discovered that the expanding sugar plantations throughout the Islands needed representatives in Honolulu who could purchase the multitude of supplies and services which were needed and in turn sell the sugar which the plantations produced. Some of these representatives helped finance their growing clients, and in several years a number of plantations discovered they were owned by their Honolulu agents.

There was no dearth of merchandise in Hawaiian stores. Trade with the East Coast fell off, but the West Coast and foreign countries were happy to fill the needs of Islanders. Honolulu newspapers regularly advertised wares from Hamburg, Bremen, London, and Liverpool. Now and then news of Hawaii-bound ships being sunk by privateers caused head-shaking. The *Contest,* a vessel well known in Hawaii, was sunk late in 1863 by the privateer *Alabama.*

All the sinkings were in the Atlantic Ocean, although there were continuing rumors that a Confederate privateer had invaded the Pacific. The potential for destruction was enormous. Two or three months might pass before it could be confirmed that an overdue ship had fallen victim to a privateer, and the marauder could be half a world away by then. Apprehensive Hawaiian businessmen feared the worst.

Near the end of June 1865 there seemed to be some basis for these apprehensions. The Hawaiian vessel *Pfiel* returned from a long cruise into the Western Pacific. On March 30 they had been stopped on the high seas by a steam vessel, and the officers who came aboard questioned the crew about the location of whaling ships in those seas. The newspaper account of this encounter concluded with the statement, "There is very little doubt but what the ship described is the *Shenandoah.*"

The *Shenandoah* and the *Alabama* shared the distinction of being the most famous Confederate privateers. Both ships had been secretly bought in England by representatives of the Confederacy. They had been manned by skeleton crews of Rebels and silently slipped from English harbors. Final preparation of the *Shenandoah* took place south of England, at a tiny island close to Madeira. James T. Waddell, formerly a lieutenant in the U.S. Navy, was in command. His ship was a sound one—220 feet long, with six-inch teak decks, two engines, and three masts. The lower half of the masts were hollow iron and the upper portions wood. It was well enough armed to deal with any merchant ship it might encounter.

The *Shenandoah's* initial problem was that she was undermanned. With every ship she captured the alternative was given the crew: join up or be locked up. Many a seaman who had no deep feelings about the Civil War took the easy way out and signed on. Before many months had passed the *Shenandoah* listed a number of Hawaiians among her crew, men who had been signed on from prizes. They were good crewmen, and Captain Waddell expressed a preference for them.

The *Shenandoah* sailed southward through the Atlantic, rounded Africa, passed through the Indian Ocean, and called at Melbourne for supplies and repairs. Australia, together with Great Britain, sympathized with the Confederate cause, and the crew was welcomed as heroes. Some crew members, however, were not so enchanted with life aboard the *Shenandoah.* Eight of them deserted, encouraged by the U.S. minister at Melbourne. Australian newspapers noted with pride that among the officers aboard were Sidney Smith Lee, Jr., a nephew of Robert E. Lee, and John Thomas Mason, the adopted son of James Mason, whom Wilkes had pulled off the *Trent*.

When the *Shenandoah* sailed from Melbourne, she carried enough "stowaways" to more than make up for the deserting crew members. The vessel moved northward, destroying Union shipping. One journal kept aboard related encountering the "P. Fiert of Honolulu," which was probably in truth the *Pfiel*, which reported being overhauled in those same seas. Because of information learned aboard the Hawaiian ship, the *Shenandoah* headed toward the Mariana Islands.

Hunting was good in the Marianas. The Confederates found four whalers, placidly riding at anchor, and destroyed three of them without hesitation. The fourth vessel, named *Harvest*, was a different matter. When the Rebels came aboard, second mate George Rowland displayed a bill of sale as proof the vessel had been sold by Americans to Hawaiians. The skeptical Confederates noted that the ship's officers were the same under Hawaiian as American ownership, although nearly all the seamen were Hawaiian. The Rebels sent the crew ashore and set the ship afire.

By the time Hawaii learned of the activities of the *Shenandoah*, the raider was far north of the Islands, making an arc across the North Pacific. The privateer probably never came closer than 1,500 miles to Hawaii, and the neutral Island kingdom certainly held no interest for the Rebel sailors. Cruising through the Sea of Okhotsk the privateer sank more ships, and the destruction continued down the coast of North America. At about this time Waddell was told the Confederacy had surrendered, but he refused to believe the news. He continued on, around South America, and finally to England, where on November 6, 1865, he became the last Rebel commander to pull down the Stars and Bars.

Many of the whalers which the *Shenandoah* sank in the Pacific carried predominantly Hawaiian crews. Periodically these crews were loaded aboard a captured vessel which made its way to the nearest port. The seamen usually landed penniless and with inadequate clothing. In August, 1865, the *Gen'l Pike* brought about fifty destitute seamen to Honolulu. Later the same month another vessel brought forty seamen to the Islands. Prior to this the *Kamehameha V* had been dispatched to the Mariana Islands to pick up the crew of the *Harvest*. The government paid the shipowners $50 for every seaman brought back. In January, 1866, the Privy Council appropriated $2,357 to aid stranded Hawaiian seamen in foreign ports.

The businessmen of Honolulu were in an uproar over the sinking of the *Harvest*. It was legally owned by three Honolulu businessmen at the time she was set afire and left to burn on a reef in the Marianas. The owners of the vessel were not only distressed by the loss of the ship, but also by the fact that she carried thirty-five barrels of whale oil. They estimated their total loss at $74,091.53.

The Confederates could not be wholly blamed for their action. Rebel privateers had been so successful that hundreds of Union-owned vessels were actually or nominally flying the flags of other countries. Any bill of sale displayed by a captain was looked at with skepticism. The most damning evidence against the *Harvest,* however, was the fact that she carried a supply of both Hawaiian and Union flags in her lockers, and an officer admitted they were not particular about which they flew. When the first mate of the *Harvest* later testified before a U.S. Senate committee, he said he did not know which flag was up at the time they were boarded.

The legal controversy over the *Harvest* continued into the 1930s. Lawyers and the descendants of the owners persisted until all hope of recovery had disappeared. The United States government would accept no responsibility for the actions of the Confederates. The Southern states no longer existed, and the only entity which could be sued was Great Britain, the nation which had sold the *Shenandoah* to the Confederacy and supplied it in the ports of her dominions. The complications were too great, and the case at last faded into history.

Captain James L. Waddell, the dark-complexioned Southern gentleman who had caused such a flurry in Hawaii, finally visited the Islands in 1876 as captain of the *City of San Francisco,* one of the new Pacific Mail Company steamers. The vessel remained overnight in Honolulu harbor, and Waddell drew no special notice or welcome. The next day, as the vessel cast off ropes, it was given the usual farewell by the Royal Hawaiian Band. The *Hawaiian Gazette* later noted that the band had played *Dixie.* The newspaper was uncertain whether this was done thoughtlessly or as a compliment to the captain, but it deplored the fact that Captain Waddell dipped his flag in response to the music.

The memory of the *Shenandoah* lingered. In mid-1924 Wallace Farrington, governor of the territory of Hawaii, suggested to the Navy that their new dirigible, named the *Shenandoah,* be the pioneer in establishing an air route between California and Hawaii. Such a good will flight would help erase the memories of the original Rebel privateer. Consideration was given the suggestion, but a year later the dirigible was rent into three pieces during a violent storm over Ohio.

The career of one Union officer was watched with particular pride by many Islanders. He was Samuel Chapman Armstrong, son of Rev. Richard Armstrong, a missionary, government official, and sugarcane grower. Young Armstrong completed two years of college work at Punahou School and went off to enter the junior class at Williams College. He was full of high spirits, of self-confidence and considerable irreverence. Life, Armstrong believed, would lead him to some extreme. He felt he was destined to become either a missionary or a pirate.

With the coming of the war, emotional tides of righteous indignation swirled about Williams College, and Armstrong was carried along, although his feelings were tempered by the fact that he considered himself a Hawaiian, not an American citizen. Nevertheless he joined up and in April, 1861, went to Troy, New York, where he was granted the right to recruit his own company. He pitched his tent in the city park and was able to fill his quota ahead of others because he was the son of a minister and religious parents were more willing to allow their sons to serve under him. His quickly became known as "the Sunday school company."

After three months of training, Armstrong's company was involved in a minor battle at Harper's Ferry where the Union forces suffered a defeat. For the next two years Armstrong performed a variety of military chores. Then, in July, 1863, the young man was promoted to major and ordered to take charge of six companies of United States black troops. Armstrong felt that the future of the black race depended largely on how their troops acted in battle, and he set about building up the pride of the unit. He took his troops into battle at Petersburg and they performed well.

The soldiering life appealed to Armstrong. From the front he wrote, "It is a splendid sight to see shelling at night, to watch a huge 13-inch mortar shell shoot far up into the heavens and then seem to glide awhile among the stars, a ball of light, then slowly descend in terror and vengeance into the heart of a great city whose spires are in sight from here. . . ."

Samuel Armstrong's most distinguished battle action came on the last day of the battle of Gettysburg. On that day General Pickett's division attacked the center of the Union lines at Cemetery Ridge. Armstrong, with five other officers and a detachment of men, took up a position on the flank of the oncoming troops. They did an effective job, pouring an unexpected fire into Pickett's men. Of the six officers only Armstrong survived. Near the end of 1864 he was put in charge of the Eighth U.S. black troops close to Richmond and promoted to full colonel. He was close to Appomattox Court House when Lee surrendered. Shortly thereafter Armstrong received the brevet rank of brigadier general of volunteers. He was twenty-six years old.

After the Civil War was over, a war in Mexico threatened to involve the U.S. and Armstrong was among those ordered to Texas to stand watch on the border. The danger soon subsided. Armstrong was offered a regular army commission, but he decided to return to civilian life. Like many other soldiers after many other wars, Samuel Armstrong was at loose ends. He toyed with the idea of business, but more and more his thoughts turned toward being "of use to my fellow men."

Armstrong had spent much of his army career associated with black troops. They had got along well together, and he had come to certain conclusions concerning the future of the blacks in the United States. He believed that simply freeing the slaves was only a beginning and that somehow they must be helped into the stream of American society. In 1865 few persons had such foresight. Most Northerners thought only in terms of freeing the slaves. After that things would take care of themselves.

In 1866 Samuel Armstrong went to work for the Freedmen's Bureau, an organization whose purpose was to help blacks adjust to their new situation. Armstrong was given the chore of administering twelve counties in Virginia. He made his headquarters at Hampton. During the early months of 1866 as many as 18,000 meals a day were dispensed by his staff. Slowly the situation improved, and Armstrong realized that there were a great many blacks in his area physically capable of working but who could find nothing to do because they possessed no trade skills. He came to believe that industrial education was the answer.

Armstrong had absorbed a certain amount of knowledge concerning the processes of education from his father, who had once been minister of education for the kingdom. As a boy he had traveled to various islands as his father inspected the school system. Armstrong particularly remembered the Hilo Boys' Training School where young Hawaiians had been taught trades. To him there was a marked resemblance between the situation in Virginia and in Hawaii, and he began to solicit funds to start a training school.

Hampton Institute was the name of the school Samuel Armstrong founded. The first funds he raised were used to purchase 159 acres fronting the Hampton River. Money was slow in coming and Armstrong continued to work for the Freedmen's Bureau for five more years to make a living while his embryo school took form. At the end of a long day Armstrong often retreated to his library, where he was surrounded with numerous pictures of Hawaii, and played the flute for relaxation. Slowly his dream gained substance.

In late January of 1870, Armstrong traveled north and met with the Hawaiian Club of Boston. The meeting was organized by an old friend, James F. B. Marshall, who had been a Sunday school teacher of Armstrong's at the Bethel Street church in Honolulu. In an adjoining room the Abolition Society was also meeting, but in their case it was for the purpose of disbanding their organization. Armstrong later reflected on this and wrote, "Their work was just beginning when slavery was abolished."

Armstrong quickly made a name for himself. He was offered the presidency of Howard University, and in 1872, the year in which he resigned from the Freedmen's Bureau to devote full attention to Hampton, he was offered the job of chief of the bureau of education of Japan at the high salary of $15,000 a year. By the time Armstrong was able to devote all of his time to Hampton, several capable men were already at the school. One was James Marshall, who came as treasurer and remained as a trustee until 1891.

Marshall also had a distinguished career during the Civil War. He had left Hawaii to return to Massachusetts, and when the fighting began he was put in charge of recruiting for the state. He became paymaster general for Massachusetts' troops and later was assigned to the Sanitary Commission, which included the hospital corps. His biggest job in this position was to care for the large number of wounded from Grant's Army of the Potomac. Like Armstrong, Marshall attained the rank of brigadier general.

Samuel Armstrong kept in close touch with the Islands over the years. They had a special place in his affections. In 1891 he was invited to give the fiftieth anniversary address at Punahou School. Less than two years later he was dead. His grave on the grounds of Hampton Institute is marked by a block of granite from the East Coast and a great volcanic boulder from the plain of Honolulu.

Following the Civil War, Hawaii saw its share of former Union Army officers. One of these was former Lieutenant Colonel Zephaniah Swift Spalding, who came in December, 1867. Spalding supposedly was on a very secret mission, known only to his father, who was a U. S. Congressman, to Secretary of State Seward, and one U. S. Senator. Spalding was to find out what effects a reciprocity treaty with the United States would have on the Islands and to describe general conditions in Hawaii. Spalding's mission might have been secret in Washington, but soon it was less than that in Honolulu. The Hawaiian government became annoyed with Spalding's pryings, but they could do little to rid themselves of him.

If the kingdom had known the kind of reports Spalding was writing, indignation would have run high. The former officer wanted annexation, not a reciprocity treaty. After his reporting was completed Spalding stayed on in the Islands and entered the sugar-growing business on Kauai. He recognized that reciprocity would greatly profit the sugar growers, and soon Spalding had changed his mind and became an advocate of such a treaty. On Kauai he did well for himself. He built a great two-story house on a ninety-acre estate and took tea in the afternoon by a waterfall while his wife played the harp. Eventually he went to Europe, where his children could receive a proper education and where his three daughters married Italian noblemen.

Another man arrived in Honolulu on January 15, 1873, bound on a secret reporting mission. This man, too, had been an officer during the Civil War. In fact he was still in the army when he visited the Islands. He was a graduate of West Point, had won the Congressional Medal of Honor during the war, and was one of Sherman's leaders and advisers during his march through Georgia. He ended the war with the rank of major general and in late 1865 was sent to Paris to settle the dispute between France and the United States over the Maximilian misadventure in Mexico. He did this successfully. For nearly a year, during the Andrew Johnson administration, he was Secretary of War. He was John M. Schofield, a popular and much honored man.

In 1872 Schofield was headquartered in San Francisco in command of the division of the Pacific. He received word from Secretary of War W. W. Belknap to go to Hawaii "for the purpose of ascertaining the defensive capabilities of the different ports and their commercial facilities, and . . . to collect all information that would be of service to the country in the event of war with a powerful maritime nation." It was believed the visit to Hawaii would "be best accomplished, if your visit is regarded as a pleasure excursion. . . ."

General Schofield spent about two months in the Islands. His announced reason for going was to recuperate from a recent siege of pneumonia. He visited the islands of Hawaii, Kauai, and Oahu. He discussed a reciprocity treaty with King Lunalilo, who must have had some intimation that the visit was more than a trip for the general's health. Perhaps only two or three persons really understood the significance of Schofield's mission. One was Henry A. Peirce, then U. S. Minister to Hawaii, and another was Charles Bishop, the banker.

Charles Bishop was a stern, upstate New Yorker who had come to Hawaii as a young man. He was industrious and honest and eventually became a cofounder and head of Bishop & Co., the only bank in the kingdom. When Schofield came Bishop was also foreign minister of the kingdom, and he assisted the general in his travels through the Islands. Bishop was an astute businessman. He knew that a reciprocity treaty could mean prosperity for the kingdom, and he knew just as well that such close ties would erode the sovereignty of the Islands.

There was another complication. Charles Bishop was married to a lovely and intelligent lady named Bernice Bishop, who was a granddaughter of Kamehameha I. Bernice was related to Hawaii's kings through her mother. Her loyalties were with the monarchy and against any entangling treaties. These differences of conviction in the Bishop household must have been one of the minor and quiet dramas of the day.

The report General Schofield sent to Washington D. C. showed that he was very impressed with Pearl Harbor, which he considered to be the only good harbor in the kingdom. He realized that the narrow mouth of the harbor had to be dredged of coral, but he thought this could be done for $250,000. As for the kingdom as a whole, John Schofield felt it would be a fine prize for the United States. Annexation, he believed, would come through evolution without overt action from the U. S. In his autobiography the general later wrote about the Americans in the kingdom: "While perfectly faithful to that government, they had lost none of their love for their native country, and looked forward with confidence to the time when the islands, like ripe fruit, should fall into the lap of their beloved mother." General Schofield's official report was not made public until twenty years later, although it was read at the time by the influential in Washington. His favorable appraisal of the Islands helped produce the climate necessary for the acceptance of a reciprocity treaty by the U. S.

The Civil War broadened the horizons of Hawaii's businessmen. Some revised their ideas concerning the potential of Hawaii and came to believe it would be helpful if the rest of the world knew more about the Islands. In Paris, in 1867, a great fair was to be held. Hawaii was invited to participate and the invitation was accepted. The kingdom had participated in fairs before, but now there seemed to be an incentive to do a bigger job.

Enthusiasm was substantial, but little happened because the government appropriated no funds, so everything had to be donated. Queen Emma and others loaned many things which could be displayed. Books in the Hawaiian language, feather leis, kapa, mats, and kahilis were sent. Samples of sugar, rice, coffee, and wool were collected. All of these things were packed in great tin boxes and shipped off in late February, 1867, but the two 15 by 20-foot rooms which had been rented at the fair were far from filled.

A call went out for additional display items, and the government agreed to stand the cost of building the needed display cases and furniture for the rooms. Henry L. Chase, a well known Honolulu photographer, contributed several Island scenes. Newspapers, furniture fashioned from Hawaiian woods, tobacco samples, lava rocks, pumice stone, and clinkers of sulfur from the volcanoes were sent off. A Bible, a hymn book, an arithmetic text, and a copy of *Pilgrim's Progress,* all printed in Hawaiian, were added.

William Martin, the Hawaiian chargé d'affaires in Paris, was a harrowed man. Display items arrived late. The cost of building the cases and furniture was too high and the workmen too slow. When the cases were finally finished, they were painted the color of sugar cane, and canopies were hung above them.

Martin prepared a folder, printed in French, which described the Islands and their people. The judges came on their rounds while the cases were still sparsely filled and the rooms unfinished. The official showing was poor. Hawaii won only four medals. The only gold medal was for agricultural products.

In a nearby building there was another reminder of Hawaii. It was the fierce image of Kukailimoku, the war god of Kamehameha I, which was a part of the display of the London Missionary Society. In the cases of the American Board of Commissioners for Foreign Missions were displayed the terrible idols which the Hawaiians had worshipped before the missionaries came.

In the 1860s Hawaii was in faster communication with the rest of the world than ever before. The big step in faster communications came in 1848 when the U. S. Congress subsidized the Pacific Mail Steamship Company. The following year service began between the East and the West Coasts. The vessels were paddle-wheel steamers, which traveled from New York to the Isthmus of Panama. Passengers and freight were carried across the isthmus and sent up the West Coast aboard another steamer. The whole trip usually took from twenty-six to thirty days. In 1855 the land part of the journey was made much easier when railroad tracks were laid across the isthmus.

The voyage between San Francisco and Honolulu took about twelve days, which meant passengers and mail from the East Coast could reach the Islands in the amazingly short time of five to six weeks. Not only was it a fantastic speed-up in communications, but there was even a nebulous kind of schedule. The Pacific Mail Steamship Company made three trips a month up the West Coast, and various vessels engaged in sailing to the Islands on a vaguely regular basis. Travel to and from the U. S. was also safer, because the hazardous voyage around South America could be avoided.

Not everyone in Hawaii was thrilled by what was happening. One was Dr. Hoffman, an obscure Honoluluan, who remembered the good old days and longed for their return. He is remembered as saying that times were much more pleasant in Honolulu when "we had the mails only twice a year round Cape Horn—ah, that was a magnificent time! Honolulu has not been the same since."

The first post office in the kingdom coincided with more reliable transportation. It was established by act of the Privy Council in late December, 1850. Before this bags of mail were taken off arriving ships and dumped on the office floor of the harbor master or a shipping agent.

Anyone who thought he might be receiving mail hurried down and sorted through the mail. Letters leaving the Islands were entrusted to a ship's captain who promised to mail them on arrival in the U. S. The normal fee the captain received was two cents a letter. Mail service between Honolulu and the mainland was on a twice-a-month basis, and service between Honolulu and the neighbor islands was about once a week.

In 1851 the first Hawaiian postage stamps were crudely printed on thin and brittle paper. They have become known as "missionaries," because the American missionaries in Hawaii used so many of them to send letters to the U. S. The three denominations which were printed were two cents, five cents, and thirteen cents. The thirteen-cent stamp allowed two cents for the captain of a ship, five cents for Hawaiian shore-to-ship postage, and six cents for postage in the United States. All three varieties have long been highly prized by philatelists, but the rarest is the two-cent denomination. Some fifteen are known to exist, and most of them are in poor condition. In 1963 a two-cent "missionary" brought $41,000 at auction in New York.

A two-cent "missionary" was the cause of a sensation in Paris during the 1890s. The stamp was owned by a Parisian, who was famous for his stamp collection. One day the collector was murdered in his apartment and no clues could be found. At last an enterprising detective discovered that the Hawaiian stamp had disappeared from the dead man's collection. One of the friends of the murdered man was also an avid philatelist. Gradually the detective worked his way into the confidence of this man under the guise of also being a collector. Eventually the detective was shown the two-cent "missionary." The "friend" of the murdered man confessed that he had killed his fellow philatelist when he refused to sell him the prized stamp.

Communications with the outside world were faster and safer, but travel between the Islands remained primitive and hazardous. The vessels which plied between the Islands were mostly small craft, from thirty-five to fifty feet in length. Their life expectancy was short, for they were the frequent victims of wild seas, boulder strewn coasts, and hidden coral reefs. The ships usually were crewed by Hawaiians—crews which passengers noted as being cavalier and unperturbed by the dangers surrounding them.

These inter-island trips were so wretched that numerous persons were moved to attempt descriptions. Walter Murray Gibson was becalmed four days between Molokai and Diamond Head. He remembered "decks crowded with natives in dress and undress, with pigs and poultry, cattle and horses, so packed together that scarce a place could be found to spread a mattress."

Theo. H. Davies, the Honolulu merchant, traveled from Honolulu to the island of Hawaii in 1859 on the schooner *Mary*. He admitted the trip was "not all stomach could wish."

The natives were scattered about the deck in small piles, and in
all stages of sea-sickness. All the ladies are carefully supplied
with very small specimens of those useful items of domestic
economy mystically promulgated by modest and retiring trades-
men, as 'chambers'. These are held in readiness for the first at-
tack of sickness, as I have abundant reason to testify, for one in-
teresting young woman being 'took bad' was waited on by a
venerable old witch, who dutifully discharged the consequences
over the vessel's side about six feet to windward of me,
sitting qualmish at the stern. I only mention it as a coinci-
dence, but it is a little strange that just as this moment
I saw divers nutritive elements flashing through space,
and felt my face spattered over with demisemidigested poi, and
other favorite viands of the aborigines of these islands.

Rev. Sereno E. Bishop reported on sailing to Honolulu on an inter-island vessel for the annual general meeting of the missionaries. The decks
were crowded with Hawaiians, calabashes, and dogs. The narrow cabins
were "intolerable for stench. I have made a two-day passage on one of the
larger of these vessels when the crowd of sitting natives was so dense that
the sailors could pass along the vessel only by walking on the gunwales of
the bulwarks. . . ."

The second steam-driven ship in the inter-island trade was a relatively large craft which went into service in 1853. The paddle-wheel vessel
came from San Francisco and in Hawaii was renamed *Akamai*, meaning
"smart" or "clever." The *Akamai* was in questionable condition when it
arrived, and by September 29, 1854, it had deteriorated further. On that
day the cargo and passengers who wanted to sail to Lahaina were substantial, and nothing was refused. The vessel took aboard between 400 and
500 passengers, nineteen horses, and other cargo. Many prominent persons
were passengers, including two royal princes. When the *Akamai* pulled
away from the pier at Honolulu, her decks were nearly awash. Between
Oahu and Maui the sea rose and the vessel sprang a leak. With great effort
the ship was brought about and made for Honolulu. Water was ankle deep
on the cabin deck and the alarmed passengers were relieved to reach the
harbor. It was the last voyage for the *Akamai*, which was later broken up
and sold as firewood.

In September, 1859, Richard Henry Dana, the distinguished maritime
lawyer, sailed for Hawaii. This was the same Dana who had come to ad-
mire the Hawaiian seamen in California nearly twenty-five years earlier.
Dana was on a trip around the world and was eager to see the Islands of

Hawaii. The first five days out of San Francisco were pleasant. Then disaster hit. A fire broke out somewhere in steerage where 175 Chinese, returning to their homeland from California, were passengers. The fire raged between decks, and the captain soon realized the ship could not be saved.

Fortunately the *Achilles* was sailing close by. The boats were lowered and passengers rowed off. Dana, an old sailor, now took command of one of the long boats which ferried passengers from the burning vessel to the *Achilles*. In the end only one passenger was lost. On board the rescue ship Dana read aloud from the Bible to the passengers and offered prayers of thanks for their deliverance.

In October Dana sailed from Honolulu for Kawaihae on Hawaii. There was a great volcanic eruption in progress at the time, and Richard Dana hired a canoe and paddlers to carry him far down the western coast of the island. At night he saw the red and yellow molten lava spill into the sea amid great geysers of steam. Dana watched the spectacle most of the night and then ordered his paddlers to row to Kailua Bay.

On the island of Hawaii, Dana had yet another narrow escape. In Hilo he went on a picnic with a group of friends. Returning, they were crossing a river on a chain bridge which gave way under the weight of their horses. Dana was hurled into the rushing river and was lucky to escape with only bruises and a fractured ankle. Later he returned to San Francisco and took passage on a vessel bound for Hong Kong. Enroute the ship passed within sight of Hawaii, although it did not stop. Seeing the outlines of the Islands, Richard Henry Dana wrote in his journal, "I do not believe I shall see, in my long journey, a place that will interest and charm me so much as this group of islands."

The Civil War created demands for supplies greater than anyone could have imagined, and machines made it possible to produce the quantities of uniforms, guns, and food necessary. Machines did jobs easier, faster, and better. The United States had been catapulted into the machine age.

The machine age did not hit Hawaii's sugar planters with the same impact as it hit Northern manufacturers and farmers. Hawaii's planters had not been driven by the urgency of a war to relentlessly seek faster and better methods. Nor was much of the machinery produced in the U. S. of value to the planters, because the growing and milling of sugar cane are unique and required unique machinery. Planters believed in the ultimate benefits of the machine, but the process of getting there was slow. Most of what was needed came through innovation and invention. It was a process of trial and error, and the failures were frequent.

In 1863 two young men arrived in the Islands from California. Their coming created a certain interest, for they carried with them a new kind of shallow pan in which to evaporate juice from cane. They said the cost of the pan was low, that it would increase yield, and use less fuel. A number of planters gathered at a plantation in Nuuanu Valley for a demonstration and were impressed by what they saw.

Newspaper stories reflected the early hopes of the planters in the new pan. Makee Plantation, it was early reported, had obtained two tons of sugar in eight hours with its use. The average mill took twenty-four hours to produce as much. Later stories indicated that the Makee report had been an exaggeration. The pan was really practical only for very small operations. The stories trailed off and the new evaporating pan was added to the long list of unsuccessful experiments.

The machine was the symbol of the new age, and the Philadelphia Exhibition of 1876 dramatically illustrated what was happening in the U. S. The exhibition was an emotional celebration as well as a practical one, for it marked the 100th anniversary of the founding of the Republic. President Ulysses S. Grant and Congress gave the event their special blessing and help. On opening day a 100-gun salute was followed by the "Hallelujah chorus" sung by a 1,000-voice choir. After these preliminaries President Grant, assisted by Emperor Dom Pedro of Brazil, opened the centennial in a manner befitting the new age. They started a huge Corliss engine, big enough to generate power for the entire exhibition. The giant machine supplied power through some forty miles of belting and twenty-three miles of shafting. For 159 days the Corliss engine did its job without fail. What, indeed, were the limits of machinery?

The list of Hawaiians who visited the Philadelphia Centennial was a long one and included many of the business leaders of the Islands. Certainly many of them must have been deeply impressed by the lesson of the machine. By midsummer of 1876 a reciprocity treaty with the U. S. was near reality, and machines would eventually make production easier. The future looked golden.

Hawaii's planters were tough and adaptable. They changed their methods and tools whenever doing so seemed to offer advantage. Eventually they would become world leaders in the growing and grinding of sugar cane. As prosperous times came closer a certain mental process took place. The planters came to believe that sugar was sufficient for the Islands in much the same way missionaries had considered religion sufficient a generation earlier. They believed everything good in the Islands had its origins in the sugar economy. The planters had thrown the cloak of righteousness about their shoulders. They were the new ruling chiefs of Hawaii.

Chapter Eleven

"AN INTELLECT THAT SHINES . . . THROUGH FLOODS OF WHISKY"

CAPTAIN JOHN CASS was sent off to China in mid-1851 to recruit workers for the plantations. Late the same year he returned with 195 Chinese from Amoy. The workers came on contracts, agreeing to remain for five years at a wage of $3 per month in addition to transportation, food, clothing, and housing. Approximately another 100 Chinese arrived in 1851, and during the fourteen years between 1852 and 1866 over 1,300 landed in Hawaii. Nearly a third came to the Islands by way of California. There were only 54 women among these immigrants, a fact duly noted by the monarchy.

The field work of the Chinese was generally acceptable to the plantation managers, but other faults were found with the newcomers. They complained that the Chinese held to their own ways and were absorbed by neither the Hawaiian nor the haole cultures. The Chinese continued to prefer their native dress, native foods, and language. Even those who married Hawaiian women altered their habits little. More distressing, the Chinese had little inclination to remain field laborers once they had served out the length of their contracts.

Miraculously, many Chinese managed to save money from their meager salaries, and with their plantation service behind them they opened stores or cultivated rice. Rice was very much in demand in California, particularly during the Civil War. In 1862 Hawaii exported nearly a million pounds.

The haole merchants bemoaned the presence of Chinese storekeepers. They said the low standard of living of the Chinese meant they could consistently undersell white merchants. The Chinese did make inroads. In 1866 Chinese owned over 27 percent of the retail merchandising stores and over 57 percent of the restaurants. Twenty-three years later Chinese owned 62 percent of the retail merchandise stores and over 84 percent of the restaurants. In addition they had moved ahead in nearly every other kind of business.

The strange ways of the Chinese made them a suspect group to most Islanders, and the fact that they could compete successfully in business did not add to their acceptance. They were considered a silent, devious lot capable of great evil, and on the morning of July 21, 1866, the predictions of the pessimists seemed confirmed. Early that day Honolulu learned of the gruesome murder of one of its best known, if not best liked, citizens.

On that July morning Jules Dudoit had been murdered in his bed and his wife had been severely wounded. Dudoit was a merchant and a long-time resident of Honolulu. He had served as French consul and in the process had provided the kingdom with numerous problems. He was bad tempered and sometimes violent. On one occasion he had beaten a child who he thought had called him a poi eater. When a woman came to the defense of the child, saying he had not been the one who had called him a name, he beat her also.

It was the misfortune of a Chinese named Asee to end up as a servant in the household of Jules Dudoit. Asee had once served aboard a British-owned vessel on the China coast, and during his service he learned a certain amount of English. He therefore had an ability most of his fellow countrymen did not possess, and so he was employed in Honolulu at higher wages under supposedly better conditions. From the beginning there were misunderstandings. Asee's working day extended from 5 A.M. to 7:30 P.M., and for this he believed he was to receive $20 a month. Asee was paid something less, and, on two occasions when the servant broke dishes, Dudoit deducted $2 from his wages. Asee also believed his ration of rice was too small, and he complained to the man who had placed him in Dudoit's house. When Dudoit learned of this, he hit Asee and pulled his ears. This treatment was repeated when Asee was caught eating peaches which had not been given him. By this time Asee wanted revenge.

On the evening of July 20 Asee went to Booth's tavern and downed half a tumbler of brandy. Then he went home and fell asleep. At about one o'clock in the morning he awoke and entered the Dudoit house through a dining room window. In one hand he held a cleaver and in the other a butcher knife. Jules Dudoit lay sleeping in the bedroom, and Asee quickly dispatched him with the cleaver. Mrs. Dudoit awakened, and Asee struck at her with the butcher knife, seriously wounding her. She ran from the house screaming for help, and Asee disappeared into the night.

Much of Honolulu's population now had proof that the Chinese were dangerous. One newspaper echoed the feelings of many uneasy residents:

It is of no use to try to conceal the fact that there is great uneasiness among our foreign residents, lest the murder committed last week prove to be only the beginning of troubles with the unruly and desperate coolies imported lately from China. It is gen-

erally admitted that they are the worst vicious coolies ever
brought here, and, according to the statements of some of them,
they had been pirates and criminals before they left Hongkong.

The marshal of the kingdom offered a $500 reward for the capture of
the fugitive, and a group of Chinese merchants, apparently believing it
wise to dissociate themselves with Asee, offered another $500 reward
for his capture. Any Chinese who gave information leading to Asee's capture would be released from his contract and given passage home to escape
the possible vengeance of Asee's friends. One aroused legislator introduced a bill which would forbid Chinese from walking the streets after 8
P.M. unless they had a special police pass. The bill was defeated.

When Asee ran off into the night, he headed up Nuuanu Valley, and
near the head of the valley he found a cave high up the cliff. For eleven
days he huddled in the cold, wet cave subsisting on wild berries. At the
end of that time he was desperate enough to venture into the valley to seek
help from other Chinese who lived there. He found some of his fellow
countrymen, but they did not give him the help he hoped for. They recognized Asee immediately, tied him up, and marched him down the valley
toward Honolulu to collect their reward. As the criminal was led toward
town, word of his capture spread, and by the time he reached the center of
Honolulu some 2,000 shouting citizens were gathered about him. Asee had
gotten his revenge. The price he paid was his own life, for he was quickly
convicted and hanged.

Most of the haoles were disenchanted with the Chinese, and laborers
had to be sought elsewhere. The planters insisted they wanted workers
from Northern Europe, but it was easier dreamed than accomplished. European males would not come without their families, and they demanded
higher wages than Asians. Other nations were seeking Europeans as immigrants, and Hawaii offered little compared to Australia, Brazil, and Ar-
gentina. In the United States the Mormons were offering settlers a farm
and the cost of transportation to Utah.

So the eyes of the planters again turned toward the Orient. This time
they thought the answer might be found in Japan. Little was known about
Japan or its people. The first look Hawaii had gotten of Japanese was in
March, 1860, when the *U. S. S. Powhatan* steamed into Honolulu harbor.
The vessel was not expected, and the seventy-two Japanese aboard were
even more unexpected. The Japanese contingent was the embassy staff on
its way to Washington, D. C., the first delegation from Japan to be assigned to a Western nation. The captain of the *Powhatan* had no intention
of stopping in Hawaii, but severe storms had caused the vessel to use great
quantities of fuel, and the ship put into Honolulu harbor to take on coal.

The Hawaiian government held an official reception for the unexpected visitors, and everyone got along well. Foreign Minister Wyllie attempted to negotiate a treaty with the Japanese, but they had no authority to deal in such affairs.

Japanese strays had appeared in Hawaii earlier. Over the years sailing vessels had brought survivors of fishing boats to the Islands. It was not uncommon for Japanese fishermen to be swept eastward by storms, and the lucky ones lived. The most famous of these fishermen was Manjiro Nakahama, who had been rescued from the sea at the age of fifteen. Manjiro went to school in New England, explored the California gold fields, and, on returning to Japan, served as translator during the visit of Matthew C. Perry.

Japanese workers sounded attractive, but they were not as easy to come by as Chinese. In the middle 1860s Japan was an isolated nation which had a great suspicion, but little knowledge, of the outside world. Japan had no precedent of allowing its people to emigrate to foreign lands. But, for the first time in its long history, Japan was open to foreigners, and the planters felt there was hope. The first step in gaining workers seemed to be the signing of a treaty with Japan. The Hawaiian government appointed Eugene Miller Van Reed to make the attempt.

Eugene Van Reed was an American citizen by birth. At an early age he moved to San Francisco, where he met a Japanese fisherman who had been rescued from a drifting boat in the Pacific. Van Reed was intrigued by the man and his stories. In 1859 he decided to go to Japan, where he subsequently made a living in a variety of ways, including the selling of munitions to warring factions within Japan.

Van Reed visited the United States in early 1865, and it seems probable that he established some important contacts in Hawaii on the way, for in April of that year the Hawaiian government named him its consul general to Japan. Van Reed was instructed to secure a treaty and to arrange for immigrants to Hawaii. He worked hard, and for a time it appeared a treaty would become a reality. In the beginning he was assisted by General Robert Van Valkenburgh, the United States minister to Japan. In the end the Japanese decided they could not honorably enter into a treaty with a foreigner who was nothing more than a lowly businessman.

Van Reed did not get a treaty, but he did secure permission to recruit 400 laborers for the sugar plantations of Hawaii. The terms of employment were $4 a month on a three-year contract. Food, lodging, and passage were provided. Before they departed from Yokohama each man was to receive an advance of $10. Each worker would be paid $2 a month cash. Another $2 would be deposited and given him when he had worked out his contract.

Van Reed had no trouble in recruiting men, since Japan was in a state of turmoil, but the recruiters Van Reed hired appeared to take the easy way out. Although they were instructed to seek out farmers, it was easier to pick up men off the streets of Yokohama, and they ended up with potters, blacksmiths, barbers, cooks, sake brewers, and printers.

Van Reed realized there was soon going to be a power shift in Japan. He had been authorized to bring about 400 Japanese to the Islands, but when he had recruited less than half that number, he loaded them aboard the *Scioto*. By the time this had been accomplished, political power had shifted from the Shogun to the Emperor, and the new government would not honor the agreements of the old. The Hawaiian consul, greatly annoyed, gave up efforts to make the departure legal. On May 17, 1868, he informed the Japanese government that the *Scioto* would sail. Later the same day the ship departed. Aboard were the first emigrants to leave Japan.

The trip to Hawaii was not altogether serene. There was a great deal of gambling aboard ship and frequent fights. The worst offenders were handcuffed and kept below decks. The passengers also spent time discussing where they were going. Some believed they were going to India while others insisted they were headed for China. Thirty-three days after leaving Japan, 148 Japanese came into Honolulu harbor.

The reception given the newcomers was warm. The newspapers greeted their arrival with enthusiasm, and Kamehameha V sent down a barrel of salted fish. The Japanese were given two weeks to adjust to their new surroundings and to recover from their ocean voyage. The newspapers used their columns to lecture the planters on how the Japanese should be treated. They reminded the planters the laborers should be given foods they were accustomed to. They instructed them what to do in case of sickness and how wages should be handled. The *Hawaiian Gazette* described the Japanese as "a very good-natured and lusty-looking set of fellows." Because they had come in the first year of the Meiji era, they called themselves "first year men."

The welcome had been generous and sincere, but the seeds of trouble had been sown before the *Scioto* left Japan. The immigrants were to receive $10 in cash before leaving Yokohama, but the money never reached their hands. It went instead to the Japanese agent there, who used it to purchase clothing for his departing countrymen. Later the laborers discovered this $10 was to be deducted from their wages. The man who acted as interpreter was a failure, and communications became a major problem. Small grievances went unanswered or misunderstood, and they often grew into major issues.

Rules on the plantations were unduly strict and some appeared to have been contrived to do the laborers out of their small wages. On Nuuanu plantation rules for the bunkhouses stated there could be no visitors, smoking, or conversation after 9 P.M. which was the time when lights had to be out. Each offense was punishable by a 25-cent fine. The same fine was levied on a worker who took a stalk of sugar cane. If tools were broken through carelessness, or if they were lost or stolen, the cost would come out of wages. Absence from work without permission was charged at the rate of two days pay for a single day not present. A like fine applied in cases where a worker was judged absent because of his own imprudence. Certainly such rules had not been explained in Japan. Some laborers ended up as near prisoners.

Planters and laborers were quick to complain. On one thing both sides agreed. No more Japanese should come to Hawaii. One of the sixteen workers assigned to Ulupalakua on Maui hung himself. His fellow workers said he had wanted to go home, and a Honolulu newspaper suggested he should have thought about that before leaving Japan.

The Japanese government had been enraged by the sailing of the *Scioto*. The new government thought the departed laborers had been kidnapped, and it demanded that Eugene Van Reed be either deported or decapitated. U. S. Minister Van Valkenburg, who had earlier helped Van Reed, was no longer of assistance. It had been pointed out to Van Valkenburg that a treaty between Hawaii and Japan might provide Hawaii with a new outlet for sugar, and this would make the kingdom of Hawaii less dependent on the U. S. Van Valkenburg should oppose a treaty, not assist in its consummation. In Hawaii the U. S. minister sent a note to the king condemning the coolie trade, which he called "inhuman and immoral."

Tales of ill treatment of the Japanese in Hawaii were circulated in Japan, and a representative was sent to investigate. The investigator sailed directly to San Francisco, where he intended to catch another ship for Hawaii. But in San Francisco he heard more stories of abuse, and he did not bother to go to Hawaii at all. Instead he returned to Japan and reported his second-hand findings. Through all of this Van Reed kept repeating that the stories were false. In December, 1869, a second group of investigators actually came to the Islands. They found that conditions were not as severe as they had expected. Finally it was agreed that the plantations would release workers who wanted to return to Japan, and the Japanese government would pay their passage home.

Forty Japanese expressed a wish to go back. When they were once more on home soil, they complained loudly of the ill treatment they had endured. When the work contracts expired, thirteen additional Japanese decided to return while the remainder either stayed in Hawaii or moved to the United States.

Japan and Hawaii were able to settle their differences at last, and in 1871 a treaty was signed. Even Eugene Van Reed was accepted again as Hawaiian consul general, although he did not have long to enjoy the honor. Two years later, at the age of thirty-five, Van Reed died at sea enroute to the United States. The treaty, however, did not provide the stream of Japanese workers which the planters had anticipated. Seventeen years would pass before the flow would start anew. In the meantime the planters had to find other sources of labor.

Prince Lot Kamehameha came to the throne in late 1863 when his younger brother died. The new king took the title Kamehameha V and was the antithesis of his predecessor both physically and mentally. Kamehameha V was a large, heavy man with an extremely strong will. The king was a man who would rule as well as reign.

Those who wanted a liberal monarchy quickly realized they would receive no support from the new king. At his inauguration he refused to take the oath to maintain the existing constitution, and in March, 1864, he read a paper to his cabinet members in which he expressed the opinion that "the prerogatives of the Crown ought to be more carefully protected . . . and that the influence of the Crown ought to be seen pervading every function of the government." He called a convention to revise the constitution. When the delegates refused to include a property requirement for voting and for election to the house of representatives, he disbanded the convention and wrote a constitution which pleased him. He proclaimed this document the fundamental law of the kingdom and took the oath to maintain it.

The arbitrary action of the king brought forth bitter protests, mostly from haoles. The native Hawaiians, whatever their feelings might have been, were intensely loyal subjects, and they accepted the constitution without opposition. During the nine years of the reign of Kamehameha V there were attempts to create a liberal opposition party, but the efforts were unsuccessful. The constitution of 1864 remained in effect for twenty-three years, longer than any other constitution under the monarchy.

Kamehameha V was a man of contrasts. He was a stern, authoritarian king, yet he rode unattended about Honolulu, freely talking with his subjects. He resented the influence of foreigners, yet he realized that trade with the United States was essential, and he tried to encourage it. He followed the general concepts of Christianity, yet he believed enough in the mystic powers of old to keep in his household a woman kahuna, a shrewd, nervous, intelligent person who had sufficient power over the king to often decide when he should make trips. Early in his reign he began to issue licenses allowing medical kahunas to practice their arts of healing. He enjoyed the hula and the ancient chants, although there were periods when he was convinced such pleasures should be banned.

Always a physically large man, Kamehameha V grew so obese in the latter years of his reign that he found it difficult to move about. One of his pleasures was visiting the plantation of John Cummins on the windward side of Oahu. The trip by horseback became too exhausting, so the king purchased a small steamboat to carry him there by water. He installed a stretch of railroad track from the dock to the plantation house so that even this portion of the journey could be covered with a minimum of exertion. He consumed great quantities of food and took little exercise. When he died his weight was estimated at 375 pounds.

Kamehameha V had once been engaged to Bernice Pauahi, but she had broken that engagement to marry Charles Reed Bishop. During his reign he discreetly approached Emma, through a second party, but that religious lady refused him, perhaps for no other reason than the fact that marriage to her brother-in-law would have brought the displeasure of the Anglican church. Kamehameha V never married, and the fact that there was no successor to the throne created particular concern during the last half of 1872. The king made his final public appearance on April 30 of that year at the opening of the legislature. After that he did not leave the palace. He had grown so heavy and so weak that he could no longer support himself. On December 11 he realized the end was near, and he summoned Bernice Bishop to his palace chambers. At the bedside of the king was John O. Dominis, who later recorded the words of the king and Bernice.

The king spoke to Bernice: "I wish you to take my place, to be my successor."

Bernice answered, "No, no, not me; don't think of me, I do not need it."

The king continued: "I do not wish you to think that I do this from motives of friendship, but I think it best for my people and the nation."

Once again Bernice said, "No, no; do not think of me, there are others; there is your sister, it is hers by right."

To this Kamehameha V simply replied: "She is not fitted for the position."

At 10:20 the same morning the king died without naming a successor. The date was December 11, 1872, the forty-second birthday of the king. As the people prepared to celebrate his birthday, they learned that he was dead.

The kingdom was without a king, and it was up to the legislature to elect a new ruler. Four persons, all of high rank, were the obvious candidates. There were William Lunalilo, a cousin of the late king, David Kalakaua, and Ruth Keelikolani, a half-sister of the late king. In addition there was Bernice Bishop, who had already refused the throne. Ruth could not speak or understand English and was not a serious contender, so the contest was between Lunalilo and Kalakaua. Both men quickly issued proclamations, each claiming to be the rightful heir to the throne because of his lineage.

Public sentiment was strongly in favor of Lunalilo, and through a shrewd maneuver he turned the contest into a rout. Lunalilo declared he would return certain rights to the people which had been taken away by the late king. He also believed the wishes of the people should be known and that a popular election should be held January 1, 1873. Even though the king was to be elected by the members of the legislature, an overwhelming popular vote for one candidate could not be ignored. The returns of the informal election were indeed a mandate. Lunalilo received 12,531 votes, and the other three candidates received a total of fifty-one votes. A week later the legislature elected Lunalilo king.

Lunalilo was enormously popular. When he learned of his election he declined a waiting carriage and walked the four blocks to the palace. He walked bareheaded, a handsome, charismatic man, accompanied and cheered by thousands of his subjects. He had promised he would be a democratic king, and now he proved it. That night torchlight parades wound through Honolulu in his honor. Three days later Lunalilo rode through the city's muddy streets in the funeral cortege of Kamehameha V. The crowds cheered him so loudly that the funeral dirges the band played were drowned out.

At the age of five Lunalilo had been sent off to the Royal School, where he remained for ten years. He had once worked for Wyllie in the foreign office, the only helpful government experience he could claim. By the time he was twenty-three, he had amply demonstrated that he could not handle his own financial affairs, which were placed under the care of a guardian. Kamehameha V would not appoint him to any important position, but he did name him a member of his staff—a position which was principally honorary. When Lunalilo was accused of boisterous conduct in church, he freely admitted the charge and turned in his uniform which marked his dismissal from even this one minor post. Lunalilo's high lineage was about his only qualification for the throne.

Like most of the kings before him, Lunalilo began testing the effects of alcohol at an early age. Celebrations often followed and on these occasions he enjoyed playing the bass drum and singing *Rule Britannia!* or perhaps reciting Shakespeare. He was engaged to two distinguished Hawaiian princesses—at the same time—but married neither. Mark Twain described Lunalilo the month he was elected: "A splendid fellow, with talent, genius, education, gentlemanly manners, generous instincts, and an intellect that shines as radiantly through floods of whisky as if that fluid but fed a calcium light in his head." To help him control his drinking many citizens joined a temperance campaign, hoping their example would lend the king encouragement. Lunalilo's deficiencies in no way reduced his popularity. He was an idol to his people, and they gave him a degree of devotion unknown to the kings before him.

In February, 1873, the newly crowned king traveled to Hilo on the U. S. ironclad, *Benicia*. Admiral A. H. Pennock was the host and General Schofield was also aboard as a guest. The town of Hilo was in an uproar over the prospect of a visit by the king. Hawaiians streamed into town from the countryside, homes were decorated with flowers and greenery, and the beach was crowded with subjects eager to welcome their king. At ten o'clock in the morning Lunalilo stepped ashore amidst the cheering and waving of his people. He walked toward the governor's house, preceded by the Hilo band and surrounded by throngs of delighted children and adults. At the governor's house the king announced he would hold a reception for his subjects on Monday.

Monday dawned a bright, warm day—a day of great expectations for thousands of Hawaiians. The reception was held at the court house, and here the king received his loyal subjects. They piled leis of maile and ohia blossoms about his neck, and during the three hours he shook hands with well-wishers there was continuous cheering. The Hawaiians were laden with gifts—pigs and fowls with feet tied, bananas, sweet potatoes, pumpkins, oranges, onions, coconuts, and money. They approached their king with awe and with an overflowing measure of love. Two thousand four hundred shook his hand, and to each the king was kind and gentle. The eighty boys of the missionary school, uniformed in white linen, formed a hollow square around the flag staff and sang the Hawaiian national anthem. Few of the spectators were untouched and many openly wept.

Lunalilo had won the affection of his people. He was the man who walked with them, an escort of children, men and women his guard of honor. He was the aristocratic one with large eyes and a melancholy look. He was the hero-chief of ancient legend—graceful, strong, the kind one, a father protector to his people. Now he was among them, and no matter what he might have asked of them they would have cheered him still, because on that February day Lunalilo was the incarnation of all that was just and true by the standards of ancient Hawaii.

The short reign of Lunalilo was marred by a distressing incident which occurred in the early part of September, 1873. The trouble arose in the barracks of the Household Troops, a body of some sixty men who

made up the standing army of the kingdom. There had been long smoldering resentments and on a Sunday morning an incident sent the troops into
open revolt. On that day seven or eight soldiers escaped from the guard
house where they had been detained for various breaches of discipline.

When Captain Joseph Jajczay, the pompous Hungarian drill master,
came upon the escaped soldiers, he ordered them back to prison. They refused to go, and Jajczay hit one of the soldiers with the flat of his sword.
The soldier knocked the captain down, and the rest joined in beating him.
Escaping from his own troops, the captain went in search of Adjutant
General Charles H. Judd, who came to arrest the offenders. Judd was also
attacked. When Governor John O. Dominis showed up to settle the matter,
he was simply ignored.

The demands of the troops were simple. They wanted Jajczay and
Judd removed from their positions. At the time of the uprising Lunalilo
was at Waikiki recuperating from chest complications which had followed
a severe cold. He was also suffering from the effects of too much alcohol.
On Tuesday he sent a message telling the troops they must lay down their
arms, vacate the barracks, and go to their homes at once. Some did as the
king ordered, but thirty-four thought the letter was simply a trick. About
forty volunteers from the Honolulu Rifles and Hawaiian Cavalry joined
the police in standing guard near the barracks. Their presence did not impress the troops or the large number of Hawaiians who milled about.
When Marshal Parke read a warrant for the arrest of the remaining mutineers, they responded by slamming the barracks door in his face.

On Wednesday three of the soldiers went to Waikiki, where the king
told them they must submit to orders and trust his clemency. The remaining troops did stack their arms but stayed in the barracks instead of going
home. On the following day a second delegation visited the king, who
promised to put into writing what he had told them. On Friday Lunalilo
sent his letter, which included the assurance, "If you shall implicitly obey
this my command, then I will be on your side, as a Father to his children,
and I will protect you from injury." After a little further discussion the
troops dispersed and the mutiny was over. As the soldiers left the barracks
they carried away ample quantities of government bedding, blankets, and
rifles. Lunalilo abolished the Household Troops except for the band.

The mutiny had the quality of a comedy, yet there were serious im-
plications which frightened and angered many. Sentiment in favor of the
mutineers was strong among the Hawaiians while sentiment against the
mutineers came from the haoles. Thus feelings ran along racial lines. Some
persons feared that one violent incident could have resulted in a race war.
Obviously the government was unable to cope with the situation. Faced
with the possibility of violence, they could only issue warrants and write

letters. In the end they had to beg the troops to give up. It was a humiliating demonstration, and the Honolulu newspapers took full note of the happenings. The *Advertiser* clearly stated what they thought of the king's ministers: ". . . dullness of apprehension, utter poverty of resources and consequent helplessness . . . where the exhibition of the opposite qualities was so immediately demanded . . ." In another column the ministers of the king were again flailed. "Neither, it may be added, will men who have thus proven themselves incompetent in a case of emergency, have the decency to go out and hang themselves—officially."

Among those who played a part in the mutiny clearly stands the figure of David Kalakaua, the recent contender for the throne. Kalakaua was involved in instigating and advising the mutinous troops. He must have gotten satisfaction from the confusion the insurrection caused in the government of his recent opponent.

Some bemoaned the annual sum of $30,000 which had supported the Household Troops. It had certainly been the worst kind of investment. Others noted the inability of the government to control violence. Admiral A. H. Pennock, who was then in Honolulu, wrote his impressions to the U. S. Secretary of the Navy. "The incidents connected with this mutiny, although farcical, have developed the fact that the authorities had not then the power to maintain order, or to give protection to the foreign residents in case of emergency."

The chest complications and constant drinking which caused Lunalilo to remain at Waikiki were no passing matters. The king was firmly gripped by tuberculosis as well as alcoholism. In November he traveled to the island of Hawaii hoping that he would benefit by the climate there. But he grew worse and in mid-January of 1874 he returned to Honolulu a weak and thin man whose voice was a mere whisper. On the evening of February 3 he died. A newspaper reported his passing with the statement that "Lunalilo, the people's choice, the liberal minded, amiable and generous-hearted king of Hawaii is no more." The night before his funeral the Hawaiians gathered at Iolani Palace to chant the ancient funeral dirges.

Although urged by his ministers to name a successor, Lunalilo had not done so. When he went to Hawaii, Emma went along too and repeatedly asked the king to designate her, but he would not. The choice of the next monarch was left to a very distressed legislature.

Since James Cook's day the Hawaiian population had been thinned by a succession of Western diseases. Venereal diseases, typhoid, tuberculosis, influenza, measles—all took their terrible toll. Honolulu newspapers lamented the certain demise of the Hawaiian race.

James King, on Cook's expedition, estimated the population of the Islands to be 400,000, a figure which appears to have been about 100,000 high. One hundred years later the total population of the Islands was just under 58,000. Of that number 47,508 were Hawaiians or part Hawaiian. This decrease in the Hawaiian population would continue, for yet another disease was now destroying the race. It was a hideous, lingering disease which often mutilated the body. It usually affected the extremities first, so that the tips of fingers lost their feeling, then the knuckles, the wrist, the forearm. Then the fingers and hands decayed and fell away. The disease was called leprosy.

It is not known how leprosy came to Hawaii. One story says it was first seen in about 1840 on a chief who had returned from a trip abroad. Sometime after that Dr. Baldwin of Lahaina treated another chief for a disease which gave the appearance of leprosy. At some early time the Hawaiians began to call the disease Mai Pake, which means Chinese sickness. The name could well point in the direction from which leprosy came, for it was a common malady in China, and travel between that country and Hawaii was frequent.

The first public concern over the disease came toward the end of 1863 when it was mentioned in the report of the Board of Health. By then the prevalence of leprosy was causing alarm. Dr. Hillebrand stated, "It is the genuine Oriental leprosy. . . . It will be the duty of the next Legislature to devise and carry out some efficient, and at the same time, humane measure, by which the isolation of those affected with this disease can be accomplished." An Act to Prevent the Spread of Leprosy was passed by the legislature and approved by the king on January 3, 1865. This act gave the Board of Health the authority to enforce the segregation of confirmed cases and to establish a hospital for suspected cases and those in the early stages of the disease.

It was decided the place where the lepers should be sent was Kalaupapa, a flat promontory of land jutting out from the north coast of Molokai. It was an isolated spot, for very rough seas usually beat against the coast on the windward side. Behind was a sheer cliff, and the only access to the rest of Molokai was along a narrow, winding path cut into this cliff. The land was purchased by the Board of Health, and the first group of lepers was put ashore in January 1866. The lepers were expected to use the houses vacated by the recent residents. It was assumed they would be relatively self-sufficient, taking over where the former owners had left off.

The government had planned poorly, if at all, for the care of the lepers on Molokai, and they obviously had no concept of the size of the problem. Those patients sent to Molokai were confirmed lepers, many in advanced stages, yet there was no resident doctor or any provision for medical treatment. What supervision there was at the settlement came from superintendents who lived there. Rudolph W. Meyer, a long-time resident of Molokai, was supposed to keep watch over the superintendents. Meyer hiked down the narrow path to the settlement once a month to look things over. Slight improvements came in 1867 when Mr. and Mrs. Walsh took over the supervision of the settlement. A small hospital was built where Mrs. Walsh did some amateur nursing. She also taught school while her husband attempted to bring some sort of order into the life of the colony. Their work was hindered by the fact that neither of them spoke or understood Hawaiian.

The lepers continued to be put ashore on Molokai as they were rounded up throughout the kingdom. By the end of March, 1870, there were 269 lepers and an undetermined number of nonlepers. The nonlepers were often the families of lepers, since the early policy of the government was to allow them to accompany the stricken one to Molokai if they wished. Some Hawaiians who had lived there before the government bought the land also remained, so the population of the settlement was swollen far beyond those who were actually diseased.

These nonlepers became known as kokuas, or helpers. Often they lived off the rations of the lepers, who were the only ones entitled to provisions. These provisions consisted of three pounds of beef and one bundle of dry poi a week—rations meager enough for a single person. Frequently kokuas were an added burden to the diseased. They depleted his food supply and often the leper had to fend for himself. Sometimes lepers were left to die when they were too ill to carry on. Many kokuas were helpful, but the general condition was so bad that their presence was repeatedly lamented by visitors.

The Board of Health also failed to realize that lepers were emotionally agitated. When a person was put aboard ship to make the one-way trip to the little settlement, his departure was considered his funeral. The courts discussed at length whether or not such lepers could be declared "civilly dead." Each leper knew that on the following day his condition would be a little worse, a day closer to a miserable death. There was no hope of being cured. It was hardly surprising that the diseased thought only of the present, of what could be enjoyed now. The report of the Board of Health for 1868 showed a slight awareness of the situation: ". . . the terrible disease which afflicts the Lepers seems to cause among them as great a change in their moral and mental organization as in their physical constitution. . . ."

In those early years the settlement was often in a state of anarchy. Supplies of food and clothing were desperately short, and the strong stole the things they wanted from the weak. Liquor was brewed from the root of a plant which grew in abundance near the foot of the cliffs, and the result was widespread drunkenness. Even the official reports admitted that "great orgies took place." Many lepers reverted to the ancient ways, resurrecting the hulas and calling on kahunas to help them where Western medicine had failed. On the half-circle of land was a small crater inside which was a very deep lake. Sometimes corpses were thrown into this lake. It was the easiest way to dispose of the dead.

Attempts were made to improve the situation, but most of them proved ineffectual. The husbands of leprous women were allowed to come and act as constables in return for rations of food and clothing. Before long some of the constables, who were supposed to be suppressing the brewing of liquor, were producing it themselves. Government agents were sent in to encourage the growing of taro so the settlement would have a ready supply of poi, but some agents cheated the lepers who had been induced to farm, and soon there were no willing farmers.

When Lunalilo became king a new Board of Health was appointed, and under their administration some changes were made. Persons who had been cheated by government agents were paid for their losses. Food rations were increased and a greater variety of food was offered the lepers. A store was established, and instead of having clothes doled out, each patient was given six dollars a year to buy clothes of his choice. In 1878 the legislature appropriated money to hire the first full-time doctor for the settlement.

Leprosy was no respecter of rank. A number of prominent persons in the kingdom contracted the disease and went to Molokai. Among these was Kahoohuli, captain of the king's guard. For a time he filled the position of superintendent at the settlement until he was incapacitated by the progress of the disease. Another was William Ragsdale, who had served the legislature for many years as English-Hawaiian interpreter. Ragsdale was also superintendent for a period. Still another victim was Peter Kaeo, a cousin of Queen Emma. Kaeo retained his seat in the House of Nobles in absentia while he died slowly from leprosy on Molokai.

The physical comforts of the residents improved somewhat, and a semblance of order was eventually brought to the settlement, but little progress was made in finding relief from the disease. In 1868 a Norwegian, Dr. Gerhard Armauer Hansen, discovered the *Bacillus leprae,* but decades passed before an effective treatment for leprosy was found. The Board of Health made an effort to assist in research by bringing a distinguished young German, Dr. Edward Arning, to Hawaii in 1883. Arning was named pathologist and bacteriologist for the board and was designated special leprosy investigator. He conducted his experiments principally from an ill-equipped laboratory in Honolulu, although he also worked on Molokai.

In 1884 Arning approached the Privy Council with an unusual request. He wanted a healthy human being on whom he could conduct an experiment. The doctor proposed to plant leprous flesh on this person. Arning had tried to grow Hansen's bacilli in a great variety of media such as rabbits, guinea pigs, rats, hogs, pigeons, and a monkey. Nothing worked. To forge ahead Arning had to study the development of the bacilli under controlled conditions, and a human guinea pig was the way to do it. Arning suggested that Keanu, a husky forty-eight-year-old Hawaiian, fill the role. In September, 1884, the Privy Council gave the doctor permission to go ahead.

Keanu's name was well known in the Islands before he unexpectedly entered the service of the medical profession, for he had recently been convicted of clubbing a man to death. The dead man's wife had been Keanu's lover, and the trial created an understandable interest in the community. Keanu was sentenced to hang, but if he agreed to allow Edward Arning to embed leprous flesh in the muscles of his right forearm, the sentence would be commuted to life imprisonment. Twenty-five months later Keanu bore the marks of leprosy over his entire body. In 1889 he was transferred from his prison cell on Oahu to a prison cell on Molokai, where he died less then four years later. Dr. Arning was not in Hawaii to see the conclusion to his experiment, for he left in the middle of 1886 after repeated altercations with the Board of Health. Other doctors were hired to pursue the investigations of Arning, but the interference continued and little was accomplished.

There was a certain group of people in Hawaii, among them several doctors, who were convinced that leprosy and syphilis were connected. Some believed leprosy was the last stage of syphilis. A large percentage of lepers were Hawaiians and, these people reasoned, since the Hawaiians were a very immoral people, the tie between the two diseases was not only logical but was also an expected and just punishment. Dr. George L. Fitch included a statement concerning this in the Board of Health report for 1882: "Syphilis was introduced here about one hundred years ago. Sixty years afterwards Leprosy appeared, or as soon as syphilis had a chance to fairly permeate the community, which among a people as licentious as these, was shortly accomplished." Dr. Arning knew there was no connection between these two diseases, but he was able to change few minds.

Stories about happenings on Molokai were repeated throughout the Islands. In being retold they lost none of their horror, and it is no wonder that many lepers decided they would die resisting anyone who tried to send them there. The most famous fugitive was a cowboy named Koolau, who took refuge in a deep valley on Kauai. He killed the sheriff who first attempted to bring him in, and later he killed two militia men who came after him. A third soldier accidentally shot and killed himself trying to escape Koolau's deadly fire. After the militia failed to flush Koolau from his valley, he was left to live out his remaining days in his stronghold where he finally succumbed to leprosy.

A leper named Ku also lived on Kauai. He was a determined, tough man and difficult to catch. One day he was invited to a feast, and in the midst of the celebration he was captured. The next day he was handcuffed, placed on a horse, and led off to prison, to await shipment to the settlement. The policeman taking Ku in was astride a nervous horse. Ku got the horse excited enough to buck the lawman off, allowing Ku to make his escape. A Chinese farmer chiseled off his handcuffs and, like Koolau, he retreated to a valley where no one dared go after him. On Hawaii, Kealoha refused to surrender and shot two policemen before he himself was wounded. He surrendered but died in jail before he could be shipped off.

The doctors who examined persons suspected of being lepers were sometimes the targets of reprisal. One night there was a knocking at the door of Dr. Jared Smith. He opened the door and the Hawaiian who stood there shot him dead. The murder was committed to prevent the doctor from signing a paper which would have sent the daughter of the killer to Molokai. In Honolulu Dr. Trousseau was examining suspected lepers when a man approached him with a double-barreled pistol. Trousseau dodged behind a post and the first shot missed. The second barrel misfired. When Marshal Parke showed up, the desperate man again fired and again missed. The newspaper account of the incident suggested that "the deprivation of his liberty and the prospect of a lingering death from leprosy may have depraved his reason."

The annual reports of the Board of Health were classic examples of the bureaucratic mentality. Many of the early reports indicated that great strides had been made and that leprosy would soon be subdued. In reality each year brought an increased number of cases, and the situation was becoming more unmanageable. On one point in particular the board was deceived. The number of lepers who remained outside the settlement was substantial. Lepers hid in isolated places and evaded the police who made periodic searches. Some who lived on the seashore swam far out to sea and stayed there until the police had departed. Most Hawaiians would not report relatives or friends. They were not troubled by the lepers about them, and they happily shared dishes, bedding, and clothing until disfigurement became extreme. It was a long time before such facts were acknowledged by the Board of Health.

In mid-1873 a Belgian priest was assigned to the parish of Molokai. He was Joseph de Veuster, commonly called Father Damien. Damien was thirty-three years old when he came ashore at the leper colony. He was a husky man, weighing over 200 pounds, although he stood only five feet, eight inches tall. His face was round, his hair black, and his voice clear. His parents had been peasants and throughout his life Damien's habits were basic and rough. His crudeness only thinly disguised a supersensitive nature which made him acutely aware of the suffering about him but also made him a difficult man to work with. Entirely by chance this unusual man went to Molokai, and there he gave comfort to the miserable lepers in a way very few others could.

Father Damien's introduction to the settlement was no different from that of the ordinary leper. He found no house to shelter him, so he camped under a pandanus tree for the first several nights. The house which did become available was adjacent to the Catholic cemetery where hundreds of bodies had been buried. The burying jobs had been haphazard, since the ground was rocky and digging a hole six feet deep was difficult. So bodies were often buried close to the surface. Pigs and dogs came to root among the graves, and the vile smell which arose permeated Damien's house day and night.

Father Damien worked hard for his church and for the lepers. He gave the Board of Health no peace, constantly badgering them for more help. He comforted the dying and encouraged the living. He was a carpenter and he turned his hand to building churches and houses. He was generous with everything he owned and did not hesitate to share his possessions with the most deformed leper in the settlement. For hundreds of people Damien was the one hopeful light in their whole abysmal underworld.

There were others who felt very differently. To them Damien was dictatorial. He allowed Catholics to live in the houses the church inherited only as long as the occupants behaved according to Damien's beliefs. He constantly attempted to usurp the authority of those in charge of the settlement. When funds were received from private donors for specific projects, he attempted to use them for projects he personally favored.

Father Damien gave no heed to his personal safety. He certainly did not believe in the germ theory of disease. No matter what chances he took, his life was in the hands of God. By 1884 he was a confirmed leper. This was known for sure when he traveled to Honolulu and Dr. Edward Arning diagnosed Damien an advanced leprosy case. That he should die of leprosy must have been Damien's unconscious and perhaps conscious wish. Four and a half years later that wish was fulfilled. During the last months of his life he lay abed, a disfigured man, tormented by the fear that he was unworthy of heaven.

Chapter Twelve

PROSPERITY, HOWEVER,
DID NOT MEAN HARMONY

THE STORY OF HAWAII from 1874 through 1890
cannot be told without becoming deeply involved with David Kalakaua,
for those were the years of his reign. To some this king was a debonair,
intelligent ruler who brought dignity and prestige to the Hawaiian throne.
To others he was a debauched spendthrift who used royal prerogatives for
personal benefit. Kalakaua is the most controversial ruler in Hawaii's history.

The King Kalakaua years were ones of enormous change. Honolulu
became used to electricity and the telephone. Sugar gave the nation a
sound financial basis, and its businessmen became affluent and sophisti-
cated. Communications with the rest of the world became faster and safer,
and the Islands were pulled into the currents of international affairs.

David Kalakaua was born at the foot of Punchbowl crater in Honolulu on November 16, 1836. With other young chiefs he attended the
Royal School. By the time he was sixteen he was an aide to Kamehameha
IV, and four days after his nineteenth birthday he was elected a member
of the Privy Council. Subsequently he was appointed to the House of Nobles and in 1863 was named postmaster general. In that year he married
Kapiolani, a granddaughter of King Kaumualii of Kauai. At twenty-eight
he was appointed chamberlain to Kamehameha V.

David Kalakaua was a thick-set man with black, kinky hair, long sid-
eburns, and a drooping mustache. His appearance was striking. His intellect and social ease surprised most who met him. He was very ambitious
and, particularly during his early years, was willing to work hard to
achieve his goals. He had opposed Lunalilo in an attempt to win the
throne in 1873, and he played a role in the revolt of the militia, an episode hardly to his credit.

Kalakaua's grandfather had been the first high chief to be executed
under the new laws which went into effect in 1840. He had been convicted

of adultery, and under the laws of the time he could not marry again until his former wife died. The grandfather of Kalakaua, however, decided he wanted to marry again and, being a chief, decided to settle things his own way. He summoned an expert in preparing poisons and killed his former wife by poisoning a bowl of kava. Both the men in the plot were tried and found guilty. A gallows was constructed over the main gate of the fort, and at 11 A.M. on October 20, 1840, the two were hanged. When Kalakaua came to the throne, some said he ordered his grandfather's bones dug from their unmarked grave and interred in the royal mausoleum.

The day after Lunalilo died David Kalakaua declared himself a candidate for the throne, and the next day Dowager Queen Emma did the same. It appears the majority of the Hawaiians favored Emma, as did the small band of Englishmen in the Islands. The pro-U. S. faction opposed Emma because of her undisguised preference for England over the United States. Kalakaua was not a great favorite of the Americans either, but he seemed cooperative and the lesser evil.

The haole backers of Kalakaua remembered vividly how the legislature virtually had been forced to name Lunalilo king after a popular election had shown him the overwhelming favorite. The best way to avoid a repetition was to move swiftly. The only steam coasting vessel in the Islands was owned by an American, and it was quickly dispatched to pick up legislators who lived on the neighbor islands. This was done without publicity, and many legislators apparently left their home islands without knowing the sentiments of the people. On Oahu mass meetings were held for both candidates, with supporters of Emma seeming stronger. Queen Emma attempted to demonstrate her popularity just as Lunalilo had. She organized a popular election, but the polling place was located at her home, and the heavy returns in her favor were hardly credible.

The mood of the town was ugly. Both the U. S. and British ministers approached commanders of warships in Honolulu harbor and asked them to have sailors and marines ready to come ashore to keep order in town. The police and the volunteer Honolulu Rifles, it was hoped, would be able to cope with the situation, but many doubted that they could handle a serious disturbance.

Nine days after the death of Lunalilo the legislature met to elect a new king. The meeting time was three o'clock in the afternoon and many Honolulu businesses had locked their doors. Two to three thousand persons, mostly Hawaiian, milled about the court house awaiting the outcome. Then the results became known. Kalakaua was king by thirty-nine votes to six. This news was just circulating through the crowd when a door of the court house opened and five legislators emerged. They had been chosen as a delegation to carry the news of the election to Kalakaua. As the delegates entered a waiting carriage, they were suddenly attacked by an angry, shouting mob of Hawaiians. The five tried to retreat into the court house, but two of them were beaten before they reached safety. The carriage was broken up and pieces used as clubs.

The alarmed legislators barred the doors of the court house as best they could. The mob smashed windows with rocks and battered at the front and back doors. One deputy marshal who was well liked by the Hawaiians tried to talk them out of violence. He was picked up, bodily passed over the heads of the mob, and deposited at the outer edge of the crowd. Most of the police stood by as spectators and others joined the rioters. The Honolulu Rifles were completely ineffective for the simple reason that only a handful answered the mobilization call. The Hawaiian members were particularly unwilling to fire on fellow Hawaiians.

Soon the doors of the court house were splintered, and the mob began smashing furniture and scattering books and papers. Most of the legislators tried to dash through the mob. Thirteen were beaten and one was killed. The haole legislators went untouched. Only those Hawaiians who had voted for Kalakaua were attacked.

Half an hour after the rioting had started the American minister requested assistance from the two U. S. warships in the harbor. About 150 sailors and marines immediately came ashore. They marched to the court house, dispersed the mob, and arrested the leaders. While the Americans were in the process of doing this, a contingent of British sailors also arrived. The Hawaiians cheered them, believing they had come to fight for Emma. When the British joined ranks with the Americans, the Hawaiians were greatly disappointed. The court house was secured and a guard mounted behind a Gatling gun.

While the riot raged two or three haoles attempted to get the queen dowager to call off the rioters, but she would do nothing. Now, with foreign troops in charge, part of the mob moved to her house where they shouted that she would be named the ruler of the Islands the next day. Their shouts were hardly prophetic, for the following day Kalakaua took the oath of office before a group of Honolulu's affluent citizens and such members of the legislature as were physically able to attend. Kalakaua was recognized as king by the representatives of the United States, Great Britain, and France. For a week U. S. troops remained ashore, guarding government buildings.

Dowager Queen Emma publicly acknowledged Kalakaua as ruler, but the wound would never heal. Some believed the Queenites would have rebelled if they had not felt U. S. and British intervention was inevitable. The new government organized the Royal Guards in case of trouble, but the public had little confidence in them. Kalakaua was a nervous ruler, and on at least two occasions rumors of impending assassination attempts alarmed him greatly. The haoles were uneasy, feeling certain that if violence came their lives and property would be in danger. Most Americans felt safer when a U. S. warship was in port. Kalakaua shared their feeling.

To gain support in his campaign to be elected David Kalakaua had changed his stand on a reciprocity treaty with the United States. He now favored a treaty with the U. S., although he was opposed to any cession of territory as a treaty provision. After his election the new king traveled to Washington D. C. President Grant honored him with a state dinner, and Congress, in joint session, gave a reception for him. Kalakaua's visit received wide publicity and his meetings with highly placed government officials created favorable impressions. Newspapers carried stories about Hawaii and its king, and Congressmen were more keenly aware of the reciprocity treaty which was before them for consideration.

A treaty was approved by both the United States and Hawaiian governments in mid-1875. In August of the following year Hawaii learned that Congress had passed the legislation necessary to put the treaty into operation. About the only Americans in the Islands who were displeased with Kalakaua at that point were those who believed in annexation. The business community expanded and prospered, Honolulu Harbor was dredged, and even a few adventurous tourists came to the Islands. Fears of rebellion by Emma's followers seemed remote. Those first years of King Kalakaua's reign appeared to benefit all Hawaii.

Many mainlanders also benefited from the reciprocity treaty. One was a ruthless, shrewd man named Claus Spreckels, who can accurately be labeled a robber baron. He was born into a poverty-ridden family in Germany and as a child was expected to do the work of an adult. At the age of eighteen he came to the United States. He worked at the grocery business in the East and was successful. Then he was lured to San Francisco by prospects of greater success. Before long he sold his grocery business to try his hand at sugar-refining. Since he knew nothing about refining, he returned to Germany and spent eight months working as a common laborer in a sugar refinery. Spreckels was successful in the refining business and in many other enterprises as well. By the time he reached Hawaii he was a millionaire.

Spreckels had opposed a reciprocity treaty between the U. S. and Hawaii, but when the treaty nonetheless became reality he was in no way hesitant in trying to gain from it. He arrived in Hawaii aboard the vessel which brought the news that the treaty had finally been approved in Washington. With his money and relentless drive Spreckels soon became the most powerful sugar man in Hawaii. His ambition for wealth and power led him into a variety of other businesses, including banking. Once Kalakaua was in his debt he was also in his grasp, and Claus Spreckels was so important to the king that anyone who opposed his various deals, including cabinet members, was soon out of office. Eventually his hold on the government and business community was broken, but during his day Spreckels was one of the most colorful men on the Hawaiian scene.

Prosperity, however, did not mean harmony. After a few years of sizing each other up, neither the haole business community nor the Hawaiian community very much liked what they saw. The breach between the two forces was an economic one. The haoles had the money and the Hawaiians did not, and so the split was reinforced and simplified by race. The Hawaiians greatly outnumbered the haoles, but they had little control or interest in the commercial enterprise of the Islands. A great portion of the taxes collected came directly or indirectly from haole business, and they also provided much of the administrative skill in the government. Because they were giving vital support to the kingdom, many haoles believed they should also control it. The Hawaiians viewed the Islands as theirs and felt that those who had settled there had done so through their generosity. Now outsiders wanted to deprive them of the right to run their own homeland.

While the haoles were pleased about the stand Kalakaua had taken on the reciprocity treaty, they approved of little else he did. He spent too much money on pompous displays, and because his personal expenses were heavy he sometimes sought to improve his fortunes through dealings which were questionable if not wholly corrupt. The haoles continuously cried out for reform, but the Hawaiians were dominant in numbers. This dominance was reflected in the legislature, which generally carried out the king's wishes. While the reformers freely criticized the actions of the king, the Hawaiians believed the king should be able to do as he wished.

The legislative session of 1880 was an explosive one. When the smoke cleared both sides knew better where they stood. Acts were introduced to float a $10,000,000 foreign loan, for the sale of the franchise to import and sell opium to Chinese, and the cabinet came under fire when a want-of-confidence resolution was introduced and hotly debated. The legislature was in a turmoil, the reformers charging the king with incompetence and bribery while the king appointed and dismissed cabinet members as he wished. It was obvious the king could be influenced by those who flattered him, and the most unscrupulous were the most ready to do this. By the end of 1880 it was clear, however, that the king continued to be the final power in the kingdom. Under the constitution he had the right to veto any legislation he wished, and he had sole control of the cabinet. The next move was up to his opponents.

At the January 11, 1881, meeting of the cabinet it was announced the king intended to make a world tour. Preparations were begun for the trip.

Charles H. Judd went with him as chamberlain, and William N. Armstrong went in the dual role of minister of state and commissioner of immigration. The stated purpose of the trip was to explore ways by which peoples from other countries could be brought to Hawaii to help reverse the population decline, but in fact little attention was paid to this.

A third attendant accompanied the king. He was Robert von Oehlhaffen, Kalakaua's valet, a man who claimed noble birth, although he had landed in Honolulu as a ship's cook. Von Oehlhaffen would cause some embarrassment on the trip because of his addiction to alcohol. Before departure impressive services were held at the Catholic Cathedral and at Kawaiahao Church. Kalakaua's last night on Hawaiian soil was taken up with singing and the hula—his subjects crowding the palace grounds and performing the whole night through.

The first stop was San Francisco, where the king was lavishly entertained. On a side trip to the state capitol at Sacramento, Kalakaua was the guest of honor at a dinner where one of the speakers talked about the coming union of Polynesia and predicted that Kalakaua, "the Colossus of the Pacific," would be the ruler of that empire. It was a heady start. From California the king traveled directly to Japan, where he unnerved Judd and Armstrong by talking with Emperor Mutsuhito about the formation of a federation of Asian nations, which would include Hawaii. He also proposed the marriage of his niece, Princess Kaiulani, to a young Japanese prince. Nothing came of either proposal, but it did cause Judd and Armstrong to keep a closer watch on the king. The grand tour continued with stops at Shanghai, Tientsin, and Hong Kong. Wherever the king stopped he was warmly received and was considered a gentleman of intelligence and good manners. They progressed to Siam, the Malay States, India, and Egypt.

The party arrived in Italy on June 30, and Kalakaua met with King Humbert and Pope Leo XIII. Then they crossed to England, where the king was warmly welcomed by Queen Victoria. He was appointed an Honorary Knight Grand Cross of the Order of St. Michael and St. George. Even the usually critical Armstrong admitted that the king's visit to England did much to impress the British with the civilization of Hawaii. He visited Belgium, Germany, Austria, France, Spain, and Portugal. He walked over the battleground at Waterloo in a driving rainstorm and inspected the Krupp gun factory in Essen. In the United States Kalakaua met with President Chester A. Arthur. He visited Hampton Institute, run by his old friend General Samuel C. Armstrong, the younger brother of William Armstrong. He stopped in Kentucky to buy horses and then went by train across country to San Francisco. He reached Honolulu on October 29, 1881, and was received by crowds who cheered his safe return.

The tour made a profound impression on Kalakaua. The power and wealth of the Oriental kings and the ceremony and dignity of European royalty certainly stiffened his resolve to maintain and even increase the prestige of royalty in his small kingdom.

When news of Kalakaua's world tour had reached the United States, Secretary of State James G. Blaine had been suspicious. Blaine had written to the American ministers in the countries the king intended to visit telling them to watch the activities of Kalakaua closely, and instructed them to inform any foreign power to which the king might offer to sell a portion of his kingdom that such a transfer would not be allowed by the United States.

There was much publicity on Kalakaua's trip in America. An editorial in the *New York Times* in mid-July was indicative of the general tone: "It is an open secret that Kalakaua, King of the Hawaiian Islands, is on a voyage around the world for the purpose of selling his kingdom. . . . If annexation ever arrives, it must take the Islands to the United States. . . ." With the first mirage of danger it became clear that if Hawaii were going to be annexed, the United States considered itself first in line.

Before Kalakaua departed on his tour he had officiated at the laying of a cornerstone for a new palace. The building would bear the same name as the old, Iolani palace, and it would be built on the same site. There were delays and much incompetence along the way, but by the end of 1882 it was completed. The palace included a basement, which extended under the whole structure, and two main floors. Six square towers rose above the second floor roof line. There were wide verandas on the four sides of the first and second floors. Kalakaua's rooms were hung with pale blue silk, and the furniture was of ebony and gold. The new Iolani palace was a handsome, impressive building.

With the palace completed, plans were pushed for a ceremony which had long been a vision in Kalakaua's mind. The king wanted a coronation, a grand ceremony, to mark the ascendency of the Kalakaua line as rulers of Hawaii. There was opposition to the idea in the cabinet, and William Armstrong, the recent traveling companion of the king, resigned in protest. The coronation was set for the ninth anniversary of Kalakaua's coming to the throne. At a cost of $5,000 the king had ordered crowns made in England for himself and his queen. A temporary amphitheater, providing seating for several thousands of people, had been built. Here the loyal subjects gathered to watch the solemn coronation rites on the morning of February 12, 1883.

The official procession started at 11 A.M. with the choir singing the hymn "Almighty Father, Hear! The Isles do Wait on Thee." The king was presented with the ancient Hawaiian symbols of office, and then the sword of state was placed in his hands. The feather cloak of Kamehameha I was draped on his shoulders, and he took the oath of office. Kalakaua lifted the crown from a satin cushion and placed it on his own head, then placed a smaller crown on the head of Queen Kapiolani. As the couple knelt, the house chaplain offered a prayer. The batteries on shore fired a salute, followed by the batteries on board the foreign warships in port. The couple then adjourned to the palace as the Royal Hawaiian Band played the "Coronation March." The *Advertiser* reported 7,000 people were there.

Few persons remained indifferent to the coronation. For royal sympathizers it was an impressive, emotional ceremony which paid the king nothing more than the honor due him. For detractors it was a teeth-grinding farce. The *Saturday Press* spoke for the latter: "If any student of government desires to see how absurd and childish are the shows and plays of a royal or imperial establishment, let him look at the coronation and the fuss and feathers of King Kalakaua." Among those who declined invitations to the coronation were Bernice and Charles Bishop and Dowager Queen Emma.

George W. Stewart wrote a long poem making fun of the coronation. It was called "The Crowning of the Dread King" and appeared in pamphlet form. Some of Stewart's statements had no basis in fact, but the tone of contempt amused the detractors.

> Not a squadron comes from Britain,
> And from France no fleet is sent us;
> Not a German flag is sighted;
> Not a dragon banner waving
> Greets the eye in thy waters,
> All thy waters, O Hawaii!

In fact, Stewart continued, there was not so much as a sail in sight from Polynesia. Later in the poem he did admit Japan sent a representative and also,

> Half a dozen souls from "Frisco,"
> All the way from San Francisco;

The poem concluded with a description of the celebration which took place that night on the palace grounds. There was singing and dancing and as the hours passed more and more drinking. The affair becomes noisier, coarser, drunker by turns, ending in "a Bacchanalian riot."

Obtaining funds for the coronation and for the statue of Kamehameha I, which stood across the street from the palace, had been the work of Walter Murray Gibson. This Gibson was the same man who had been viewed with suspicion when he arrived in Honolulu during the early days of the Civil War. He had gone through the motions of being a Mormon, which gave him the opportunity to defraud the church and end up with extensive lands on Lanai. The domain of Lanai, however, was a dry, lonesome place with a diminishing number of subjects. Gibson turned his attention to business endeavors in Lahaina and in 1878 ran for the legislature.

Walter Murray Gibson was a shrewd man, and he won an impressive victory in his first attempt at elective office. During his first term he worked hard and effectively. He flattered the king and fought for the appropriations the king wanted. His ability quickly brought him to the top at a time when incompetence and indolence were the rule. On May 20, 1882, Gibson won his prize. King Kalakaua appointed him premier and minister of foreign affairs. Only Claus Spreckels could contend that Walter Gibson was not the most powerful haole in the kingdom.

Gibson knew where the votes came from. He had mastered the Hawaiian language and knew much of the history and mythology of the Islands. His emotion-filled speeches were designed to raise the spirit of nationalism and racism in the hearts of Hawaiians and he was eminently successful. His cry was "Hawaii for the Hawaiians," and in the absence of a strong leader of Hawaiian blood the Islanders flocked to the support of the white-haired, white-bearded man.

King Kalakaua and Gibson were a fearsome pair. Gibson had the imagination to dream grand schemes and the persuasiveness to sell them to large numbers of important people. Kalakaua could easily visualize himself as the hero in these dreams, and he was eager to do all in his power to bring some substance to them. There was shrill opposition to the Gibson-Kalakaua reign, but for five years Gibson was able to frustrate his enemies and push plans ahead. And in the end their enemies had to go outside the law to tumble Gibson and render the king ineffectual.

The list of endeavors Gibson and the king arranged and consummated is a long and complicated one. Some of them certainly were well intentioned, but the reformers had made up their minds that all government activity which involved these two was dishonest. The truth of the matter was that the king was under great financial pressure, because his personal indebtedness was getting farther and farther out of reach. To pay the bills many things were for sale which should not have been. For a price lepers could be exempted from being shipped to Molokai, customs duties could be avoided if goods were marked for the king's use, and lands were illegally leased to the crown without auction. All brought badly needed income. And there was the bank charter for Claus Spreckels, the Hawaiian silver coinage, the various loan acts—all probably brought money into the personal treasury of the king.

The reformers were a morally righteous group, and the continuing flow of suspicious events was as irritating to them as an ocean tide washing salt into an open wound. Two particularly unpleasant happenings finally shook them into action. The first was an absurd attempt to establish an Empire of Polynesia, with Kalakaua as ruler, and the second was accepting money for the license to import opium from two different individuals. The tolerance for such activity on the part of the reformers was now small, and those first steps were taken which soon would seal the fate of the kingdom.

King Kalakaua had vague wishes to extend his influence or his kingdom or both. In 1880 a resolution was passed in the legislature which created a Royal Hawaiian Commissioner to represent the government to the peoples of Polynesia. Three years later the government sent copies of a policy statement to twenty-six nations stating that the various islands of Polynesia should be allowed to govern themselves and not be annexed by any major power. Most nations ignored the statement. In December, 1886, Kalakaua and Gibson were ready to make their first real attempt at wielding influence in the South Pacific when John E. Bush was named envoy to Samoa and Tonga.

At that time Samoa was internally split. Two chiefs were vying for control of the country and Germany, Great Britain, and the United States were all interested in annexing the islands. Bush signed an agreement of confederation with one of the chiefs, and the document was approved by Kalakaua. News of the confederation was received by the three major powers with annoyance. Meanwhile the unrestrained personal life of Bush was losing him and Hawaii support in Samoa at a rapid pace.

If Hawaii was to become a Polynesian power, it needed a navy, and so a British copra and guano steamer was purchased toward the end of 1886. It was fitted out with six brass cannons and two Gatling guns and named the *Kaimiloa,* meaning "the far seeker." The captain was a drunkard, the officers were inexperienced, and half the crew were reform school boys who were supposed to learn their seamanship enroute to Samoa. Before leaving Honolulu there was a drunken brawl aboard the *Kaimiloa* which resulted in the discharge of three officers. On June 15, 1887, the vessel at last reached Apia. The *Kaimiloa* made a good impression on arrival, but things soon deteriorated. The sailors were unmanageable and drunken. When the captain of a German naval vessel sent a detachment of men aboard the Hawaiian ship to keep mutinous crew members from blowing up their own vessel, it was clear to everyone that the *Kaimiloa* and the Hawaiian legation were capable only of playing a comic role in the tense Samoan situation. Eventually the vessel found its way back to Honolulu harbor. It was the end of the short-lived Hawaiian navy.

The full story of what was going on in Samoa was not public knowledge in Honolulu in mid-1887, but rumors about the opium monopoly were enough to keep the reform party in a state of agitation. The legislature of 1886 gave the government the right to grant an opium monopoly for the entire kingdom. Such a monopoly would be extremely lucrative and at least several persons were interested in it. On May 17, 1887, the *Hawaiian Gazette* published a story taken from a series of affidavits by a Chinese rice planter named T. Aki and others. The story confirmed some of the wild rumors which had been circulating. Aki had paid $71,000 to a flunky of the king to secure the opium monopoly. The money had been accepted, but the monopoly went to another person who had paid a larger sum. When Aki demanded the return of his money, he was told it had been spent. The king did not bother to deny the story, and reform indignation swelled to a new high.

Toward the end of December, 1886, the Hawaiian League was formed. The goals of the League varied with individual members, but there was unanimous agreement that changes in the government had to be made. The conservative members simply wanted to force Gibson out of office, while the radicals wanted to overthrow the monarchy and establish a republic or seek annexation to the United States. Members took an oath to keep the existence of the League a secret and to defend others endangered by membership. The Hawaiian League was made up of haole reformers with a very sparse sprinkling of part Hawaiians.

The Honolulu Rifles was organized anew as the League was growing. Many men were members of both groups. Arms and ammunition were imported. The companies were drilled by Lieutenant Colonel Volney V. Ashford. Ashford was a man of considerable military experience, having served through the Civil War in the Union army, later in the Indian wars, and then in the Canadian army. Volney Ashford had a very direct solution to the problems of the time. He thought the Honolulu Rifles should hold a marksmanship competition and Kalakaua should be invited to present the winner with a prize rifle in the presence of the companies. As the king stood before the troops, the order would be given to shoot him. Ashford's suggestion was vetoed, but it so upset several of the conservative members that they resigned.

Because the Honolulu Rifles was an official government volunteer organization, its rapid growth and training were public knowledge. The Hawaiian League was supposed to be a secret organization, but with a membership of some 400 secrecy was hardly possible. Both Walter M. Gibson and Kalakaua certainly knew of the activity of this organization and the king, at least, did not take it lightly. He ordered platforms built behind the eight-foot-high wall surrounding Iolani palace so soldiers could fire on an enemy. He had loopholes cut in the tall iron stairs at the front and rear of the palace so other soldiers could cover these two approaches should the enemy break through the wall. At night the palace grounds were illuminated by electric lights. The government knew that arms were being imported into the Islands, but it was too frightened or inept to do anything about it.

The Hawaiian League grew in numbers and became better organized. Nowhere along the line did they meet open opposition from the government, and this undoubtedly emboldened them. Toward the end of June, 1887, Gibson and the king became alarmed by the constant rumors which came to their ears. By June 27 the king knew something drastic was about to happen. That evening he requested the U. S. minister to come to the palace and tell him what he must do. He was told, as others had told him, that he must get rid of Gibson and the rest of the cabinet and he must stop meddling in the government. By 1 A.M. on the morning of June 28 he had secured resignations from all his cabinet members. Kalakaua had hopes of placating his enemies before they became violent.

A succession of events had frightened Kalakaua into action. One unnerving fact was the arrival in Honolulu of a large shipment of arms which had been ordered by the Hawaiian League, whose members boldly went down to the dock to pick them up. The League no longer made any attempt to keep its membership or movements secret. Now well armed, they called a mass meeting for June 30. Kalakaua had an active imagination, and he undoubtedly feared he would come to some bloody end during that last week in June.

Success had come easily and without cost to the Hawaiian League, and they could no longer be appeased by the resignation of the cabinet. On the afternoon of the mass meeting business houses closed. At 2 P.M. some 2,500 men gathered at the armory of the Rifles to listen to numerous speakers voice their opinions. Because of the possibility of violence the Honolulu Rifles had officially been called out to stand guard. The cooperation of the government in making the presence of the Rifles legal is curious, for it would have been an act of rebellion for them to have stood guard over government buildings if not officially ordered to do so. Kalakaua certainly knew the Rifles would take orders from the League and not from him. Members of the Rifles not on duty elsewhere were drawn up outside the armory.

Lorrin A. Thurston, a grandson of the missionary Asa Thurston, read a set of resolutions which had been prepared. The demands called for a new cabinet, which would write a new constitution, the return of the $71,000 owed Aki, and the pledge of the king that he would not interfere in elections or in the working of the legislature or cabinet and that he would not use his position for private gain. A committee of thirteen was named to present the demands to the king, who was given twenty-four hours in which to reply. Among the speakers at the meeting was Charles Bishop, a most conservative man, who was opposed to the overthrow of the monarchy. Even he was moved to state flatly, "There is no confidence in the King." It was a noisy group, applauding those who demanded immediate action and booing the speakers who called for caution.

While the mass meeting was in progress, Lieutenant Colonel Ashford, commander of the Rifles, was on personal business. Only days before the mass meeting Volney Ashford had been selected by the Gibson administration to go to Canada to negotiate a reciprocal trade agreement with that country. His commission was delivered to him just two days before the public meeting. While the mass meeting was in progress, Ashford was collecting $4,000 of a $5,000 fee for this job. He received $1,500 from the government and the remainder from Kalakaua's personal funds. The strange timing of Ashford's business dealings raised some serious questions as to whether or not he was selling "protection" to Kalakaua. Ashford never went to Canada, and he returned only the $1,500 which came from the government, pocketing the $2,500 which had come from the king. Ashford's explanation of the affair, however, seemed to satisfy most League members.

After the meeting had run its course the committee of thirteen called on the king and presented their demands in written form. The king was ready to agree to them immediately, but the committee members said that twenty-four hours was the time allotted and twenty-four hours he must take. The king was distraught. At noon of the following day Kalakaua called in the ministers of Great Britain, France, Portugal, Japan, and the United States and stated that his country had been taken over by armed men and that he wanted to place the kingdom in their hands. The foreign representatives could not accept such a proposition, of course, and that same afternoon the king acceded to the demands of the League.

The new cabinet included Lorrin A. Thurston and Clarence W. Ashford, brother of Volney. Both were League members and had addressed the mass meeting. Thurston did the major work on the new constitution, which was presented to the king for his signature on July 6. The new document took a great deal of power away from the monarch. In essence Kalakaua became a ceremonial figure. While he could still appoint his cabinet, the members would now be responsible to the legislature. Cabinet members could only be removed through a want-of-confidence vote by a majority of the legislature. While the king still had veto power over legislation, it could now be overridden by a two-thirds vote of the legislature. Nobles were to be elected and no longer appointed. To be eligible to run for the House of Nobles a candidate had to own property worth $3,000 or have an annual income of $600. There was a lesser property requirement to run as a representative.

To be eligible to vote for nobles voters had to possess the same amount of property or income as if a candidate for that office. American and European males could vote if they took an oath to support the constitution and laws regardless of whether they were citizens of the kingdom or not. Asians could not vote. What the new constitution did was increase the number of haoles who could vote and drastically limit the number of Hawaiians who could vote for nobles, because of the relatively high property or income requirements. The objective in all this was to give the reformers the edge they deemed necessary to control the legislature and thus the government.

Why did Kalakaua not resist? He had the backing of the great majority of the Hawaiians. He had fortified Iolani palace and he had troops, arms, and ammunition. There appear to be several reasons why he so quickly accepted the demands of his enemies. One reason was that the Gibson-Kalakaua regime had sheared the government of leadership. There simply was no one around capable of resisting the aggressive League. With Gibson gone the king had no one to counsel with, and in desperation he turned to the representatives of foreign countries. The Hawaiian troops not only lacked leadership, but no one knew better than Kalakaua that they could be subverted. He had played that role himself in the mutiny of 1873. Perhaps the most important reason for his quick surrender was the simple fact that Kalakaua was not a brave man in the face of physical danger.

At 4 P.M. on the afternoon of July 6 a group of League members brought the new constitution to the king. He listened in sullen and somewhat stunned silence as the document was read. He hedged and stalled, but according to Clarence Ashford, who was there, "little was left to the imagination of the hesitating and unwilling Sovereign, as to what he might expect in the event of his refusal to comply with the demands made upon him."

The morning following the mass meeting Walter Gibson and his son-in-law, Fred Hayselden, were taken into custody by the Rifles. At first they were held prisoner in a waterfront warehouse. Here it was that Lieutenant Colonel Ashford threatened to hang Gibson from the yardarm of a ship as an example to others. He was prevented from carrying out his threat by the executive committee of the League. Later in the day the two were taken to Gibson's house, where they were placed under guard, and on July 5 they were packed off to Oahu jail. The charge of embezzlement of public funds was brought against the pair, but it was dropped for want of evidence. On July 12 Walter Murray Gibson sailed for San Francisco.

The Hawaiian League was not the only problem Gibson had run into during the trying summer of 1887. Perhaps less dangerous, but certainly very vexing was a breach of promise suit brought against him by a Mrs. Flora Howard St. Clair. The scandal was a delight to Gibson's numerous enemies.

Mrs. St. Clair, a widow, had come to Honolulu in February, 1886, from San Francisco. The ship's roster listed her as Mrs. Howard, the name she customarily used in her business as a bookseller for A. L. Bancroft & Co., of San Francisco. With Flora came a sister, Alice Caldwell, who also sold books and for that purpose used the name Alice Waite.

Some six weeks after coming to the Islands Flora made an appointment to see Gibson and showed him some art books which she hoped would interest him. Gibson purchased books from time to time, and apparently Flora received introductions to various prominent people in Honolulu through him. Matters did not long remain on a business basis, however, for Gibson soon asked to walk her home and to call at the boarding house where she and her sister stayed. Flora later testified, "I liked him, thought him very nice and entertaining, and felt sorry he was so old." At this time Flora was twenty-eight and Gibson was sixty-three or sixty-four. Toward the end of December, 1886, Flora was greatly surprised when Gibson proposed to her. Nonetheless, she accepted his proposal.

The prime minister explained to Flora that there was a problem. It revolved around his daughter, Talula, and son-in-law, Fred Hayselden. Gibson asked Flora to keep their engagement a secret until an opportune time came and he could break the news to them. Somewhere along the line his daughter and son-in-law had heard of Gibson's romantic ideas, and it was no secret that they strongly opposed them. Gibson continued to see Flora and she came to his house on at least two occasions when he was ill. Somehow he never quite got around to discussing Flora with his daughter and son-in-law, and no public announcement was made of their engagement.

In March a short item appeared in a gossip column in the *Hawaiian Gazette,* a newspaper which delighted in ridiculing Gibson and Kalakaua. The columnist ". . . believed old Nosbig really meditated taking unto himself a wife soon. . . . Things squint that way at present. Well, who'd have thought it. . . ." The prime minister, known as Nosbig by his enemies, was upset. He called on Flora, telling her he could not afford to have his name the subject of gossip. Items continued to appear, and Gibson no longer showed up at Flora's residence. On April 26 the columnist felt ". . . sure that the ceremony will soon take place, unless lightening should strike the old fraud, or Providence or some one else intervenes." The following week the columnist reported having talked to Flora: ". . . she blames Sonny-in-law for her troubles with the gay old fraud. . . . She said, 'You bet, and that ceremony will have to come off soon or I will raise—well, I'll make it warm for the old man, that's all. . . .' "

When Walter Gibson ceased to call, Flora became upset. She wrote him three agitated letters, the last of which was dated May 5, 1887: "You know in your heart that we are engaged . . . Unless you renew your visits to me, and freely admit our engagement not later (Monday, May 9th) I shall as [I must] conclude that you are insincere in your professions and promises." Gibson ignored the letters. By May 19 Flora St. Clair had the case in the hands of a lawyer, who sent Gibson a letter stating that Flora would drop the whole matter if Gibson would write her a letter acknowledging the fact that he had asked her to marry him and that she had accepted. The lawyer pointed out that Flora would not seek financial damages if such an acknowledgment were made, since she was not impelled by "mercenary motives, but feels that circumstances have made it necessary for her to take this course for her vindication and protection."

On May 21 Gibson's lawyer wrote an answer stating that Gibson "declines to make such an acknowledgement not having made any proposals of marriage to the lady in question." On the same day the prime minister was served a summons. The charge was breach of promise, and the damages asked were $25,000. The case was set for the July term. With the issuance of a summons, the news of Gibson's personal troubles moved from speculation to fact. It was the most tantalizing conversation piece in a long, long time.

Gibson was spared the indignity of being in Honolulu for a July trial, thanks to the Hawaiian League and the Honolulu Rifles. With Gibson out of the kingdom his lawyer succeeded in having the trial date postponed to October, because of the prejudice which then existed against the former prime minister. When October came, Gibson was seriously ill in St. Mary's Hospital in San Francisco—too sick to give a deposition, much less consider returning to Honolulu. The trial opened October 25 and lasted two and a half days. During this time the slim, dark-haired, dark-eyed Flora spent ten hours on the stand. When the evidence was all in, the jury adjourned, returning in less than two hours. The verdict was unanimous in favor of Flora Howard St. Clair, who was awarded $10,000 damages.

Flora settled for $8,000, possibly with the understanding that Gibson's lawyers would not press for a new trial. The bookselling sisters had expressed a wish to leave the Islands, and the threat of a new trial would have delayed them longer. In December Flora sailed for Japan and sister Alice returned to San Francisco. What happened to Flora after her Hawaii adventure remains a mystery.

A San Francisco reporter interviewed Walter Murray Gibson at St. Mary's hospital when the verdict had become known. Asked if he had made a promise of marriage to Flora, Gibson said, "I never dreamt of doing such a thing." The former prime minister was quite ready to cast a shadow over Flora's character. He recalled that when she showed him art books she had said "that the charms of Venus could be totally eclipsed by women of the present day. She also, in her vanity, compared her form with that of Venus, and intimated that the comparison was in no wise disparaging to her." In the final analysis Gibson believed his political enemies had really been the ones who had done him in: ". . . the Chief Justice and the jury which tried the case were my most bitter enemies. I have no doubt these men had great satisfaction in bringing a verdict against me. . . . The whole suit was the outcome of political enmity which I had incurred, and Mrs. Flora Howard St. Clair was the willing tool of the conspirators."

Flora St. Clair was born in Sacramento County in California. At the age of twenty-two she married, but two years later her husband died. She went to work for A. L. Bancroft & Co., a company she had worked for before her marriage, and sold books in the San Francisco and Los Angeles areas. By the time she reached Hawaii she had worked for the company about four years.

In investigating Flora's past on the mainland, Gibson's lawyers could find no damaging evidence acceptable in court. Flora Howard St. Clair seems to have been an industrious, calculating woman who was determined to make a living for herself in an age when it was difficult for women to do so. At this point in Gibson's life he was a much harassed, sick, lonely old man. The attractive widow was a comfort to him, but when his daughter heard of the affair and when newspapers began to ridicule him, Walter Gibson backed off. Flora felt doubly stung. She had missed financial security which marriage would have brought and she also believed, according to the mores of the day, that her good name was endangered. She demanded Gibson admit he had proposed to her. Suspicions that she was out to swindle the old man are largely dispelled by the fact that initially her lawyer did not ask for money, but only recognition of their relationship.

There was little time left for Walter Murray Gibson. Tuberculosis finally killed him on January 21, 1888. His remains were shipped back to Honolulu and carried ashore in a coffin draped with the Hawaiian flag. His body was placed on view in Honolulu and a long line of curious people filed past the casket. Among them were Lorrin Thurston, Sanford B. Dole, and his brother George. Thurston described what happened in his memoirs: "When I got to a place where I could look down into the coffin, I was shocked to see that an embalming fluid, with which the body had been treated, had turned it coal black. Against that color, the snow white hair and beard presented a startling contrast. While we went into the street, we were silent for some minutes. Then Sanford asked: 'What do you think of it?' After a pause, George Dole said deliberately: 'Well, I think his complexion is approximating the color of his soul.' "

The Catholic Cathedral in Honolulu was crowded with Gibson's friends and enemies who came to hear mass sung over his remains. Among them was the man who had once wanted to hang him. The casket was placed in a Honolulu cemetery and later removed to Lahaina, where a special vault had been constructed. The casket has since disappeared and the vault lies empty.

In the summer of 1888 Robert Louis Stevenson sailed from San Francisco in the ninety-five-foot yacht *Casco*. He was bound for the South Seas, hoping to regain his failing health through a sea voyage into warm climes. With the emaciated, tubercular author were his wife, Fanny, his stepson, Lloyd Osbourne, Stevenson's mother, a cook, and a maid. The sailing crew consisted of four hands under Captain Albert O. Otis, a long-time sailor who dreaded going to sea with women and a sickly author. Stevenson looked so frail that the captain secretly made the necessary preparations for a burial at sea.

The owner of the *Casco* was a Dr. Merritt, who had been opposed to renting his vessel to an author, but Stevenson's charm had convinced the doctor that he was sound in mind if not in body. The rent was set at $500 per month plus repairs and incidental costs. The yacht was luxurious. The main cabin was fitted out with tassels, carvings, and mirrors—everything Victorian decorators could crowd into the limited space.

The *Casco* made for the Marquesas and then sailed on to the Society Islands. At Tahiti the travelers were delayed five weeks while the two masts were repaired for a serious case of dry rot. On Christmas day 1888 they sailed north, bound for the Hawaiian Islands. Calms and headwinds alternately bedeviled them, slowing their progress to sixty or seventy miles per day. A week passed between the time they sighted the island of Hawaii and the day they were blown into Honolulu harbor.

On three occasions the vessel had been so close to Honolulu that special celebration dinners had seemed appropriate. On each occasion the passengers awakened the next morning to discover that contrary winds had driven them farther away than on the previous evening. Then a strong wind caught the *Casco* and careened it into the harbor at a frightening speed. The voyage had lasted thirty days.

The arrival was doubly pleasant for Fanny Stevenson. Her daughter, Isobel Strong, and a grandson named Austin came off port in a small boat to meet them. It was the happiest of reunions because the *Casco* was so long overdue that some considered it lost. The Joseph Strongs had been living in Honolulu since September, 1882, when he had come to the Islands to do a painting for the Spreckels Sugar Company. Joe had been in Honolulu before, as a boy, when his father was minister of the Fort Street church. Now Joe and Isobel were part of the Kalakaua crowd, a group much frowned upon by many of Honolulu's respectable people. Joe had been selected for the ill conceived expedition to Samoa where he was supposed to collect artifacts and make sketches of native life.

The ocean voyage did much for Stevenson's health, and he felt better than he had for years. In Hawaii he was a celebrity, for he was the famous author of *Dr. Jekyll and Mr. Hyde, Treasure Island,* and *Kidnapped.* Two days after arrival Stevenson was introduced to Kalakaua and before long the king called on the author. As Kalakaua was entertained aboard the *Casco,* he amazed Stevenson by downing five bottles of champagne and two bottles of brandy during a four-hour visit. This kind of performance was repeated on subsequent visits, and Stevenson later wrote to a friend, "Why a bottle of fizz is like a glass of sherry to him. . . ." Before long the rush of callers at the Stevenson cottage became such a trial that a notice appeared in the newspaper announcing they would be "at home" between 2 and 5 P.M.

Robert Louis Stevenson had to get down to the business of writing. When he arrived in Honolulu he was nearly broke, and he spent some anxious weeks awaiting funds from his publisher. He released the *Casco* and moved out to Waikiki, about four miles from Honolulu, a comfortable distance to put between himself and prying people. Waikiki consisted of some twenty to thirty wooden buildings, scattered along the beach, most of them summer houses. He moved into a house in the shadow of Diamond Head and designated a shack off the main building as a work room. Here Ah Fu, the cook who had stayed with them when the *Casco* departed, brought him tea and toast in the morning. In this dilapidated place he worked as hard as his health would allow and finished *The Master of Ballantrae.*

The Stevenson household was a strange, informal place. The author often worked through the day in his pajamas, and when he went out he usually dressed in a velveteen jacket and wore a red sash about his waist. The first emotion many persons felt on seeing him was pity. He weighed less than a hundred pounds and appeared to be little more than a shell. His hollow chest, the narrow face, blue veins showing in his forehead, and his burning eyes created a startling impression. Fanny quickly adopted the muumuu and holoku and went about barefooted. She had cut her hair short and incessantly smoked cigarettes. Stevenson's mother was a contrast. She was a very proper person who customarily wore a starched, white, Victorian widow's cap. Isobel and Joe Strong, with their son, usually joined the Stevensons on weekends. In the evening Stevenson might read aloud or the family might join in home-made music, with Stevenson playing the flageolet. When Fanny noticed her husband tiring, she would politely but firmly suggest that guests leave.

The family was not without its problems. The constant social whirl which characterized Kalakaua's reign was not the sort of life Joe Strong should have been exposed to. He drank excessively, ran up bills he could not pay, and was generally unreliable. These shortcomings brought on emotional scenes of banishment which in turn moved Joe to equally emotional periods of repentance. Joe was a competent artist when he worked at it, but the gaps between efforts were frequent and prolonged. The generous Stevenson helped support the young couple during his Honolulu stay. Later, when he moved to Samoa, the Strongs joined him. But, at last, their marriage ended in divorce.

For King Kalakaua the presence of Robert Louis Stevenson appeared to be an opportunity. The king had suffered great humiliation when the constitution of 1887 was forced on him, and he wanted all the friends he could find. A world-famous writer would have been a great catch. The writer and the king spent many hours together. Kalakaua explained Hawaii's ancient legends and the two pored over the notebooks of the king. They became genuinely fond of each other, and the king was disappointed when he learned that Stevenson was not going to become a permanent resident of the Islands.

Stevenson was an avowed monarchist and the sad plight of Island royalty touched his heart. Like other writers before him, he lamented the presence of a Western civilization which had fastened its moral and mercantile codes on the Polynesians. Before he had ever set foot on the Islands someone had influenced Stevenson against the prevailing social situation, and he had described the Islands he had never seen as "a boiling pot of disagreeables." After he had been in Honolulu for several months he wrote a friend, ". . . we live here, oppressed with civilization, and look for good things in the future." Although he apparently made one verbal offer to write a pamphlet in opposition to the reformers, he did not become actively involved in Island political affairs. Very likely he felt matters had deteriorated too far. There was no turning the tide.

Stevenson believed the climate of Hawaii was too cold for him. At first he had felt good enough to swim at Waikiki, but he tired easily and frequently hemorrhaged. Before departing, the author visited the Kona coast of Hawaii, where he obtained the background material for the short story which he called "The Bottle Imp." On his return trip from Kona he received permission to go ashore at the leper settlement on Molokai. He arrived a month after Father Damien's death, which he much regretted. Stevenson probably had heard glowing accounts of the priest during his visits with fellow writer Charles Warren Stoddard in San Francisco. He stayed at Kalaupapa for a week, and the horror of the experience made a deep impression. He played croquet with the leper girls and talked to many persons about Damien. When he returned to Honolulu he had a $300 piano sent to the settlement for the use of the girls who had been his croquet partners.

On June 24, 1889, the Stevensons departed Honolulu on another chartered yacht. Stevenson was still searching for that climate which would add a few years to his life, and the South Seas was his destination. The king added his good wishes for the voyage. When the vessel was about to depart, Kalakaua and several members of his band rolled up in carriages. The king was amply supplied with champagne. Toasts were drunk and as the sailing ship slipped from the dock the king waved and the musicians serenaded the voyagers.

The turn of events willed that Robert Louis Stevenson should create a great commotion in Hawaii when he was thousands of miles away and six months gone. In Sydney, Australia, the author read a letter written by Rev. Charles M. Hyde of Honolulu in a church newspaper. The letter was a personal one, not intended for publication, and it was just one paragraph in length. It had been written in response to a request for information on Father Damien's work at the leper settlement, and the Protestant clergy-man's response was less than flattering to the priest.

The letter by Hyde ignited all of Stevenson's sympathy for the lepers and all his dislike for the haoles. In a passion Stevenson wrote an open let-ter to Hyde which was widely reprinted in the United States and Europe. It is still considered a classic in denunciation. In defending Damien, Ste-venson lashed out at Hyde in a personal and bitter way. Even the author realized his letter was libelous. He showed it to his family and told them it could result in a law suit which might mean great financial loss, but his family encouraged him to publish it. Fortunately for the family, Reverend Hyde brushed the affair off, refusing to make an issue of it. Stevenson later regretted the personal aspects of the letter, calling it "barbarously harsh." The letter stands as a discordant note among the writings of a man who was generally acclaimed as a kind and gentle person.

Robert Louis Stevenson made a second trip to Hawaii in 1893. He took his lodgings again at Waikiki, this time at a hotel managed by a Greek named George Lycurgus. He visited the deposed Liliuokalani but avoided all political involvement. A brief incident illustrated the frailty of his health. His carriage driver had acquired a new horse, and for some reason the animal suddenly ran wild. The driver brought the horse under control quickly, but the experience so upset the ailing Stevenson that he took to his bed. Fanny rushed to Hawaii to nurse him. Somewhat re-covered he sailed home to Samoa, where he died in 1894.

The control of the government was slipping away from the native Hawaiians. This did not immediately affect the lives of many, but it did hurt the pride of most. Historically the Hawaiians had been politically sensitive—keenly aware of the fine gradations of power which their chiefs possessed. Now they were losing hold. There were men willing to fight to regain their prerogatives, but no leader appeared.

The best man to come forward was Robert W. Wilcox. His father had been an American sailor who had married a Hawaiian chiefess. They lived on Maui and there Robert was born in 1855. He was a bright boy, and by the time he was twenty-two he was teaching school. Five years later he was elected to the legislature. That same year Robert Wilcox was selected by Kalakaua as one of the Hawaiians who should go to Italy to receive a military education. When the king was shorn of his power in 1887, the money for educating these men was withdrawn, and Wilcox returned to Hawaii.

Wilcox did not return alone. With him came his wife, the former Gina Sobrero, a daughter of a noble and distinguished Italian family. During his years of absence Wilcox must have magnified his importance, at the same time forgetting the unpleasant aspects of Hawaiian life. It is certain that he was shocked to learn what the situation was in the Islands. The Hawaiian League dominated the government, and there was little sympathy for a person who had been benefiting from the largess of Kalakaua.

Life in Honolulu was miserable. Somewhere along the line Gina Wilcox told Liliuokalani she wished she had never married Robert. Sympathetic friends raised funds to enable the couple to go to San Francisco, and this they did in 1888. She taught Italian and French while he worked as a surveyor. It was neither the kind of life she was used to nor the sort of life he hoped for. Robert Wilcox returned to Hawaii in 1889. His wife and infant daughter returned to Italy sometime later. The daughter died and Mrs. Wilcox was granted an annulment by Pope Leo XIII in 1895.

Back in Honolulu Robert Wilcox opened a surveying and civil engineering office. When work was scarce, he charged the reformers with boycotting him. Wilcox's continuing misfortunes made him determined to change things, and the obvious first thing to change was the constitution of 1887. He took note of the way the opposition was organized, and he founded the Kamehameha Rifle Association. He also started a secret organization whose purpose was to restore the old system of government. He raised money, recruited men, and bought guns. The organization included several Chinese members who helped supply the money.

By mid-July, 1889, rumors about the secret organization were heard throughout the Islands. Kalakaua knew of it and told the cabinet. One story related that Robert Wilcox not only wanted to establish a new constitution, but also wanted to replace Kalakaua with the king's sister, Liliuokalani. The government did little to frustrate Wilcox, believing he would take no action until after the elections of February, 1890. Kalakaua tried hard to stay out of the entanglements. While he certainly would have liked to regain his old authority, he knew that he could not afford to end up on the losing side. The persistent stories which prophesied he would be replaced on the throne by his sister must have made him uneasy. And no one knew better than the king that the reformers were not going to yield up their gains easily.

Early on the morning of July 30 Robert Wilcox made his move. With some eighty followers he marched on the palace. Some of his men were dressed in red shirts, and Wilcox wore his Italian military uniform. In his pocket he carried a copy of a new constitution. The weapons his men shouldered were an odd assortment of rifles and small-bore shotguns. As they marched along spectators joined the parade, and at about 4 A.M. they reached the palace grounds and easily gained admittance. The King's Guard retreated to the palace itself, leaving Wilcox in possession of the grounds between the palace building and the outer eight-foot-high coral rock wall. Wilcox had command of four small-bore cannon which were brought out of storage and set up to command the four gates.

The king was not at the palace, so Wilcox sent the royal carriage to Queen Kapiolani's private residence to bring him back to sign the constitution. Kalakaua would not come and moved to his boathouse on Honolulu harbor. Wilcox sent messengers twice more, but the king gave evasive answers. Militarily Wilcox was in an untenable position. He was within the walls of the palace grounds, but his men did not have the protection of the palace itself, which continued to be held by the King's Guards. He had the protection of a sturdy eight-foot-high wall, but rising above this wall outside the grounds were three buildings. From the roofs of these buildings riflemen could sweep the palace grounds. Before long members of the Honolulu Rifles were doing just this.

Sometime between 10 and 11 in the morning the first shot was fired and the fighting began. Wilcox's men tried to use a cannon against the opera house, which was one of the buildings commanding the grounds, but they were quickly driven from the cannon by rifle fire. With inadequate weapons and little protection, it was no contest. Some of the insurgents surrendered to the King's Guard at the palace. Wilcox and others took refuge in a flimsy wooden bungalow, but they were driven out when sticks of dynamite with spikes tied to them were hurled onto the roof. Seven insurgents were killed and a dozen wounded.

Later Wilcox said he had counted on the support of the King's Guard and that Kalakaua had earlier agreed to sign the new constitution. Robert Wilcox was tried by a native jury, as the law required, and was acquitted.

The verdict infuriated his enemies. His plans had been juvenile and when put into action they were disastrous, but he had dared to try. To the Hawaiians he was a hero.

Kalakaua and Liliuokalani disavowed any part in the Wilcox revolt, although they both must have been consulted. Kalakaua was a nervous man who was not going to take risks he could avoid. His refusal to cooperate with Wilcox probably saved him the throne. Liliuokalani was also in a delicate position. If it were known she had plotted against her brother, if indeed she had, it could lose her the support of many Hawaiians. If the haoles thought she had attempted to bring back the old prerogatives of the sovereigns, she would have had little chance eventually to gain power. The only course for Kalakaua and Liliuokalani was to shake their heads and plead ignorance.

In 1890 David Kalakaua was sick. He sailed for San Francisco in November and again there were rumors that he was going to sell his kingdom. England instructed its Washington and Honolulu ministers to protest such action if it took place. In San Francisco the king was entertained by old friends. His every move was reported in the newspapers, and if his own kingdom showed him little respect, the homeland of his enemies paid him much honor. He journeyed to Southern California in a private car supplied by the Southern Pacific railroad. It was a relaxing trip. Kalakaua enjoyed sitting on the rear platform of the car smoking his pipe. At each stop people gathered to look at a real king.

Returning to San Francisco, Kalakaua stopped at Santa Barbara, where one of his entourage noticed the king had difficulty lighting his pipe. He had suffered a mild stroke. In San Francisco his social commitments were curtailed. Dr. G. W. Woods, medical inspector for the U. S. Navy, now became his personal physician, and he ordered Kalakaua to bed. The king's condition worsened. He ran a high temperature and at last he responded only when spoken to in Hawaiian. Two Hawaiian women nursed him and Dr. Woods was moved by their loving care. "It was perfect in its character—such as no foreign servants could have given."

By January 19 Kalakaua was unconscious, but communion services were conducted in his room. The next day Dr. Woods recorded that the king's life was maintained by pouring glycerine and brandy into his mouth. Charles Reed Bishop and Claus Spreckels came to his room in the Palace Hotel. Rev. J. Sanders Reed read passages from the Bible, hymns were sung, and everyone knelt in prayer. At 2:35 P.M. the king was dead. Two days later services were held in Trinity Church. As the procession moved from the church to the wharf, a San Francisco reporter estimated that 100,000 persons lined the streets. Among the things which killed Kalakaua were cirrhosis of the liver, uraemia, and cerebral damage from strokes. His enemies said he killed himself with drink, and his friends said the reformers killed him through persecution.

Kalakaua's body was returned to Hawaii aboard the *U.S.S. Charleston*. Islanders knew their king was due to return aboard this vessel, and when the warship appeared off Diamond Head plans for welcoming him home were put into action. Guns boomed a welcome before it was noticed that the *Charleston* ran her flag at half mast and that the spars and part of the hull were draped in black. Festive decorations were pulled down, and the flower arch through which Kalakaua was to step ashore was hastily covered with black.

As the band of the *Charleston* played dirges and sailors and marines moved in measured step, the body of Kalakaua was brought to Iolani Palace. Queen Kapiolani saw the procession wend toward the palace steps, and she had to be restrained from throwing herself from the second floor upon the metal steps below. A San Francisco newspaper reporter who was there was terrified by what happened. When the coffin was placed in the throne room, the queen ran down the stairs. "More mad than otherwise," the reporter wrote, "she threw herself upon the coffin and beat it with her clenched fists, venting at the same time a series of frightful cries which seemed not of the earth, but of the regions of despair."

NOW, A SINGLE SHOT
LAUNCHED THE COUP D'ÉTAT

T HE NEW RULER OF HAWAII was Queen Liliuoka-lani, the fifty-two-year-old sister of the late king. Shortly after her birth Liliuokalani had been adopted by the Paki family. She became a fast friend of Bernice and, later, Charles Bishop. By the time Liliuokalani took the oath of office Bernice was dead, but Charles remained an interested and true friend. At the beginning of her rule Bishop volunteered some practical advice: "I regard the moral influence which you can exert upon the community, and especially upon your own race as of much more importance than anything you can do in the politics or business of the country. . . . You will live longer and happier and be more popular by not trying to do too much."

If heeded these suggestions might have kept the monarchy intact for additional years, but Liliuokalani was a determined woman with definite ideas. She had been critical of her brother because he gave up his royal rights without a fight, and she had no intention of following that path. It was clear she would not be a rubber stamp monarch when she refused to hold over the cabinet of the late king. She insisted on naming her own ministry, and the supreme court upheld her wish.

During the first months of Liliuokalani's reign the press treated her kindly. *The Friend* wrote of "Her gentle and gracious demeanor, her good sense, and her fine culture. . . ." In the same article the editor also clearly indicated in what direction the kingdom was headed. "It can hardly be doubted by any one that this Kingdom is advancing through a period of transition from Monarchy to government by the people."

In August, 1891, John Dominis, husband of the queen, died. Dominis had filled several high government offices over the years, including that of governor of Oahu. He was a mild, conservative man whose quiet counsel was an important counterbalance to the queen's aggressive tendencies. Liliuokalani recognized this and later wrote that Dominis died at the time she needed his wisdom the most.

One of those who hoped to gain power and prominence under the new regime was Robert Wilcox. He wrote to the new queen early in 1891 seeking the position of chamberlain. In fact, he was willing to make a concession if the job came his way. His letter to the queen included the sentence, "This manner of immoral living I can discard at any time, when I see for the best."

Robert Wilcox was denied the position, so he attempted to gain power by establishing the Liberal party, which he hoped would control the legislature. Wilcox himself had no trouble in winning election in 1892, but other Liberal party members fared poorly. Honolulu was tense on that election day. Liliuokalani wrote in her diary that preparations had been made to quell any riots incited by the Liberal party. She feared Wilcox might try to force her from the throne.

No one was satisfied. The reformers had believed they could control the government as a result of the constitution of 1887, but they were mistaken, for the legislature was still beyond their control. They wanted a safe, stable government and they did not have it. Some discussed the idea of buying out the monarchy. The sum of $250,000 was suggested, but Lorrin Thurston considered it too small unless the queen felt very insecure. Other thoughts crossed Thurston's mind. If the monarchy were overthrown, might not the U. S. ask the Hawaiian legislature to vote approval of annexation? He felt that few of the Hawaiian legislators could be convinced to vote for annexation through argument, but if they were "subsidized" by sums of between $500 and $5,000 their votes could be obtained. Thurston believed support could be gained from other Hawaiian leaders in like fashion.

The legislative session of 1892 was a turbulent one. Those who supported the queen and her program favored a bill for a national lottery, but they could not muster the strength needed to pass it. Liliuokalani was determined it should pass, and she held the legislature in session into 1893. When certain legislators who opposed the lottery bill went off to tend to their personal businesses, the way suddenly became clear for passage. It was quickly passed on January 11, and the next day a want-of-confidence in the cabinet resolution was also passed. Most legislators agreed the cabinet members were men of ability, but they would not carry out the wishes of the queen and so they had to go.

On January 13 Liliuokalani named a new cabinet, and the next day it was announced she had signed the lottery bill. That morning she awarded royal orders to the two men who had successfully maneuvered her bills through the legislature. At noon Liliuokalani crossed from Iolani Palace to the government building to adjourn the legislature. It was a colorful, impressive procession, for she was accompanied by the Household Guards, her court ladies, chamberlain, and kahili bearers. She wore a coronet studded with diamonds and her chair was covered with a feather cloak. In her short remarks the queen invited all those present to come to the palace grounds that afternoon.

Why had the queen invited the legislators to the palace? The reason soon became known. The queen intended to proclaim a new constitution which would restore to the throne many of the rights taken away in 1887. Liliuokalani had planned well, but at the last moment a maddening problem arose. Two of the new cabinet members would not sign the new constitution. That afternoon a procession of Hawaiians came into the palace grounds as expected. They were led by a dignified man, resplendent in high silk hat, who solemnly bore a copy of the new constitution. To this gathering the queen was forced to announce that she would not be able to carry through her plans for a few more days. Some angry supporters made wild speeches from the palace steps damning those who dared thwart the queen's will.

The wrath of the queen was monumental. One of the cabinet members who received the full impact was John F. Colburn, the newly appointed minister of the interior. With the anger of the queen, who considered him a traitor, and the mounting emotion of the crowd Colburn felt lucky to escape. He went directly to the office of William Owen Smith, a law partner of Lorrin Thurston. Smith later reported, "Colburn's manner was that of a scared man—frightened—very much in earnest." John Colburn was not a friend of Thurston or Smith or the reformers in general, but in this time of stress he apparently could think of no other group who could give him protection. Why Colburn refused to sign the new constitution is not known. Perhaps he was aware of the intense feelings of the reformers while other members were not.

John Colburn confirmed the fact that the queen wanted a new constitution, and the crowd of men who quickly gathered in Smith's office were highly incensed. A committee of public safety was formed on the spot, and there was open talk of abolishing the monarchy once and for all. John Colburn was advised to continue to refuse to sign the new constitution. That evening a meeting was held at Thurston's home. Some men feared they did not have the strength to overthrow the monarchy. One of the facts which encouraged them to go on with their plans, Sanford Dole later wrote, was the fact that "We knew that the United States minister was in sympathy with us." The reformers had forced the monarchy to do its bidding in 1887, and they believed that power could now be wrested from the existing order. Hopes of success seemed bright enough to risk treason. The few persons who talked of maintaining the monarchy were drowned out. Now it was revolution.

On Sunday and Monday the reformers scoured the town for arms and ammunition. A mass meeting was called for Monday afternoon, but the course of events had been determined before most of the haole businessmen gave their approval. The supporters of the queen tried to minimize the mass meeting by calling a meeting of their own at the same time at Iolani Palace. That afternoon the committee of public safety requested U. S. Minister Stevens to land troops from the *U.S.S. Boston* to protect United States citizens and their property. One hundred and sixty-two U. S. sailors and marines marched ashore that evening carrying full packs and double cartridge belts, toting two pieces of artillery and two Gatling guns and accompanied by a hospital unit. Most of these men were stationed at Arion hall, across the street from the palace and just seventy-six yards from the government building. A majority of the American citizens and their property were located across town.

On Monday evening the reform leaders met again. They asked Sanford Ballard Dole, a man respected by the Hawaiians, to head the new government. Dole suggested a regency be established until the heir to the throne, Princess Kaiulani, should come of age, but such talk met with quick rejection. The idea was to overthrow the monarchy, establish a republic, and immediately seek annexation to the United States. Sanford Dole then proposed that Thurston head the government, but he was considered too radical and controversial. The next morning Dole agreed to serve. Strangely, at this point, four of the key persons in this drama took to their beds, too ill to continue. Lorrin Thurston and two other reform leaders were unable to take an active part in the events which were about to unfold, and John Stevens also was ill, seeing only a few of those who called on him.

Tuesday was the day of action. The plan was to take over the government building, proclaim the monarchy dissolved, and announce that a provisional government would run the country until annexation by the United States. After lunch the key leaders gathered at Smith's office and nervously awaited the time when they would begin the three-block walk to the government building. On the way to Smith's office Sanford Dole stopped by the home of U. S. Minister Stevens to deliver an advance copy of the proclamation dissolving the monarchy. Dole quoted Stevens as saying, "I think you have a great opportunity."

The revolutionaries at Smith's office were somewhat unnerved by a group of Hawaiian policemen who stood in the street watching the office. They made no attempt to arrest anyone, but their presence was a threat. The monarchy's failure to take positive action against the reformers was due either to an abysmal ineptness or to fear of the U. S. forces ashore and the warships in the harbor. Apparently the monarchy made only feeble attempts to reduce the mounting odds. The marshal of the kingdom had talked to Lorrin Thurston in an effort to persuade him to call off the mass meeting of Monday, and cabinet members had asked John Stevens to withdraw the troops he had ordered ashore. Liliuokalani had also promised to abide by the old constitution. But words were no longer effective.

Now, a single shot launched the *coup d'état*. A block away from Smith's office a wagon load of arms and ammunition rumbled up Fort street. When the wagon halted to allow a tram car to pass, a Hawaiian policeman grabbed the reins of the team. Captain John Good, ordnance officer for the reformers, was in charge. He drew his revolver and shot the policeman in the shoulder. The wagon rolled on, but the sound of the shot drew an excited crowd, including the policemen who had been watching the office of W. O. Smith.

With the policemen gone, Dole and his followers safely left the office and proceeded toward the government building. People ran in the opposite direction, toward the sound of the shot, and the reformers walked to the seat of government without the slightest difficulty. Captain Good's shot had triggered events slightly ahead of schedule. The takeover of the government building occurred about twenty minutes ahead of time, and no militia had arrived to support the reformers. But there was no opposition, for the only persons in the building were an assortment of clerks. Cabinet members and other officials of rank were making their headquarters at the police station. A lengthy proclamation, dissolving the monarchy, was read from the steps of the government building. No one was there to listen except a handful of reformers and a few curious Hawaiians.

At about 2:45 P.M. a messenger was sent off to Stevens requesting recognition of the new government and the help of American troops in preserving the public peace. The messenger pressed for an answer, and when he got it he went to the police station and presented it to Samuel Parker, minister of foreign affairs. The note said the United States had extended *de facto* recognition to the new government. Later, two ministers of the queen claimed Stevens had told them U. S. soldiers would intervene if loyalist forces attacked the reformers. Since Stevens had rushed recognition to the new government and since U. S. troops were the most powerful force in Hawaii, the queen decided to surrender to the U. S., not the reformers.

While the proclamation was still being read from the steps of the government building, the volunteer militia began to arrive. The first group to come were former German nationals under the command of Captain Ziegler. With a strong force on hand, Dole felt the building was secure. Mar-

tial law was declared, and the queen was called upon to surrender the police station. All saloons in town were closed, and recognition was
requested from other foreign consuls.

At some time after the Provisional Government had been proclaimed,
but before Queen Liliuokalani had surrendered, Samuel Damon and C.
Bolte called on her. The visit had no official sanction and probably was
due to the kindness of Damon, who had long been a friend of the queen
and had belatedly joined the revolutionists. He was convinced that resis-
tance on the part of Liliuokalani was useless, and perhaps he wanted to
make the death of the monarchy as easy as possible. Later events indicate
Damon gave the queen the impression that she could remain in the palace
and continue to fly the Hawaiian flag after she surrendered. If, indeed,
Damon had made such a statement, the new government was in no way
bound to honor it.

In surrendering the kingdom to the United States, Liliuokalani followed the path Kamehameha III had taken when he surrendered the kingdom to Queen Victoria under pressure from Lord George Paulet. She
wrote, "That I yield to the superior force of the United States of America
whose Minister Plenipotentiary, His Excellency John L. Stevens, has
caused United States troops to be landed at Honolulu and declared that he
would support the said Provisional Government." The queen yielded her
authority until such time as the United States investigated the facts and
reinstated her. Sanford Dole accepted this surrender to the U. S. and not
to the Provisional Government.

The monarchy had fallen. Only one shot had been fired, and not a life
had been lost. There was no disorder in the kingdom the night the monarchy died, although there was intense frustration among the Hawaiians.
The victors felt a variety of emotions. Some thought they had won because
their cause was just. Others believed the monarchy was so decadent that it
fell at the first serious challenge. The president of the new Provisional
Government, Sanford Dole, knew they had also been lucky. He wrote
about that momentous day, "We certainly owed much on that first day, to
circumstances entirely out of our control."

Now that the monarchy had been toppled, a five-man mission was
speeded off to Washington D. C. on a chartered vessel to seek admission
to the Union. The queen wished to send her representatives on the same
ship, but the request was refused. As soon as the chartered vessel reached
San Francisco, the commissioners began a publicity campaign on behalf of
the new government. Lorrin Thurston, one of the commissioners, was particularly active. He visited newspaper editors and influential businessmen
in an effort to build support for the cause. Thurston was a strong-willed,

convincing man, and he gained support as the train moved from city to city toward Washington.

The goal of the commissioners was to bring Hawaii in as a territory or, if that failed, as a protectorate. At no time was the possibility of statehood mentioned. President Harrison and Secretary of State John W. Foster were both agreeable to the idea of Hawaii becoming a part of the Union, although Foster had to talk the president out of conducting a popular vote on the matter in Hawaii. A treaty was drawn up quickly and sent to the Senate. At this point there was no discussion concerning the part U. S. forces might have played in the overthrow. Harrison did not push the treaty, since President-elect Grover Cleveland would soon take office.

Queen Liliuokalani was not allowed to send representatives on the ship chartered by the Provisional Government, but she was allowed to send a letter to Grover Cleveland. In this letter she said she had not fought against the reformers because it would have been futile to fight against the United States. She put her confidence in Cleveland, "and the certainty which I feel that your government will right whatever wrongs may have been inflicted upon us. . . ." The envoys of the ex-queen could not get passage to the United States until February 2. The two men sent to represent her were attorney Paul Neumann and Prince David Kawananakoa. Archibald Cleghorn and others paid for the passage of E. C. Macfarlane to protect the interests of the heir to the throne, Princess Kaiulani, Cleghorn's daughter.

The royalist representatives were afflicted with the same ineptness which had characterized the monarchy for so long. Instead of deploring the fact that a kingdom had been stolen from a defenseless woman and that American sailors had protected the thieves in their crimes, the royalists talked freely of the possibility of annexation and admitted some Hawaiians did not oppose it. They did not demand the restoration of the monarchy, but rather seemed interested in getting the best financial deal possible for the ex-queen and ex-princess. By contrast their opponents were determined, aggressive men who sold the benefits of annexation in a positive way to anyone who would listen.

The most articulate spokesman for the monarchy was a man who had no official capacity there, an Englishman, Theo. H. Davies, the very successful Honolulu merchant. Davies brought the lovely Kaiulani from England to Washington to try and influence the course of history. The protestations of Davies were heard with some suspicion since he was English. His efforts did not meet with success. His pamphlet and letter writing, however, were calm and kind, and his words infuriated many of his fellow businessmen in Hawaii. He proclaimed the royalists as being morally right

—a tack which galled the reformers, who customarily flaunted their moral superiority.

Davies stated that the new government "is not the Government of the people, nor of the Constitution." The new rulers, moreover, dared not ask the nation to speak. For a small handful of rebels "to attempt to transfer the nationhood, would be betrayal." The monthly missionary publication, *The Friend,* came in for particular criticism, and Davies found its editor, Rev. Sereno E. Bishop, was having a very difficult time justifying the revolt. Davies noted: "The coarsest and most revolting language has been used against the lady who was, until this year, outwardly honoured in all the Churches, and not one word of rebuke has been heard from the *Friend* or any of its correspondents. . . ." Then the Englishman quoted a statement by the Evangelical Association which he thought offered little comfort to the Hawaiians: "Painful as may be to the Hawaiian this loss of the prestige which came to his native Court, we may believe he will yet come very generally to see in it the wisdom and goodness of God to him."

The Friend indeed had done a remarkable about-face. The editor had written that Liliuokalani "commanded the high regard of the foreign community" and that she was a gentle and gracious person, but less than two years later he blamed the court for the fact that a large proportion of the Hawaiian people had "reverted to superstition, and are slaves to their sorcerers and to the lowest forms of vice, and it is evident why their sympathies are so largely with a royalty of their own sort." In the issue of *The Friend* which followed the revolt, Reverend Bishop became enchanted with the events which had taken place. The lead article told of the sailing of the "gallant" commissioners for Washington. They were "followed by prayers and tears and ardent hopes, and beyond doubt, by the bitter curses of kahunas and lottery pirates." Liliuokalani had inherited the impurities of Kalakaua's court, and editor Bishop was not prepared to say how much she "secretly cherished these poisonous palace growths."

The verbal battles surged back and forth, and it is unlikely anyone was converted by the endless columns of prejudiced stories. On occasion tempers did boil over. Paul Neumann, who had gone to Washington for Liliuokalani, and William Cornwell, a member of the last cabinet, beat up the editor of the *Advertiser* as he walked to work one morning. The two believed they had been slandered by the newspaper.

Among those who were severely buffeted by conflicting winds of opinion were the native Hawaiian Protestant ministers, who were told by the church hierarchy that the queen was vile and that no Christian could support her. Their congregations were largely Hawaiian and royalist in sympathy. Some ministers who preached the doctrine of annexation were threatened with expulsion by their congregations while other ministers had their salaries cut off.

In the days following the revolution Honolulu was full of rumors concerning attempts at counterrevolution. Troops from the *Boston* moved into a downtown hotel to keep close watch. Sanford Dole and his wife moved out of their home, fearing reprisals. The concern of the new government was so great that they asked John Stevens to accept the job of preserving the Provisional Government while awaiting the decision of Washington. Stevens readily agreed, and on February 1, 1893, the American flag was raised over government buildings. U. S. marines took over the guard duty which had previously been performed by the volunteer militia. It was an admission by the revolutionary forces that matters were not really under control.

In Washington affairs were not proceeding well for the Provisional Government. President Cleveland withdrew the treaty which had been sent to the Senate. He ordered a special commissioner to Hawaii to investigate and issue a report on what had really happened there. The man chosen for this job was James H. Blount, a Confederate war veteran. He arrived in Honolulu March 29, 1894, and was greeted by a large number of persons who waved American flags and wore annexation club buttons. His first action was to order the American flag down and the sailors and marines back aboard their ships.

Representatives of the Provisional Government as well as royalists were on hand to provide him with whatever he might wish, but Blount distressed everyone by remaining aloof from all advances. During his time in Honolulu James Blount personally conducted interviews with numerous persons and in general kept his own counsel. Near the end of 1893 his report was printed. It ran to 684 pages, and the conclusion was that John Stevens and the U. S. armed forces gave substantial help to the reformers in the overthrow. When the report became known in Hawaii, the press reacted by bitterly attacking Blout and President Cleveland. The Provisional Government continued to declare the U. S. forces had nothing to do with the success of the revolution.

President Cleveland was opposed to annexation throughout his term of office. He believed taking the Islands was immoral, and without his support annexationists had no hope. The Provisional Government, however, did not cease to push their cause in Washington—in fact, the vocal Thurston pushed so hard that he was declared *persona non grata*.

When the Cleveland administration rejected annexation, it requested the Provisional Government to restore the monarchy. This request created additional hard feelings in Hawaii, and the new government flatly refused to comply. For a time it appeared that U. S. forces might now be called upon to wrest power from the Provisional Government, but the request was not unduly pressed by the United States and matters quieted down. The Provisional Government now became the Republic of Hawaii. A new constitution was written and the Islands settled down to await more favorable times.

A battle of words raged across the U. S. in the nation's newspapers. Many newspapers supported the royalists while others hailed the Republic. In San Francisco *The Call* warned that the annexation of Hawaii "will be the open door through which the least desirable elements in Japan will enter upon American citizenship." The *New York Journal* and *Advertiser* thought Hawaii belonged to the United States: "The acquisition of Hawaii is an imperative patriotic duty."

The most powerful opponent of annexation was the sugar trust, which was made up of the sugar refiners. The sugar trust was divided into an Eastern and Western camp with Claus Spreckels controlling the West. The refiners subsidized many sugar planters in the country, and they not only were able to name the price mainland farmers received for their crops, but they pretty well controlled the retail price of sugar as well. The admission of Hawaii created many questions, and the refiners feared a breach in their monopoly. Perhaps high-grade Hawaiian sugars would not need refining. Certainly all hope of a tariff barrier would be gone, and it was possible Hawaiian sugar could be produced at lower costs. All of these things loomed as threats.

The sugar trust lobby in Washington was a powerful one, and its weight was felt in Congress. The lobbyists also conducted a campaign aimed at turning the U. S. public against acquiring the Islands. One of their favorite suggestions was that a popular vote on annexation be taken in Hawaii. This the Republic of Hawaii wanted to avoid at all costs.

As the pros and cons of annexation were being shouted back and forth, a man appeared who would supply the rationale for bringing Hawaii into the Union. He was a thoughtful, deliberate man, and the answers he gave were often qualified and seldom extreme. The Hawaiian Islands, specifically, were not his concern. He looked at things in a world-wide context. His approach was that of a scientist who studied the evidence and then made pronouncements concerning his findings. This man, Alfred Thayer Mahan, was a naval officer.

Mahan had grown up thinking about the movement, maintenance, and equipping of military forces. His father had been a West Point professor and had written a book on strategy and tactics which became the textbook for both sides during the Civil War. In 1885 Alfred Mahan was on a cruise, and he spent his leisure time considering the role naval power had played in history. He thought of how differently things might have turned out if Hannibal had been able to muster sufficient naval strength to invade Italy directly instead of crossing through the Swiss alps and attacking the Roman Empire from the north. What an advantage it would have been for Hannibal if a fleet had been able to stay in communication with Carthage and bring him supplies.

A theory began to form in Mahan's mind. Control of the seas had often controlled the destinies of nations. In 1890 Captain Mahan's first book appeared. It was titled *The Influence of Sea Power Upon History,* and its effects upon the Western world were enormous. Alfred Mahan was soon considered the leading naval thinker in the world.

In the 1890s most naval vessels ran on coal, and vast amounts of this fuel were needed for long cruises. If any nation aspired to world importance, it needed stations where its ships could refuel, thus giving its fleet range and mobility. Hawaii was an obvious refueling station. In March, 1893, Alfred Mahan wrote a magazine article in which he said Hawaii possessed "unique importance—not from its intrinsic commercial value but from its favorable position for maritime and military control." To Theodore Roosevelt Mahan wrote, "Do nothing unrighteous, but as regards the problem, take the islands first and solve afterwards." This kind of thinking appealed to Roosevelt, who replied, "If I had my way we would annex those islands tomorrow."

Captain Mahan believed that sea power was the most important factor in the making or breaking of nations. No matter how gifted a nation might be, it could not attain its highest potential without a powerful fleet. Mahan's theories dovetailed perfectly with those popular writers of the day who spoke of the manifest destiny of the white Christian nations. They were the superior nations and were responsible for the triumph of morality in this world. Mahan was greeted with enthusiasm. Theodore Roosevelt and Henry Cabot Lodge consulted him frequently. The British took his writings to heart and modernized their fleet. The Kaiser believed Mahan's theory of sea power and created a powerful fleet.

If it were the destiny of the white Christian nations to extend their morality and control over the rest of the world, the annexing of Hawaii was an inevitable and even insignificant step in the grand scheme of things. In fact, the haole minority in Hawaii had already shown its superiority by wresting the kingdom away from the nonwhite rulers. Minor irregularities were unimportant along this road toward inevitable destiny.

From the beginning the new government had been nervous about a counterrevolution. Iolani Palace was sandbagged and garrisoned. Government reserves were on alert. By the end of 1894 the news was indeed unsettling, for there was an increasing number of reports of mysterious men and ships. Somehow the police were never quite able to lay their hands on the shadowy persons behind it all. On Saturday night, January 5, 1895, a group of these shadowy men gathered beyond Diamond Head. Rifles, which earlier had been smuggled ashore and buried in the sand, were distributed. Late the next day the attorney general was told that a band of men was moving toward Honolulu.

An armed government force hurried to the area. As they prepared to search a house near Diamond Head, they were fired on by royalists who were hiding in a nearby boathouse. Charles Carter, a young lawyer on Dole's staff and a former commissioner to Washington, was hit and died the following morning. The royalists fled up Diamond Head, and the next day those who remained there were bombarded by two field pieces, one aboard a tug sent out from Honolulu harbor. The remaining royalists scattered, a number of them retreating up Manoa Valley. They were pursued by the soldiers of the Republic, and in a few days it was all over. The royalists had started out with the idea that they would secure provisions and equipment when they captured Honolulu. Their abortive attempt displayed the familiar failures—poor planning, poor leadership, and little discipline. In the end 190 prisoners were tried and all but three found guilty. Some severe sentences were initially announced, but by the end of 1895 all had been released from prison.

The leader of the royalists was that compulsive revolutionary, Robert Wilcox. Under pressure from the U. S. minister and Sanford Dole, the court commuted a death sentence to thirty-five years at hard labor and a $10,000 fine. By the end of the year Wilcox too was out of prison, and by 1898 he had a full pardon.

On January 16 Liliuokalani was arrested at her home. She was imprisoned in two second-floor rooms of Iolani Palace and was put on trial for knowing of the revolt and not reporting it. In the yard of her home arms and ammunition had been uncovered. The former queen insisted she knew nothing of the royalist plot, but she was sentenced to five years at hard labor and a $5,000 fine. The hard labor portion was commuted and she was soon released. The nature of the sentence, however, indicates the deep animosity many leaders of the Republic felt toward the former queen. While imprisoned Liliuokalani signed her abdication as queen of Hawaii and took the oath of alliegiance to the new government.

During the royalist revolt Captain Black was on duty at the "front" in Manoa Valley. On his rounds he came across a strange looking man wandering through the underbrush. The lone stranger wore leather leggings and a broad sombrero and his hair reached to his shoulders. Black could not arrest the man for his appearance, but he carried no government pass, and that was reason enough to escort him back to Honolulu. At headquarters, located in the old bungalow on the palace grounds, the eccentric man was identified as Joaquin Miller.

Miller was something of a minor celebrity in Honolulu. In California he was known as the poet of the Sierras. He had come to Hawaii toward the end of 1894 as a correspondent for *Overland* magazine and several newspapers which were pushing annexation. Miller's poems had appeared in Honolulu newspapers as early as 1873, and his showing up in the Islands was duly noted. When the revolt broke, Miller promptly offered his services to the government. He visited the "front," sending off eyewitness dispatches to *Overland* and his newspapers. In Honolulu he was quoted as saying that the government men "fought like tigers," but later in California he wrote caustically of the army of the Republic.

The physical beauty of the Islands enthralled Joaquin Miller more than its politics. The wild mountains which rose so steeply into clouds he described as "cloudcapped peaks where thunders slept." His enchantment at seeing the Islands for the first time were reflected in his words, "I tell you, my boy, the man who has not seen the Sandwich Islands, in this one great ocean's warm heart, has not seen the world."

President and Mrs. Dole invited Joaquin Miller to their home, and apparently they spent a pleasant evening together. Later, however, Anna Dole learned that Miller and a very pregnant Mexican girl were living in adjoining rooms in a Honolulu hotel. Joaquin Miller introduced the girl around town as the wife of his plumber in California and said she just happened to be alone and in Honolulu. Mrs. Dole was shocked. Shortly Miller was advised to leave the Islands. The advice must have been strongly put, because in order to buy passage as quickly as possible he pawned a diamond ring.

The girl was Alice Oliver. She had earlier been sent to the Islands by Miller when she became pregnant. The poet soon followed her, and in Honolulu they again enjoyed each other's company. Alice remained in Honolulu until a baby boy was born, and then she too returned to California.

The leaders of the Republic of Hawaii were disappointed that the United States did not accept the Islands with gratitude, but they were not the kind of men who allowed bruised feelings to dishearten them. If the U.S. did not want the Islands, they must be made to want them. One suggestion was to ask Canada to annex Hawaii. Then, some believed, the U. S. would come running.

When William McKinley assumed the presidency in 1896, the Republic of Hawaii believed prospects for annexation to be brighter, since the new president was an expansionist. But some special impetus was needed—some dramatic event—which would illustrate that the U. S. needed Hawaii. That dramatic event came in April, 1898, in the form of the Spanish-American war. For the first time the United States had to fight a campaign in the distant Pacific, because the Philippine Islands were occupied by the Spanish.

News of the war reached Hawaii twelve days after it was declared. Although Sanford Dole had previously inquired in what way the Republic could assist the U. S. if war did come, there was considerable discussion in Honolulu over what role the nation should choose. Some felt the Republic should remain neutral, particularly since Spain had a Pacific fleet which could conceivably bombard the Islands. Lorrin Thurston, who was once again in Washington, was furious at the indecision of his fellow Islanders. He dashed off a letter which appeared in the *Advertiser* in June. "The trouble with you is that you are ready to take all the benefits of American connection as long as there is no danger in sight. . . ." Two days before the news of Admiral Dewey's destruction of the Spanish fleet at Manila reached Hawaii, Dole sent a letter to Washington informing the U. S. that it had the unreserved backing of Hawaii.

That dramatic moment the Republic of Hawaii needed was close at hand. The *New York Herald* noted, "In view of the impending naval conflict with Spain over the Philippine Islands the United States government must have a base of supplies in the Pacific Ocean. Unless Commodore Dewey is able to take Manila and finds the expected coal supply there he will be obliged to retreat to our own coast for supplies. The Philippine Islands are 6,520 miles from San Francisco. . . ." Alfred Mahan was right. If the United States would become a Pacific power, it needed bases, and Hawaii was a good starting point. In Washington two Senators and former Secretary of State John Foster called on President McKinley and asked him to annex Hawaii immediately.

The first war vessel to appear off Hawaii was the familiar *U.S.S. Charleston*. It was preceding three troopships which arrived in Honolulu on June 1, 1898. The *Advertiser* noted that "From end to end of the city 'Old Glory' floated from every housetop," and patriotism streamed "from each nook and corner of Honolulu." The citizens treated the U. S. troops generously, spreading a great luau for them on the grounds of Iolani Palace two days after their arrival. The next morning a mass of people lined the docks to bid Godspeed to the first troops bound for Manila.

The annexation of Hawaii appeared to many Congressmen as a step which would speed the war against Spain. A joint resolution of annexation passed the House of Representatives on June 15, and the Senate approved it on July 6. The next day President McKinley affixed his signature. There was substantial opposition to annexation in both houses, and a large number of Congressmen refrained from voting. Nonetheless annexation had been achieved at last.

On August 12, 1898, the Republic of Hawaii became a territory of the United States. A relatively simple ceremony marked the event at Iolani Palace. Sanford Dole and U. S. Minister Harold M. Sewall spoke. The Hawaiian national anthem was played, colors were sounded, a twenty-one-gun salute was fired, and the Hawaiian flag was slowly lowered. The United States flag was then pulled up, "The Star Spangled Banner" was played, and again there was a twenty-one-gun salute. Dole was sworn in as chief executive, and sailors from two warships in the harbor marched in review.

That August 12 was a strange day. The highest hopes of the Republic had been realized, yet there was little rejoicing. Perhaps the victors had become too wearied through long efforts and the final consummation brought little pleasure. The many Chinese and Japanese who crowded the palace grounds that day watched in interested silence, not feeling any strong loyalty to either the new or the old. As for the Hawaiians, one writer reported that "throughout the day's exercises the Hawaiians were, comparatively, sparsely represented, except as silent and distant spectators —and who could blame them?" In later years it was rare to find a Hawaiian who would admit he had been there.

The U. S. troopships kept coming, stopping for a few days to grant leave for soldiers, to take on fuel and provisions. The Islanders continued to greet the troops with enthusiasm, and most of the soldiers left with kind memories of Honolulu. There were times, however, when the exuberance of men on their way to war got out of hand. The usual quota of drunks and fights were easily handled and overlooked, but molesting civilians on tram cars and beating up shopkeepers reminded one newspaper man of the whaling crews of old. "Since the arrival of the troops, there have been many exhibitions of the same crimson nature," the writer noted, but "they have been, so far of a milder type and far less aggravating." Less than two months after annexation an exhibition took place which in turn amused and angered Honolulu's citizens.

On the night of October 3 at about 11:30—the hour the downtown saloons closed—First Lieutenant Wheelock and Second Lieutenant Merriam sallied forth on their adventure. Wheelock was provost marshal and on duty that night. Merriam, who was off duty, was a junior aide-de-camp to Brigadier General Charles King, the commander of the U. S. Army in Hawaii. The two men must have been imbibing freely, and very likely nothing serious would have happened if Wheelock had been off duty. As it was, he had a dozen mounted military police awaiting his orders.

The exact sequence of events is not too clear, but apparently Wheelock soon got into a fight with a sailor. The army officer did not have the sympathy of the sailors and civilians who circled about the brawl. Wheelock was loudly booed, and at this point he proclaimed Honolulu to be under martial law by order of General King. The mounted soldiers were told to clear the streets and the sidewalks of both civilians and military.

At one point Wheelock galloped off toward the waterfront in pursuit of a pack of jeering sailors. Merriam insisted martial law was indeed in effect while his companion was chasing his tormentors. At about 1 A.M. General Charles King was roused from bed and informed of the state of affairs. He ordered his adjutant general to bring the two officers to his headquarters in the Hawaiian Hotel. *The Independent* for October 4 reported: "Two young officers, who evidently had looked at the wine when it was very red, succeeded in making perfect asses of themselves last night."

General King was a distinguished soldier from a successful family. He had volunteered at the age of sixteen as a drummer boy during the Civil War. Later he graduated from West Point and fought in the Indian wars until a bullet shattered a bone in an arm, forcing him to retire. His great-grandfather was a member of the Continental Congress and his grandfather was president of Columbia University. After the Indian wars King turned his talents to writing and was both popular and prolific. When the Spanish-American War came, he was named Brigadier General of Volunteers.

The citizens of Honolulu tried to be tolerant about the episode, and General King apologized in the press. He stated he would have given $20,000 if the affair had not taken place and that he had relieved Wheelock of duty. Wheelock, he said, was the real culprit, since he was on duty at the time. Merriam was pictured as having been led astray. The general was investigating the incident, and most citizens were satisfied, although there was talk of a civil suit being filed against the two offenders.

Then General Charles King became ill and remained abed for three days. The episode itself could have been easily handled, but possibly the general was ill over the identity of one of the men involved. Lieutenant Merriam happened to be the son of Major General Henry Clay Merriam, commander of the department of California and the commanding officer of King. Charles King was in a very delicate position. He explained that he did not have authority to conduct a court martial of officers and that he had sent a report on to his superior, Major General Henry Merriam.

Troubles in Honolulu did not come singly for General King. Two weeks after the martial law episode the general was out for exercise with two of his officers. They were horseback riding beyond Diamond Head. During the course of the day the three soldiers became lost. In fact, they did not find their way back until the next day, and this humiliating fact was duly recorded in the press. General King was becoming irritated.

Two days later newspapers reported the comments of Judge W. Luther Wilcox. Two U. S. soldiers had been brought before him, and the judge lectured the offenders. "If there was any prospect of your paying a just penalty before a military court, I would let you off easy here."

General King did not believe such words could go unchallenged. He wrote a letter to Judge Wilcox protesting the untruth of his remarks. The general expected a public apology, but Wilcox was not about to make one. Letters went back and forth, each duly printed in the newspapers. Soon there were editorials commenting on the merits of the case. In exasperation the general returned a Wilcox letter unopened.

This conflict was just cooling down when the Honolulu press received copies of *The Call* from San Francisco which carried a story on the report King had written on the Wheelock-Merriam affair. The report admitted Merriam had not acted as an officer and gentleman, but the real blame lay with Wheelock, who had a dozen troopers under his command. He was the one who had lost his head. General King also sent a letter to Major General Henry Merriam saying that he had the highest regard for his son and that he was not drunk on the night of the disturbance. To the *Advertiser* it sounded very much like a whitewash job for Lieutenant Merriam.

Before this report became public knowledge the *Advertiser* had been somewhat critical of Judge Wilcox and his remarks, but now their sympathies for him grew. Near the end of a long editorial the newspaper referred to the letter King had written to General Merriam which stated the young lieutenant was not drunk on that fateful night. "An educated officer who declared, under the circumstances, that martial law had been declared was, so far as men may fairly judge, either drunk or insane."

General King was undoubtedly glad to receive orders to move on to Manila, where he faced only enemy bullets. King served for a time in the Philippine Islands, but ill health forced him again to retire. He returned to writing, a profession which he followed successfully for many years.

In 1885 the Japanese immigration to Hawaii started once again. After years of polite negotiations both governments realized that immigration to Hawaii had advantages for them. Hawaii badly needed laborers while in Japan a severe depression had driven many farmers into bankruptcy, and they desperately wanted work. In 1886 the two countries agreed on a convention, and the flood gates of immigration were opened. Wages were $9 per month on a three-year contract, in addition to housing, food, and medical care. A wife received $6 a month if she worked. A work month consisted of twenty-six days of ten hours in the fields or twelve hours in the mill. Twenty-five percent of the wages of each worker was turned over to the Japanese consul in Hawaii, who deposited it in a governmental postal bank account.

The man who smoothly arranged this immigration in Japan was a meticulous, self-assured American named Robert Walker Irwin. In 1881 he was appointed permanent Hawaiian consul general to that country. Irwin was a well established businessman in Japan, who had married a Japanese lady from a wealthy family. Under his direction 28,691 Japanese came to Hawaii. He was paid at the rate of $5 a head, and undoubtedly other fees came his way. Irwin understood the Japanese extremely well, and he made thoughtful suggestions to the planters about the treatment the new workers should receive. When his suggestions were ignored, trouble often followed. Paia plantation on Maui was one of the unfortunate examples. There, five Japanese died from a combination of bad treatment and disease. The situation was so tense that all Japanese were withdrawn from the plantation.

Robert Irwin worked hard to protect the rights of the Japanese he recruited. He recommended that Japanese be employed as overseers, pointing out that each company of immigrants had elected a head man before reaching Hawaii. Irwin also tried to have immigrants segregated by prefecture so that families and friends might stay together. Once the newcomers had gone off to the plantations, however, they were in the hands of the plantation managers whose temperaments varied greatly.

It was soon apparent that liaison was needed between the immigrants and the government, so the Bureau of Inspection of Japanese Immigrants was established. G. O. Nakayama, who had come aboard the first ship under the new agreement, was given the job of heading the bureau at a salary of $100 a month. This was soon raised to $250 a month and then to $500 a month, a sum which brought much complaining since it was more than any government officer under cabinet rank received. Nakayama's staff consisted of fourteen inspectors and interpreters and five doctors. As the number of Japanese increased, so did the personnel in the Bureau of Inspection. Nakayama had quickly graduated from laborer to bureaucrat.

The planters bemoaned the existence of the Bureau of Inspection. They said inspectors would break down discipline on the plantations. The inspectors, in fact, cooled down the workers and helped settle disputes. They probably helped the planters more than the workers, and eventually their role was accepted. The cost of the Bureau of Inspection, however, rankled the planters, and in 1887 this was modified. After that only the salary of Nakayama and one other bureau man were borne by the government. The bulk of the cost for running the Bureau of Inspection was collected from the immigrants.

The recruitment of Japanese was concentrated in southwestern Japan, in the prefectures of Hiroshima, Yamaguchi, Kumamoto, and Fukuoka. This area was overpopulated with farmers, and during the depression of the late 1880s and 1890s these people were particularly hard-pressed. Robert Irwin paid close attention to the persons who were selected, and he did well by the planters, for the Japanese who came to the Islands were a hardy, outdoor lot, well suited to the strenuous work in the mills and fields. By 1894 the Japanese had become the backbone of plantation labor, making up approximately three fifths of the total plantation labor force.

Financially the immigrants fared poorly. Nakayama and his bureau did little to help. In fact, some bureau men were illegally making money off their fellow countrymen. They took money from workers for the transportation of wives or brides from Japan to Hawaii. Such passage was normally paid by the government, but apparently some workers did not know this, and the money was pocketed by bureau men. Sometimes workers had trouble collecting the 25 percent of their wages which had been deposited in a government postal bank. Plantations were often lax about depositing the money in the first place, and workers had to wade through red tape before they could collect. Most plantations had a system of fines for the infraction of rules, and these diminished the small earnings of the workers. Those who got into trouble with the law often suffered severely. In 1894 nine Japanese were convicted of gambling by a judge on the island of Hawaii. They were fined the mammoth sum of $200 each. They had no money to pay the fines, so each man had to spend sixteen months at road work.

The Japanese who came to Hawaii under labor contracts faced three years of hard work under drab, harsh conditions. Usually housing was bad and the food was unfamiliar and of poor quality. The ratio of women to men was about one to four. The immigrants lived under strange conditions and were governed by rules they often did not comprehend. Under these circumstances many Japanese customs, of necessity, disappeared. When the three-year contract had been served, the laborer could choose one of three options. He could return to Japan. He could seek other employment in Hawaii. He could continue on the plantation, usually with an increase in pay and possibly in position.

Those who left the plantations to open stores or start farms tended to throw off the Western customs which had been forced on them on the plantations. They reverted to Japanese food and Japanese dress. The brides who came from Japan reinforced the old customs. They organized the home in the familiar ways and raised the children by Japanese standards. They remained a very closely knit group.

The haoles were alarmed over the large Japanese population, but the pressure for workers in the expanding sugar industry was unceasing. In the 1890s they again turned to China for workers, but the Chinese were Oriental also, and what was really wanted was an increase in the haole population. From 1880 through the early 1900s the planters searched the world over for non-Oriental laborers. They tried Norwegians, Russians, Americans (including a shipment of American blacks from Tennessee), Germans, Spaniards, and Portuguese. In varying degrees the planters were displeased with all of them. The cost of importing people from Europe was high, and the wages and standards they expected far exceeded those acceptable to Orientals. Plantation labor continued to be predominantly Oriental.

In 1894 Robert Irwin and the Republic of Hawaii parted ways. The Republic wanted Irwin to do his job at a reduced price, and Irwin was unwilling. More than cost was bothering the men of the Republic. The simple fact was that the Japanese population in the Islands was getting too large. They feared Hawaii was being overwhelmed and that the dominant standards and customs of the Islands would become Japanese. Somehow this migration had to be checked, and somehow the Japanese already in Hawaii had to be kept from voting. By 1896 there were over 24,000 Japanese in Hawaii, nearly 25 percent of the population.

The government minimized the Japanese vote by holding up naturalization for a time, and in June, 1896, a sake law passed the legislature. This punitive law raised the tariff on the favorite alcoholic drink of the Japanese from 15 cents to $1 a gallon. At the same time wine from the U. S. was imported duty-free. In 1897 many Japanese immigrants were turned back when the Republic decided to enforce certain laws which had formerly been ignored.

Strong notes were passed back and forth between Hawaii and Japan. By this time Japan had built a navy of consequence, and naval vessels frequently appeared in Honolulu harbor to remind the little Island government that they were dealing with a powerful nation. In the U. S. the large number of Japanese in Hawaii was an argument both for and against annexing the Islands. Some feared that if the U. S. did not act, Hawaii would eventually fall to Japan and that nation would then be a menace to the West Coast. Others argued that Hawaii should not be annexed because of the large number of Orientals who would become U. S. citizens.

Once annexation came, the fears of the haoles were greatly reduced. The standards and customs of Hawaii would be those of the Western world, not of Japan, and no matter what the numerical odds might be, this condition appeared to be secure. Once again the gates were opened wide to immigration, and the Japanese poured into Hawaii. By 1900 there were over 61,000 Japanese in the Islands, about 40 percent of the population.

The closing years of the nineteenth century had brought monumental changes. Honolulu harbor was improved, streets were paved, trees were planted. Telephones were common, regular tram service ran through town, and by 1903 the Islands were linked to the mainland by cable. The monarchy had been swept away, the propertied haoles became the ruling elite in name and fact, and Hawaii was a possession of the United States. Of all those who played a part in this, three persons had left a particular mark on the age. Their names were Queen Liliuokalani, Sanford Ballard Dole, and Lorrin Andrews Thurston.

Queen Liliuokalani was a big-boned, solid woman. Her character matched her physical appearance, for she was resolute and aggressive. Following the overthrow she was subjected to much abuse by the victors, who were continually frustrated by their inability to destroy her dignity. When Liliuokalani was no longer a threat to the new government, they hoped she would lend the prestige of her support to them, but with the possible exception of Dole she held in disdain those who participated in the uprising for the rest of her life. She died in 1917 at the age of seventy-nine.

Sanford Dole was a curious person. He was a tall, lean man, and throughout his adult life he wore a long beard which effectively hid a receding chin. He had a highly developed sense of right and wrong. The respect he commanded among the Hawaiians made him a very valuable man to the reformers. Like Thurston he was a missionary descendant, spoke Hawaiian, and was a lawyer. Dole led the government well during his years in public office. His self-control and courage cooled the vindictive ardor of those who wanted to see the former queen suffer. He took pleasure in sailing and horseback riding. He escaped Honolulu as often as possible to visit the ranch of Eben Low on the island of Hawaii, where he spent hours riding over the vast grassy plains.

Dole's endless patience must have been tested by his wife, Anna. She had come from Maine, and during the years of their marriage she spent a good portion of her time on the mainland. Anna was obsessed by illness. The thought of leprosy so terrified her that she would not open a door in her own home without first covering the doorknob with a handkerchief. She spent a great deal of time painting Hawaiian flowers, but she apparently had little comprehension or interest in other things Hawaiian.

Lorrin A. Thurston was the propelling force of the rebellion. He was the incendiary and without him it is doubtful that the 1893 uprising would have taken place. He was an organizer, a leader, a doer. He was outspoken and willing to do what was necessary to win. Few people felt indifferent toward Lorrin Thurston. Some considered him a great and effective leader. Others hated him as ruthless and arrogant. He bought the *Advertiser* after annexation, and he editorialized that Hawaii was not ready for statehood. Statehood should not come, Thurston believed, until "we revise our moral and political standards, *upward*. . . ." Through the years the enemies of statehood repeated these sentiments.

One thing the new rulers of Hawaii could not do was control the popular vote. In 1900 the first delegate to Congress from the Territory of Hawaii was elected. The winner was the chronic revolutionist, Robert Wilcox. After his election his enemies tried to unseat him by accusing him of bigamy, of sending treasonable letters through the U. S. mails, and of having been improperly elected. Once in Washington he was accused of appointing only non-haoles to the U. S. military academies. In the election of 1902 his enemies put up Prince Kuhio as an opposition candidate. Kuhio was the adopted son of Kapiolani, the wife of Kalakaua, and he had sufficient appeal to win the most important elected office in Hawaii away from Wilcox. A year later Robert Wilcox was dead.

Chapter Fourteen

HYSTERIA HIT HONOLULU

IN 1906 A SMALL COLONY OF RUSSIANS settled on Kauai. They were Molokans, a pacifist-religious sect. During the Russo-Japanese war the Molokans had steadfastly refused to serve in the army or navy, and, to escape the persecution which followed, some 5,000 emigrated to Southern California. A handful of these Molokans thought Hawaii a better place yet, and they went to Kauai, where they hoped to establish again a kind of isolated village life. The government agreed to sell them land so they could become independent farmers, but the experiment was a dismal failure. Six months after they had arrived all the Russians had departed.

The men of the sugar industry were well aware the Russians had left disillusioned. Yet they desperately wanted white workers for the plantations. In fact, the urgency was so great that three years later the planters were willing to pay the passage of other Russians who were willing to come as plantation laborers.

In October, 1909, a Russian contingent of some 250 arrived. They had been recruited in Manchuria. Perhaps they had earlier been urged to go to Manchuria by the Czar, who hoped to so inundate that country with Russians that it would peacefully fall into Russian hands. The Czar's scheme failed, and most of the Russians were left to scratch out a bare living through exhausting labor. They learned that they could migrate to Hawaii, and the idea sounded alluring, especially as explained by the promoter of the scheme.

A. W. Perelstrous was the promoter. He was a contractor by profession who had helped build the Trans-Siberian railroad and the naval drydocks at Port Arthur. He became interested in recruiting Russian workers when he heard of Hawaii's labor shortage from a former plantation manager who was visiting Vladivostok. In midsummer 1909 A. W. Perelstrous came to Hawaii, talked to Governor Walter Frear and the Board of Immigration, and inspected several plantations on Oahu. After this he declared the Russians would adapt well to plantation life.

What happened when the Russians reached Hawaii was a repetition of what had happened to other immigrants of varying races. The first introductions were friendly enough with the planters expressing optimism. Then the new workers went off and discovered what plantation life was like. They usually found there was little relationship between promises and reality. Then came a time of disillusionment. Most of the earlier immigrants had been willing to suffer out their contracts, unhappy though they were. The Russians, however, were not willing to stay. By February, 1910, a great many had drifted back to Honolulu.

The Russians protested that they were paid less than half of what they had expected, that goods in plantation stores were of inferior quality, and prices were too high. They had been led to believe it would be possible to own a home after three years work, but now found that such dreams were preposterous. Twenty-seven of the Russians were angry enough to send off a joint protest letter which was printed by newspapers in Manchuria and circulated among Russian consuls in the Orient. The letter asserted that the plantations "have cheated us in every word."

Many of the dissatisfied Russians were in Honolulu on February 17 when another shipload of immigrants came into the harbor. When the government learned that the first Russian contingent meant to warn the newcomers about accepting work contracts, they would not allow the two groups to meet. In an effort to warn their fellow countrymen several Russians tried unsuccessfully to swim across Honolulu harbor to Quarantine Island where the immigrants were detained.

Honolulu newspapers were happy about the latest batch. "The young fellows are a likely looking lot, clean and bright faced. The men are mostly middle-aged and are strong broad-shouldered men, all appearing to have great physical power. . . . Many of the young men and girls were comely and rather pretty." The arrival was not a happy one for the Russians. When their baggage was unloaded, they discovered that much of it had been damaged aboard ship. Money, locked in trunks, had been stolen and family heirlooms ruined. On the Honolulu docks the baggage was left unguarded in the rain. At last, word was smuggled through to the new Russian contingent about the bad plantation conditions, and they refused to sign the contracts offered them.

Some of the Russians had kept the booklets which Perelstrous had distributed promising an hour of free schooling a day and listing prices at half of what they really were. The *Advertiser* commented editorially, "that in the minds of some, the complaints justify charges of injustice and misrepresentation on the part of the agents who brought the Russians here." Affairs were at an impasse. The government did nothing, the planters would make no concessions, the Russians increased their demands, and promoter Perelstrous was far away in the Orient.

A language barrier added to the troubles. Both sides searched for persons who could communicate with the other. Nachrin, a Russian who had once run a boarding house along the Siberian railroad and who had a dubious command of English was pressed into service. He could speak enough English to retain Joseph Lightfoot, a Honolulu attorney who had once represented the earlier Russian immigrants. Eva Alvas, a song and dance artist at the Empire theater, was discovered to have new talents. Eva could speak Russian, and she was recruited to find out what was going on.

On February 24 a newspaper story said that all the newly arrived Russians had been quarantined, because cases of diphtheria and measles had appeared. The following day seventy more Russian immigrants arrived in Honolulu, and on March 7 another ship put ashore 249. Before the last load arrived, a cable had been sent to Manchuria ordering a stop to all immigration. All the Russians had to go into quarantine and the number was so great that the medical detachment of the national guard was called out to help.

Royal Mead, head of the planters' labor bureau, stated that he did not want useless talk and that no concessions would be forthcoming. The Russians became more suspicious and withdrawn. They sent a cable to the Russian ambassador in Washington D. C. asking for help. When the Socialist party of Honolulu adopted a resolution of protest "against enslaving of the Russian brethren for the enrichment of the capitalists of the Islands," the planters began to view the immigrants as being not only disobedient children, but as having dangerous sympathizers.

By the middle of March the conservative part of Honolulu's community began to be frightened by the Russians. With a little imagination these peasants could be visualized as diabolical. Many of the men, indeed, fitted the stereotype of the dreaded bomb-throwing anarchist of the time. They had shaggy beards, baggy pants, wore army caps pulled securely down on their heads, and tramped about in ponderous boots. And who knew what thoughts lay behind those expressionless faces? Nachrin was singled out as a particular troublemaker. It was now revealed that earlier he had been fired from a plantation on Hawaii for selling liquor illegally.

Toward the end of March A. W. Perelstrous arrived in Honolulu from Kobe, and a front page headline predicted "Perelstrous As Peace Maker." It did not happen. The recalcitrant Russians refused to talk to him, and after a meeting with the governor at Iolani Palace, Perelstrous was cursed and chased off the grounds by a crowd of Russian women.

Governor Frear became the mediator. At his urging the planters made token concessions, and the governor in turn told the Russians they should go to work. The *Advertiser* believed differences had been settled. But it was not so simple. After Governor Frear had addressed the Russians a man named Vasileff gathered them under a big tree on the palace grounds, "and made one of his impassioned and flamboyant speeches and in five minutes undid all the work of days." A headline read "Vasileff Queers the Game," and perhaps he did. The hearts of both the immigrants and the government were hardening. The government decided not to feed them after Monday. "The men may starve and nobody will shed many tears, but the poor women and little children are an entirely different problem."

Vasileff, it was disclosed, also had been fired from a plantation, because his energies in the fields went into singing revolutionary hymns and not into cutting cane. One newspaper regarded him as "an eloquent speechmaker . . . who has clean, white, tender hands, very different from those of a field laborer, who is educated and well dressed as compared to the rest, but who came here fare paid under the fraudulent pretense that he was a laborer." Attorney Lightfoot decided he could do little for the Russians, and he resigned as consul. His parting opinion was that Perelstrous had lied to them.

On April 4, 1910, the remaining Russians at the quarantine station were expelled. They joined others who had left earlier in setting up a camp of canvas and box tents in Iwilei, on the barren west fringe of town. The Russians climbed the mountains behind Honolulu in search of fruits and berries to add to their food supplies. Iwilei was a poor neighborhood, but many residents brought the Russians food, and the U. S. soldiers at Schofield barracks collected $162 for their aid. It was reported that conditions in their makeshift camp were less than marginal and an epidemic was feared. For about a hundred of the people, the situation had become so desperate that they at last accepted work on the plantations.

The police watched closely. They assured the public the Russians would be arrested as vagrants if they did any stealing. By now all sorts of dark suggestions were rumored. Some of the Russian women were not really the wives of the men they were living with, and if this was true the White Slave act would apply. The Russians would start throwing bombs if the police attempted to enforce vagrancy laws. One of the most emotional and inaccurate of the newspaper stories reported the Russians were selling their children.

On April 28 Perelstrous was quoted in a front page story as saying, "Why don't they hand this Vasileff up? What are they waiting for? Are they waiting until someone is killed and then it will be too late?" The simple Russians assumed the suggestion of Perelstrous would be carried out. The next day they sent a delegation to call on the governor. They asked when Vasileff was to be hanged and who would hang with him.

The following day Vasileff and three cohorts were arrested. A crowd of Russians gathered outside the police station. Their presence seemed menacing, and the police charged the crowd with clubs, turned a fire hose on them, and finally three mounted police armed with whips drove the few remaining men from the street. Again a delegation called on the governor to find out why Vasileff had been arrested and why the police had attacked them. They learned only that Vasileff had been charged as a vagrant. The Russians released their frustrations by drawing a large picture of a policeman on a board with the words "American Liberty" below it and then throwing stones and mud at it.

The police were nervous and suspicious. When a group of Russians appeared at the prison bearing food for Vasileff and his fellow captives, the police allowed only cans of sardines to be passed to the prisoners and refused to accept several loaves of bread which were also offered. The police feared the loaves might have bombs inside.

The Honolulu Socialists again came forward with advice. "We assure you that our sympathies are with you and that we appreciate the fact that by the brave fight you have made against capitalist brutality you have rendered valuable service to the entire working class. . . ." But the Socialists believed nothing more could be gained by holding out, and they recommended that the Russians "go to work on the plantations and to try to improve your conditions as occasion presents itself."

Matters were coming to a quick conclusion. The immigrants were near the end of their resources, and by the middle of May most had found jobs in town or accepted the conditions of plantation life. A number of Russians—those who could scrape the money together—bought passage to California. There was little the immigrants could do for Vasileff and his three companions. Each was sentenced to three months in jail.

The Vasileff name appears once again in Hawaiian annals. In May, 1911, the Russian embassy in Washington passed on a memorandum to the U. S. Secretary of State asking that assistance be given in returning five families to Russia. Among the names in the memorandum was that of Vasileff, his wife, and two children. The memo stated these five families were not suited to plantation life.

The district where the Russians had set up their makeshift camp, Iwilei, was an area much talked about long before the Russians came, and the name was synonymous with depravity. Iwilei was the place where open, organized prostitution flourished.

The Iwilei establishment dated back to the end of the nineteenth century. Three men, Eugene P. Sullivan, J. M. Kanematsu, and T. Masuda, planned the construction of the buildings and the maintenance which would be necessary. Before they went ahead with their plans they consulted the high sheriff of the territory regarding their scheme. The high sheriff told them it would be tolerated as long as the stockade was run according to police and Board of Health regulations. The area became known as Iwilei stockade.

Land was leased from two Chinese. They were paid an outright sum of $9,000 and promised a quarterly rental of $150. The entire cost of setting the place up totaled about $30,000, which included the construction of a number of small bungalows which were occupied by the prostitutes. Maintenance costs ran about $300 a month, including bookkeeping help, collection of rents from the prostitutes, janitor services, and electricity. The maintenance costs did not include the salary of a police officer who was stationed on the premises to enforce the police regulations which were posted at the five entrances to the stockade. A grand jury report in 1901 stated that the net income ranged between $1,160 and $1,650 per month.

That same year the attorney general wrote a letter to the acting governor stating that there were 144 registered prostitutes at Iwilei. The women had to be examined by a doctor regularly to determine if they were diseased, and no woman could legally work in Iwilei stockade if she did not possess a current certificate. The existence of Iwilei pricked the conscience of the attorney general just as it periodically upset other sensitive citizens. The attorney general closed his letter with an apology. "Whether wise or unwise it is an honest attempt to lessen the evils of an infamous traffic, which human laws, at least under conditions existing here, are powerless to eradicate."

Indignation over Iwilei stockade intermittently burst forth, but the stockade continued to exist. In 1905 a civic group in Honolulu published a pamphlet which stated that venereal diseases were not being controlled by legalizing prostitution at Iwilei. This had been the rationalization all along, and it was now declared that the theory was not working. But little happened. Periodically a rush of public indignation pushed the police into raiding the stockade. In May, 1908, *The Friend* noted: "A vile resort known as Iwilei closed by Sheriff Iaukea." In 1913 thirty-seven women were arrested. The prostitutes who were aliens were escorted to the immigration station and deported.

The following year a group of citizens issued a *Report of Committee on the Social Evil*. The report noted that the number of women at Iwilei fluctuated between fifty-two and 188. At the time of one inspection by the committee there were eighty-two Japanese prostitutes, fourteen Puerto Ricans, six French, and five Americans. The report pointed out that in spite of Iwilei there were sixteen houses of prostitution in Honolulu and three at Waikiki. The conclusion was that every effort should be made to bring prostitution to an end. But more than mere repression was needed. The prostitutes must not be treated as criminals. They should rather be helped back to a productive life. The report showed an understanding not common in that time.

World War I made the problem more obvious. As military camps burgeoned so did Iwilei. In late 1916 the citizens of Honolulu decided to crack down and to close Iwilei permanently. Just before the ax fell, Somerset Maugham arrived in Honolulu. During his stopover Maugham visited the stockade. His report was not very different from others who had walked the muddy paths between the bungalows. Maugham thought Iwilei a desolate, unattractive place. Gramophones blared. Women not busy at the time stood on the porches of their bungalows, exposing their breasts and inviting passers-by to come in. One woman obviously had acquired a great reputation, because there was a line of men extending some seventy-five feet in front of her door.

As a result of the 1916 raids 108 women were given suspended sentences. If any of them were convicted again, Judge Clarence Ashford threatened to sentence them to up to a year in prison. Thirteen male procurers were allowed to leave the Islands. Not all the women charged appeared in court. When Somerset Maugham sailed from Honolulu, apparently one of these prostitutes took passage aboard his ship. She seems to have been the prototype for his story *Miss Thompson,* which gained fame as the motion picture *Rain.*

Ever since the Hawaiian Islands had been discovered by Westerners, there were people interested in seeing what the place looked like. The journals of early voyagers were the travel books of their age, although few persons could afford the time, the money, or the risks of traveling to such an exotic place as Hawaii. But as early as the 1840s and '50s there were a few who were rich and bold enough to travel to Hawaii.

Perhaps Henry Whitney was the first man to think of tourism as being a distinct business in itself. In 1875 he wrote *The Hawaiian Guide Book.* The book was in enough demand for varied editions of it to keep appearing for the next twenty-five years. The 1890 version began: "The Earthly Paradise! Don't you want to go to it? Why of course." The book sold for 60 cents, and the round-trip fare from San Francisco to Hawaii was $125.

Tourism was becoming a substantial source of income for Hawaii during the last days of the monarchy. From 1883 through 1887 between

500 and 750 tourists visited Hawaii annually, and the estimated income from this was $500,000. In 1887 a man was hired in San Francisco to promote tours to the Islands, but the service was ahead of its time and not successful. The following year James Williams, a photographer, started a magazine called *Paradise of the Pacific*. This slick paper publication carried many illustrations, and well into the 1950s it continued to depict Hawaii as a land of brilliant sunsets, palm fringed lagoons, and friendly maidens.

In 1901 a section of the Moana Hotel was completed on Waikiki beach. It was the first big building on what would eventually become the most famous stretch of beach in the world. Before the fall of the monarchy a Hawaiian Bureau of Information was formed. Through various name changes it evolved into the Hawaii Visitors Bureau.

At the beginning of the twentieth century there wasn't much to do in Hawaii unless one had initiative or local friends. The folders described the view from the Pali, on Oahu, but Kilauea crater on the island of Hawaii received the biggest build-up. Waikiki attracted only a few. It was essentially a broad sandbar with the ocean on one side and a swamp behind. Some Islanders considered it an acceptable place for weekend houses but little more.

After World War I there was much discussion about the tourist business. Many Islanders thought that the image of the hula girl in a grass skirt was not only dishonest but would give Hawaii a bad reputation. But the hula girl, the imported ukulele, and a jazz kind of music came to be the popular symbols of the Islands during the 1920s and 1930s. By 1923 the number of tourists had risen to 12,021 and in 1931 to approximately 16,000. Tourism was meriting the interested glances of Island businessmen.

When World War I erupted there were a number of British, German, and Japanese merchant and passenger ships at sea in the Pacific. When the war declarations came over their radios, many vessels headed at full speed for neutral harbors where they could safely remain while deciding what the next move should be. Before long it became clear that German strength in the Pacific was small, and so Allied ships ventured onto the high seas once again. Most German captains realized the odds were steadily rising against them, and they kept their ships inside neutral harbors.

The first German vessel to appear at Honolulu was the steamer *Setos*. It arrived just three days after war was declared. Other German vessels arrived from time to time, and soon the harbor became so crowded that permission was asked of Washington to send some of the vessels to Pearl Harbor. The request was refused.

On October 15, 1914, the government was faced with a new problem when the German gunboat *Geier,* followed by her collier, came into the harbor. Under neutrality regulations merchant and passenger ships could remain in port indefinitely, but warships could remain for a maximum of only twenty-four hours unless they were in need of repairs. Captain Grasshof of the *Geier* claimed the boilers and machinery on his ships were in need of extensive repairs. An inspection was made of the ships, and Grasshof was allowed three weeks to get the work done. Six days after the Germans arrived the Japanese battleship *Hizen* appeared just beyond the three-mile limit off the harbor. The Japanese captain said he planned to remain until the German war vessels came out of the harbor. Soon a cruiser arrived to give the *Hizen* support.

Honolulu residents heard the sound of guns fired in anger on October 24. The boom of cannon and the brightness of a searchlight brought many to the shore that night. It was not the *Geier* trying to escape, but rather a small German-owned sailing vessel attempting to get into Honolulu harbor. The small ship was captured by the *Hizen*. The Japanese took off the crew and then used the vessel for target practice. The waterfront reverberated with the sound of cannon, but the damage did not match the noise. The Japanese were unable to sink the ship with their guns. Finally it was set afire.

The deadline for the departure of the *Geier* and her collier was midnight November 7. As that day approached tension rose. Some Japanese in Honolulu protested that the repairs were taking too long and that the warships should be forced to put to sea. While making repairs the Germans were also keeping an eye on the enemy battleship. Each day the chief officer of the *Geier* mounted to the roof garden of the Alexander Young Hotel, where he watched the movements of the *Hizen* as he sipped tea. At nightfall November 7 the German ships still lay at their piers, and thousands of persons crowded the shore to watch the fight which must come if the Germans sailed. The spectators were disappointed, for Captain Grasshof knew he was heavily outgunned, and in spite of the earlier inaccurate shooting of the Japanese he remained in the harbor after midnight and his ships were interned.

Old-timers in Honolulu remembered the *Geier*. It had been in the harbor fourteen years earlier. Then the vessel was on its way to the Boxer Rebellion in China. The reception it received in Hawaii on that earlier occasion was indeed friendly. A newspaper greeted the crew's arrival with a front page story in German, and a great luau was spread for them ashore. The vessel was serenaded by bandmaster Berger on its departure, and a newspaper wrote, "mayhap some day the noble little craft will return to these waters with the smile of victory ennobling the sun-burned countenances of her gallant crew."

In 1914 few in Honolulu, outside of a handful of German nationals, wanted to see the "smile of victory" on the faces of the crew of the *Geier*. But at that early point in the war the U. S. was a declared neutral and anti-German sentiment had not yet swept the nation. Even a year later, in December, 1915, the crew of the *Geier* could come ashore for a Christmas party and be joined by a large number of Islanders. Some 500 persons joined in the celebration. The band from the *Geier* played and George Rodiek, one of Honolulu's most prominent businessmen and also German consul in Hawaii, addressed the crowd. Money was raised during the evening and donated to the Red Cross.

As months passed stories of German atrocities crystallized sentiment in favor of the Allies. By the end of January, 1917, Germany had declared unrestricted U-boat warfare in the seas surrounding the Allied nations. On the day this declaration was made smoke drifted from the funnels of the German vessels in Honolulu. A few days later smoke poured from the deck of the *Geier*. When city fire equipment arrived at the dock, the *Geier*'s crew refused assistance, and later an offer to tow the ship away from the pier was likewise refused. A day earlier Germany and the United States had broken diplomatic relations.

The German crews were attempting to inflict the greatest possible damage to the machinery of their ships so they would be worthless if the U. S. joined the Allies. The crews drained the water from the boilers and stoked up the fires in an effort to burn out the boilers. Gauges and cocks were smashed, cylinder heads cracked, and navigating instruments thrown overboard. When the government realized what was happening, they took the crews of all the ships into custody, but orders soon came from Washington instructing the territory to return the crews of the merchant ships to their vessels. The men of the *Geier* and her collier were the only exception. They were kept ashore in custody.

As the U. S. and Germany moved ever closer to war, the presence of the German ships in the harbor appeared as a serious threat. The vessels could be blown up at their piers, wreaking havoc upon harbor facilities. Perhaps the ships could even be towed to the narrow mouth of the harbor, where they could be sunk and so close the harbor for months. Newspapers pointed out the danger and pressure was put on the governor to take action. The governor asked Washington, but no approval came either to anchor the ships outside the harbor or tow them into Pearl Harbor. The federal government was concerned with handling all matters with Germany on a strictly legal basis, while the people of Hawaii were concerned lest serious damage be done their harbor.

Deeply involved in the controversy of the ships was the firm of H. Hackfeld & Company, which acted as agent for the German merchant vessels. As agent, Hackfeld & Company successfully blocked every effort to move ships or remove their crews. They did allow inspectors to go over the vessels carefully to search for explosives, but this did little to ease the mind of many citizens.

When the U. S. Congress passed a war resolution on April 5, 1917, the German merchant ships were still berthed essentially where they had been three months earlier. On the same night the war resolution was passed the ships were seized under instructions from Washington. Most members of the crew were sent to the mainland and were interned for the remainder of the war, although some sailors were sent to work on Kipahulu plantation on Maui. There were no attempts either to blow up the ships or block the harbor entrance. The damaged machinery aboard eight merchant ships in Honolulu and one vessel in Hilo was repaired and the vessels put into service under the American flag. The *Geier* and her collier were also repaired and eventually joined the U. S. Navy.

Anti-German sentiment in Hawaii rose steadily from early 1917. Several dramatic events in Honolulu helped fuel the feeling. In the summer of 1917 a Honoluluan was accused of playing a role in a grandiose and impractical German plot which was supposed to result in a revolution against the British in India. Honolulu was shocked by the name of the accused, for it was George Rodiek, first vice president and ranking officer of H. Hackfeld & Company, the largest company in Hawaii. He was also German consul, which was an incidental job, and president of the powerful Hawaii Sugar Planters' Association. Indicted with Rodiek was Heinrich Schroeder, a Hackfeld employee and former secretary of the German consul. The part these two men played in the India plot now seems trivial and vague, but in those emotional times it seemed monstrous.

The India plot had touched Hawaii in 1915, while the U. S. was still very much of a neutral. An essential part of the plot was to get arms and ammunition to the would-be rebels. One load of weapons was supposed to be transferred from one ship to another at a point south of the Hawaiian Islands during the summer of 1915. The ship which was to receive the arms was named the *Maverick*. It put into Hilo harbor and was met by Rodiek and Schroeder. Perhaps Rodiek carried messages to the captain of the *Maverick*. The two men, in their consular capacities, certainly helped the ship buy supplies in Hilo. Two years after meeting the *Maverick* Rodiek and Schroeder were accused of breaking neutrality laws and were ordered to stand trial in San Francisco. Both pleaded guilty of violating neutrality laws, although Rodiek claimed he did not know he was violating the laws at the time.

In December, 1917, the diary of Captain Grasshof of the *Geier* was made public. It made interesting reading. It showed that the *Geier* had sent and received radio messages after it was interned. Under the laws of neutrality the radio was supposed to be sealed. The diary described how men from the *Geier* were given false passports and secreted off to the mainland, from which they continued their attempts to get back to Germany. Mentioned in the diary were the names of Captain Boy-Ed and Captain Franz von Papen, both of whom had been expelled from the U. S. The names of Rodiek and Schroeder also appeared in Grasshof's diary, although it is not clear in what connection.

The assumption of many of Honolulu's vocal citizens was that Rodiek and Schroeder were guilty of numerous foul acts, and there was a roar of indignation. Rodiek was fined $10,000 and lost his American citizenship, while Schroeder, who turned state's evidence, was fined $1,000. The newspapers complained that the sentences were much too light. In cooler times the revoking of Rodiek's citizenship seemed severe, and four years later he was given back his citizenship by President Wilson.

Hysteria hit Honolulu. If the head of the largest company in Hawaii had aided the enemy, other treasonous acts certainly were taking place. The *Star Bulletin* editorialized, "we must be prepared to stand firm against any hint of mounting hysteria. . . ." But hysteria had already taken hold. The superintendent of Queen's hospital was charged with pro-German feelings. He resigned, although an investigation failed to substantiate charges which had been made by a disgruntled nurse. Newspapers published letters asking Carl Du Roi, manager of a large department store, to confirm or deny whether he was pro-German. U. S. Marshal J. J. Smiddy was accused in a front page story of being pro-German.

The hysteria quickly infected the school system. All public-school teachers had to sign a loyalty letter which included the statement: "Good American citizenship is more important than scholarship." Miss Maria Heuer was a teacher of German at the University of Hawaii and was also a German citizen. In response to demands for her dismissal, she stated she had never said anything against the U. S. When asked about the war she replied that she was against all war. There were howlings in the community that she be fired, but the University would not do so. Matters became very bitter and Maria Heuer finally resigned. The teaching of German was not resumed at the University of Hawaii until 1927. German language courses were dropped from public high schools.

On January 2, 1918, The Hawaiian Vigilance Corps of the American Defense Society was organized. The leader was George R. Carter, a former governor of Hawaii, who had visited the East Coast and was convinced that Hawaii did not realize the importance of the war. The purpose of the Vigilance Corps was to break down hostile influences and maintain the morale of the citizens. Each new member of the corps had to be endorsed by an older member who must stand ready to answer for the loyalty of the newcomer. Membership was much sought, since it amounted to certification as a superpatriot.

Many persons in Hawaii helped the war effort in calmer ways. Liberty bonds were bought by the citizens in great quantities, and women labored on behalf of the Red Cross and Belgian Relief. At the beginning of 1918 some 200 Islanders were overseas. They were ambulance drivers, nurses, and members of all branches of the armed forces. In August, 1917, the first military unit composed of men of Japanese extraction to be organized under the American flag became a part of the Hawaii National Guard.

Curiously, many of the social and business leaders in the Islands were the least immune to war hysteria, and the result was persecution. Any person with a German name was fair game. Some persons advocated interning all persons who had been born in Germany for the duration of the war, and others added that all persons of German origin were potential enemies, no matter how exemplary their earlier conduct. John Soper, who was in charge of the militia during the overthrow of the monarchy, predicted there would be vigilante hangings if the federal forces in Hawaii were not more severe. It was easy to fire a person with a German name for imagined reasons. Newspapers carried front page stories of suspected disloyalties or of a suspected lack of patriotic zeal. Near the end of the war the situation became bad enough for the attorney general's office in Washington to write to George Carter and through him reprimand the citizens of Hawaii for "persecuting alien enemies." During the war years and immediately after a large number of Germans left the Islands, many of them moving to California.

The intensity of feeling brought bloodshed on April 14, 1918. The two men involved were S. J. Walker, a forty-eight-year-old mechanic who worked at Pearl Harbor, and Henry Allen, a one-armed navy veteran who was proprietor of a soft drink stand in Aala Park. The two men had long known each other. Both men were bachelors and they had shared rooms during an earlier time when they were friends.

Each morning Henry Allen hoisted the navy ensign above his soft drink stand, and on that tragic April morning, Allen reported, Walker called his flag a dirty rag. It must have been the ultimate insult in a bitter relationship, for Allen pulled a gun and fired. The shot missed and Walker turned away, but Allen fired again. This time he hit his enemy in the stomach. Walker died without uttering a word.

The *Advertiser* quoted Allen: "I just had to shoot him . . . there was nothing else I could do. I have known for some time that he was a Hun, but did not report him to the authorities because I was gathering evidence against him and did not want to alarm him by premature exposure. But when he insulted my flag, the Flag I enlisted under in the United States navy, he went too far and I shot him."

Henry Allen was indicted for second degree murder. In court he claimed that Walker had said he hoped all U. S. troops in France would die. It was also claimed that Walker had refused to take off his hat when the flag was carried by. The Vigilance Committee was not critical of Henry Allen. John A. Balch, a businessman and one of the leaders of the Vigilance Committee, however, was critical of local police officers for not doing their duty. He noted that Walker was a member of the International Workers of the World. According to Balch, "Local authorities have failed to carry out their sworn duty. If they continue their laxity there will be more murders unless every Hun and I.W.W. is placed behind barbed wire."

In April, 1918, there was only one possible verdict for Henry Allen. He was declared innocent. After court had been dismissed a crowd of people paraded Allen through Honolulu. The *Star Bulletin* editorially admitted that Allen ". . . was freed on sentiment."

One of the business casualties of the war was the firm of H. Hackfeld & Company. From the beginning of the war the company had been blacklisted by the British, who considered the firm to be the center of German influence in the Pacific. After George Rodiek was accused of being a part of the India conspiracy, the U. S. government refused the company the right to use radio or cable facilities. The problems of Rodiek, the role the firm had played in protecting the interests of the German merchant ships in Honolulu harbor, and the employment of many Germans on plantations and in the head office of the firm brought H. Hackfeld into disrepute with a substantial segment of Hawaii's population.

H. Hackfeld & Company had 40,000 shares of stock outstanding. Of this something over 27,000 shares were owned by German citizens. In October, 1917, President Wilson signed the Trading with the Enemy Act, which allowed the U. S. government to take over property held by the enemy for the duration of the war. This act made it possible for a majority of the shares of H. Hackfeld to be seized and then sold. A group of Island businessmen bought most of these shares, and H. Hackfeld was now dominated by them. It had passed from German to American control.

The new ownership brought numerous quick changes. The name of the company was changed to American Factors, Limited, and B. F. Ehlers & Company, the department store owned by Hackfeld, was renamed Liberty House. The manager, whose loyalty had once been questioned, was replaced. On August 2, 1918, a double-page advertisement appeared in a Honolulu newspaper inviting the public to come to the Liberty House at 3

P.M. to witness the removal of the old name. A headline stated: "All Traces of Teutonism Within and Without Will be Removed. . . ." That, indeed, was the first objective of the new management.

After World War I ended Johan Friedrich Hackfeld, who had returned to Germany many years earlier, and who was the largest shareholder in the company, filed several suits in an attempt to regain funds which he believed were his. He claimed that he was a U. S. citizen, because he had been given a certificate by the Republic of Hawaii which gave him all the privileges of citizenship without requiring him to give up his German citizenship. When Hawaii became a territory of the United States, all citizens of the Republic automatically became citizens of the U. S. Between 1924 and 1931 Hackfeld was paid some $3,700,000 under presidential order. Litigation continued into the 1940s. The substantial interests which the Isenberg family held in H. Hackfeld & Company likewise resulted in suits. After each contestant had had his say, the Germans ended up winning certain financial concessions, but the company which had become American Factors, Limited, remained in the control of Americans.

On the morning of May 18, 1907, the smooth slopes of Mauna Kea were spotted by the crew of the *Snark*. The craft was forty-five feet long and had cost its owner, Jack London, $30,000 to build. Two days after sighting land the *Snark* lay off Honolulu, where a tug was hired to pull the yacht into Pearl Harbor. It had taken twenty-seven days to reach Honolulu from San Francisco. The arrival of the famous author was proclaimed in a banner headline in the *Evening Bulletin:* "Jack London Makes Pearl Harbor His Port." A reporter who rowed out to the *Snark* was not impressed by what he saw. He noted the decks were littered, the engine had failed enroute, and no one aboard could repair it.

The trip to the Islands had been slow, because winds were weak. But the voyage had not been unpleasant. The Londons had stowed hundreds of books aboard, and there was a phonograph to provide music. Such time as was left was passed in playing cards. Jack decided the voyage could be a challenge in more than one way. Out of San Francisco he determined to use the trip to lick the cigarette habit, and he dumped his entire supply of tobacco overboard. Ashore in Honolulu Jack quickly got his hands on cigarettes again, and he chain-smoked while talking to a reporter. After this one last orgy he declared he would cut down to five cigarettes a day.

Jack London had been in Hawaii before. In 1904 he had paused in Honolulu going and returning from the Russo-Japanese war, and he claimed he had come to Honolulu even earlier—in 1893 as a hand aboard a sealing vessel. In 1907, however, he had his first real look at Hawaii.

The *Snark* required extensive engine repairs, and London had been so eager to depart from San Francisco that parts of the vessel were still unpainted. While this work was being done Jack and Charmian lived in a cottage at Pearl Harbor. Soon the Lorrin A. Thurstons invited the Londons to spend some time at their home in town and also at their cottage on Tantalus. On outings at Waikiki Jack was introduced to the sport of surfing, and he became a fast friend of Duke Kahanamoku, the Hawaiian boy who would become famous as an Olympic swimming champion.

Whether aboard ship, at his Pearl Harbor cottage, visiting the Thurstons, or camping at Waikiki, Jack London kept a very strict morning schedule. He could not be lured away from his morning writing, and he did not put down his pencil until he had written 1,000 words.

The crater of Haleakala on Maui intrigued London. This giant mountain rose more than 10,000 feet. Its summit was shaped like a vast bowl which held symmetrical volcanic cinder cones and fields of volcanic cinder, all in a startling variety of color. Haleakala is a beautiful, unearthly place, and Jack London wanted to see it.

Lorrin Thurston wrote to Louis von Tempsky, who managed Haleakala ranch on Maui. Could they come? Von Tempsky replied that any man who could write *The Call of the Wild* was welcome at the ranch. The Londons and the Thurstons set out for Maui on the *Claudine,* a vessel Thurston knew well, since it was the ship the revolutionists had chartered to carry the commissioners to the United States in 1893.

Louis von Tempsky's wife had died earlier, and the children had grown up in the informality of ranch life. They were in the saddle as soon as they could grasp the pommel. They spent days riding the gentle, grassy slopes of Haleakala and within the crater itself. Two teen-aged von Tempsky girls, Gwen and Armine, decided to join the expedition.

The party included the Londons, the Thurstons, Louis von Tempsky, his daughters Gwen and Armine, and two cowboys who brought up the pack horses. The first day's ride took them to a cabin 6,500 feet up the mountain side. The next day they reached the peak of Haleakala and then made their way down a cinder trail to the floor of the crater. By nightfall they had crossed to the northern rim, where they pitched their tents.

The northern corner of Haleakala is the one wet part of the crater. The travelers had the choice of getting soaked or spending their time under cover. They elected to remain in the tents, playing cards. During breaks in the weather they went goat hunting to help supplement their food supplies. Two days later they rode out through Kaupo gap, which is a break in the south rim of Haleakala crater. They rode to sea level and followed the trail to the village of Hana. Hana was one of the most isolated places in the Hawaiian Islands, but it did have a sugar plantation and even the amenities of a primitive hotel.

The village of Hana is buried in the great rain forest of eastern Maui. It is on the narrow coastal plain below the stern mountains which rise to form the rim of Haleakala. Clouds, laden with moisture, sweep onto the coast and deluge the land. When the bright sun pours its rays on the wet jungle, steam rises in a haze. Through this humid jungle, which seemed to hold every tint and shade of green, rode the Londons and their friends. It was a hazardous trip during dry weather, but when the Londons were there the rains poured down.

The slopes of Haleakala are serrated, with steep valleys cutting deeply into the mountain wall. A narrow, slippery path was the one route along the mountainside. This path joined a trail which followed a ditch that carried water to the sugar plantations on the dry, central plain of Maui. Under ideal conditions the ditch trail scared most people, but the Londons were there when the trail was very nearly a stream. When they came to the fragile, shaky bridges which stretched across yawning valleys —bridges without rails—even the relaxed Hawaiian cowboys dismounted and respectfully led their horses across. At nightfall the sodden company reached the house of the ditch tender at Keanae Valley, above the peninsula where the Mormon missionaries had made their first mass conversion years earlier.

Weary and soaked as they were, there was constant good humor and fun between Jack London and the von Tempsky sisters. They raced their horses and splashed each other with mud. Much later Gwen remembered Jack London as a well mannered man, who drank a good deal, rode his horse poorly by strict Maui standards, and, above all, was an intriguing, virile man.

For Armine the presence of a famous writer strengthened her inclination to pursue her own writing. She had made attempts at writing, schoolgirl efforts which Jack thought were terrible, but he told her to keep at it. Perhaps his words of encouragement were important, for Armine von Tempsky later became one of Hawaii's most successful novelists.

Charmian London was hardly a beautiful woman, but she was vivacious and usually a match for Jack. Numerous problems plagued their marriage, and one of the reasons it endured was Charmian's willingness to attempt any adventure which interested her husband. After Jack died Charmian returned to Hawaii and to the ranch on Haleakala, and she wrote about the good life they had enjoyed in the earlier years.

The warm relationship between the Thurstons and the Londons was strained in 1910 when Thurston decided some of Jack's stories, which included leprosy as part of the plot, gave distorted views of the Islands. A series of letters went back and forth between Thurston and London, who was then on the mainland, and these letters were printed in the *Advertiser*. Thurston charged London with the same general crimes which James Michener would be charged with after publication of *Hawaii* nearly half a century later.

> *You came to Hawaii and absorbed local color enough to give realism to your tales. You then began a series of gruesome stories in which leprosy was the theme and Hawaii the setting. None of them were true. They were pure fiction; but like the historical novel, worked in so much fact with the fiction, that they give the impression to the uninitiated that they are more fact than fiction, the net result of which is to create an untrue impression, injurious to Hawaii, that this is an unsafe and undesirable place to live in.*

In March, 1915, Charmian and Jack London were back in Hawaii. They rented a cottage at Waikiki and settled in for a three-month stay. Jack talked about his great house in the Valley of the Moon, which had burned, and how he planned to rebuild it. He wanted to use some Hawaiian woods in the interior. With the Londons came Yoshimatsu Nakata, whom the Londons had signed aboard in Hilo eight years earlier. Nakata was a man of all trades in the London household, and he did most of Jack's manuscript typing. Yoshimatsu pondered the possibilities of becoming a writer, but London encouraged him to become a dentist. The advice was followed, and Nakata eventually became well known in his profession in Honolulu.

The social life of the Londons was frantic. They were taken off to the island of Hawaii to look at the volcano. They were the guests of former Queen Liliuokalani, and Jack lectured the Honolulu Ad Club on the dangers of holding out the hand of friendship to visitors while privately discrediting them. Jack was trying to press forward on two novels, but the flow of visitors and entertainment slowed him down. To control the situation the Londons announced visitors would be received only after 2 P.M. In spite of the interruptions it was good to be in Hawaii. Jack reported, "The old charm of Hawaii has come back on me a hundred fold."

The Londons returned to the mainland in July, 1915, but by December they were again in Hawaii. Gwen von Tempsky remembered that Jack was a sick man. He would not follow his prescribed diet of boiled vegetables and salads. Instead he preferred feasts of under-cooked duck, and there was a lot of drinking. Hawaii had a special fascination for him. To a daughter he wrote, "I grow more and more in love with Hawaii, and I am certain, somewhere in the future (not too remote) that I shall elect to make Hawaii my home."

On July 26, 1916, Jack and Charmian London left the Islands so he could attend the annual Bohemian Club gathering at Pacific Grove in California. Jack was thirty-five pounds overweight and was suffering from uremia and rheumatism. His ankles and legs were painfully swollen. He hoped to return to Hawaii soon. Perhaps his next book might be about the Islands. But Jack London was not destined to see Hawaii again. His physical condition worsened and his will to live flowed from him. He was in constant pain and in November 1916 he died after taking a massive overdose of narcotics.

Ever since Captain Cook's visit the number of part-Hawaiians had rapidly increased. Were these hybrids Westerners or were they Hawaiians? Whatever their individual feelings might have been, most part-Hawaiians really had little choice. The easiest drift was into the Hawaiian community where racial restrictions were minimal. There were a few part-Hawaiians, however, who had money enough to choose the kind of life they wanted to live. Among these few were the children of Robert Holt.

Robert Holt came to Hawaii in the 1830s aboard a trading vessel. He was an Englishman who was related to Honolulu residents John Dominis and William Aldrich. Aldrich had been a partner of Charles Bishop in several business enterprises and Dominis was the husband of Liliuokulani. Robert Holt decided to settle in Honolulu. He became a partner in a shipyard business. Holt was a plodding man, who played a quiet role in the community.

Robert Holt retired from the shipyard company under pressure from his partners. It was noted that he drank excessively in his old age, but when he wrote his will several of Honolulu's knowledgeable citizens were pleased to witness it. Among them was Charles Bishop. He knew how much money Robert Holt had on deposit in his bank. Bishop and others attested to the authenticity of Holt's shaky signature. Shortly after this Robert Holt died, and it was revealed that not only did he have a sizable amount of cash in the bank, but he owned a hotel and some 12,000 acres of choice lands on Oahu.

Robert Holt had married Wati Robinson, a part-Tahitian lady who was the stepdaughter of one of his shipyard partners. Of the three sons Wati bore, Owen appeared to have the best business potential. Owen was tall, slender, handsome, blue-eyed, fair-skinned. He was sent to the mainland to study animal husbandry. He returned with a knowledge of animal care and a decided dislike for Americans.

Robert Holt had divided his 12,000 acres into three ranches, one for each of his sons. The ranches covered the areas known now as Wahiawa, Schofield, and Makaha. Soon Owen was running all three, but Makaha was his favorite. Makaha is a cathedral-like valley near the northwest tip of Oahu, and here Owen built a grand establishment, English style. He constructed an enormous two-story house, numerous guest houses, servants' quarters, and at the beach a large pavilion for those who wanted to fish or swim. He planted orchards of citrus trees. Among the trees ran turkeys, and Kamehameha V added peacocks as a gift. There were blooded race horses in the stables, and a race track was laid out on the valley floor. The gardens were plentiful in ivy geraniums, which were woven into leis and worn by the Holt women.

Makaha could accommodate about a hundred guests, as well as the numerous servants who were brought along. The dining room was forty feet wide and sixty feet long. It was carpeted in red, with red upholstered chairs and red and gold drapes. In this room the important people of Hawaii were entertained. Owen imported a great tallyho coach from England. It was driven by a liveried Englishman and pulled by six pairs of matched horses. There was room inside for twelve people and another six could ride atop.

The woman who ruled the establishment at Makaha was Owen's wife, Hanakaulani. She was strong-willed, aristocratic, and possessed great dignity. Hanakaulani was slender, with high cheek bones, fine black hair, and large, dark eyes. Her appearance was the more impressive, because she stood nearly six feet tall. Hanakaulani's mother was a Hawaiian chiefess, perhaps a direct descendant of Kamehameha I. Her father was Lord George Paulet, the English captain who had run up the British flag in 1843.

Hanakaulani shared her husband's dislike of Americans as well as his appreciation for the ways of the landed English gentry. She largely followed English customs and manners and considered herself an English noblewoman. Of her eighteen children only eight lived to adulthood. They were brought up under a curious combination of English and Hawaiian influences. Each had a kahu, a person who looked after his every want, and at dinner a kahu sat next to each child. Hawaiian fashion, a name song was composed for each child. Sunday dinner consisted of the English staples of roast beef and yorkshire pudding. When guests arrived the children greeted them in a fashion befitting young ladies and gentlemen.

A crack in this idyllic life came in 1891 when Wati Holt died. Owen had been extremely close to his carefree, part-Tahitian mother. Her death was more than he wanted to bear. After the funeral he locked himself into his room and refused food. Six days later Owen Holt was dead. His excessive grief was well understood by the Hawaiians. In his time of great strain

Owen had chosen the Hawaiian way. Hanakaulani lived on for thirteen years, surrounded by her brood of children and insulated from reality by the wealth of her husband.

Anne Holt was one of the daughters of Owen and Hanakaulani. It was expected that all the Holt children would prefer English customs, but Anne, perhaps, responded most enthusiastically. She longed to be an English lady and to be recognized as the granddaughter of Lord Paulet. In 1900 a man arrived in Hawaii who seemed able to turn her dreams into reality. His name was Lawrence Kentwell, born in Shanghai, of English father and Chinese mother. Anne and Lawrence were married and in 1906 they put Hawaii behind them. Eventually they settled in England, in a cottage in Oxford.

Life in England did not turn out to be all Anne had hoped for. The Paulet relationship, of course, was not acknowledged. Lawrence spent four years in the British army during World War I. After his discharge he did not long remain with Anne. He returned to Shanghai and spent the rest of his days there. Anne continued to enjoy her rose garden and afternoon tea. She lived out her life in England. In contrast to her father, the English blood in her veins dominated the Hawaiian.

In the fading years of the 1800s and the opening years of the 1900s a few select businessmen in Hawaii acquired great fortunes. These men were engaged in a variety of businesses, but they had one thing in common. The source of their wealth, whether direct or indirect, came from sugar. Usually the closer the connection with sugar, the faster and greater the wealth. The few families which accumulated these fortunes became the power elite of Hawaii, and they continued to dominate the social, political, and economic life of the Islands until after World War II.

Sugar stocks had great reputations during this era, and middle and upper management customarily invested in them as a sure way to enjoy retirement years. From 1915 through 1925 Kekaha Sugar Company paid no less than a 25 percent dividend and one year it paid 60 percent. From 1906 through 1937 dividends from the plantation at Onomea never dropped below 12 percent. In 1920 Hawaiian Agricultural Company might have set a record. They paid out $1,340,000—a 67 percent dividend.

Among those who qualified as the very rich was Charles Montague Cooke, a son of the missionary-teachers Amos and Juliette Cooke, those two patient persons who had run the Chiefs' Children School for so many years. Amos Cooke had left the mission to become a partner in a business house which became known as Castle and Cooke. In time Amos became a competent businessman, but the son far outshone the father. Charles

Cooke was incredibly successful—perhaps the most successful business-man in Hawaii's history.

By the time he was twenty-five, Charles Cooke pretty well knew where he was going. Behind him was a stint at Amherst Agricultural College. He was married to Anna Rice, the daughter of a missionary family. And he was employed as a bookkeeper at Castle and Cooke. Charles did not stay with his father's company, however, because he felt it was the preserve of an older brother who worked there. Charles Cooke left to join Lewers and Dickson, and in 1877 he borrowed $6,000 to buy a quarter interest in that company.

During his early business days Charles Cooke held two jobs. His second job, which he pursued after regular business hours, was that of auctioneer, and the money he earned enabled him to begin his career as a financier. His first investments were in shares in sailing vessels—shares which brought him a percentage of the profits of a voyage. Cooke was able to place cargoes bound for Lewers and Dickson aboard vessels in which he had an interest, and this helped make his investments profitable. Cooke also knew who the competent captains were, and his money went with the best. Occasionally a ship was lost and Cooke suffered, but profits far outweighed losses. Later, some termed Charles Cooke a gambler, and gambler of sorts he was, but the odds were heavily in his favor, for he had not only inside information but inside influence.

Charles Cooke diversified his investments. He bought shares in sugar plantations and in various Honolulu companies. By 1882 he could afford to invest the sizable sum of $10,000 in a single plantation. Five years later he bought two of the fourteen shares in Lihue plantation from Charles Bishop. It cost him $100,000—a monumental sum. But the dividends from Lihue plantation were so great that he quickly earned back his total investment.

In 1894 Charles Cooke decided to retire. He was only in his mid-forties, but he was a man of wealth. He moved to Oakland, California, because he thought the climate there was better for his son, Richard, and because he would be close to those children who were attending college. Very soon, however, his wife was a virtual widow, for the businessmen of Honolulu missed the golden touch of Charles Cooke, and they constantly lured him back to Honolulu.

Four years after this premature retirement the Cooke family returned to Honolulu. Charles was named president of the newly founded Bank of Hawaii. He also opened banks on the islands of Hawaii, Maui, and Kauai and in 1899 was named president of C. Brewer and Company. Charles Cooke had been a wealthy man when he retired in 1894, but the flurry of activity which followed his return to the Islands quickly made him fabulously wealthy. Perhaps Hawaiian Agricultural Company was an indication of the kind of wealth he was amassing. In 1899 Cooke collected an estimated $84,000 in dividends from this plantation alone, and it was just one of his many investments. Alone it was a fortune, for in that day round steak sold for five cents a pound and no one worried about income taxes.

If impressive stature or athletic ability were evidence of financial astuteness, Charles Cooke would have been a failure. He was a rotund man who stood five feet five in height. The game of golf always defeated him. He rather had the mind of a mathematician and the ability to appraise quickly and accurately the value of a company or a field of sugar cane. In business, as in chess, he made an appraisal and moved fast. A continuing optimism supported his ever enlarging investments in the Islands. When the faint-hearted moaned that Hawaii's economy was sinking, Cooke offered to buy out the faint-hearted. He believed in the economic growth of Hawaii, and such setbacks as might come were only temporary inconveniences. He strongly supported those who overthrew the monarchy, and he went to Washington to push annexation, but politics frustrated him and he left it to others as soon as he could.

The newspaper stories which followed the death of Theo. H. Davies distressed Cooke. The stories included a listing of the wealth of Davies, and Cooke believed this was highly inappropriate. To avoid this Charles Cooke established Charles M. Cooke, Limited, and transferred the great bulk of his wealth to this company. His wife and children benefited from this arrangement, and when Cooke died there was no listing of his possessions or his value. Not only did such an arrangement prevent disclosure of personal wealth, but it bound the family together.

When Charles Cooke died in 1909, he was president of C. Brewer and Company and of the Bank of Hawaii. His entire salary from C. Brewer went to the employee pension fund, and he gave half his salary at Bank of Hawaii to their pension fund. He had more than he needed, and once he had gained his wealth he shared generously. He donated a fortune to libraries, hospitals, churches, and a variety of other causes. On their silver wedding anniversary Charles and Anna gave a total of $100,000 to a long list of charities. He established an aquarium at Waikiki, and after his death Anna endowed the Honolulu Academy of Arts. The fibers of his character can hardly be dissected, but they seem to blend the best of missionary resolve with the admirable generosity of the Hawaiians.

Chapter Fifteen

PARADISE FOR A SELECT FEW

T̲HE PRAYERS intoned in Honolulu churches on Sunday morning, March 28, 1915, were unusually fervent. The supplications asked for the safe return of twenty-one men trapped in a submarine which lay on the ocean bottom somewhere off Honolulu Harbor.

The missing craft was one of four submarines in a flotilla which had gone out to practice diving on the morning of March 25. Only three submarines returned to Honolulu Harbor, and after several hours passed, a search was ordered. The missing craft had been christened the *Skate,* but it was commonly known as the F-4.

It was the first submarine the United States Navy had ever lost, and the navy had no idea how to locate the F-4 or how to raise it if it were found. Ships crisscrossed the seas above the area where they guessed the submarine lay. An oil slick was discovered about three quarters of a mile off shore, and it was presumed that it came from the F-4. But how to find the exact location of the submarine? The ends of a great long chain were secured to the stern ends of two vessels. The ships then ran on parallel courses with the loop of the chain dragging along the ocean floor. In the process they hoped to hook onto the F-4. On shore hundreds of people watched as the ships continued their search day and night.

Shortly after six o'clock Saturday evening, the chain hit a metal object on the ocean floor. Gray paint rubbed off onto the chain, and it was presumed it came from the hull of the F-4. The gray paint, however, was from a giant anchor which had been lost by a ship several years earlier. On Monday morning, March 29, Rear Admiral C. B. T. Moore announced there was no hope the trapped sailors could be found alive.

Navy men refused to abandon hope. They worked without rest to locate the submarine. A diving bell seven feet tall and four and one-half feet in diameter was built at Honolulu Iron Works. The bell was not used, perhaps because navy divers were descending to such great depths. Jack Agraz went down 215 feet wearing a helmet but no diving suit. The gallant efforts were in vain. By April 1 the most optimistic recognized that the men of the F-4 were dead.

Eight giant pontoons were constructed at the Mare Island Navy Yard and rushed to Hawaii aboard the battleship *Maryland*. Five divers also came aboard the battleship, including the man who held the world's record, a descent of 274 feet.

About mid-April the F-4 was finally located a mile and a half off Honolulu Harbor at a depth of 305 feet. A thin stream of air bubbles and oil led to its discovery. Navy diver Frank Crilley went down to the submarine and in doing so set a new world record. Later, diver Loughman descended to the sub. As he was being brought up he became fouled in the cables. He was caught fast at a depth of 275 feet for about four hours. At last Crilley went down and released him. Loughman survived pneumonia and a case of the bends. Crilley won the Congressional Medal of Honor for his daring work.

The navy did not believe they could raise the F-4 from a depth of 305 feet, so they dragged the sub toward shore with chains and cables. By the time the submarine had been pulled to the sixty-foot depth, the hull was terribly broken and on the verge of disintegrating. The sixty-ton pontoons were now used to raise the F-4. The hull was upside down when it broke the surface, and it was towed to Honolulu Harbor in that position. The submarine was brought to the surface on August 30, more than five months after she had disappeared.

There was a gaping hole in the side of the F-4, and when the wreck was examined in dry dock a sickening smell came from the compartments. Curious citizens watched as the remains of the sailors were separated from the battery plates, furniture, engine fittings, and sand. The Navy had appropriated $20,000 to raise the F-4. The final cost was over $126,000.

It was impossible to determine what sank the F-4, but investigations indicated battery leakage which probably eroded part of the hull structure, including the top section of a forward ballast tank. The controls of the F class submarines were known to react slowly, and more water poured in through corroded plates than could be pumped out. As the submarine sank deeper, pressure on the hull increased. More and more water came in. The crew apparently had time to react, because all diving apparatus was set in the rise position. The engine room was probably the last compartment to be flooded, because remains of fifteen of the twenty-one men aboard were found there.

The F-4 disaster caused a great stir across the United States. *The New York Times* demanded that the F class submarines summarily be removed from service. They were outdated and dangerous. The navy earnestly began developing safety devices for submarines and ways to locate and reach them if they lay disabled on the ocean floor. The 1916 annual report of the Navy Department made a recommendation as a result of the F-4 disaster. Since only four of the bodies in the F-4 could be identified after its recovery, it was suggested that sailors be required to wear aluminum identification tags in the future.

The F class submarines were not removed from service with the fleet, and two years later disaster struck again. The location was off Point Loma, California. Fog made visibility poor that day, and in changing course the F-1 was rammed amidships by the F-3. Five men were able to escape, but nineteen plunged downward with the submarine. The depth of the ocean was 600 feet. No attempt was made to raise the F-1.

By 1915, the year of the F-4 disaster, the United States Navy was finally becoming established in Hawaii. A major reason for acquiring the Hawaiian Islands had been to establish a strong naval base there, but after the end of the Spanish-American War some argued that the major base for the United States in the Pacific should be the Philippine Islands. While Congress debated the navy used its meager dock facilities in Honolulu Harbor. Coal and other supplies could be loaded aboard ships, but there were no facilities for major repairs.

Some urgency was added to the development of a Pacific naval base after the Russo-Japanese War of 1904. The victory gave Japan new confidence, and it viewed with disapproval the presence of the United States in the Philippine Islands. Other things also irritated the Japanese. There was discrimination against Japanese on the West Coast of the United States, including an instance in 1906 when Japanese children were segregated in San Francisco schools.

One of the ways President Theodore Roosevelt decided to impress Japan with the power of the United States was to parade his Great White Fleet around the world. From the West Coast the first portion of the fleet sailed for Hawaii. In July, 1908, people from Honolulu drove their buggies to Diamond Head to watch the fleet come in. They were not disappointed by the sight. Twelve great battleships and assorted smaller vessels steamed past in single file, and for days newspapers could talk of little else. "Magnificent beyond any spectacle of the kind these waters have ever seen," the *Advertiser* commented.

Twenty-four hundred sailors paraded through Honolulu, and each was presented a flower lei. Buildings were decorated with flags and bunting and crews were lavishly entertained by Honolulu's citizens. The arrival of the Great White Fleet clearly showed the inadequacy of naval facilities in Hawaii. Fewer than half of the ships of the fleet could fit comfortably into Honolulu Harbor. The rest anchored outside or joined the contingent which sailed to Lahaina. If the United States seriously intended to become a Pacific power, they badly needed naval facilities.

At last Congress decided Hawaii would be its major Pacific naval base, and in 1908 it appropriated $1,000,000 to begin. There was no doubt where the base should be located. Pearl Harbor was the obvious choice. The harbor was big, deep, landlocked, with room for extensive shore facilities. Priority went to building a dry dock, but even before that would be usable the narrow, shallow channel which led into the spacious harbor had to be deepened. As early as 1903 some dredging had been done, but capital ships were unable to enter. Hawaiian Dredging Company won the contract to dig the channel deep enough to accommodate the largest ships of the day.

In late 1911 the deepening of the entrance to Pearl Harbor was completed, and on December 11 the harbor was officially opened. The cruiser *California* steamed up the passage, its bow cutting a great ribbon which spanned the channel. Aboard the *California* was Rear Admiral Chauncey Thomas, and among his guests were Liliuokalani and Sanford Dole.

Oahu Railroad Company carried 500 people to Pearl Harbor aboard a special train for the occasion. As the warship glided through the channel, a telephone call alerted Honolulu, and the town celebrated with a general blowing of steam whistles.

Congressional concern brought another change to Hawaii in 1908. The navy constructed a wireless station on Oahu which made it possible for the first time to contact ships at sea. Islanders could keep track of the locations of ships and learn the exact time they would arrive in Honolulu.

The United States and Japan were allies during World War I, but this brought no lessening of tension between the two countries. After the Allied victory Japan benefited by gaining some of Germany's Pacific possessions. Some of these new island holdings were turned into Japanese naval bases. When Japan and China again began warring in the early 1930s, it seemed all the more reason to develop Pearl Harbor even further.

The United States Army also came to Hawaii. Its first base was Camp McKinley, set up at the foot of Diamond Head during the Spanish-American War, and it was adequate until 1907. Then Fort Shafter was established to the west of Honolulu. The biggest post was Schofield Barracks, which was started in 1908. This coincided with the choosing of Pearl Harbor as the naval base in the Pacific, for it was the army's job to protect the base. Schofield was named after General John Schofield, who had surveyed Pearl Harbor in 1872. The base included over 14,000 acres on the middle, upland plain of Oahu. From this central location the army could move to any point on the island to repulse an attack. The first unit stationed at Schofield was the 5th Cavalry Regiment, which disembarked from a transport in Honolulu Harbor in January, 1909, and rode out to its new home.

The day the 5th Cavalry Regiment rode out to Schofield Barracks the *Advertiser* noted editorially that this was the greatest influx of American blood the Territory had ever seen. It was the newspaper's hope that the soldiers would "help Honolulu grow along traditional American lines." In plain language, the editorial was saying that the Americans would help reinforce American standards as opposed to Oriental standards in the Islands.

By the 1920s the military was not only reinforcing American standards in the Islands but were also providing another source of income. Civilian employment by the various services and spending by the military and their dependents became vital to the economic well-being of the Territory. Even this economic boon could not smooth the ruffled relations which sometimes upset both military and local residents. Islanders sensed that the military felt Hawaii was a foreign land and that the citizens of the Territory were somehow inferior. The military believed servicemen were often discriminated against and that the economic benefits the military brought were ignored.

An irritating and continuing cause for friction was prostitution. The large concentration of men in Hawaii made prostitution a flourishing business. In the early twentieth century immigrant laborers as well as the military were predominantly single males. In 1930, for example, males outnumbered females 222,640 to 145,696.

Periodically the Territorial government took some action, like raiding the stockade at Iwilei, but for the most part they tried to ignore the problem. Most military commanders preferred to allow prostitution in designated areas. They believed that if they knew where the prostitutes were, they could regularly have them examined by doctors and venereal diseases could be curtailed. Often the Territory was more than happy to let the military worry about the problem, hoping that prostitution would not become too blatant and so become an issue for noisy reformers.

In May, 1927, Charles Lindbergh stirred the imagination of the world by flying across the Atlantic Ocean in a single-engine airplane. The Pacific remained unconquered. In Honolulu Riley H. Allen, editor of *The Honolulu Star Bulletin,* and Joseph Farrington, managing editor of the same newspaper, decided they would try to do something about it. They believed that if a prize were offered to the winner of a California to Hawaii flight, it would undoubtedly speed the day when that crossing would be made.

An attempt had been made earlier to fly to Hawaii even before the

Lindbergh Atlantic crossing. Three navy seaplanes were scheduled to leave San Francisco Bay on August 31, 1925. The seaplanes were to follow a line of naval vessels which were stationed about 200 miles apart pointing the way to Hawaii. During the day the ships blew black smoke from their funnels, and at night they turned on searchlights. Of the three seaplanes one was unable to get off the water, another landed at sea 300 miles westward, and only Commander John Rodgers and his crew were airborne. Approximately 200 miles northeast of Maui the navy fliers ran out of gas and glided down to a water landing. Ships rushed to the area, but they found no trace of Rodgers and his crew.

After several days most people gave up hope. Then, nine days later, the plane was sighted off the island of Kauai by a submarine and was towed into Nawiliwili Harbor. The fliers had rigged a sail on their seaplane from fabric cut from the wings, and they were only several hours' sailing time from Kauai when they were found. In Honolulu the navy men were welcomed by some 5,000 people at Iolani Palace, but they failed to qualify as the first to fly from the mainland to Hawaii. The challenge of flying to the Islands remained.

In 1927 the Lindbergh flight kindled new interest in flying. The two newspapermen, Allen and Farrington, believed that James P. Dole, president of Hawaiian Pineapple Company, was the man who could best promote a flight to Hawaii. Dole had turned the growing and canning of pineapple into a very successful business. His name was familiar to anyone who walked through the aisles of food markets in the United States. In 1927 Dole had undertaken his first national advertising campaign, and it seemed natural that he could benefit from the publicity which would come from sponsoring a mainland to Hawaii flight.

Two days after Lindbergh had flown the Atlantic, Allen and Farrington sent a radiogram to James Dole, who was then traveling toward the East Coast aboard the Overland Express. In part the radiogram read, "IN VIEW LINDBERGHS ATLANTIC FLIGHT PACIFIC REMAINS ONE GREAT AREA FOR CONQUEST AVIATION STOP SITUATION THIS MOMENT RIPE SOMEONE OFFER SUITABLE PRIZE. . . . THIS WILL PUT YOUR NAME EVERY NEWSPAPER IN WORLD." The radiogram suggested Dole might offer $25,000 to the winner of an air race to Hawaii.

Dole certainly recognized the value of world-wide publicity, but he was also an imaginative man, and the idea of linking Hawaii to the mainland by air struck him as a beneficial thing for the Territory. With enthusiasm Dole sent a radiogram to Honolulu. Not only would he sponsor an air race to Hawaii, but in addition to the $25,000 first place prize he would add a $10,000 second place prize. On July 25 he sent a long radiogram to the *Advertiser*. In part it said, "CONSIDER THE HELP GIVEN TO HAWAIIS

PROGRESS BY THE CABLE THE RADIO THE AUTOMOBILE AND TRUCK. . . . WHAT WOULD WE DO WITHOUT THEM TODAY. . . ." Then referring to his sponsorship of the coming flight he said, "SOMEONE HAS TO DO IT THE FIRST TIME AND I HOPE THE REWARDS WILL HASTEN ITS ACCOMPLISH-MENT."

The story of Dole's offer did not appear in *The Honolulu Star Bulletin* until all the directors of Hawaiian Pineapple Company had agreed that it was a good idea. One director suggested that a condition of the race be that the winning airplane be required to drop a letter on the island of Lanai, which was a Hawaiian Pineapple plantation, but the idea was rejected because of adding one more risk to the flight.

When the news of Dole's offer became known, it caused a sensation in the United States and Europe. James Dole hoped that Charles Lindbergh would be the first man to enter the race. He sent a radiogram to the flier aboard the *USS Memphis,* which was then carrying the young hero home from Europe. Dole closed his invitation by saying, "I WANT YOU TO KNOW THAT MY OFFER TO AIRMEN WAS INSPIRED BY YOUR MAGNIFICENT FLIGHT TO FRANCE."

Charles Lindbergh did not enter the race to Hawaii, but letters from a wide assortment of other people poured into James Dole's Honolulu office. There were many requests for financing—from both men and women pilots who wanted to compete but had no money to buy airplanes. One letter came from two young Swiss men who not only needed an airplane but asked Dole to pay for their flying lessons first. A woman pilot offered to secretly make out a $10,000 life insurance policy to Dole if he would buy an airplane for her. There was a letter from a man who reported he had perfected a steam engine which could power an airplane. All he needed was financing.

Newspapers across the country labeled the race the Dole Derby, and as publicity mounted the number of letters Dole received increased. The writers of the letters asked questions, and some hard decisions had to be made. The most pressing decision concerned the basic rules for the flight. It was decided that this should be placed in the hands of the National Aeronautic Association. The Hawaii chapter and the Oakland, California, chapter, where the flight would start, agreed to set the rules.

Very soon James Dole became worried about the safety standards for the flight. Perhaps the mail he received alerted him. It was evident that many of those who wrote were neither personally qualified as pilots nor had airplanes capable of flying to Hawaii. It was obvious that if the only requirement for entering the race was the $100 fee, the Dole Derby could be a disaster.

The rules for the race were finalized with the emphasis on safety.

Every plane had to carry both a pilot and navigator, and each had to pass tests administered by the NAA. Each plane had to carry fifteen percent more gas than was necessary to reach Hawaii. These simple rules eliminated many incompetents, but Dole continued to worry. Were the rules strict enough? No one knew, because there had never been anything like the Dole Derby before.

The take-off date for the Dole race was set at August 12, but soon there were rumors that an attempt to fly to Hawaii would be made sooner, not in hope of winning the prize money, but for the honor of being first. On June 28, 1927, the attempt was made. Army lieutenants Lester Maitland and Albert Hegenberger took off from Oakland in an army three-engine Fokker named *Bird of Paradise*. They made the flight to Oahu in twenty-five hours, forty-nine minutes. The *Bird of Paradise* carried the best equipment then known. In spite of this, Maitland and Hegenberger not only missed Oahu but nearly overshot the northern tip of Kauai. In mid-July the first civilian crossing to Hawaii happened when Ernie Smith and Emory Bronte crash-landed on the island of Molokai. They cut forty-seven minutes off the time set by the army pilots.

The success of the two lieutenants and of Smith and Bronte only heightened interest in the Dole Derby. Stories about the race continued to appear on the front pages of every sizable newspaper in the country. As the starting day drew closer, however, it became apparent that the machines and the men who would fly them simply would not be ready by August 12. On August 11 a radiogram reached Honolulu advising that "NO ENTRANTS QUALIFIED YET." James Dole was opposed to postponing the race, but there was little he could do. All the pilots agreed they would be ready by August 16.

The San Francisco manager for Hawaiian Pineapple Company, Henry MacConaughey, kept James Dole informed of what was happening. At first MacConaughey shared the enthusiasm of nearly everyone else, but when the first flush of excitement faded, he too worried about the safety standards which had been set for pilots and planes. MacConaughey worked closely with the two military officers who were testing the pilots and navigators. On August 10 his worries flooded forth in a letter to James Dole. "I can say to you from the bottom of my heart that I will be glad when this flight is over. . . . I do not hesitate to say to you that if I had had any realization of what was coming when you made the offer, I certainly would have voted 'no.' " MacConaughey was, however, pleased by the continuing publicity. He noted that the August 12 issue of *The Examiner* mentioned the Dole name fifty-two times and *The Chronicle,* for the same day, carried the Dole name twenty-four times.

On the day of departure, August 16, Henry MacConaughey stood at the starting line at the Oakland airport, watch in hand, to help time the departure of the airplanes. The airfield was supposed to be grass-covered, but it had been dragged to make it smoother, and as a result departing planes blew up clouds of dust, making it difficult for MacConaughey and others to see what was happening. Estimates of the number of spectators at Oakland airport varied between 50,000 and 100,000.

At 12:01 P.M. the *Oklahoma* left the runway and headed westward, but by the time it reached the Golden Gate it developed mechanical problems and returned. Next came the *El Encanto,* which rose about four feet into the air and then crashed down on the runway, demolishing its left wing. In third place was the *Pabco Pacific Flyer,* which also crashed to the ground after rising several feet in the air. Fortunately, there were no injuries.

The fourth plane off was the *Golden Eagle,* which was backed by George Hearst, publisher of the *San Francisco Examiner.* It made a safe departure and was followed by the *Miss Doran.* The *Miss Doran* was the only plane to carry three persons, the extra passenger being Mildred Doran, a twenty-two-year-old Michigan teacher who wanted to be the first woman to fly the Pacific. Shortly the *Miss Doran* returned because of a mechanical problem. It was corrected and the plane took off again. Then the *Woolaroc* safely departed, followed by the *Aloha,* piloted by Martin Jensen of Honolulu.

The next airplane scheduled to take off was the *Airking,* but it was disqualified at the last minute because it could not carry enough fuel to reach Oahu. Then the *Dallas Spirit* took off, only to return shortly with torn wing fabric. The *Pabco Pacific Flyer* had been hastily repaired, and a second take-off was attempted. It crashed again, demolishing part of a wing. It was out of the race.

Eight planes were poised to participate in the race on the morning of August 16, but in the afternoon only four were in the air. Of those four only the *Woolaroc* had a two-way radio, the same one used by Smith and Bronte on their earlier flight to Hawaii. The *Golden Eagle* had a receiving set, but the *Aloha* and *Miss Doran* had no communications and so could receive no radio beams. They had to navigate by compass and sextant only.

Probably the best equipped team in the Dole Derby was the crew of the *Woolaroc.* The pilot was Arthur Goebel, a rangy, confident man who thrived on the danger which the new machines of the early twentieth century provided. After a stint in the army during World War I, Goebel tried his hand at motorcycle and automobile racing. Aviation was the next challenge and he became a Hollywood stunt flyer.

Arthur Goebel was thinking of attempting the flight to Hawaii after he read about Lindbergh's trip to Paris and before he saw a poster announcing the Dole prizes. Goebel immediately decided to enter the race, and he found the backers to help him buy a suitable four-seat monoplane. The engine had 220 horsepower and was similar in appearance to the one flown by Charles Lindbergh. Goebel needed a navigator, and through a friend he was put in touch with a young naval officer and Annapolis graduate by the name of William Davis.

Davis was a pilot as well as an experienced navigator and radio man. He agreed to go as the navigator. If they won, pilot and navigator would each receive $10,000 and the remaining $5,000 would go to their backers. Davis knew his radio equipment perfectly, and he carried such spare parts as he might need to make repairs.

From the beginning they faced many unknowns. The first question was: could they get off the ground? The plane was so heavily loaded with gasoline that getting into the air was a real question. Goebel and Davis decided that if they were not off the ground by the time they reached a spot well down the runway, Goebel would cut the engine. A man was stationed at the designated spot to signal them if the wheels were still touching as they passed.

Goebel and Davis did get airborne, and they wasted no time in heading for their destination. Some of the other pilots flew out into the Pacific through the Golden Gate to wave at the crowd gathered there, but Goebel and Davis considered this a waste of time. They flew over the hills of San Francisco and as straight for Hawaii as they could.

Two of the four seats in the *Woolaroc* had been removed to make room for extra gas tanks, and the two men could communicate only by means of a pulley system. They wrote notes, put them in a tin can tied to the pulley, and pulled them back and forth. Davis attended to his radio, talking with several ships enroute and staying on the radio beam between San Francisco and Maui. Davis carried four compasses and a bubble sextant for sun and star observations. Goebel flew at altitudes of up to 6,000 feet to avoid the heavy clouds. It was very cold and very lonely. Chicken sandwiches and coffee satisfied their hunger and thirst.

The experience and carefulness of Goebel and Davis won the prize for them. The first land they sighted was Maui—they were dead center on navigation—and as they turned toward Oahu, Davis celebrated by tossing smoke bombs from the plane and shooting a Very pistol off into the sky. They passed Diamond Head, were picked up by an escort of army and navy planes, and touched down at Wheeler Field, next to Schofield Barracks. Some 20,000 people waited there to welcome them. The flight lasted twenty-six hours and seventeen minutes.

The first person to reach Arthur Goebel as he climbed down from his airplane was Mrs. Martin Jensen, wife of the pilot of the *Aloha*. Mrs. Jensen was frantic about the safety of her husband. Goebel could only report that he had seen no airplanes during his long trip. Governor Wallace R. Farrington and James Dole reached the pair, and then they were encircled by a crowd of military. One hour and fifty-eight minutes after Goebel and Davis arrived the *Aloha* circled Wheeler Field and landed. Jensen's wife was weak with relief.

The Goebel and Davis flight had been uneventful, but Jensen and his navigator, Paul Schluter, had had more than their share of close calls. The *Aloha* carried no radio and so the San Francisco-Maui radio beam was of no help. They flew in clouds for much of the way, and only when they were able to climb above them could the navigator shoot the sun. For a good portion of the way Jensen flew 100 feet or less above the water. On one occasion he dipped too low and the wheels of the *Aloha* hit a wave. Water shot up and tore open the fabric which covered the plane's wing. When Jensen landed at Wheeler Field, gauges showed the plane had just five gallons of gas left.

By the time Jensen arrived there was serious concern about the fate of the *Golden Eagle* and the *Miss Doran*. Both airplanes had taken off ahead of Jensen, and it was reluctantly assumed they had gone down. James Dole immediately offered a $10,000 reward to anyone locating any of the missing persons. Governor Farrington asked the people of Hawaii to unite in prayer for the safety of the missing fliers.

Forty-two ships and airplanes joined in the search. The *Dallas Spirit,* which had dropped out of the Dole Derby because of torn wing fabric, volunteered to search. It crashed into the sea, as did an army airplane also on the search team. The last heard from the *Dallas Spirit* was a terse statement transmitted over the plane radio. The pilot said they were in a tail spin. They were never found.

The total number of lives lost because of the Dole Derby added up to an even dozen. Two planes preparing to enter the race crashed before reaching Oakland, killing three persons. Two planes were lost in the actual race, killing five, and two airplanes were lost during the ensuing search, killing four more.

James Dole was shaken by the loss of life in the race he had sponsored. Some persons associated with Hawaiian Pineapple Company feared the vast amount of publicity the Dole name had been receiving would now affect them adversely. Their fears were unfounded. Very few blamed James Dole or his company for the deaths of the fliers.

The general feeling in the 1920s was that airplanes were flying coffins and anyone who ventured aloft was in danger of sudden death. There was ample evidence. John Rodgers, who had eventually reached Hawaii, was killed a year after his Pacific flight. When Hegenberger and Maitland sailed from Honolulu Harbor to return to the mainland after their successful flight, three army airplanes flew out to give them a farewell. As the two men watched, one of the planes crashed into the sea, killing its pilot. On a single day Arthur Goebel served twice as a pall bearer for flier-friends who died in separate accidents.

What was the result of the Dole Derby? Most important was the realization that expert equipment and well trained men were essential to air safety. The Dole flight showed how little men knew about the dangers of long flights. The participants in the Dole Derby passed certain tests, eliminating many in the process, but the tests of men and equipment were not severe enough. It took more than courage to fly long distances successfully.

The Dole Derby was a symbol of the 1920s. It represented a general optimism, and specifically a great faith in the new mechanical marvels of the age. The most impressive of these mechanical marvels were the airplane and the automobile. These were bringing new speed, new freedom, a sense of adventure and daring to the nation.

Who was responsible for developing these wonderful machines? Unquestionably they were the products of the great American business complex. That complex was not only building exciting new machines, but it was providing employment for millions of men and women. The more goods it produced the better, because it meant more jobs, more sales, more profits—cycles of endless, self-perpetuating growth. The public could even share in the earnings of companies by buying stock. And additional profits would come as the stock rose in value. Some prophesied this system was destined to at last wipe the age-old scourges of poverty and unemployment from the earth. Few questioned the workings of this magical business system. Why should they? It was producing goods in a volume and variety the world had never before known.

This optimism about business and the wonderful age of the airplane and automobile was as popular in Hawaii as elsewhere. After all, business expertise and the development of the right machinery had made both the sugar and pineapple industries possible. This confidence in business and the machine was reflected in the banner headline of the *Advertiser* on the morning of October 23, 1929. It read: "HAWAII ZEPPELIN LINE FORMED." Among the very substantial backers were W. A. Harriman & Co., and Lehman Bros., Bankers. Two zeppelins were proposed as a starter, each capable of carrying 100 people. The trip from California to Hawaii would take an estimated thirty-six hours.

The zeppelin line, like many another scheme originated in late 1929, never materialized. On the same day the headline appeared in the *Adver-*

tiser the stock market went into a tailspin and business activity everywhere was threatened.

On October 25 the stock market crash made front page headlines in Hawaii. The story beneath the headline reported that nearly 13,000,000 shares had been traded on the previous day, by far the largest volume in the history of the New York Stock Exchange. A subhead read: "Scores of Traders are Ruined," and a description of the panic on the floor of the Exchange was given. On October 29 the activity of the previous day was again reported in detail. Over 9,200,000 shares had been traded. U.S. Steel dropped 17½ points and Standard Gas & Electric dropped 40½ points. Radio Corporation stood at 40½. Ten days earlier it had sold for 87.

The newspaper stories in Hawaii were little different from those appearing across the nation. Each day it was expected that the stock market would firm up and that prices would again continue their upward march. On October 30 the *Advertiser* reported that a new record had been established the previous day. Over 16,400,000 shares of stock had been traded. On that day U.S. Steel dropped 12 points and Standard Gas & Electric fell 25¼.

On October 31 a newspaper noted editorially, "There are right here in Honolulu many men who are today wiped out financially because they thought to play a long-distance game of speculation." The editorial went on to estimate that some $250,000 of Island money had been lost by persons who had been wiped out of the market. The editorial concluded, "Nothing of real value has been affected, but . . . [some] have been badly singed." The press maintained its confidence. Things were improving, they reported, and they took great heart from a New York release which stated that bankers were uniting to shore up the failing stock market. In Hawaii, as elsewhere, it would take years for the public to understand that some long established, basic economic beliefs were being shattered.

Undoubtedly the New York stock market crash affected a certain selected few in Hawaii—mostly the affluent ones—and some had to sell Island stocks to cover the margin calls from their mainland brokers. Initially Island stocks were affected very little. The economic convulsions which the mainland was going through were watched with awe by Island businessmen, but few felt the actual pain of financial loss during the beginning years. Historically, economic changes on the mainland touched Hawaii on a delayed basis and with diminished violence.

Because the softening of business activity in Hawaii was rather gradual, it was more difficult to understand what was happening. Most business leaders believed that, somehow, things had gone a bit off course and that some slight adjustment would quickly set everything right again. In late October, 1931, *The Honolulu Star Bulletin* quoted Roger Babson, a favorite prophet of the time. "The present trouble with business is under-consumption, not over-production," Babson said. How could this condition be cured? Advertising was the way. Advertising would make people want goods and services and they would start spending money again. Then the whole economic life of the world would take heart and soar upward.

Business did not soar. In fact, it declined despite repeated stories in the newspapers which told of increased sales by bakers, automobile dealers, and furniture store operators. Finally in late 1931 some practical businessmen admitted that conditions were bad. There was unemployment. There was a depression. It had to be recognized and it had to be dealt with. In December, 1931, a Territorial report showed there were 4,015 people out of work in Honolulu and that another 1,321 had only part-time work. The figures were probably very low, because many people were too embarrassed to admit unemployment. At Christmas the Salvation Army gave food baskets to 400 needy families in Honolulu.

By April of 1932 it was estimated that about 10 percent of the employable people in Honolulu were out of work. Again the figure was undoubtedly low and no attempt was made to discover what unemployment was outside the city of Honolulu. Many of the unemployed were destitute. One direct step to reduce unemployment was taken in 1932 and 1933. During those years over 10,000 Filipino laborers, who had come to the Islands as field workers, were sent back to the Philippine Islands. The newspapers offered advice to the public. Home owners were asked to hire an unemployed person to make home repairs. The unemployed were urged to plant vegetable gardens, and some of them climbed the slopes behind Honolulu, where they planted gardens and built huts from wooden crates.

Sugar was the economic backbone of Hawaii, and the plantations suffered along with everyone else. Profits fell so drastically that some plantations operated in the red during the depression years. In spite of the low price sugar was bringing, crops were substantial and few workers were laid off, although in some instances workers were put on short hours and short pay. Some sugar plantations even hired some of the unemployed pineapple workers. The continuing construction work at Pearl Harbor and other military installations loomed larger than ever in the Island economy.

Hardest hit in Hawaii was the pineapple business. Canned pineapple was a luxury item, and when pocketbooks were squeezed across the country, luxury items were left on the grocer's shelf. At Hawaiian Pineapple Company the warehouses became crowded with cases of canned pineapple. It was unwise to can even more. The number of field workers was cut back as pineapple acreage was reduced and the big seasonal canning crews went unhired. To help move the inventory some long-time employees walked house to house selling canned pineapple.

James Dole's Hawaiian Pineapple Company, the giant in its field, was particularly hard hit. Losing money was a new experience for Hawaiian Pineapple. From its earliest days the company had been a profitable one. In 1922 the island of Lanai had been bought as a pineapple plantation for the enormous sum of $1,100,000 in cash. The next year the company reported net profits of $2,760,000. Three million cases of pineapple were grown and packed in 1926. In 1929 the old cannery was replaced with a new one which cost $1,500,000. In 1930 the company packed a record 4,577,091 cases. It was this pineapple pack which crowded Hawaiian Pineapple Company warehouses when the depression hit hardest. In late October, 1931, the directors of Hawaiian Pineapple Company voted to omit their quarterly dividend. It was the first time they had failed to pay dividends in twenty-four years. In 1931 the company suffered a net loss of $3,875,000.

Hawaiian Pineapple had to borrow $5,000,000 to stay in operation, and in 1932 the company was reorganized. James Dole was ousted as president, although he was named chairman of the board, a title with no authority. The company produced under 1,000,000 cases of pineapple in 1932, although conditions quickly improved. In 1934 the company was in the black with a net profit of nearly $1,000,000.

Both the Territorial legislature and the counties appropriated money for the unemployed. The money went to pay wages to men and women who worked on public projects. Workers were allotted from two to five days of work a week, according to the number of dependents they had. Local funds were augmented by funds from the federal government. In January, 1934, Washington awarded Hawaii $421,000 for a Civilian Conservation Corps, and in the same month the Territory was granted $15,-000,000 in Public Works Administration funds. Helpful as all the federal and local projects were, Hawaii continued to have a frustrating unemployment problem until the shadow of World War II increased defense spending in the Islands.

The economic low point for the Islands came in 1932, and by late 1933 conditions began slowly to turn. The fluctuation of Island stocks was a good indicator of how things were going. In 1929 American Factors, Ltd., sold for a low of $40.75 a share. In 1932 the low fell to $19.50, but by 1936 the low for the year had risen to $40. C. Brewer was another example. The low for the year 1929 was $305 per share. In 1932 the low was $150, but by 1936 it was back to $300 per share.

The year 1932 must stand as one of the grim years in the history of Hawaii. As the Islands were suffering the worst pains of the depression, the famous Massie case set nerves on edge in Honolulu and brought damning publicity across the country.

Thalia Massie was the central figure. She was a slight, shy girl, the daughter of a well known East Coast family. At the age of sixteen Thalia married Thomas Massie, an Annapolis graduate. Three years later Lieutenant Massie was aboard a submarine stationed at Pearl Harbor. On the evening of September 12, 1931, the Massies and two other couples went to the Ala Wai Inn, a club on the edge of Waikiki, and a popular weekend gathering place for navy couples. At about 11:30 P.M. Thalia became bored with the triviality of the evening and went for a walk.

What happened after she left the Ala Wai Inn became the subject of the most sensational court case in Hawaii's history. According to Thalia's story she was walking along a road some two blocks from the Ala Wai Inn when a car pulled up beside her. Two men jumped out, hit her, and dragged her into the automobile. They drove to a deserted area, perhaps a mile away, where she was repeatedly raped. When her abductors left, Thalia managed to find a road and flag down a passing motorist who drove her home.

At the Ala Wai Inn Lieutenant Massie was not concerned about Thalia. He presumed she had joined other friends at the Inn, and when he unsuccessfully looked for her he assumed she had gone home with neighbors who lived nearby in Manoa Valley. Massie drove to the neighbor's house, but Thalia was not there, so he called his own home. Thalia answered. The conversation was brief. She asked her husband to come home. "Something awful has happened," she said.

Tom Massie rushed home. After his wife sobbed out her story, he called the police. When the police arrived they found a woman with a bruised, swollen face. Subsequently it was discovered she had suffered a double fracture of the jaw. It was dark, Thalia said, and she was not sure if she could identify her attackers, although she did say they were native Hawaiians. At Queens Hospital Mrs. Massie was examined by Dr. David Liu. He noted that Thalia had suffered no vaginal injuries, but his report did not clearly state whether or not she had been raped. Later on Sunday Thalia was admitted to Queens Hospital, where she remained for a week.

The suspected assailants of Thalia Massie came into police custody in a strange way. At about 12:35 A.M. on the night of the attack on Thalia Mr. and Mrs. Homer Peeples were driving through Honolulu. Their automobile was nearly hit at an intersection by a touring car which ran a stop sign. Angry words were exchanged, and both cars pulled over to the curb. Agnes Peeples got out of the car and was struck on the side of the head by a husky Hawaiian who had jumped from the touring car. Mrs. Peeples got back in her car, and her husband drove the short distance to the police station. Agnes Peeples had the presence of mind to write down the license number of the touring car, and at approximately 12:50 A.M. a call went out on the police radio to pick up the car. The occupants were wanted for assault.

At about 1:50 A.M. the police radio broadcast the few known facts about the assault on Thalia Massie. There apparently was confusion between the two incidents, which were both called assault cases. It was assumed by some, at least, that the men in the touring car were wanted for the attack on Mrs. Massie. Once the touring car occupants were found, the police apparently made no further serious search for suspects.

The Ford touring car was owned by the sister of Horace Ida. Ida had just returned from the mainland. He borrowed his sister's car for the evening, and as he drove about town he picked up an assortment of old friends. They included Henry Chang, Hawaiian-Chinese, Joseph Kahahawai, Hawaiian, Benny Ahakuelo, Hawaiian, and David Takai, Japanese. Joseph was a boxer, and Benny, in addition to being a boxer, was a football player. All were in their early twenties and all were unemployed, a fact which could hardly be held against them in the depression days of 1932. The five, however, hardly qualified as ideal citizens. Three had prison records, and on the night of September 12 they had been drinking as they wandered about town.

The license number supplied by Agnes Peeples led the police to the Ida home. Horace Ida, it was quickly learned, had been driving the car. He was routed from bed and taken to police headquarters. At first he denied he had been out that evening, but in the end he admitted he and his friends had an altercation with the Peeples. He denied any connection or knowledge in the Thalia Massie episode.

A quick check of the various stops made by Ida and his friends showed they had stopped by a public dance, sponsored by the Eagles, which was held along the same road where Thalia claimed to have been abducted. The police went off to pick up Ida's companions. It was an easy job since none of them were in hiding or resisted arrest. The police assumed they had the men who had not only been in a near collision with the Peeples, but who had attacked Thalia Massie.

The five suspects were interrogated individually, and they each gave very nearly the same account of their activities of the previous night. The assistant district attorney was the leader in the interrogations. As he pieced the story together, he must have realized it was something less than a solid case. His hopes must have been dampened when the suspects were shown to Thalia and she could identify only Henry Chang with certainty as one of her attackers.

While the police and the assistant district attorney were gathering their evidence, Thalia Massie was suffering mentally and physically. To wire her fractured jaw together properly and to allow her to take nourishment through a tube, a molar had to be extracted. It was all very painful and she cried for hours at a time. Through most of this her husband was with her. Finally Thomas Massie took his wife home, at her insistence and against the advice of her doctor. Tom acted as night nurse for her, and he said she continued to cry much of the time. On October 13 Thalia entered Kapiolani Maternity Hospital to abort a possible pregnancy, since her menstrual period was overdue. The results of the operation indicated she was not pregnant.

Lieutenant Massie was enraged by the gossip which circulated through Honolulu. One persistent rumor suggested that Thalia was having an affair with a naval officer friend of her husband and that he had hit her during an argument. To cover her activities she had manufactured a wild story of rape. Some naval officials suggested the Massies leave the Islands for their own peace of mind, but Thomas Massie was not about to do that. The time of vindication and justice would come with the trial of the five suspects.

The trial began on November 16, 1931. The prosecution rested primarily on the shoulders of the assistant attorney general while the defense was carried by three capable lawyers. The defense produced witnesses who saw the accused at the various places at which they had stopped on that Saturday night. One man saw the accused about midnight in the parking lot next to the public dance. A friend saw them driving toward town after the dance, and two people testified they stopped by their house, where a luau had been held earlier, at about 12:14 A.M. At approximately 12:35 A.M. it had been established that the suspects had a run-in with the Peeples. Thalia stated she had left the Ala Wai Inn at 11:35 P.M. at the earliest and possibly much later. The defense claimed that even if she had been abducted as early as 11:40 P.M., it would have been impossible for her to have been driven to a deserted area, raped by five men, and for those same men to have casually appeared at the public dance by midnight.

After the lawyers made their final appeals, Judge Alva E. Steadman instructed the jury that "the prosecution must prove to your satisfaction and beyond a reasonable doubt that the defendants were present at the time of the alleged commission of the offense." After ninety-six hours of deliberation the jury reported that they could not reach a verdict, and they were dismissed.

Thomas and Thalia Massie were terribly upset and frustrated. They certainly had not been vindicated—in fact Thalia's account of the happenings of that Saturday night had been rejected by a jury. Equally upset was Thalia's mother, Mrs. Granville Fortescue, who was on her way to visit her daughter when she received news of the assault. Mrs. Fortescue was a determined, capable woman, and the verdict of the jury simply was not acceptable to her.

Rear Admiral Yates Stirling, the ranking naval officer in Hawaii, was also becoming very angry. From the beginning he had shown a deep interest in the case. The prosecution, he believed, had been pitifully weak. It was an obvious miscarriage of justice, and Stirling was not willing to allow it to end that way. The admiral recommended that the five men be held in jail, since their appearance on the streets of Honolulu might result in violence, but there was neither the willingness nor the legal means to hold them.

An uneasiness ran through military ranks, both officer and enlisted. Many servicemen worried about the safety of their wives and daughters while they were away on duty. Hundreds of women armed themselves with pistols, carrying them in their purses during the day and laying them beside their beds at night.

All of this alarmed Hawaii's businessmen. They realized the economic importance of the military, and they understood the tremendous power Admiral Stirling possessed. To show their concern a group of businessmen pushed for a retrial. Resentment was not limited to the military in Hawaii. It was fast becoming apparent that the Massie case had aroused people across the nation.

In mid-December there was trouble. A group of sailors kidnapped Horace Ida, led him into a cane field, and lashed him with leather belts in an attempt to force a confession from him. When no confession was forthcoming, they left him unconscious by the side of the road. He was picked up by a motorist and driven to the police station in Honolulu. When Admiral Stirling heard the news, he sent marines into Honolulu who ordered all sailors to return immediately to base. His action might have avoided violence. By that time police cars were equipped with submachine guns and military and civilian tempers were nearly out of control. Admiral Stirling suggested the time had come for decent elements in Hawaii to do something about the lawless elements.

Again the businessmen gathered together to discuss how matters could be worked out. The Honolulu Chamber of Commerce put up $5,000 to hire a lawyer and detectives to further investigate the Massie case. A Law Enforcement Committee formed by the Chamber asked Governor Lawrence M. Judd to call a special session of the Legislature to bring about police reforms.

The new year, 1932, brought more bad news for Hawaii. On New Year's Eve two men climbed the fence of Oahu Prison and escaped. One was a murderer and the other a burglar. Escape from the prison was not a particularly difficult thing, since the institution was run in a very casual way, but with all the current excitement about law enforcement the timing if not the escape was most embarrassing.

Just how embarrassing the escape could be was realized on January 2. On that day Lui Kaikapu, the escapee who was a convicted burglar, broke into a home, tied up a Caucasian woman with her husband's neckties, then beat and raped her. Kaikapu made little attempt to hide. In fact, he wandered about downtown Honolulu while the police were searching for' him, and he was soon captured. The second escapee did try to hide, and it took a month before he was returned to prison.

The government acted with nervous haste in the case of Kaikapu. Five days after he committed his crime he was sentenced to life imprisonment. But much more than this was needed to calm those who now believed they had positive evidence that law enforcement was criminally inadequate and that the local population included a large number of sex maniacs. Governor Judd took action. He ordered an investigation of the police department, called on Major Gordon Ross to recruit men from the National Guard for police duty, and fired the head of Oahu Prison.

The mounting frenzy in Honolulu probably made Thomas Massie and Grace Fortescue more determined than ever that someone was going to pay for the attack on Thalia. When Mrs. Fortescue inquired about a new trial, she was told that new evidence was needed. The most telling kind of evidence, of course, would be a confession from one of the five. Thomas Massie and Grace Fortescue decided that was exactly what they would get. Their job was made a little easier by a rumor which suggested that Joseph Kahahawai was about to confess.

Mrs. Fortescue laid out a plan. Joseph Kahahawai and his four companions had to report each morning to the probation office in the judicial building. Mrs. Fortescue, Lieutenant Massie, and two seamen he had recruited from the submarine service would wait in front of the courthouse in a rented car. The service men, of course, would wear civilian clothes. When Kahahawai emerged from the building, he would be presented with a counterfeit summons. When he had been persuaded to get into the car, they would drive him to the Fortescue home. There he would be induced to confess.

The abduction worked to near perfection. The fake summons was presented to Kahahawai as he left the judicial building by one of the sailors, and the Hawaiian readily got into the rented Buick which was driven by Massie. The only flaw was that a cousin walked from the judicial building with Kahahawai, and when Joseph disappeared into the Buick and was quickly driven away, the cousin became suspicious. The police were alerted.

The Hawaiian was questioned in the living room of the Fortescue home while one of the sailors pointed a pistol at him. It was soon apparent that the rumor about Kahahawai being ready to confess had no basis in fact. Sometime during the emotional strain of the interrogation the trigger of the gun was pulled. A .32 caliber slug slammed into Kahahawai's chest, and he died stretched across a chaise longue. His body was pulled into the bathroom where as much blood as possible was washed off in the bathtub. Then the body was wrapped in a sheet and put on the back floor of the Buick. The intention, apparently, was to dispose of it somewhere along the southeast coast of Oahu, because Massie was racing the Buick in that direction when he attracted the attention of a policeman. A chase followed and finally the Buick was forced to the side of the road. In it were Massie, Grace Fortescue, and one of the sailors. Sticking out from under the sheet was the leg of the dead man. Police took the three into custody, then rushed to the Fortescue home, where they collected a good deal of evidence, including the fake summons.

A grand jury was convened in the courtroom of Judge Albert M. Cristy to view the evidence and hear arguments for an indictment against Massie, Mrs. Fortescue, and the two sailors. After deliberation the jury returned to the courtroom, and the foreman announced the evidence was not sufficient to connect the four with the kidnapping or murder of Kahahawai. Judge Cristy was stunned. He would not accept the decision. He lectured the jury on their duty, then told them to reconsider and come back with a better decision. Finally Cristy succeeded in getting the jury to bring an indictment for second degree murder.

The outcry against Cristy was immediate and great. In Washington D.C. Senator Kenneth McKellar thought Cristy should be impeached by act of Congress. In Honolulu Admiral Stirling was disgusted. If Judge Cristy did insist on his murder charge, the admiral could insist that the four defendants should not remain in the hands of the police while they awaited trial. The admiral succeeded in having the accused quartered at Pearl Harbor, promising to return them at any time the Territory requested them. Thalia gladly joined her husband within the safety of the naval base.

The indictment by the grand jury brought a tremendous wave of sympathy from the mainland. Offers of help poured in from across the country. Flowers came by the carload. Newspapers headlined the injustices the Massies had been subjected to and applauded their courage in taking the law into their own hands. Hearst newspapers across the country printed front page editorials in bold type and called it "The Honor slaying."

John Russell of the *Los Angeles Herald and Express* came to Hawaii to write a series on what was happening. He believed it was not the pure

Hawaiians who were the villains. It was rather the persons of mixed blood. "It should be made clear to the American public that the filthy hoodlums and woman attackers of Honolulu are not Hawaiians. There is not a full-bred Hawaiian among them. The problem rests in one of the strangest and most fantastic potpourris of alien blood that was ever mixed into a hell's broth and forced on an innocent race."

Instead of a retrial for the four remaining men it was now a trial of the former prosecutors. One thing was sure. Thomas Massie and Grace Fortescue were not going into court with the same caliber of legal help which had served as the prosecution in the rape trial. With the help of friends they contacted the famous Clarence Darrow and asked him to come to Hawaii and handle their defense. Darrow, who was seventy-four years old and retired, accepted the offer, perhaps as a means of recouping some of the losses he had suffered during the depression. With him came George Leisure, a New York lawyer. Clarence Darrow's fee was purportedly $30,000.

Reporters converged on Honolulu representing newspapers across the United States and from as far away as the *Times* of London. Courtroom seating for the public was limited to seventy-five, and on Sunday, April 3, the day before the trial opened, people began to line up at the door of the judicial building, hoping to be fortunate enough to get a seat. As the trial opened in Honolulu, the United States Congress as well as the press debated what restrictive actions must be taken to insure order and justice in Hawaii.

It took a week to select a jury and in the end the racial composition did not please Darrow. Before leaving the mainland for Hawaii the famous lawyer had announced that it would be unfortunate if the trial became a racial one. But as he studied the jury he felt his only hope was to try the case for the press. Darrow constantly referred to the rape of Thalia Massie. When Thomas Massie testified, Darrow inferred that Massie had shot Kahahawai in a moment of blank insanity after the Hawaiian admitted he had attacked Thalia.

Clarence Darrow's summation took four hours and twenty minutes. His talk was broadcast direct to radio stations across the United States. Before the jury left the courtroom to make its decision, the judge told them no one has the right to take the law into his own hands. The jury had little choice, since the four defendants admitted they had kidnapped and murdered Kahahawai. The verdict was guilty, with a recommendation for leniency.

News of the verdict brought a wave of indignation from the mainland. A large group of Congressmen sent a joint radiogram to Governor Judd urging him to pardon the four. Military personnel boycotted the firms which employed the jurors. Many persons expected Hawaii to be placed under martial law.

Governor Judd had to make a fast, hard decision. If he did nothing on behalf of the convicted four, Congress would certainly pass strong measures limiting Hawaii's self-government. On the other hand, if he granted pardons it would be equal to reversing the verdict of the court and the whole trial would appear a sham. More bills were introduced in Congress, editorials continued to appear across the country. Judd was well aware of his predicament. Then the ultimate pressure was applied. A telephone call came from President Herbert Hoover. If Judd did not find a way to keep the four out of prison, Congress would authorize Hoover to pardon them.

With the help of Clarence Darrow, Judd came up with a solution. On May 4 Grace Fortescue, Thomas Massie, and the two enlisted men appeared at the judiciary building for sentencing. Each was given ten years at hard labor. Immediately afterward the four crossed the street to Judd's office in Iolani Palace. With the four within the governor's office, Judd went into the hallway to meet the press. He told them the sentences of the four had been commuted from ten years to one hour. The one-hour sentence would be served in Judd's office.

Part of the agreement was that the four leave Hawaii as soon as possible and that there would be no retrial of the four surviving men accused of raping Thalia. On May 8, 1932, the Massies and Grace Fortescue sailed from Honolulu.

The events which began with the attack on Thalia came very close to bringing down the wrath of Congress on Hawaii. Congressmen were disturbed by the handling of the rape trial. They were incensed by the hung jury which allowed the five suspects to go free. When Joseph Kahahawai was murdered and an indictment of second degree murder was brought against Grace Fortescue, Massie, and the two sailors, Congress was further outraged.

It was after the murder of Kahahawai that Senator Hiram Bingham of Connecticut, Chairman of the Committee on Territories and Insular Affairs, and a descendent of Rev. Hiram Bingham of Honolulu, made an ominous statement. He said: "I hope it will not be necessary for Congress to enact legislation restricting the present powers of the islanders. But we will certainly have to do so if they fail to remedy the situation promptly." Floyd Gibbons of the Hearst newspapers called for the President to appoint only inactive or retired military as the governors and secretaries of Hawaii. If Judd had not commuted the sentences of the four, Hawaii very likely would have lost some portion of its home-rule powers.

Many Islanders resented the action of Governor Judd. His decision to commute the sentences was a reversal of the decision of the court. One who spoke out was Princess Abigail Kawananakoa. She asked the question, "Are we to infer from the Governor's act that there are two sets of laws in Hawaii—one for the favored few and one for the people generally?"

Lawrence Judd was not satisfied with the investigation of the Thalia Massie attack case. He wanted a thorough, impartial study, and he hired the Pinkerton Agency to make it. Clues were long cold by the time the Pinkerton men arrived on the scene, but they did delve deeply into the case. They summed up their findings in a covering letter which accompanied the full report. The Pinkerton investigators believed that the evidence ". . . makes it impossible to escape the conviction that the kidnapping and assault was not caused by those accused. . . ."

The Pinkerton report expressed strong disapproval of the Honolulu Police department, and many in Honolulu agreed. The police could not answer some very embarrassing questions. Why were the clothes worn by Thalia on that Saturday evening not immediately recovered to test for signs of semen? Why did the examining doctor fail to take a sample discharge from the vagina of Thalia to determine the presence of semen? Why did the police take the touring car, which Ida had driven earlier, to the place where the alleged attack took place and drive around the dirt area looking for tire tracks? As they crisscrossed, familiar tire marks quickly multiplied. Perhaps most important of all, why was the search for new suspects not pushed when no confessions came from the five accused and when the evidence against them grew thinner and thinner?

What had happened to the police department? The police department in Honolulu, like that in many another isolated community, was a tight-knit, closed club. The force was made up largely of Hawaiians or part-Hawaiians. They were affable and tolerant, but such meager training as they received was picked up on the job.

In the deeply interrelated community of Honolulu a large portion of the cases which came under police scrutiny could be handled on a personal basis. It was likely that someone on the force would be a relative, school mate, or friend of the accused. Through this intricate network of racial, cultural, and blood relationships the police usually could quietly control the problems which faced them.

Then along came the Massie case. It suddenly presented them with a whole new set of standards, and old rules were terribly inadequate. There was no way to quietly smooth over the Massie case. Critics were loud and powerful and the police were expected to be impersonal, professional. It was something the police could hardly understand, much less practice. The system which served them well in the past suddenly appeared to be amateurish and ridiculous.

In early 1932 Seth W. Richardson, assistant attorney general of the United States, was ordered to Hawaii to investigate the administration and enforcement of criminal law. His searching into the corners of a variety of affairs annoyed many Islanders, but they had little to fear. Richardson's final report was kind. Hawaii, he indicated, was a law-abiding community. But Richardson pulled no punches about the law enforcement and judicial systems: "We found a condition of inefficiency in the administration of justice which, in effect, constituted an invitation to the commission of crime, and which had largely destroyed the morale of the law enforcement agencies. . . ."

Reforms did come. The offices of police chief and public prosecutor became appointive rather than elective, and this was a decided improvement. It was not easy to undo the vast amount of bad publicity Hawaii had received. For years the Islands were considered by many as a place noted for sex crimes and lackadaisical law enforcement.

What happened to the surviving four who had been acquitted of attacking Thalia Massie? With time they faded into obscurity in Hawaii. Through the years they all stoutly maintained they had played no part in the Massie attack. And the four defendants in the murder trial? Mrs. Fortescue returned to the East Coast and rejoined her social circle. Two years after the murder of Joseph Kahahawai, Thomas and Thalia Massie were divorced. Thomas resigned from the Navy and settled into a business career on the West Coast. He remarried. Thalia twice attempted suicide. She remarried also but again was divorced. In July, 1963 Thalia died of an overdose of barbiturates. The two sailors who helped Thomas Massie were quietly transferred to the mainland. Both continued their careers in the submarine service.

The game of polo came to Hawaii early and immediately became popular. The first match was played in 1880 near Honolulu between an Island team and officers off *H.M.S. Gannet.* The sport quickly was taken up on the neighbor islands, and in 1902 an Inter-Island Polo Association was formed.

To play polo well the best horses are a necessity. To breed and train these sensitive animals is very expensive. By 1920 it was clear who had the money and interest to pursue the game seriously. On Oahu the leader was a wealthy businessman, Walter Dillingham, whose company had won the contract to dredge the entrance to Pearl Harbor. On Maui, Frank Baldwin, descendant of the missionary-doctor Dwight Baldwin, was the moving spirit. The Dillinghams and the Baldwins owned some of the finest polo ponies in the world.

The Dillinghams and the Baldwins did not have to look far to find good men to ride their horses. Dillingham rode with his sons, Gay, Lowell, and Ben. On Maui, Frank Baldwin brought up his sons, Edward, Lawrence, and Asa to ride with him. A cousin of theirs, Richard, also added strength to the team. When the Dillingham and Baldwin sons went off to complete their schooling on the East Coast, they often led their collegiate polo teams. By any standards they were good players.

Each year the inter-island tournament was held on the fields at Kapiolani Park in Honolulu. In addition to Maui and Oahu, the U. S. Army usually fielded a team, with Hawaii and Kauai also entering on occasion. In 1935 an awesome contender from the mainland entered the tournament. It was Midwick Country Club from Southern California, led by Eric Pedley, one of the finest international players. Another respected Midwick player was Hal Roach, the Hollywood producer. The Midwick team obviously meant business. They arrived with thirty polo ponies. Midwick was the heavy favorite and large silver trays were selected as winning trophies, because it was felt that Hawaiian prestige would suffer if Midwick won and returned to California with the usual small cups awarded inter-island champions.

Both Walter Dillingham and Frank Baldwin retired from active competition in 1935, and the teams of their respective islands relied mainly on their sons. Midwick was anchored by Eric Pedley. The fourth team in the 1935, tournament was army's, led by Lieutenant Colonel George S. Patton, Jr. Patton believed a good army officer should seek danger, and he played polo with a reckless abandon. Patton and his teammates might have had a special kind of courage, but they could not overcome the disadvantage of riding ponies inferior to their competitors'.

The teams were well matched. Maui beat army eight to five. Then they beat Oahu seven to six and thus became the only possible challenger to the powerful Midwick team. Riding with the Maui team of Edward, Richard, and Lawrence Baldwin was Harold ("Oskie") Rice. Oskie was hardly outside the Baldwin family. His mother was a Baldwin and the Rice family had social credentials of their own. They were wealthy Maui ranchers and Oskie's great-grandfather was the missionary who had founded the Protestant church in Hana, Maui. Edward Baldwin was captain of the Maui team and is considered to be the finest polo player Hawaii has ever produced.

George Patton called them the "Maui cowboys." Patton was not being complimentary, but he came close to being accurate. The Maui players spent much of the day in the saddle, making the rounds on the great ranches they owned on the slopes of Haleakala. They rode their horses with authority and grace.

On a Sunday afternoon in August, 1935, the largest crowd in the polo history of the Islands gathered at Kapiolani field to watch the vaunted Midwick team claim their silver trays. Once the game was under way it was clear that the Maui team had not shown up just out of courtesy. They could not gain the lead, but they never fell far behind. At halftime the score was tied three to three.

Maui never led, but they managed to keep the score tied. As the match drew near the end of regulation time, a newspaper account stated that the crowd was "on its feet and in a frenzy of excitement." At the end of regulation time the score stood five to five, and in keeping with polo rules the match continued until one of the teams scored. It was Lawrence Baldwin who put in the winning goal. That winning goal was the only time Maui led during the entire match.

The crowd ran onto the field, surrounded the Maui team, and pulled them from their horses. Oskie Rice remembers fans grabbing at his shirt, mallet, and helmet as souvenirs. The next day a nostalgic reporter wrote: "There probably never will be another polo match in the islands with a finish like that one."

Frequently, well known individual players came to the Islands and often went to Maui. Usually the visit brought about a polo match. In 1934 Will Rogers played on Maui and the following year Winston Guest came. In 1936 George Patton and the army team arrived for a July 4 match. Army lost. Patton did not win on the polo field, but he did turn out to be a crowd pleaser at the party which followed the game. That evening, at the Baldwin's beautiful Ulupalakua Ranch, George Patton filled a glass with scotch, bourbon, and gin—then stood on his head with his feet braced against the sides of a doorway and proved he could defy gravity by emptying the glass.

Polo continued in Hawaii in all its splendor until 1941. The symbolic end of the game came on December 7 of that year. Because the wide expanse of the polo field at Pukalani, on the lower slopes of Haleakala, appeared to be an ideal place for Japanese planes to land, logs were hauled across the field. Before the war was over the stables and club house had burned down. Polo continued after a fashion in Hawaii, but the days of grandeur, which required great wealth and leisure, were gone.

The 1920s and the 1930s were a time of paradise on earth for a select few in Hawaii. Seldom has any group of people lived so securely, with such great freedom, or developed such an appealing life style.

The select few were the haole elite. They were largely the descendants of missionaries and successful businessmen, and by the early 1900s they were profiting enormously from the vision or labor of their pioneer parents and grandparents. The economic and political world of Hawaii was their pond. Richard Cooke, a son of Charles Montague Cooke, was an example of the breed. Cooke had long been a leader in the business world of Honolulu, and when he spoke Island leaders listened carefully. They had good reason to, for Richard Cooke was a powerful man. When he died in 1940 he was president of eight corporations and a director of seventeen.

These ruling families sent their sons to Ivy League schools. Sometimes when the boys returned to Hawaii, they married the daughters of other prominent families, which further consolidated money and position. If sons lacked ambition or intelligence, a safe, respectable position was usually available for them in Island companies.

Ties with the mainland states were ideal for maintaining the system. Radio and cable allowed instantaneous business or personal communications, but it took time and money to travel to the Islands. For most Islanders a mainland trip was an important event planned far in advance. For the same reasons the tourists who visited Hawaii tended to be wealthy people.

Some people's religious background prescribed church on Sunday morning and quiet contemplation in the afternoon. But the stern ways were fading fast. Most enjoyed weekends filled with parties, polo matches, and excursions to beach or mountain houses. There were occasions for swimming, hiking, fishing, hunting, and trips to the neighbor islands where the leaders of Honolulu were welcomed into the spacious homes and privileged lives of relatives or plantation managers.

Only a few of the elite could be described as decadent. Most were rather democratic and benevolent as long as their interests were not threatened. Some, indeed, were generous and kind, and if there were instances of arrogance and despotism there were also instances of inconspicuous help, such as paying for the education of a bright but poor child and providing care for the elderly or sick.

The middle management of Island business was mostly haole, with a sprinkling of Orientals and Portuguese. They too could afford such amenities of life as servants and spacious homes in the cool valleys behind Honolulu. Daily demands were not great and life was pleasant as long as a person was not overly ambitious or sought to upset the status quo. The man or woman who preached ideas which ran counter to the established ones found Hawaii small and hostile.

The independent merchants in Hawaii included many Chinese and a growing number of Japanese. Business could be profitable, but again it was wise to avoid anything which the big companies would consider competitive. If a small merchant dared to challenge the long established business houses, he quickly learned in how many ways he was vulnerable.

It is a truism that no one ever considers a current situation as ideal, and the economic rulers of Hawaii were no exception. The problems of their time were difficult. There were serious plantation strikes in the 1920s, there was the Massie affair, the depression, battling with the federal government for increased sugar quotas. But past problems had been successfully overcome, and there was no reason to doubt that future problems could be solved as well. The existing system had brought profit, material comforts, and a healthier life for a large number of people. No basic changes were needed in the system.

Change, of course, is imperceptible in the beginning. In the twenties and thirties it was happening among the Japanese, most of whom were still on the plantations. There were over 139,000 of them living in Hawaii in 1930, comprising by far the largest racial bloc in the Islands. Over 75 percent of these Japanese had been born in Hawaii. Only a few had visited the homeland of their parents. They attended public schools where American history and government were taught. They found it convenient to adopt Western first names even if their parents had not bestowed them officially. Even the Japanese they spoke had taken on Hawaiianisms and sounded strange to relatives from Japan.

These young people were pulled between two cultures. Most parents did not want their children to be anything except Japanese in thought and action. They sent them to Japanese language schools after public school, and homes were maintained as much like homes in Japan as possible. If the young people were pulled toward the Japanese way by emotion and a tradition of parental obedience, they were pulled toward the American way because the prevailing system of values in Hawaii was American. The American ideals taught in school allowed the young Japanese to hope they could escape the hard life of the plantations, allowed them to hope for more education, for a more rewarding and prosperous life.

The Americanization of the Japanese in Hawaii had begun and that meant change. Normally that change would have been generations in coming, but it was enormously speeded up by the advent of a war. In 1940 that war was clearly forming on the horizon.

Chapter Sixteen

"WE KNOW BUT ONE LOYALTY . . ."

D URING THE FIRST DAYS OF DECEMBER, 1941, war news dominated Honolulu newspapers. Singapore was placed on a wartime footing. In Washington talks between United States and Japanese representatives appeared fruitless. The Japanese were massing a great army along the borders of Thailand. The question was not peace or war, but rather how quickly would war come.

The news from Hawaii was also dominated by military activities. Honolulu newspapers filled pages with lists of army and navy promotions, details on maneuvers, and grim warnings about the future. Sandwiched between the military events were stories about happier events. The *Lurline* had left at noon on December 5 for San Francisco carrying a record number of passengers together with a load of Christmas mail. Punahou's football team left Honolulu for Maui the same day to play Baldwin High School. The *Advertiser* warned football fans to get to Honolulu stadium early on December 6 for the annual Shrine charity game pitting the University of Hawaii against Willamette.

On December 6 downtown Honolulu was decorated for Christmas with strings of lights spanning the streets. In the evening there were parties following the University of Hawaii's victory. The following Saturday Hawaii was scheduled to meet San Jose State, a team which had already arrived in the Territory. People flocked to the Princess Theater to see Charlie Chaplin in *The Great Dictator*.

Several hundred miles to the northwest Japanese warships were tuned in to Honolulu radio station KGMB on December 6. The Japanese hoped they might pick up some warning signal from the station if their presence so close to the Islands had been discovered. There was no indication that they had been discovered. KGMB continued its regular broadcasting. Aboard the Japanese carrier *Akagi* tension and emotion mounted when a very special flag was hauled up. It was the same flag Admiral Heihachiro Togo had flown when he won his great victory over the Russians in 1905. In the early morning hours of December 7 a code message came to the Japanese fleet. The message contained three words: "East wind, rain." It meant proceed with the attack against Oahu.

At 3:42 in the early morning blackness of December 7 the United States minesweeper *Condor* sighted a periscope just off the entrance to Pearl Harbor. It was an area where United States subs were required to be on the surface, and the *Condor* flashed a message to the destroyer *Ward*. The *Ward* searched for an hour but could not find any trace of a submarine. At 6:40 another naval vessel reported a submarine near Pearl Harbor and the *Ward* again went in search. This time the sub was sighted and the *Ward* opened fire with deck guns and dropped depth charges. The captain of the *Ward* reported the sub was sunk.

At approximately 6 A.M. the first waves of airplanes leaped from the Japanese carriers some 230 miles northwest of Honolulu. Near Kahuku Point on Oahu two army men manned a mobile radar station. They were supposed to be picked up by an army truck at seven o'clock, but the truck was late so they continued to work the equipment. A blip came on the screen. Suddenly it appeared to be an enormous flight of airplanes. The two soldiers thought something had gone wrong with the equipment, but after checking they decided it was in perfect working order. They estimated the airplanes to be 137 miles north of Oahu. At 7:20 they telephoned headquarters. The lieutenant on duty decided it must be the flight of Army B-17s which was due in from the mainland that day or perhaps a flight of planes off a United States aircraft carrier.

At approximately 7:57 the first waves of Japanese planes dived on Oahu military bases. The next two hours would be the most disastrous in United States history. During that time 2,325 United States servicemen were killed, 188 airplanes were destroyed, and eighteen naval vessels were severely damaged or sunk. In addition fifty-seven civilians were killed. The Japanese lost twenty-nine airplanes, one large submarine, and five midget submarines.

The realization that a war was on came quickly enough for the men on the military bases. Bombs and bullets drove them to their battle stations, and they fought back quickly and well. For most civilians the comprehension came more slowly. Even those in sight of Pearl Harbor with its funnel of black smoke rising upward and the flights of airplanes overhead thought it was just another maneuver, certainly the most realistic to date, but still a sham battle. For some civilians the realization that they were in the middle of a massive attack came when antiaircraft shells exploded in their neighborhoods. At the time they believed them to be bombs dropped by the enemy.

At 8:04 radio station KGMB interrupted a concert program to order all military personnel to their bases. The order was periodically repeated. At 8:40 came the first announcement of the attack. KGMB was flooded with telephone calls. An exasperated announcer shouted into the microphone: "This is the real McCoy!" Orders became more frequent and urgent. Doctors and nurses were instructed to report to hospitals or emergency stations. Firemen and policemen were called to duty. Defense workers were ordered to the bases. A total blackout was ordered that night. An announcer instructed, "Turn out your lights and do not turn them on for any purpose whatsoever." Governor Poindexter declared a state of emergency over station KGU.

At 11:41 A.M., by order of the army, commercial radio stations went off the air. The reason—enemy planes could follow radio beams to Honolulu. Islanders were now cut off from news reports and it was easy to imagine the worst. Periodically the stations broke silence to make a terse announcement. At 8:52 P.M. on December 7 the last order came over the radio. All workers in retail firms which did business with the army engineers were ordered to report to their offices immediately.

At sea the *Lurline* received the news of the attack and went on a zigzag course. At night she was blacked out. On Maui the commanding military officer on the island canceled the Punahou-Baldwin football game scheduled for that afternoon. Because the Philippine Islands had been invaded by the Japanese, he feared any gathering which would bring large numbers of Filipinos and Japanese together might end in violence.

At ten minutes past noon on December 7, Major General Walter C. Short called on Governor Joseph Poindexter and asked him to declare a state of martial law. Poindexter was reluctant. He did, however, agree with Short that the situation was desperate, and he was genuinely worried about the loyalty of the local Japanese. Governor Poindexter wanted to talk to President Franklin Roosevelt before reaching a decision. By 12:40 P.M. Poindexter had talked with President Roosevelt, who believed martial law was a good safety measure. At 4:25 in the afternoon Honolulu's radio stations broke silence to announce that the Hawaiian Islands were under martial law. It was the first time martial law had been declared on American soil during a war.

Courts were closed on December 8 and cases were heard by a military judiciary. Martial law, however, meant much more than the closing of the civilian courts. The military could do anything it wished. Among its various actions was a tight press censorship. Not only were stories about the war in the Pacific censored, but so was all news about happenings in Hawaii. After December 8 Honolulu newspapers made very dull reading.

The military was quick to seize power in Hawaii but most reluctant to release it, even when all reasonable need for martial law terminated and the writ of habeas corpus was restored. Blackout and curfew regulations stayed in effect until July, 1945.

During those early days the Islands were awash with foolish rumors. Japanese paratroopers had been dropped in the mountains of Oahu. Island Japanese-Americans were blocking the road to Pearl Harbor. And there were some near-tragic mistakes. Army planes, out looking for the enemy, sighted the United States cruisers *Minneapolis* and *Portland* to the south of Oahu. The pilots thought they could only be the enemy and dropped their bombs. The *Portland* narrowly missed being hit.

A tragic mistake did happen on the evening of December 7. At 7:15 P.M. the antiaircraft gunners at Pearl Harbor opened up on a flight of planes which was coming in low. The planes were American, not Japanese, and their coming had been known. Some nervous gun crew, however, opened fire and four of six navy planes from the carrier *Enterprise,* trying to land on Ford Island, were shot down. To the people of Honolulu, who sat in darkness imagining the worst, the boom of guns and the thin line of searchlights meant Pearl Harbor was again being bombed.

On the night of December 7 few people in Honolulu slept. They kept their radios turned on, although no sounds were forthcoming. Nervous sentries patrolling utility installations and other vital communications centers fired shots at shadows in the darkness. People on the neighbor islands knew even less than those on Oahu. Their communications systems were few. Only Hilo had a daily newspaper and only Hilo and Lihue, Kauai, had radio stations. In an effort to stop possible sabotage volunteer guards were posted at check points along roads and lookouts watched for airplanes and surface vessels.

Long before the smoke cleared over Oahu, military leaders were considering the gigantic clearing and building job which had to be started immediately. Defense workers were pressed into service, and the sugar and pineapple plantations responded to a government plea by sending men and equipment to military bases. The brunt of the burden, however, had to be borne by the Army Corps of Engineers. The job of clearing wreckage, building airfields, barracks, shore fortifications, warehouse facilities, and a thousand other necessities was staggering.

To accomplish these tasks the engineers needed a headquarters large enough to hold the number of people necessary to run their operation. Somehow they were pointed in the direction of Punahou school, the highly regarded private grammar and high school which had been started just one hundred years earlier by Protestant missionaries. At 2 A.M., in the darkness of December 8, the truck convoy of the engineers pulled up to the gates of the spacious campus. They demanded the gates be opened, and once inside they demanded the keys to all the buildings. When the keys did not come quickly enough, doors were smashed open.

At 5 A.M. the lady in charge of the school's dining hall was ordered to prepare breakfast for 750 men. Boarding students, both boys and girls, were ordered to vacate the dormitories. Barbed wire was strung over the stone wall surrounding the campus, and members of the Willamette and San Jose football teams, who had been recruited for guard duty, patrolled the boundaries. At first all Japanese employees of Punahou were ordered off the campus, but this so depleted the caretaking staff that the order was rescinded.

All the schools in the Territory, both public and private, were closed on December 8. Teachers were put to work registering the civilian population and issuing ration cards. When schools were allowed to reopen, Punahou classes met in garages, on lanais, and in other assorted rooms which were offered them in Honolulu. Teachers moved from home to home to teach, thereby easing the transportation problem. Later, when the enrollment of the University of Hawaii dropped drastically, part of the university campus was rented to Punahou school.

The days following December 7 were filled with dozens of unfounded rumors of sabotage by Japanese-Americans. A potential threat, according to the military, was any small boat in the waters around the Islands. Such boats could carry saboteurs to the shores of Hawaii, and an order was issued on December 7 declaring that all unidentified boats approaching the Islands would be attacked. Hawaii's commercial fishermen were the persons who suffered. A number of them were at sea on December 7. They did not know a war had begun, because they did not listen to their radios or because Honolulu radio stations had been silenced. Most captains were unaware of danger. As the vessels made for home ports, many were strafed by military airplanes. At least six fishermen were killed and more were wounded.

The enemy was not in sight, but there was ample evidence of his lurking presence. Through the month of December lifeboats carrying survivors from torpedoed ships found their way to Island beaches. On the night of December 30, 1941, the ports of Hilo, Kahului, and Nawiliwili were briefly shelled by Japanese submarines. Little damage was done, but the psychological impact was substantial. Near the end of January, 1942, an army transport was torpedoed in the channel between Maui and Hawaii. The people of Hawaii were apprehensive. By April, 1942, a token number of troops were sent to the neighbor islands. Before then the neighbor islands depended on such volunteers as they could raise backed by a handful of regular military.

During that month of April a happening of enormous importance was unfolding at Pearl Harbor. Navy Commander Joseph J. Rochefort and his dedicated staff had deciphered the Japanese code, and they were piecing together bits of information from intercepted Japanese radio messages. The Japanese were planning a major offensive, but where and when was not clear.

Where would the thrust be aimed? After days of analysis Rochefort concluded the target of the attack would be the island of Midway, the small atoll northwest of Oahu. Some did not agree. They believed Oahu would be attacked. Other military men believed the West Coast of the United States would be bombed or invaded. Admiral Chester Nimitz accepted Midway as the target, and he began to plan how the Japanese could be defeated.

On May 25 Pearl Harbor naval intelligence intercepted a radio code message which listed all the units the Japanese would employ and the dates for the attacks on Midway. Admiral Nimitz went into action. He recalled warships from the South Pacific, where the battle of the Coral Sea had just been fought. B-17's were flown in from the mainland and were dispatched to Midway. Supplies and men were sent to the atoll until there was no room to accommodate airplanes or store more munitions.

The carriers *Enterprise* and *Hornet* arrived at Pearl Harbor on May 26. They were provisioned and sent to sea again. On May 27 the *Yorktown* arrived. She had taken a direct hit in the battle of the Coral Sea when a bomb had smashed downward through four decks before exploding. Internal damage was enormous. The Japanese believed the *Yorktown* sunk. The crew was weary. They had been at sea for over three months and were looking forward to shore leave. It was estimated it would take three months to repair the damage.

At Pearl Harbor the *Yorktown* went directly into drydock. Workers swarmed onto the ship. Admiral Nimitz came aboard. He was not interested in estimates of how long it would take to repair the ship. He gave an order. The *Yorktown* must be ready for sea in three days. Sailors got no shore leave. Instead they worked around the clock storing provisions. The fliers aboard had suffered heavy losses in the South Pacific, and new air units had to be readied. Welders and others worked forty-eight hours at a stretch in dim, smoky compartments below decks where temperatures ran to 120 degrees. Men collapsed at their posts.

In the late morning on May 29 the drydock was flooded and the *Yorktown* was slowly pulled into the harbor. Many workmen were still aboard, hard at their labors. At 9 A.M. the next morning the engines turned over and the carrier moved slowly toward the channel of Pearl Harbor. The last workmen went over the side as the ship headed through the narrow passage which led to the open sea. That afternoon the newly organized air groups for the *Yorktown* rendezvoused with her at sea.

Although there was strict censorship on all news media, the people of Honolulu did not miss the alarming signs of activity which appeared about them. The large number of airplanes coming in from the mainland, the frenzied activity at Pearl Harbor, army pilots remaining on duty in the cockpits of their airplanes—all of these facts quickly spread through the tense community. Such patients as could be released from hospitals were sent home, presumably to make room for the expected wounded.

On the afternoon of June 3 the army urged women and children to leave the downtown section of Honolulu. Leaves for servicemen were canceled and those men off base were ordered back. Volunteer units of all kinds were sent to their posts. Pearl Harbor was sealed off. Within the base men stood by their guns and fire-fighting units rested next to their equipment. There was a persistent rumor that a great invasion fleet was headed for Hawaii.

On June 4 the navy announced that Midway was under attack. The next day the *Star Bulletin* ran a banner headline: "MIDWAY FIGHT GOES ON!" On June 6 the news of the victory at Midway was announced. Four Japanese carriers had been sunk by navy aviators. The United States had lost the gallant *Yorktown*. For the first time in nearly seven months the citizens of Hawaii slept free of the fear of invasion. Later the battle of Midway would be called the turning point in the war with Japan.

The workers that swarmed over the *Yorktown* in Pearl Harbor and who helped repair the damage after December 7, as well as build a myriad of new facilities, had largely been recruited on the mainland. They started to come in large numbers in early 1941. They were mostly Caucasians, many first learning of work possibilities in the Islands from posters on the bulletin boards of post offices and other government offices across the country. The reasons they came were varied. Some thought they would earn big money, others were inspired by patriotism, some were enticed by the romance of the South Seas, and many came to escape problems which plagued them on the mainland.

The defense workers did a job which had to be accomplished, but generally they were not happy in doing it, and Islanders were not happy with them. There were many malcontents. Most were unmarried males who added to the age-old problem of prostitution. Many suffered a degree of cultural shock when they came to Hawaii. Never had they imagined that such a mixture of races could live and work on a relatively equal basis. Decent housing was hard to find. The barracks which were built for them offered little privacy. There was constant complaining about living conditions and the quality of food served in the mess halls.

When the war started, additional hardships and disillusionment descended on the defense workers. Work hours were longer than ever, and curfew regulations kept them indoors at night. It became difficult to accomplish such necessary tasks as banking or getting laundry washed. Most workers did not consider Hawaii their home—rather they considered their time in the Islands in much the same way as the military did. They were on a tour of duty. Workers came to refer to Oahu as "the rock." Most Islanders considered them as necessary but unwelcome intruders.

For Hawaii's people of Japanese ancestry the attack of December 7 brought difficult problems. Most Japanese-Americans were deeply shamed by the attack. Some of them stayed away from their places of employment, particularly if their bosses were Caucasian. Many were fearful of reprisal. Some believed that martial law was a means whereby they would be punished for the deeds of the enemy. Many expected Filipinos in the Territory to attack them. All the possibilities were grim.

On December 7 Hawaii's Japanese did their duty along with everyone else. They reported to their military units, volunteered as doctors and nurses, and performed all the duties everyone else did. A portion of the non-Japanese community, however, was very distrustful of Hawaii's Japanese. They viewed them as fifth columnists, ready to sabotage Hawaii's war efforts.

The military had long been worried about the large number of Japanese-Americans living in Hawaii. Before hostilities began the military, the local police, and the Federal Bureau of Investigation carefully scrutinized Hawaii's Japanese. On the day the war started those Japanese who were considered dangerous in any way were arrested. Buddhist and Shinto priests, Japanese language school teachers, and commercial fishermen came first. There were also some 200 consular agents in the Territory—unpaid representatives who did an occasional, usually trivial job for the consul in Honolulu. These men were taken into custody also.

With Hawaii under martial law, the army and navy could do as they wished. Japanese language radio programs were ordered off the air, and Japanese newspapers were forbidden to publish. Japanese language schools, Buddhist temples, and Shinto shrines were closed. Japanese could not possess weapons, cameras, shortwave radios, binoculars, or anything which could be used as a signaling device. Not more than ten persons could legally gather together.

If the military and some civilians in Hawaii were nervous about Island Japanese, leaders in Washington were even more anxious. President Franklin Roosevelt was in favor of shipping many of the Japanese to the mainland. Secretary of the Navy Frank Knox believed that some 100,000 of Hawaii's 160,000 Japanese should be interned on the mainland, or if that were not possible, then they should be confined in camps on a neighbor island, perhaps Molokai.

Lieutenant General Delos Emmons, who replaced Lieutenant General Walter C. Short ten days after Pearl Harbor, thought the wholesale moving of the Japanese impractical and probably unnecessary. There had been no cases of sabotage in Hawaii, contrary to rumors, and besides the Japanese were needed as war workers. The shipping necessary for the moving of 100,000 persons to the mainland was unavailable. All Japanese workers who were moved would have to be replaced. And if the Japanese were moved to a neighbor island, it would mean building housing for them, feeding and clothing them, and at the same time losing the benefit of their efforts as war workers. Most of the people around President Roosevelt continued to believe Hawaii's Japanese should be moved and interned just as the West Coast Japanese had been interned. The two reasons why this did not happen were the facts that shipping was not available and workers were not at hand to fill the vacancies.

General Emmons, who was also the military governor of the Territory, assured the Japanese-Americans that they had nothing to fear as long as they remained loyal. The statement was hard for some to believe. Nisei, or second-generation Japanese, who were members of the Hawaiian National Guard were disarmed and relieved of duty. Japanese-Americans who were members of the University of Hawaii ROTC were likewise relieved of duty. Japanese defense workers were not allowed in certain areas which were considered sensitive. The identification badges issued them were different from others. Outside their photograph, which was in the center of the badge, was the word "Restricted." There was resentment over this discrimination, but the opening months of World War II obviously was not a time for Hawaii's Japanese to complain.

Arrests of Japanese continued into the early months of 1942. Those arrested were mainly men who occupied positions of leadership in the Japanese communities. The usual pattern was to arrest a man at his home and detain him under guard until he could be questioned. Questioning panels consisted of several prominent non-Japanese members of the community and several military officers. Occasionally a person would be released after being questioned, but it was a rarity.

George Hoshida was one of those arrested in Hilo on February 6, 1942. George was active in Buddhist churches on the island of Hawaii and in teaching judo. Apparently his interest in judo is what made Hoshida a suspicious person. He and seven other men, all active in a judo organization, were arrested the same day. Ironically, the man ordered to arrest the eight was George's brother-in-law, a detective on the Hilo police force. They were detained at Kilauea Military Camp, near Kilauea volcano, which had been a military rest camp since World War I.

Yotaro Hoshida, George's father, had come to the island of Hawaii in

1907 to work on a sugar plantation. Like so many others, Yotaro came in the expectation of acquiring a small fortune and returning to Japan. When he realized this was not possible, he borrowed all the money he could and brought his wife and two sons to Hawaii. He could not borrow enough money to bring another son and a daughter, who never were able to join the family in Hawaii, because immigration from Japan was closed by the time the family could afford their passage. George was four years old when he arrived in the Islands.

Yotaro Hoshida eventually was able to buy some land of his own on which he grew sugar cane which he sold to a neighboring mill. It was a hard life and George had to leave school after the ninth grade to work in the fields. He injured his back while carrying bales of sugar cane and went to Hilo in search of a less strenuous occupation. Eventually George became an appliance salesman for Hilo Electric Company. He married Tamae Takemoto, whose family lived on a nearby plantation. Over the years they saved enough money to make a down payment on a small home. Three daughters were born to them. There was no affluence, but they were making financial progress.

After his arrest George Hoshida was allowed to correspond with Tamae, and it was during this time that George learned his wife was pregnant. About a month after being taken into custody George was told it was time for him to appear before a panel in Hilo. Tamae somehow found out her husband was coming, although such information was supposed to be secret. Tamae and her family gathered on the lawn outside the federal building, hoping to get a glimpse of George.

The Hoshida family, together with the families of other men who had been arrested, searched the windows of the federal building, hoping to catch even a fleeting glance of a loved one. George was one of those escorted to the third floor. They were warned to stay away from the windows, but George slipped aside for a moment and looked down on the lawn. There was Tamae. She saw him, waved, and pointed to her slightly bulging stomach. George felt "both happy and sad."

The interview with the panel did not go well. Some of the men on the panel insisted that judo promoted loyalty to Japan. Hoshida could not agree and he said so. He was marked for internment and removal to the mainland. Later he believed he "may have gotten out clear" if he had patiently listened to the lecture a panel member gave him instead of disagreeing.

In the early part of May, George was shipped to Honolulu. During this interval he was not allowed to see Tamae or his children. In Honolulu his group was detained at the old immigration station on Sand Island on the western edge of Honolulu Harbor. Japanese from other islands joined them there, and two weeks later they were put aboard a ship which zig-zagged across the Pacific to San Francisco. Several days after arriving they were sent by train to San Antonio, Texas, where they were herded into a camp which included German and Italian nationals, as well as Japanese from Alaska. The Alaska Japanese were clothed in army fatigues with big PW's on the back of their shirts. The Hawaiians soon learned that the Alaskans did not understand the Japanese language.

Ten days later the Japanese were moved to a camp near Lordsberg, New Mexico. They were assigned to barracks, each of which held some thirty men. It was very dry and whirlwinds of dust blew through the camp. The barracks were surrounded by double fences of barbed wire. Guard towers were spaced along the fences where soldiers watched with loaded rifles.

Life at Lordsberg was tense. As the internees went about their chores, they were guarded by soldiers. George Hoshida talked to some of the soldiers and discovered that they believed they were guarding dangerous men guilty of subversive activities. George explained this was not true, that they had not acted against the government, and that many believed they owed much to the United States. After this tensions were lessened and the inmates at Lordsberg were treated less like criminals.

Some of the guards remained nervous and ready to shoot. When a mainland group of Japanese arrived at the nearby railroad station, two of the newcomers were too ill to walk the mile to camp. As they waited at the station for a car to pick them up, a guard shot and killed both of them. The guard later explained he thought they must have been trying to escape. Within the compound a man from Hawaii could no longer stand the confinement and tension. In desperation he tried to climb the fence and was shot and killed. When a new camp commander was assigned to Lordsberg, conditions improved.

George Hoshida had taken correspondence courses in commercial art, and he did pen and ink drawings of some of his fellow internees. The demand for portraits was great, many persons sending them to their families. It became more than George could handle. He started an art class in which some thirty persons enrolled. Soon other classes were offered, a dramatics club was formed and baseball became the favorite sport.

Repatriation to Japan was offered to the persons at Lordsberg just as it was offered to internees at other camps. Those who wished could go to Japan in exchange for Americans who had been caught in Japan when the war started. It was a dilemma for many. Most had some ties in Japan, even though remote. Only in rare instances did they feel any loyalty to Japan. Yet the country of their adoption had not trusted them. They had been put behind barbed wire and found loaded guns pointed at them. They had been treated as prisoners of war. Some wondered what they could lose by repatriation to Japan.

George Hoshida toyed with the idea of repatriation to a country he had not seen since he was four years old. He wrote his thoughts to Tamae. After he had written his letter, he had a dream. He saw his wife, standing with a telephone in her hand but unwilling to speak to him. She looked at him with great displeasure. Tamae's feelings were just as George had dreamed they were. As soon as she received his letter, she sent a radiogram to George. It said: "Do not expatriate. Stay where you are." George no longer considered going to Japan.

When George was interned Tamae came on difficult times. She had three young girls to care for, and she was pregnant with a fourth child. Although she had help from her relatives, she was terribly worried about what was happening to their family. She was unable to work and had to accept welfare. The small checks she received were not enough to cover the most basic expenses. To compound the burden their eldest daughter was a total cripple. As an infant she had been badly injured in an automobile accident. She was blind, partially paralyzed, unable to walk or to talk. She required constant attention.

The pressure was so great that Tamae suffered a nervous breakdown. Friends came to her rescue, but most important was the fact that Tamae herself was not willing to give up. She made the hard decisions which were necessary. On the advice of a social worker she sent the crippled daughter to a home in Honolulu for retarded children.

On October 20, 1942, another daughter was born to Tamae and several days later she was informed that she would have to evacuate to the mainland. She tried every means she knew to be allowed to stay a little longer so she and her child could better stand the trip, but there was no recourse. Shortly before Christmas she was told she would have to leave in three days. In that period of time she sold their home and nearly all their possessions. Nothing went for its true value. When Tamae left she had accumulated only about $1,000.

The voyage to the mainland on an overcrowded ship and the trip by train to a camp in Jerome, Arkansas, was a nightmare. It was a matter of standing in line for every necessity, from meals to using the toilet. She slept during moments when it was possible and cared for sick children without the aid of a doctor. Tamae was usually so burdened with children and possessions that she could not wipe the tears from her cheeks. When she reached Arkansas it was early January, and the unfamiliar blasts of winter blew through wide cracks in the barracks walls.

It was a year before clearance could be obtained allowing Tamae and George to be reunited. After that life was bearable, although sad news reached them in July, 1944. The Hoshidas learned their oldest daughter, the crippled child who had been taken to a home in Honolulu, had died. Later it was discovered the child had been left unattended in a bathtub and had drowned.

Money was a constant worry. The $1,000 which Tamae had realized from the sale of family possessions eventually disappeared as they purchased needed items. George did such work as he could, but the wage he received was a miserable 10 cents an hour. When the family was returned to Hilo in 1945, they were nearly penniless.

When George returned to his home, he had to start life over again. He filed claims against the government for the property he had lost, but in the end he was awarded $500, a small part of what he had lost. George Hoshida and the others who had been condemned to live out the war behind barbed wire lost not only their possessions but also valuable years from their lives.

On December 7 Hawaii's governor ordered such military organizations as existed to report for duty. The most important of these was the Hawaii Territorial Guard. Its nucleus was the University of Hawaii ROTC as well as some high school ROTC units. By 10 A.M. most of these men had reported to the Honolulu armory. They were ordered to guard utilities and communications centers. Many of these young men were Japanese-Americans, but few people worried about this during those first anxious days after Pearl Harbor. On January 21 of the new year, however, 317 members of the Hawaii Territorial Guard were discharged without explanation. All of them were of Japanese ancestry.

On the same day the Japanese-Americans were relieved of duty, the Businessmen's Military Training Corps was organized. It was made up of businessmen, over military age, who trained with army equipment. They stood guard duty and served as a back-up force for the regular army. A majority of these men had some previous military training. Membership was restricted to Caucasians and Caucasian-Hawaiians. The chief concern of the Businessmen's Military Training Corps was the loyalty of the Japanese-Americans, and a major function was to watch them closely. To do this they collected data on suspicious persons and drew detailed maps of those areas of Honolulu where the Japanese population was concentrated.

The Japanese-Americans who had been discharged from the Territorial Guard were very much offended. One hundred and fifty of them, mostly University of Hawaii students, sent a joint letter to the commanding general in Hawaii. The letter stated, "Hawaii is our home; the United States, our country. We know but one loyalty and that is to the Stars and Stripes. We wish to do our part as loyal Americans in every way possible, and we hereby offer ourselves for whatever service you may see fit to use us."

Such a plea was hard to ignore. The volunteers were put to work with the Army Corps of Engineers. They were moved to Schofield Barracks, where they lived under military discipline, although technically they remained civilians. They became known as the Varsity Victory Volunteers. In late May, 1942, the Schofield contingent together with other Japanese-American army men in Hawaii were ordered to the mainland for training. Washington had decided it would permit the formation of a regimental combat team. On June 5, as the battle of Midway raged to the northwest, 1,300 Japanese-Americans sailed from Honolulu for training on the mainland. They did not know where they were going or what was intended for them.

These men differed from the average United States soldier in more than the color of their skin and the slant of their eyes. They were smaller in stature, weighed less, and were older than the average. As a group they averaged five feet, four inches in height and twenty-four years of age. Their average IQ was high. At 103 it was only seven points below that required for officer training.

The destination of these Islanders was Camp McCoy in Wisconsin. Once settled in they took their training seriously. The right to fight for their country had been slow in coming, and many of the men felt a sense of mission. They spent their own money to buy books on tactics and training. They felt they were being watched by the nation and that they had to excel. Perhaps the thing they resented most was being called Japs. The use of that word often resulted in a fight. They were designated the 100th battalion.

In January, 1943, the War Department decided to accept volunteers from among the Nisei for a special combat unit. Originally the War Department had hoped to get 1,500 men, but when the call went out in Hawaii nearly 10,000 volunteered. Finally 2,686 were selected from the Islands and some 1,500 more volunteers came from the mainland. The volunteers were sent to Camp Shelby, Mississippi, where the 100th battalion had been transferred.

The new recruits formed the 442nd Regimental Combat Team. Their shoulder patch showed a hand raising a torch of liberty against a blue field. The motto read "Go for Broke." It was an Island saying which probably originated with gamblers but which had been adopted by nearly everyone who wanted to express the idea that they were going "all out."

The 100th left Camp Shelby in late summer, 1943, and landed in North Africa September 2. They were moved to Italy, where they saw their first action at Salerno. Then followed engagements at Salerno, Volturno, the Rapido River, Cassino, and Anzio. It was some of the bitterest fighting of the war, and casualties were high. In June, 1944, the 442nd arrived and later that month went into action north of Rome. The 100th joined them as their first battalion.

The Japanese-Americans quickly gained a good fighting reputation. Their bravery in combat was no less impressive than their training record had been. In September the 442nd was sent to southern France where they became a part of the 36th division, which was made up principally of Texans. They moved northward through rain and mud. Once again casualties were high.

The 442nd was in need of rest, but they were not given that luxury. A Texas infantry battalion had been cut off by Germans two miles east of Biffontaine, and the 442nd was one of the units called to attempt a rescue. They marched out in the pre-dawn of October 27. It was cold. Rain turned the ground into a mire. Each man had a piece of white paper pinned to his back so the man behind could more easily follow. Soon after 8 A.M. they met the first German fire. Progress was slow through the day.

At dawn the following day they moved forward again. The going was as difficult as the day before. The cold was intense, the rain kept falling. Vehicles slipped about in the mud and became useless. Ammunition and other supplies were carried forward on men's backs. Stretcher bearers slipped in the mud as they carried the wounded to the rear. On the third day the 442nd cut a corridor through the last German mine field and reached the lost battalion. The Texans had been isolated for seven days. They were exhausted and some of their wounded had died because of the lack of medical attention. Later the Texans sent the 442nd a bronze plaque of appreciation and proclaimed their rescuers honorary Texans.

Tadao Beppu vividly remembers the three days it took to reach the Texans. Tadao had grown up on a sugar plantation on Maui. He was a University of Hawaii graduate, and in 1943, when the call came for Japanese-American volunteers, Tadao stepped forward. Unlike some of the others, Beppu did not feel he had to prove anything. He wanted to do his duty, but he also wanted to get his military service out of the way.

The three-day march to rescue the Texans was the toughest fighting Tadao remembered. The Texans were lodged on a steep hill, and the 442nd had to move upward through wooded country to reach them. At first the Germans were in front of them, but as they advanced the enemy appeared on both flanks. As they moved forward, cannon and mortar shells burst in the treetops spraying fragments over a wide area. Nearly every German shell resulted in at least one casualty.

Like most of the other men in the 442nd, Tadao Beppu came home from the war with a collection of medals. One of his was the Purple Heart.

He received it when a piece of shrapnel from a German 88 hit him in a shin in November, 1944, as they were moving north into France. For Beppu the war was over.

With the war in Europe won, the 442nd was returned to the United States. On July 15, 1946, they marched in Washington, D.C., through rain toward the White House, where they were drawn up at attention on the White House lawn. President Harry Truman reviewed the men and attached the seventh presidential citation to their colors. "You fought not only the enemy but you fought prejudice—and you have won," Truman said. The price of winning was 650 dead.

The 100th and later the 442nd received the glare of publicity because they were unique units made up solely of Japanese-Americans. They were very newsworthy and the press covered them extensively. For other Islanders of all racial backgrounds who served with equal distinction, the continual praising of the 442nd was galling. Among those most annoyed was another group of Japanese-Americans, those who served in the Pacific theater.

As United States forces took the offensive and moved westward in the Pacific, it was quickly discovered that few people could speak or read Japanese. There was a desperate need for men who could interrogate prisoners, translate documents, and broadcast to the enemy. Japanese-Americans were asked to volunteer. Those who accepted faced special kinds of danger. Japanese soldiers often wore remnants of United States uniforms and sometimes tried to infiltrate United States lines clad as American soldiers. Any man with brown skin and slanted eyes was in danger of being shot even in his own camp.

Some of these interpreters volunteered for duty far beyond what could have been expected of them. One such man was Sergeant Hoichi Kudo of Maui. On Saipan Kudo climbed unarmed into a cave where nine Japanese soldiers were holding 120 Saipan natives hostage. He convinced the soldiers that if they did not surrender they would die. The soldiers accepted his advice and surrendered, saving not only their own lives but probably the lives of many of the Saipanese.

A month after the parade in Washington, D. C., there was another victory parade, this time in Honolulu. The leader of that parade was not a member of the 442nd. Rather he was Alexander Kahapea, a part-Hawaiian who won the honor of being Hawaii's most decorated soldier. Kahapea was an infantry captain. He had been wounded five times in combat in France, where he received a battlefield commission. The marchers ended up at Kapiolani Park, and that night celebrations were held throughout the city. The war was officially over for Hawaii.

Islanders began thinking as civilians again, and many looked for those prewar events in which they had previously found pleasure. One of those events was obviously missing: boat day, the day when the *S.S. Lurline* arrived in Honolulu Harbor. The *Lurline* was a great white ship of the Matson Navigation Company, and for generations Island people had taken pride and bestowed special affection on vessels bearing that name.

In 1887 the first *Lurline* came to Hawaii. It was a brigantine named for a daughter of Captain Matson. In 1933 the largest and most luxurious of the *Lurline*s made her maiden voyage to Hawaii. It was called the "Great white palace of the sea" in an editorial. The *Lurline,* more than any other single object, represented Hawaii in the minds of Islanders. The sight of the *Lurline* raised emotions of nostalgia and protection. On boat day hundreds of people came to the wharves to watch her arrival and departure.

At the beginning of World War II the *Lurline* was commandeered, and through the war she served as a troop transport in the Pacific. During those years Islanders occasionally caught sight of her when she stopped in Hawaii. She was hardly recognizable under a layer of dark gray paint. Then, in January, 1946, with the war over, the government returned the *Lurline* to Matson.

After five years of war service as a troop transport the *Lurline* was in ragged condition. In fact, the interior of the vessel was in such disrepair that it had to be entirely rebuilt. The job was not completed until early 1948, at a cost of $18,000,000. The original cost of the vessel had been $8,500,000.

In April, 1948, Honolulu prepared for the return of her favorite ship. It was a time of real excitement. The governor proclaimed the day of arrival as *Lurline* day. A king and queen were elected to welcome the ship. As she appeared off Diamond Head on the morning of April 21, army, navy and marine airplanes flew over in a salute. Musicians, dancers, and a crowd of dignitaries boarded the *Lurline* off Waikiki. Nearly a hundred boats escorted her toward Honolulu Harbor. At the harbor entrance a fleet of thirteen outrigger canoes, crews dressed in Hawaiian attire, greeted the ship. In the center canoe stood the king and queen of *Lurline* day.

Whistles and sirens in the city blew a welcome. David Bray, who mixed the Christian religion with ancient Hawaiian beliefs, blessed the vessel. An eighty-foot lei was draped over the *Lurline's* bow. Special editions of newspapers listed the names of all 709 passengers. An estimated 100,000 persons watched the *Lurline* sail along the coast and into the harbor. An editorial in the *Advertiser* reported "Ships have personalities to islanders who depend upon them for their existence. . . . Long live the Queen."

EPILOGUE: THE HERITAGE WILLED
TO ALL OF US

THE RETURN OF THE *Lurline* brought back memories of prewar days, but it could not bring back an era which had unequivocally passed. World War II was the beginning of a new age for Hawaii's people.

The war had exposed Islanders to the rest of the world in a way no other event could. Men and women from Hawaii traveled around the world and proved they were the equal of people anywhere. At the same time the Islands served as the major base of the United States in the Pacific, and millions of mainlanders came through Hawaii. By the time the war ended Hawaii's people had won a high degree of self-confidence.

The GI bill of rights made it possible for servicemen to attend the finest universities on the mainland—something many of them could not have afforded or would not have dared in an earlier time. They returned with degrees which qualified them to enter the professions.

These people believed they were capable of making their own way and that the paternalistic system which had dominated the Islands for over 100 years was no longer acceptable. Changes were demanded in the power structure of Hawaii. Such changes are never willingly made by those in power.

Among the powerful forces responsible for bringing change to the Islands were the labor unions. Labor activity of a sort dated back to the latter 1800s when occasional uprisings, nearly spontaneous, erupted over some grievance on a plantation. These demonstrations were usually brought to an end quickly and decisively. In the 1920s and 1930s there were active attempts to organize labor. For the most part workers could be brought together for a particular cause, but once the problem was settled unity melted away. The effectiveness of labor organizations was diminished by the fact that they were unified more by race than by cause.

In 1937 a break came for labor. In that year the United States Supreme Court ruled that the National Labor Relations Act was constitutional. This opened the way for collective bargaining. Of the several unions in the Islands the most militant and most successful was the International Longshoremen's Warehousemen's Union. By 1941 the ILWU had succeeded in organizing the dock workers in both Hawaii and San Francisco. This meant they were able to control the flow of goods to and from Hawaii. The Hawaiian Islands depended on shipping for their very existence, and with a hold on this vital flow the ILWU had become a serious power.

World War II and martial law in Hawaii brought an end to overt action by Hawaii's unions, but even if men were frozen in their jobs and strikes illegal, planning for future organization went forward. Once martial law was lifted the ILWU moved ahead with ever increasing success. They organized not only the longshoremen but also the sugar and pineapple workers. It was only a matter of time before management and unions would clash, facing each other in a test of strength.

That test came on September 1, 1946. On that day some 21,000 workers on thirty-three plantations left their jobs. There had never been anything like it before in Hawaii's history. Negotiations began, but little was accomplished. Feelings ran high and logical arguments persuaded no one, because opinions of Island people had long since polarized. At last Castle and Cooke, one of Hawaii's big factoring companies, reached a point where they would suffer greater losses on their sugar plantations by holding out than by making concessions to the union. They gave in and were followed by Hawaii's other plantation holding companies. The strike had lasted seventy-nine days.

The ILWU had not won all its demands, but they were unquestionably the victors. Their success stands as a milestone in Island history. No reasonable person could deny that a new, powerful force had established itself on the Island scene.

Change of another kind was brewing. Ever since Hawaii had become a possession of the United States, it had been dominated by the Republican party. The Democrats, in fact, had been so notoriously weak that even Democratic Presidents of the United States had appointed Republicans as governors of the Territory. After World War II many persons believed the quickest way to make the Islands more democratic was through legislation, and they became involved in politics for the first time. A large number of these persons were Japanese-Americans, and they found little welcome when they knocked at the door of the Republican party. The Democratic party door, however, was opened wide to them. When the ILWU realized the Democratic party could be another means of adding to their strength, they attempted to capture party leadership. They failed to control the party, although they came close in the beginning and they continued to be a powerful influence.

During these years the Democratic party had one common, unifying objective. It wanted to overthrow the existing power structure—and that meant the Republicans. This unifying objective was enough to bring the diverse segments of the Democratic party together. On one extreme was the radical ILWU, and on the other end of the spectrum was a group of conservatives. In the end the radicals and the conservatives were the losers. Those who occupied the middle ground were destined to control the party.

Even middle-ground Democrats were radicals by Republican standards. In the 1954 elections the Republicans attempted to define Democrats and communists as one and the same, hoping particularly to link the ILWU faction with the communist investigations which caused a furor in the Islands during the early 1950s. The tactic was a dismal failure. For the first time in history Democrats gained control of both houses of the Territorial legislature.

The only Republican in prominent office was Samuel Wilder King, who was appointed governor of the Territory by President Dwight D. Eisenhower. Republicans were sure the 1954 elections were an abnormality, and Governor King reflected this feeling. He blunted Democratic legislative efforts by using his veto power seventy-one times in the 1955 session.

Many Republicans continued to believe that 1954 had simply been abnormal, but after a second Democratic sweep in the 1956 elections it was obvious the earlier win had been no fluke. Again the Republicans had tried to link the Democrats with odious communists. Again it had not worked. In 1957 the legislature repassed many 1955 bills. This time Governor King exercised restraint in the use of his veto.

More than Island politics was changing. World War II had revolutionized the development of airplanes, and in 1947 United Airlines became a competitor to Pan American World Airways. Pan Am had been the American pioneer in the Pacific, forging an air link all the way to the Orient in the 1930s with their famous China clippers. Postwar air travel, however, brought new competition and improved equipment which reduced prices as well as flying time. If the *Lurline* and other vessels of Matson's great white fleet remained the sentimental favorites in the Islands, they by no means held a monopoly on travel to and from Hawaii.

One of the two great barriers to travel to Hawaii had been removed for the first time. If the cost of reaching the Islands remained high, the barrier of time had been reduced dramatically and with finality. Prospects for Hawaii's long talked about tourist industry took on a new glow. Hawaii's Visitors Bureau advertised the Islands across the country, and hotels and other tourist-related businesses responded with cautious optimism.

In the early 1950s no one guessed what a change the airlines would bring. By 1960 a visitor from the Middle West could fly to and from Hawaii, plus spending ten days in the Islands, for the amount of money transportation alone had cost several years earlier. Waikiki sprouted high-rise hotels, set among gift shops and restaurants. Many visitors who had come to Hawaii in prewar days were disillusioned by the commercialism which engulfed Waikiki, and they recaptured their dreams by visiting the neighbor islands.

The tourist boom of the middle 1950s was only the beginning. The continued affluence of the United States and the coming of the giant jet planes resulted in yet another revolution in Hawaii. Time and cost were drastically, dramatically cut. A vast number of Americans could now afford to come to Hawaii if they really wanted to, and hundreds of thousands did come. Many of these people were budget tourists, and the average length of stay and the amount of money they spent was less than it had been ten years earlier.

During the middle 1950s, when Hawaii's economy was growing and diversifying, the drive to achieve statehood was gaining momentum both in Hawaii and in the nation's capital. Statehood had been talked about before Hawaii became a territory of the United States, but it was not truly a serious matter until after World War II. The war had demonstrated that Hawaii's people were loyal and capable. What reasons could be given to deny them the full rights of citizen status in the Union? The question was hard to answer even for those who did not want to see non-Caucasians become full-fledged citizens of the United States.

Tadao Beppu, the one-time infantry sergeant and a legislator, remembered how the basic question had changed. Before World War II the Congressional investigating teams which came to the Islands repeatedly asked the question, "Are they loyal?" In the 1950s such a question could not be taken seriously. The recurring question then was "Can they be assimilated as Americans?"

For most people in the Islands the fact that Hawaii was not a state was galling. Hawaii had waited patiently and politely for justice. It had waited longer than any other territory of the United States had waited. Continuing Territorial status had meant Island people could not vote for the President of the United States and that they had no representatives in Washington except a delegate who was elected in Hawaii but had no vote in Congress. As long as Hawaii remained a Territory, Congress had enormous powers. They could even abolish the Territorial legislature if they wished.

There were some in Hawaii who had grave fears about statehood. They gave a variety of reasons. Business tycoon Walter F. Dillingham thought Island people would elect the wrong kind of representatives to Washington. Some Hawaiians and part-Hawaiians feared that statehood would remove them yet another step from the days of the monarchy and would surely mean that Orientals would dominate the life of the Islands.

In Washington there were a number of Congressmen who found ample reasons why Hawaii did not deserve statehood. It was too far away; it was Oriental, not Western in thought; it was dominated by communists. There were more than enough ways of delaying a vote in one or the other house of Congress, and when the House did pass a bill approving statehood the Senate voted it down.

In the early 1950s the Territory of Alaska surfaced as a serious contender for statehood. People discussed at great length how this would affect the chances of Hawaii. Finally it was agreed that Hawaii and Alaska should join together in waging their battles on the theory that Congress would be hard pressed to vote one in and keep the other out.

Alaska's time came in 1958 when Congress approved statehood for her. The fact that the Alaska bill moved before the Hawaii bill annoyed some in the Islands, and Delegate John A. Burns, who was running for re-election that year, had to face his critics at home. The strategy, however, was sound. On March 11, 1959, the Senate passed its bill and the next day the House passed an identical bill. Statehood for Hawaii was at last a reality.

Word was flashed to Hawaii and people paraded in the streets, business firms closed, bells were rung and sirens blown. Only the formalities remained. The people of Hawaii had to ratify the action of Congress. This they did in late June by a margin of seventeen to one. President Eisenhower performed the last official act when he signed a proclamation on August 21 admitting "the state of Hawaii into the Union on an equal footing with other states of the Union. . . ." At last Hawaii's people were first-class citizens.

Unnoticed in the general celebration were the few who were saddened. On March 13 services were held at Kawaihao Church to commemorate the coming of statehood. The old, coral stone church, which had witnessed so much history was crowded. Extra chairs were placed in the aisles, every seat was occupied in the lofts, and people gathered outside to hear the words of Reverend Abraham Akaka over a loudspeaker system.

"There are some of us to whom statehood brings great hopes; and there are some to whom statehood brings silent fears," Reverend Akaka said. "One might say that the hopes and fears of Hawaii are met in statehood today. There are fears that statehood will motivate economic greed toward Hawaii, that it will turn Hawaii into a great big (as someone has said) spiritual junkyard filled with smashed dreams, worn-out illusions—that it will make us lonely, confused, insecure, empty, anxious, restless, disillusioned—a wistful people."

But Akaka believed all would be well. He remembered an ancient Hawaiian chant which said, "but there is salvation for the people, for now the land is being lit by a great flame." Hawaii had much to give to the nation which had now seen fit to make her an equal member. The greatest contribution was the gift of aloha. Akaka remembered that as a child he had heard the words, *"Aloha ke akua."* Aloha is god. He told his congregation that "when a people or a person live in the spirit of aloha, they live in the spirit of God."

Reverend Akaka neared the end of his sermon: ". . . aloha is the spirit of God at work in you and in me and in the world." Then Hawaii's moving anthem, *Hawaii Ponoi,* was sung. In a back corner of the choir loft stood a tall, proud Hawaiian man. He sang the words with great feeling while tears flooded down his cheeks.

In 1959 a special election was held in Hawaii to fill the offices which came with statehood. William F. Quinn, who had been appointed governor by President Eisenhower, now won the office by popular vote. Oren E. Long, an educator who had served as the appointed governor during the Truman administration, was elected to the United States Senate, as was Hiram Fong, a long-time political power in the Islands. Daniel K. Inouye, who had won fame for his World War II exploits, was elected to the House of Representatives.

The economic growth and diversification which was beginning in the 1950s was enormously stimulated by statehood. Mainland businesses which had hardly considered Hawaii worthy of their notice arrived to investigate the possibility of opening branch offices. Tourism boomed, great shopping centers were erected, and the business section of downtown Honolulu became dotted with high-rise office buildings. The jet planes which rounded Diamond Head came in ever increasing numbers.

Not all the people who filled the seats of those jet planes bought round-trip tickets. There were thousands who came to see if what they had read about Hawaii was true and if they liked what they saw they intended to stay. In the middle 1950s the population of the Hawaiian Islands was approximately 500,000. Ten years later it stood at over 700,000.

The great majority of these newcomers to Hawaii were young haoles from the mainland. They came as the Tahitians had once come and the Marquesans, followed by all the other racial groups which settled in Hawaii. They are the newest wave of immigrants, and they will leave their mark on the Islands.

There were all types in those earlier influxes of population and the same was true in the 1960s and 1970s. There were indolents who lived on the beach, not discernibly different from the beachcombers who appeared in the late eighteenth century. There were new kinds of missionaries preaching beliefs which earlier missionaries would have believed were deserving of hell fire. Some fled from overcrowded cities, just as Polynesians long ago fled from over populated islands, knowing there had to be a better place to live. Some were rapacious exploiters, seeking to deceive, loot, and leave. Hawaii has known them by the thousands through the years.

In viewing the newest invasion it is helpful to call back the voices and records of the past to help evaluate what must be preserved if we treasure these Islands.

Most important is the preservation of that particular quality which is Hawaii's first right to fame. That quality is summed up in a sense of tolerance, a willingness to accept others who do not hold a particular tradition and who look different physically. It is the quality of being willing to listen when instinct says to lash out. These are the qualities which make Hawaii unique.

Those who make the Islands their home, wherever they came from originally, are indebted to maintain this quality. It is the heritage willed to all of us by the native Hawaiians.

BIBLIOGRAPHY

THE BIBLIOGRAPHY AND CHAPTER NOTES are for persons wishing to look more deeply into certain episodes which are touched on in this volume. Both the bibliography and notes have been compiled to provide the necessary direction to pursue additional research. Where sources could adequately be identified in the notes, I have listed such sources there only and have not repeated them in the bibliography.

A brief explanation is necessary for the abbreviations used. ABCFM stands for American Board of Commissioners for Foreign Missions. AH represents Archives of Hawaii. BPBM is the Bernice P. Bishop Museum. HHS is the Hawaiian Historical Society. HMCS stands for the Hawaiian Mission Children's Society, UC for University of California at Berkeley, and UH for University of Hawaii.

Throughout the notes I have referred to the newspaper, the *Advertiser,* simply with that one word. Through its long history the *Advertiser* has had several name changes, but always the word *Advertiser* has been a part of the name. Likewise, I have written *Star-Bulletin,* when the complete name of the newspaper is the *Honolulu Star-Bulletin.*

Adams, C. *Richard Henry Dana.* New York, 1895.

Addleman, W. *History of United States Army in Hawaii 1849–1939.* Typed copy AH.

Adler, J. *Claus Spreckels: The Sugar King of Hawaii.* Honolulu, 1966.

Alexander, W. "Incidents of the Voyage of the Heros." HHS Report 4, 1896.

———. "The Oahu Charity School." HHS Report 16, 1908.

———. *History of the Later Years of the Hawaiian Monarchy.* Honolulu, 1896.

Allen, G. *Hawaii's War Years.* Honolulu, 1950.

Aller, C. *Labor Relations in the Hawaiian Sugar Industry.* Berkeley, 1957.

Altman, A. "Eugene Van Reed, a Reading Man in Japan 1859–1872." *Historical Review of Berks County.* Winter issue 1964–1965.

Anderson, B. *Surveyor of the Sea.* Seattle, 1960.

Anderson, C. *Melville in the South Seas.* New York, 1939.

Andrade, E. "The Hawaiian Revolution of 1887." MA thesis, UH, 1954.

Annual Report of the Navy Department for the Fiscal Year. Washington D.C., 1915, 1916.

Anthony, J. *Hawaii Under Army Rule,* Palo Alto, 1955.

Armstrong, W. *Around the World with a King.* New York, 1904.

Ayer, F. *Before the Colors Fade.* New York, 1964.

Bailey, T. "The World Cruise of the American Battleship Fleet." *Pacific Historical Review.* Vol. 1, 1932.

Balfour, G. *The Life of Robert Louis Stevenson.* 2 vols. New York, 1901.

Bancroft, H. *The Works of Hubert Howe Bancroft.* Vol. 24. San Francisco, 1890.

Barber, J. *Hawaii: Restless Rampart.* New York, 1941.

Barnes, R. *United States Submarines.* New Haven, 1944.

Barrere, D. *The Kumuhonua Legends.* Honolulu, 1969.

Beaglehole, J., ed. *Journals of James Cook.* 3 vols. Cambridge, 1955–1967.

Beckwith, M. *Hawaiian Mythology.* New Haven, 1940.

———, ed. *Kumulipo.* Chicago, 1951.

Berrett, W. *The Restored Church.* Salt Lake City, 1961.

Bingham, H. *Residence of Twenty-One Years in the Sandwich Islands.* Hartford, 1847.

Bird, I. *Six Months in the Sandwich Islands.* Honolulu, 1964.

Bock, M. "Church of Jesus Christ of Latter Day Saints in the Hawaiian Islands." MA thesis, UH, 1941.

Bosworth, A. *America's Concentration Camps.* New York, 1967.

Bradley, H. *American Frontier in Hawaii: The Pioneers, 1789–1843.* Palo Alto, 1942.

Brooks, V. *The Confident Years: 1885–1915.* New York, 1952.

Brown, J. *Reminiscences and Incidents of Early Days of San Francisco.* San Francisco, 1933.

Bryan, E. *The Hawaiian Chain.* Honolulu, 1954.

Buck, P. *Vikings of the Sunrise.* New York, 1938.

———. *Arts and Crafts of Hawaii.* Honolulu, 1957.

Burrows, E. *Hawaiian Americans.* New Haven, 1947.

Bushnell, O. "Dr. Edward Arning: The First Microbiologist in Hawaii." *Hawaiian Journal of History.* 1967.

Byron, George Gordon, Lord. *Voyage of HMS Blonde to the Sandwich Islands in the Years 1824–1825.* London, 1826.

Caldwell, E. *Last Witness for Robert Louis Stevenson.* Norman, Oklahoma, 1960.

Campbell, A. *Voyage Around the World, 1806–1812.* Edinburgh, 1816.

Cannon, G. *My First Mission.* Salt Lake City, 1882.

Carruthers, J. *Captain James Cook, R.N.* London, 1930.

Chamberline, L. Journal. Typed copy. HMCS.

Chen, Ta. *Chinese Migrations, With Special Reference to Labor Conditions.* Bulletin of US Bureau of Labor Statistics 340. Washington D.C., 1923.

Chinen, J. *Great Mahele.* Honolulu, 1958.

Coman, K. *History of Contract Labor in the Hawaiian Islands.* New York, 1903.

Conroy, H. *Japanese Frontier in Hawaii.* Berkeley, 1953.

Cook, J. and King, J. *Voyage to the Pacific Ocean, 1776–1780.* 3 vols. London, 1784.

Cooke, A. Journal. Ms. HMCS.

Cooke, C. *Charles Montague Cooke 1849–1909.* Honolulu, 1942.

Curti, M. *The Growth of American Thought.* New York, 1943.

Coulter, J. and Chun, C. *Chinese Rice Farmers in Hawaii.* UH research publication 16. Honolulu, 1937.

Davies, T. *Personal Recollections of Hawaii.* Typed copy. AH.

————. *Letters Upon the Political Crisis in Hawaii.* Honolulu, 1894.

Davis, W. *Seventy-Five Years in California.* San Francisco, 1929.

Daws, G. *Shoal of Time.* New York, 1968.

Dibble, S. *History of the Sandwich Islands.* Lahainaluna, 1843.

Dillon, R. *Fool's Gold.* New York, 1967.

Dole Collection. AH.

Dole, S. *Memoirs of the Hawaiian Revolution.* Honolulu, 1936.

Dominis, J. "Correspondence Relating to the Last Hours of Kamehameha V. A Letter by the Late Governor J. O. Dominis."

Doyle, E. *Makua Laiana; the Story of Lorenzo Lyons.* Honolulu, 1945.

Dwight, E. *Memories of Henry Obookiah.* Elizabethtown, 1819.

Elbert, S. and Pukui, M. *Hawaiian-English Dictionary.* Honolulu, 1957.

Ellis, W. *Narrative of a Tour.* Reprint of the 1826 edition, Honolulu, 1963.

Emory, K. "Origins of the Hawaiians." *Journal of the Polynesian Society.* Vol. 68, No. 1, March 1959.

————. "Religion in Ancient Hawaii." *75th Anniversary Anniversary Lectures.* Honolulu, 1965.

Fornander, A. *Account of the Polynesian Race.* 3 vols. London, 1878–1885.

Frankenstein, A. "Royal Visitors." *Oregon Historical Quarterly*. March 1963.

Furnas, J. *Voyage to Windward*. New York, 1951.

Gelett, C. *A Life on the Ocean*. Honolulu, 1917.

Gerstaecker, F. *Narrative of a Journey Around the World*. New York, 1853.

Gihon, J., Nibet, J., and Soule, F. *Annals of San Francisco*. San Francisco, 1854.

Golovnin, V. *Tour Around the World . . . 1822*. Translated from Russian by E. Embree. Typed copy. UH.

Greer, R. "Mutiny in the Royal Barracks." *Pacific Historical Review*. November 1962.

Gurko, M. *Clarence Darrow*. New York, 1932.

Haddon, A. and Hornell, J. *Canoes of Oceania*. 3 vols. BPBM Special Publications 27, 28, 29. 1936, 1937, 1938.

Hafen, L. *The Overland Mail*. Cleveland, 1926.

Halford, F. *Nine Doctors and God*. Honolulu, 1954.

Handy, E. *The Native Culture in the Marquesas*. BPBM Bulletin 9, 1923.

Handy, E. and Pukui, M. *The Polynesian Family System in Ka'u, Hawaii*. Wellington, New Zealand, 1958.

Handy, E.S.C. *History and Culture in the Society Islands*. BPBM Bulletin 79. 1931.

Harvey, A. *Douglas of the Fir*. Boston, 1947.

Henry, T. *Ancient Tahiti*. Honolulu, 1928.

Hines, G. *A Voyage Around the World*. Buffalo, 1850.

Holman, L. *Journal of Lucia Ruggles Holman*. BPBM Special Publication 17. Honolulu, 1931.

Horvat, W. *Above the Pacific*. Fallbrook, 1966.

Hosokawa, B. *Nisei*. New York, 1969.

Humphrey, H. *The Promised Land*. Boston, 1819.

Humphreys, A. *Herman Melville*. New York, 1962.

Hunnewell, J. "Honolulu in 1817 and 1818." Excerpts from a journal edited by his son, J. Hunnewell. HHS Report 8, 1895.

———. *Journal of the Voyage of the "Missionary Packet," Boston to Honolulu*. Charleston, 1880.

Hunt, C. *The Shenandoah: The Last Confederate Cruiser*. New York, 1867.

Ii, J. *Fragments of Hawaiian History*. Honolulu, 1959.

Jackson, F. "Koloa Plantation Under Ladd and Company, 1835–1845." MA thesis, UH, 1958.

Joesting, E., ed. "A Scotsman Views Hawaii: An 1852 Log of a Cruise of the Emily Bourne." *Journal of the West,* Vol. 4, Number 2, April 1970.

Johnstone, A. *Recollections of Robert Louis Stevenson in the Pacific.* London, 1905.

Judd, A. "Lunalilo, The Sixth King of Hawaii." HHS Report 44, 1935.

Judd, B. "Koloa: a Sketch of its Development." HHS Report 44, 1935.

Judd, G. *Dr. Judd: Hawaii's Friend.* Honolulu, 1960.

Judd, L. *Sketches of Life, Social, Political and Religious in the Hawaiian Islands from 1828 to 1861.* Honolulu, 1928.

Kamakau, S. *Ruling Chiefs of Hawaii.* Honolulu, 1961.

Kemble, J. *The Panama Route.* Berkeley, 1943.

Kenn, C. "Descendants of Captain Sutter's Kanakas." *Proceedings of the Second Annual Meeting of the Conference of California Historical Societies.* Stockton, 1956.

Kent, H. *Charles Reed Bishop.* Palo Alto, 1965.

Kotzebue, O. von. *Voyages of Discovery, 1815–1818.* 3 vols. London, 1821.

Kuykendall, R. *Hawaiian Kingdom.* 3 vols. Honolulu, 1938–1967.

————, and Gill, L. *Hawaii in the World War.* Honolulu, 1928.

Larkin, T. *The Larkin Papers.* edited by G. Hammond. 10 vols. Berkeley, 1951–1964.

Latourette, K. *The History of Early Relations Between the U.S. and China 1784–1844.* New Haven, 1917.

Lewis, O. *Sutter's Fort.* Englewood, 1966.

Lind, A. *Hawaii's Japanese.* Princeton, 1946.

Lisiansky, U. *Voyage Around the World, 1803–1806.* London, 1814.

Lloyd, C., ed. *The Voyages of Captain Cook.* London, 1949.

London, C. *Our Hawaii.* Honolulu, 1917.

London, Jack. *The Cruise of the Snark.* New York, 1928.

London, Joan. *Jack London and His Times.* Seattle, 1968.

Loomis, E. Journal. Ms. UH.

Lord, W. *Day of Infamy.* New York, 1957.

————. *Incredible Victory.* New York, 1967.

Luomala, K. *Menehune of Polynesia.* BPBM Bulletin 203, 1951.

————. *Voices on the Wind.* Honolulu, 1955.

Lydecker, R. "Memorandum on the Introduction of Foreign Laborers into the Hawaiian Islands." Typed copy. AH.

Lyman, C. *Around the Horn to the Sandwich Islands and California 1845–1850.* New Haven, 1924.

Lyman, H. *Hawaiian Yesterdays.* Chicago, 1906.

Lyman, R. "Recollections of Kamehameha V." HHS Report 3, 1894.

MacDonald, G. and Abbott, A. *Volcanoes in the Sea*. Honolulu, 1970.

Mackay, M. *The Violent Friend*. New York, 1968.

Mahan, A. *Naval Strategy*. Boston, 1911.

Malo, D. *Hawaiian Antiquities*. BPBM Special Publication 2, Second edition, 1951.

————. *Ka Po'e Kahiko*. BPBM Special Publication 51, 1964.

Marberry, M. *Splendid Poseur*. New York, 1953.

Marshall, J. "An Unpublished Chapter of Hawaiian History." *Harper's Magazine*. September, 1883.

McClellan, E. "John M. Gamble." HHS Report 35, 1927.

McGhie, F. "The Life and Intrigues of Walter Murray Gibson." MA thesis, UH, 1958.

McGraw, M. *Stevenson in Hawaii*. Honolulu, 1950.

McLaren, N. "Russian Immigration: Hawaii." MA thesis, UH, 1951.

Meares, J. *Voyages Made in 1788–1789*. London, 1790.

Mehnert, K. *The Russians in Hawaii 1804–1819*. Honolulu, 1939.

Menard, W. *The Two Worlds of Somerset Maugham*. Los Angeles, 1965.

Miller, W. Journal. Ms. AH

"Minutes of Meeting of Commissioners Held 12th March, 1843." HHS Report 14, 1906.

Moore, G. "Hawaii During the Whaling Era." MA thesis, UH, 1934.

Morgan, M. *Dixie Raider*. New York, 1948.

Morgan, T. *Hawaii, A Century of Economic Change 1778–1876*. Cambridge, 1948.

Morison, S. *The Maritime History of Massachusetts*. Cambridge, 1961.

Mouritz, A. *Path of the Destroyer*. Honolulu, 1916.

————. *A Brief History of Leprosy*. No publisher listed. 1943.

Muir, A. "John Ricord." *The Southwestern Historical Quarterly*, July, 1948.

Munford, J., ed. *John Ledyard's Journal of Captain Cook's Last Voyage*. Corvallis, 1963.

Murphy, T. *Ambassadors in Arms*. Honolulu, 1955.

Neumann, P. *Biennial Report of the Attorney General to the Legislative Assembly* of 1884. Honolulu, 1884.

Parke, W. *Personal Reminiscences of William Cooper Parke*. Cambridge, 1891.

Potter, W. *The Punahou Story*. Palo Alto, 1969.

Paske-Smith, M. "Early British Consuls in Hawaii." *The Mid-Pacific Magazine of the Pan-Pacific Union*. Honolulu, October–December 1936.

Paty, W. Journal. Ms. AH.

Peabody, F. *Education for Life*. New York, 1919.

Pierce, R. *Russia's Hawaiian Adventure, 1815–1817.* Berkeley, 1965.

Pitman, A. *Fifty Years.* Norwood, 1931.

Pleadwell, F. "Voyage to England of King Liholiho and Queen Kamamalu." 1952. Typed copy. AH.

Polynesian Cultural History. Honolulu, 1967.

Porter, D. *Journal of a Cruise Made to the Pacific Ocean.* 2 vols. New York, 1822.

Portlock, N. *Voyage Around the World, 1785–1788.* London, 1789.

Report of Committee on the Social Evil. Honolulu, 1914.

Rolle, A. *An American in California.* San Marino, 1956.

Rossetter, A. "Report of the Pinkerton National Detective Agency, Inc." Typed copy. AH.

Ruggles, E. *Prince of Players Edwin Booth.* New York, 1953.

Rydell, R. *Cape Horn to the Pacific.* Berkeley, 1952.

Samwell, D. *Captain Cook and Hawaii.* San Francisco, 1957.

Schofield, J. *Forty-Six Years in the Army.* New York, 1897.

Sheldon, H. "Reminiscences of Henry L. Sheldon." Ms. AH.

Sherman, W. *Memoirs of General William T. Sherman.* 2 vols. Bloomington, 1957.

Shineberg, D. *They Came for Sandalwood.* Melbourne, 1967.

Simpson, A. *The Sandwich Islands.* London, 1843.

Smith, B. *Americans from Japan.* New York, 1948.

Snowbarger, W. "The Development of Pearl Harbor." Doctoral dissertation, UC, 1950.

Squires, Z. *The Planters' Mongolian Pets, or, Human Decoy Act.* Honolulu, 1884.

Stearns, A. *Geology of the Hawaiian Islands.* Honolulu, 1946.

Sterling, Y. *Sea Duty.* New York, 1939.

Stevens, S. *American Expansion in Hawaii 1842–1898.* Philadelphia, 1945.

Stewart, G. *The Crowning of the Dread King.* Honolulu, 1883.

Stoddard, C. *The Lepers of Molokai.* Notre Dame, 1885.

Sullivan, J. *A History of C. Brewer & Company, Limited.* Boston, 1926.

Swails, T. "John McAllister Schofield—Military Diplomat." MA thesis, UH, 1966.

Talbot, E. *Samuel Chapman Armstrong.* New York, 1904.

Tate, M. *United States and the Hawaiian Kingdom: A Political History.* New Haven, 1965.

Taylor, A. "Historical Notes." HHS Report 38, 1929.

Taylor, C. "The Fabulous Holts." A series of 89 articles which appeared in the *Star-Bulletin* commencing June 3, 1954.

Thurston, L. *Life and Times.* Michigan, 1882.

Thurston, L. A. *Memoirs of the Hawaiian Revolution*. Honolulu, 1936.
————. ed., and Farrell, A. *Writings of Lorrin A. Thurston*. Honolulu, 1936.

Tinker, R. Journal. Ms. HMCS.

Underhill, R. *From Cowhides to Golden Fleece*. Palo Alto, 1939.

United States Naval Medical Bulletin. Washington, D.C. 1916.

Van Slingerland, P. *Something Terrible Has Happened*. New York, 1966.

Vancouver, G. *Voyages of Discovery to the North Pacific Ocean, 1790–1795*. 3 vols. London, 1798.

Vandercook, J. *Great Sailor*. New York, 1951.

Wagner, H. *Joaquin Miller and His Other Self*. San Francisco, 1929.

Wakukawa, E. *History of the Japanese People in Hawaii*. Honolulu, 1938.

Watanabe, S. "Diplomatic Relations Between the Hawaiian Kingdom and the Empire of Japan." MA thesis, UH, 1944.

Westervelt, W. "The Passing of Kamehameha I." HHS Report 31, 1923.

Wilbur, M., ed. and translator. *A Pioneer at Sutter's Fort 1846–1850*. Los Angeles, 1941.

Wilson, C. "Some Social Aspects of Mainland Defense Workers in Honolulu." *Social Process in Honolulu*. November 1943.

Wilson, F. *David Douglas, Botanist at Hawaii*. Honolulu, 1919.

Withington, A. *The Golden Cloak*. Honolulu, 1953.

Wolcott, R., ed. *The Correspondence of William Hickling Prescott 1833–1847*. New York, 1925.

Yzendoorn, R. *History of the Catholic Mission in the Hawaiian Islands*. Honolulu, 1927.

Zimmerman, E. *Insects of Hawaii*. Vol. 1. Honolulu, 1948.

Zimmerman, H. *Account of the Third Voyage of Captain Cook 1776–1780*. Translated from German by U. Tewsley. Wellington, New Zealand, 1926.

Zollinger, J. *Sutter*. Gloucester, 1967.

BIBLIOGRAPHIC NOTES

Chapter One

Beckwith and Fornander wrote on the beliefs of the ancient Hawaiians concerning the creation of the Islands; MacDonald and Abbott, Stearns, E. Zimmerman, and Bryan on the geological creation of the Islands; Buck, Ellis, Emory, *Polynesian Cultural History* on the origins of the Polynesians; Henry on the Society Islands; Suggs, Handy on the Marquesas Is-

lands; Feher, Buck, Haddon, and Hornell on the Polynesian canoe; Buck
and Handy concerning Raiatea.

Chapter Two

Bryan has written on plants and animals; Elbert and Pukui on place
names; Luomala and Barrere about the Menehune; Kamakau on later ar-
rivals from Tahiti, on the Ka'u rebellion, and on Umi; Handy and Pukui
plus Ii on family life; Kamakau and Malo concerning the first impressions
made on Hawaiians by Westerners.

Chapter Three

Cook and King, H. Zimmerman, and Ledyard (see Munford) were among
those who kept journals on Cook's third voyage. Samwell, Beaglehole,
Kuykendall, Lloyd, Vandercook, Carruthers were later commentators on
Cook's visit to Hawaii. Malo, Kamakau, and Ii wrote about the reactions
of the Hawaiians to the English; Kamakau concerning Lono.

Chapter Four

Kuykendall, Kamakau, Malo, Portlock, Meares, and Vancouver are valuable sources about Hawaii before 1800. *The Columbian Centinel,* Boston,
printed a detailed account of the Olowalu massacre on November 30,
1791. This account was reprinted in the *Advertiser* on September 3, 1928.
The Vancouver journals and Anderson discuss the Vancouver visits to Hawaii. Lisiansky, Golovnin, von Katzebue, Mehnert, Pierce, and Alexander
wrote about Russian activity in Hawaii. Campbell, Vancouver, Kamakau,
Malo, and Westervelt are important sources on Kamehameha I.

Chapter Five

See Dwight on Obookiah. Humphrey's ordination sermon was published in
1819. L. Thurston, Bingham, the files of the ABCFM, and particularly the
library of the HMCS provide much information on missionary activities.
Holman, Bingham, and Halford wrote about the difficulties between the
Holmans and the mission. Ellis and Dibble discussed the development of a
written Hawaiian language. See Byron, Frankenstein, Pleadwell on Kamehameha II visit to England; Loomis journal on the decadent haoles; Yzendoorn on the Catholic mission; Alexander, Kuykendall, Pleadwell on
Rives; Kuykendall and Bradley on the French; Kuykendall and Tinker on
the school system.

Chapter Six

See Morison, Rydell, Bradley, Latourette on New England trading in the Pacific; Bradley, Shineberg, Kuykendall, *Hawaiian Annual,* for 1905, 1906 on sandalwood; Hunnewell on Hunnewell voyages to Hawaii; Moore, Gelett, Davies on whaling; The *Polynesian* for November 1852 and Parke on sailors' riot of 1852; Humphreys and C. Anderson on Melville; *Hawaiian Annual* 1904, British Commission papers AH, *The Friend,* August 1873, concerning Montgomery and relation with Melville; Jackson and B. Judd on Ladd and Company; Wilson, Harvey, James Tice Phillips Collection AH on Douglas; Kuykendall and Daws on Boki.

Chapter Seven

Larkin, Bancroft, Underhill and Morgan have written on Hawaii-California relationships to 1850; Alexander and Underhill on California children at Oahu Charity School; Davis and Rolle on Davis; Dillon, Zollinger, *Sandwich Island Gazette* April 6, 1839, Lienhard (see Wilbur), and Lewis concerning Sutter; *Polynesian, The Friend* for 1848, 1849, 1850, Doyle, Morgan, and H. Lyman, on effects of Gold Rush on Hawaii; C. Lyman, Brown, Davis, Kenn, Gihon, *Polynesian* and also *The Friend* for 1848, 1849, 1850 concerning Hawaiians in California; Berrett and Parke on Brannan; Joesting on *Emily Bourne.* Hines, C. Lyman, Sherman, Muir, and G. Judd throw light on Ricord.

Chapter Eight

See Bradley, Paske-Smith, *Polynesian* February 21, 1846, and letter from Kamehameha III to the King of England dated November 16, 1836 AH concerning Charlton; Cooke, Bradley, Marshall, Miller, Simpson, British Foreign Office Records AH, "Minutes of Meeting of Commissioners held 12th March 1843," Paty, British Commission Records AH, *Polynesian* September 7, 1844, Wyllie-Paulet correspondence AH, *Paradise of the Pacific* June 1909, G. Judd, and Forbes on Paulet; Chamberlain, *Polynesian* December 12, 1857, Tice Phillips Collection AH, *The Friend* August 1843; Paske-Smith, Privy Council Records March 11, 1851 AH, Miller, Gregg to Secretary of State Marcy Dispatch 83 March 24, 1855 AH, and Wolcott on Miller; *Advertiser* February 28, 1861, Gregg to Secretary of State Marcy Dispatch 89 April 13, 1855 AH, Dispatch 102 June 18, 1855 AH, Sheldon on seamens' hospitals; G. Judd, Kuykendall, Bradley, L. Judd, on French intrusion; Bradley, Chinen, Malo, Withington, Kamakau, Parke, and Gerstaecker on Kamehameha III; Kuykendall, G. Judd, and Bradley on Judd.

Chapter Nine

See Kuykendall, Kamakau, *The Friend* July 1931, letter from Malo to Kaahumanu (Kinau) August 18, 1837 AH, *The Friend* April and July 1931, and letter from Alexander to Armstrong October 25, 1853 AH on Malo; the *Advertiser* for late November and for December 1856 on Risley circus; Ruggles, *Hawaiian Annual* 1903, *Advertiser* September 5, 1893 on Booth; typed copies of letters dated between June 28, 1849 and October 25, 1859 from Neilson to his father, mother, and brother AH, letter from Wyllie to Kamehameha IV September 24, 1862 AH, Gregg diary February 12, 1862 AH on Neilson; McGhie, Cannon, Gregg diary AH, Bock, and Gibson on Mormons; Coman, Morgan, Stevens, Aller on sugar; *The Garden Island* December 6, 1949, *Star Bulletin* March 9, 1935 on Lihue plantation; *Star Bulletin* April 17, 1937 and *The Garden Island* December 6, 1949 on Isenberg.

Chapter Ten

The *Polynesian* for November 16, 1861 carried the news of the completion of the transcontinental telegraph line. See Kuykendall and Sheldon on reaction of Americans in Hawaii to the Civil War; *Hawaiian Annual* 1924, letter from Wyllie to Spencer December 27, 1861 AH, letter from Wyllie to Kamehameha IV December 1, 1861 concerning Spencer; Pitman on Pitman; *The Friend* August 1915 on Emerson; *Paradise of the Pacific* March 1962, May 1963 on Ward; M. Morgan and Hunt on the *Shenandoah;* Kent on Marshall; Kent, Schofield, and Swails on Schofield; dispatches between William Martin and deVarigny between January 18 and November 8, 1867 on Paris Exposition of 1867 AH; Kemble and Hafen on transportation to Hawaii; *Hawaiian Annual* 1925, 1930 on postal service; Davies on inter-island trip; *Hawaiian Annual* 1889 on the *Akamai;* C. Adams, *Advertiser* November 3, 1859, *Polynesian* October 1, 1859 on Dana. Issues of the *Polynesian* during May 1863 discuss interest in the new evaporating pan. Parrington and Curti described changes which followed the Civil War.

Chapter Eleven

Coulter and Chun, Squires, Lydecker, Neumann, Chen, *Hawaiian Annual* 1890, 1894, 1896 include material on Chinese. See record of a conversation between Kekuanaoa and Dudoit May 12, 1840 AH, *Hawaiian Ga-zette, Advertiser* July 28, August 4, 1866 on Dudoit and Asee; Watanabe, Smith, Kuykendall, Wakukawa, Coman, Conroy on Japanese; Altman on Van Reed; Kuykendall, Dominis, A. Judd, and R. Lyman on Kameha-meha V. *Paradise of the Pacific* July 1910 contains Twain quote on Lunal-ilo. Letter from Charles Castle to his wife December 30, 1873 HMCS, Bird, Kuykendall, A. Judd, mention Lunalilo. Greer, *Hawaiian Gazette* September 10, 17, 1873, letter Kalakaua to Dominis September 1–15, 1873 AH, *Advertiser* September 13, 1873 give details on the revolt of the troops. See *Report of the Board of Health to the Legislature* for 1868, 1872, 1874, 1884, Mouritz, *Advertiser* April 5, 1873, April 18, 1874 on leprosy; Privy Council Records Vol. 14 August 13, 20, 1884 AH, Mour-itz, Bushnell on Arming; Stoddard, Mouritz on Damien.

Chapter Twelve

See Dole, Kuykendall, Withington, Kent, Daws on Kalakaua in general; *Polynesian* October 24, 1840 and *Hawaiian Gazette* October 12, 1894 on hanging of Kalakaua's grandfather; letters from Alfred Castle to his wife February 11, 15, 23, 1874 HMCS, *Hawaiian Gazette* February 18, 1874, Kuykendall on election of Kalakaua; Kent, Kuykendall, Daws on reciproc-ity treaty; Adler on Spreckels; Armstrong and Kuykendall on tour of Ka-lakaua; Stewart, *The Saturday Press* February 17, 1883, *Advertiser* Febru-ary 13, 1883, Withington on coronation of Kalakaua; Andrade, Kent, Kuykendall on revolt of 1887; *Hawaiian Gazette* October 28, 29, Decem-ber 6, 1887, L. A. Thurston, Law 2501 AH, Adler on Gibson; Caldwell, Furnas, Mackay, McGaw, Balfour, Johnstone, *The Friend* June 1923, No-vember 1927, *Advertiser* June 24, 1889, July 19, 1936, April 14, 1902, November 10, 1940 on Stevenson; Andrade, Dole Collection AH, Sundry Documents on Overthrow AH on Wilcox; report by George P. Blow AH, report by Dr. George W. Woods AH, *Daily Bulletin* January 29, 1891 on death of Kalakaua.

Chapter Thirteen

See Liliuokalani Collection AH, letter from Wilcox to Liliuokalani Febru-ary 24, 1891 AH, letter from Bishop to Liliuokalani March 5, 1891 AH regarding Liliuokalani; L. A. Thurston, Dole, Davies, William Owen Smith Collection AH, Sundry Documents on Overthrow 1893 AH, Alex-ander, letter from Thurston to Hopkins December 12, 1892 AH, *Adver-tiser* February 18, 1896, Papers of Frank M. Hatch, Minister of Foreign Affairs under the Provisional Government AH, Dole Collection AH on

:he overthrow of the monarchy and annexation; Mahan, Brooks, Tate on Mahan; *Advertiser* June 16, 1912, Marberry, Wagner on Miller. The exploits of Wheelock, Merriam, King were covered in the Honolulu newspapers of the day. Burrows, Watanabe, Wakukawa, Coman, and Conroy have written on Japanese immigration.

Chapter Fourteen

See McLaren, *Evening Bulletin, Advertiser* from February through June 1910, Broadside for Socialist party May 1912 AH in connection with the Russians; *Advertiser* April 27, 1901, Menard, *Report of Committee on the Social Evil, Advertiser, Star Bulletin* for December 1916, Stainback Territorial File AH on Iwalei; *Advertiser, Star Bulletin* for month of December 1917, also April 15 through May 1918, Kuykendall and Gill, *Advertiser, Hawaiian Star* July 28, 30, 31, 1900, *Advertiser* October 1914, February, March, April, May, June, October 1918, *Star Bulletin* for December 1917 on World War I; L. A. Thurston, C. London, Jack London, Joan London, *Advertiser* May 1910, *Star Bulletin* February 18, 1939, personal interviews with G. Rothrock and K. Emory on Jack London in Hawaii; C. Taylor, and personal interviews with Holt descendants on Holt episode; Sullivan, Cooke, *Manual of Hawaiian Securities* for appropriate years, *Paradise of the Pacific* September 1909 on Cooke.

Chapter Fifteen

See *Advertiser, Star Bulletin* from March 26 through April 1915, August 30 through September 1915, *Hawaiian Annual* 1916, *United States Naval Medical Bulletin* January 1916, *Annual Report of the Navy Department for the Fiscal Year* 1915, 1916, Barnes, *The New York Times* September 2, October 28, 1915 on the F-4; *Advertiser* July 17 through July 23, 1908, Bailey on Great White Fleet; Barber, Snowbarger, *Advertiser* December 13, 14, 1911 on Pearl Harbor development; Addleman, Barber on Army in Hawaii; *Star Bulletin* November 29, December 2, 1916 on prostitution; *Hawaiian Annual* 1926 and Horvat on Rodgers. Original source material for the Dole Flight came from the Dole Hawaiian Pineapple Company library, Honolulu. Details of the *Woolaroc* flight were obtained in personal interviews with Goebel and Davis in Honolulu. See *Hawaiian Annual* 1932, *Manual of Hawaiian Securities* 1929 through 1936, *The Friend* April 1933 on depression; Van Slingerland, Gurko, Rossetter, Stirling on Massie case; *Hawaiian Gazette* November 10, 1880, *Paradise of the Pacific* December 1935, Ayer, personal interviews with R. Baldwin and H. Rice on polo.

Chapter Sixteen

See Potter, Allen, Lord on pre-December 7, 1941 activities and on events of December 7; Anthony on martial law; Lord, Murphy, Allen on Battle of Midway; Allen and Wilson on war workers; Allen, Lind, Murphy on Japanese in Hawaii during the war; Bosworth, Lind, letter from Hoshida to Joesting February 2, 1971 on internment of Japanese; Allen, Hosokawa, Murphy on 100 and 442. Personal interview with T. Beppu.

INDEX